On Social Closure

On Social Closure

Theorizing Exclusion, Exploitation, and Elimination

JÜRGEN MACKERT

OXFORD
UNIVERSITY PRESS

Oxford University Press is a department of the University of Oxford. It furthers
the University's objective of excellence in research, scholarship, and education
by publishing worldwide. Oxford is a registered trade mark of Oxford University
Press in the UK and certain other countries.

Published in the United States of America by Oxford University Press
198 Madison Avenue, New York, NY 10016, United States of America.

© Oxford University Press 2024

All rights reserved. No part of this publication may be reproduced, stored in
a retrieval system, or transmitted, in any form or by any means, without the
prior permission in writing of Oxford University Press, or as expressly permitted
by law, by license, or under terms agreed with the appropriate reproduction
rights organization. Inquiries concerning reproduction outside the scope of the
above should be sent to the Rights Department, Oxford University Press, at the
address above.

You must not circulate this work in any other form
and you must impose this same condition on any acquirer.

Library of Congress Control Number: 2024034801

ISBN 978–0–19–778168–5

DOI: 10.1093/oso/9780197781685.001.0001

Printed by Marquis Book Printing, Canada

To Rima

Contents

Acknowledgements   xiii
Preface   xv
List of Abbreviations   xvii

Introduction: A New Approach to Social Closure   1
   I.1   Social Life as Collective Struggle   1
   I.2   Social Closure: An Almost Forgotten Theoretical Concept and Analytical Idea   2
   I.3   Critical Aspects of the New Approach to Social Closure   6
   I.4   Global Dynamics and Life Chances / Chances of Survival   7
   I.5   Social Closure: Overcoming Conceptual, Theoretical, and Methodological Problems   11
   I.6   Key Issues of a New Theorizing of Closure   13
   I.7   Structure of the Book   17

PART I   THE MISGUIDED PATH OF THE THEORY OF SOCIAL CLOSURE

1. A Critical Discussion of the Theory of Social Closure   21

2. Frank Parkin: Social Closure as Exclusion and Usurpation   25
   2.1   The Framework for an Analysis of Social Closure   25
      2.1.1   The Social Closure Equation   26
      2.1.2   Strategies of Social Action   27
      2.1.3   Bringing the State into the Analysis of Social Closure   28
      2.1.4   Closure and Exploitation   29
   2.2   Social Closure as Exclusion   30
      2.2.1   Private Property and Credentialism   30
      2.2.2   Collectivist and Individualist Strategies of Exclusion   34
   2.3   Social Closure as Usurpation   37
   2.4   Dual Closure   39

3. Raymond Murphy: Rules, Structures, and Forms of Social Closure   41
   3.1   Elaborating on (Neo-)Weberian Closure Theory   41
   3.2   A Model for the Analysis of Social Closure   43
   3.3   A Conceptual Framework for Closure Theory   47
   3.4   The Rationalization of Closure   48

4. Critical Shortcomings of the Theory of Social Closure — 50
   4.1 Closure: A Concept in a Procrustean Bed — 50
      4.1.1 Closure as an Economically Restricted Concept — 51
      4.1.2 The Two Sides of the Social Closure Equation — 52
      4.1.3 Closure as Teleological: Towards an Iron Cage of Closure — 53
   4.2 The Lack of Group Action — 55
   4.3 Power: A Missing Concept — 56
   4.4 Methodology: A Dead End — 58

5. Going Beyond the Theory of Social Closure — 59

PART II BASIC TERMS, CONCEPTS, AND METHODOLOGY FOR CLOSURE THEORY

6. Reconsidering, Problematizing, and Introducing Critical Concepts for Closure Theory — 65

RECONSIDERING MAX WEBER'S APPROACH

7. Max Weber's Critical Basic Terms for Theorizing Social Closure Reconsidered — 69
   7.1 The Ontological Idea: Social Life as Struggle — 69
   7.2 Communal and Associative Relationships — 73
   7.3 Open and Closed Relationships — 74

8. Max Weber's Closure Analyses: Three Contexts — 77
   8.1 The Economic Relationships of Communities — 77
   8.2 The Distribution of Power within the Community — 78
   8.3 Relations between Ethnic Groups — 81

9. Beyond Max Weber: Towards a New Idea of Social Closure — 84

NEW CONCEPTS FOR CLOSURE THEORY

10. Group Action and Acting in Solidarity — 89
11. Power in Closure Analysis — 93
    11.1 Heinrich Popitz: Processes and Mechanisms of Organizing Power — 95
       11.1.1 Premises of Conceptualizing Power — 95
       11.1.2 The Concept of Power — 96
       11.1.3 Power Formation — 100
       11.1.4 Discussion — 106

11.2 Anthony Giddens: Socio-Theoretical Considerations of Power	108
11.2.1 Agency	108
11.2.2 Structure: Rules and Resources	110
11.2.3 Duality of Structure	113
11.2.4 Discussion	115
11.3 Michael Mann: The Social Sources of Power	116
11.3.1 Ideological Power	118
11.3.2 Economic Power	120
11.3.3 Military Power	120
11.3.4 Political Power	122
11.3.5 Discussion	122
11.4 Elements of a New Concept of Power for Social Closure	123
12. Life Chances / Chances of Survival: The Real Goal of Closure Struggles	127
12.1 A Critical Idea but Rudimentary Concept	127
12.1.1 Life Chances and Chances of Survival in Weber's Closure Analyses	128
12.2 Life Chances / Chances of Survival and the Opportunity Structure	129
12.2.1 Life Chances as Related to the Opportunity Structure	130
13. Discussion	133

PART III THEORIZING SOCIAL CLOSURE

14. A New Approach to Social Closure	137

CONCEPTUALIZATION

15. Three Forms of Social Closure	143
16. Power and Social Closure	145
16.1 Power, Contexts, and Social Relations	145
16.2 Structural Elements of Resources of Power in Closure Struggles	148
17. A New Concept of Life Chances / Chances of Survival in the Opportunity Structure	154
17.1 The Dynamics of the Opportunity Structure	154
17.2 Dimensions of Life Chances / Chances of Survival	155

x CONTENTS

18. Reorganizing Relations of Social Closure: The Two Critical Mechanisms *Denial of Access* and *Intervention into Community Closure*   158

19. A New Concept of Social Closure   164

TYPOLOGY

20. A Typology of Social Closure   169

EXPLANATION

21. Towards an Explanation of Social Closure   175
    21.1 The Critical Role of Events   175
    21.2 The Explanatory Model: Strategies, Mechanisms, Outcomes   178

22. Explaining Social Closure   180
    22.1 Analysing and Explaining the Reorganization of Social Relations of Exclusion   180
        22.1.1 Context: Neoliberalism and Marketization   181
        22.1.2 Event and Principal Strategy   186
        22.1.3 Mobilizing Predominantly Politico-Legal Structural Elements of Power   190
        22.1.4 The *Politics of Austerity* as a Strategy of Social Closure: Processes and Mechanisms   191
        22.1.5 Outcomes, Stabilization, and Legitimation   215
    22.2 Analysing and Explaining the Reorganization of Social Relations of Exploitation   216
        22.2.1 Context: The Capitalism-Slavery Nexus   217
        22.2.2 Event and Principal Strategy   222
        22.2.3 Mobilizing Predominantly Economic Structural Elements of Power   227
        22.2.4 *Global Labour Value Chains* as a Strategy of Social Closure: Processes and Mechanisms   229
        22.2.5 Outcomes, Stabilization, and Legitimation   256
    22.3 Analysing and Explaining the Reorganization of Social Relations of Elimination   258
        22.3.1 Context: Settler Colonialism   259
        22.3.2 Events and Principal Strategy   265
        22.3.3 Mobilizing Predominantly Ideological and Military/Violence Structural Elements of Power   270
        22.3.4 *The Politics of Erasure* as a Strategy of Social Closure: Processes and Mechanisms   273
        22.3.5 Outcomes, Stabilization, and Legitimation   305

23. The Explanatory Logic of Social Closure   308

Conclusion: Social Closure and the Global Struggle for
    Life Chances / Chances of Survival   312

References   317
Index   359

Acknowledgements

Over the years, many friends and colleagues have been kind enough to listen to my early ideas and initial thoughts on a new approach to social closure and to discuss them with me. My heartfelt thanks go to Eddie Hartmann, who read substantial parts of the manuscript and took the time to discuss them with me in detail and to push me to constantly rework the argument by persistently asking questions. His theoretical and analytical rigour forced me to reconsider and revise considerable parts of the argument and to rethink the way of making the theoretical ideas empirically plausible. I also profited a lot from many discussions on what has been called the *theory of social closure* with Max Oliver Schmidt, who, himself a specialist in closure theory, gave me important hints regarding severe problems with this approach. I am also deeply thankful to Tariq Dana, who read and commented on the chapter on the social relations of elimination. I learned a lot from him as he shared his profound historical and politico-economic knowledge about the repressive and eliminatory politics of decades of the settler-colonial occupation of Palestine with me. Finally I would like to thank James Cook, Emily Mackenzie Benitez, and Keith Cline at Oxford University Press as well as Hinduja Dhanasegaran at Newgen Knowledge Works for guiding me with kindness and highest professionalism through the whole process of making a book out of a manuscript.

This book is dedicated to my wife, Rima Issa, for sharing her life with me, for her intellectual inspiration and her daily support over the years, and for revealing to me what it really means for her Palestinian people to live under Zionist settler-colonial occupation. Witnessing the daily brutality and violence the occupation uses against the Indigenous Palestinians has opened my eyes to the everyday human suffering caused by the White settler-colonial regime, a brutal regime that has oppressed the Palestinian people for decades with the full support of the 'civilized' West. Her exposing me to this experience has not only changed my life but also my understanding of what sociology should encompass and led to the creation of this book.

Preface

Like many books, this one has a long history. Its beginnings date to the mid-1990s when, while writing my doctoral thesis, I discovered the *theory of social closure*, which offered a way to discuss citizenship as a mode of social closure. While sociological theory had always seen citizenship as the very institution of inclusion into the *communal society*, in the face of migration processes and nation-states' denial of inclusion by rejecting migrants, sociological theory seemed to be at odds with social reality. I was interested in the ways this modern institution also operates as an instrument of exclusion. Where there is inclusion, we also find exclusion, like two sides of a coin; this is something students of sociology learn pretty early on, and with regard to citizenship there was a lot of exclusion to see.

However, while the theory of social closure allowed me to discuss citizenship from a new perspective, working with it brought a lot of frustration, too. I was dissatisfied with how it had been developed; my seminars on closure theory were not the best, to say the least, and I increasingly had the feeling that something was basically not working. Over the years, I tried to develop certain aspects of the theory, realized that concepts were unclear or missing, and found that it was theoretically developed in a much too narrow sense, while finding it still interesting to use and apply certain ideas of social closure to issues as seemingly distant as terrorism and torture.

Being busy with other topics for some years, I actually came back to thinking about closure and, once I realized that closure, or as Max Weber put it, *open* and *closed* social relationships, was not simply an idea to be applied to social phenomena of a status or class system, but needed to be seen as, I believe, the most basic processes in social life, a new perspective seemed possible. Somehow I was seeing a little light at the end of the closure tunnel.

Over the years, another dissatisfaction with sociology was growing, which is the still vivid obsession with modernity and the West as somehow cut off from the rest of the world because of a deeply ahistorical and isolated understanding of them. It is strange to see why sociology has proven to be so inflexible with respect to broadening its scope, and rethinking its theories and methodologies, after having been confronted with postcolonial thought for decades now. Still, and this may be an impression mainly influenced by the state of sociology in my own country, sociology still mainly addresses 'modern', 'advanced', and Western societies, while there seems to be only limited interest in disastrous living conditions in the Rest of the world—not to mention how profound developments, dynamics, and processes in the West have led and continue to lead to these distortions, both as a long-term historical effect and also today in the twenty-first century.

Struggling with these two dissatisfactions, at a certain point in time I began to assume that if it was correct that closure processes were the most basic processes in social life, then theorizing about them should not be confined to national societies or the West but offer a perspective from which to think about such processes everywhere as being connected. However, while postcolonial thought has opened a perspective to do so and reveals still existing power asymmetries that originate from colonial times, these debates have widely remained on the level of analysing discourses. Yet, while Edward W. Said, the forefather and, to my mind, the most significant figure in these debates, has not only sparked *postcolonial* thinking, analysing, and challenging dominant Western discourses, he also emphasized *settler colonial* thought and analysis. For a sociologist interested in 'facts on the ground' that *settler colonialism* has produced in more than five hundred years, this analysis provides a new dimension. In this book, I aim to introduce the settler colonial paradigm to theoretical sociology and political sociology. This approach provides a basic sociological tool for analysing serious social problems and distortions. By adopting a historical and global perspective, I developed a new theoretical approach to social closure, which culminates in this book. I hope this work broadens sociology's perspective and helps make sense of today's world.

Abbreviations

ACRI	Association for Civil Rights in Israel
Adalah	The Legal Center for Arab Minority Rights in Israel
Addameer	Prisoner Support and Human Rights Organisation
B'Tselem	The Israeli Information Center for Human Rights in the Occupied Territories
CAP	Common Agricultural Policy
DAWN	Democracy for The Arab World Now
DCIP	Defense for Children International-Palestine
ECB	European Central Bank
ECHO	European Commission Humanitarian Aid Offices
EIGE	European Institute for Gender Equality
EU	European Union
EWASH	Emergency Water Sanitation and Hygiene Group in the Occupied Territories
FEANTSA	European Federation of National Organisations Working with the Homeless
FEPS	Foundation for European Progressive Studies
GBVH	Gender-Based Violence and Harassment
GCC	Global commodity chain
GCIV	Fourth Geneva Convention
GDP	Gross Domestic Product
Gisha	Legal Center for Freedom of Movement
CLVC	Global labour value chain
GPN	Global production network
GSC	Global supply chains
GVC	Global value chain
HRW	Human Rights Watch
IDF	Israeli Defence Forces
ILO	The International Labour Office
IMEMC	International Middle East Media Center
IMF	International Monetary Fund
IOM	International Organization of Migration
MEMO	Middle East Monitor
NFA	New financial architecture
NHRC	National Human Rights Committee
NPL	Non-performing Loan
OCHA	United Nations Office for the Coordination of Humanitarian Affairs
OECD	Organization for Economic Co-operation and Development

OHCHR	Office of the High Commissioner for Human Rights
OMCT	World Organisation Against Torture
OPT	Occupied Palestinian Territories
P.C.H.R.	Palestinian Centre for Human Rights
REDER	Red de Denuncia y Resistencia
SEC	Securities and Exchange Commission
TASC	Think Tank for Action on Social Change
UNCTAD	United Nations Conference on Trade and Development
UNESCO	United Nations Educational, Scientific and Cultural Organization
UAWC	Union of Agricultural Workers Committees
UPWC	Union of Palestinian Women's Committees
UNRWA	United Nations Relief and Works Agency for Palestine Refugees in the Near East
WAFA	Palestine News & Info Agency
WFP	World Food Programme
WHO	World Health Organization
WRC	Worker Rights Consortium
WTF	World Trade Forum
WTO	World Trade Organization

Introduction

A New Approach to Social Closure

I.1 Social Life as Collective Struggle

In recent decades, we have observed a typical development all over the world: social, political, economic, ethnic, religious, language, gender, and Indigenous groups have become the targets of both governments' and powerful actors' strategies to deprive them of rights or prevent them from accessing resources and further options that human beings need to survive and to participate in public and the economy, in politics and culture. To defend or fight for their life chances, at times only for their chances of survival, people raise their voices or even rebel against social marginalization, political disenfranchisement, economic exploitation, and cultural repression. This is true in neo-liberalized, hollowed-out democracies where citizens are rarely able to make meaningful political decisions anymore, in authoritarian regimes with even narrower corridors of action for social groups, or in dictatorial ones that most brutally try to repress dissent. More than ever before, today we see that social life is collective struggle.

Questions of exclusion, of radicalized exploitation that often turns into new forms of slavery, and of eliminatory strategies threatening the survival of groups and collectives are pressing today. We observe movements that shape social struggles against processes of *exclusion* that range from identity politics on US campuses or women's fight for abortion and their reproductive rights in countries such as Poland (The Guardian 2021) and the United States to the desperate situation of social groups such as the elderly, the homeless, the (chronically) sick, the poor, single-mother households, and disabled persons, who are all facing high insecurity and poverty risks in the face of neoliberal politics. They also shape struggles in a period of radicalized *exploitation* that for many millions has already turned into slavery, including the Manchester capitalism-like working conditions for labourers in countries such as India, Ethiopia, or Bangladesh. Yet, also for seasonal workers or illegalized migrants in the United States, the United Kingdom, and the European Union, working conditions can only be considered a new system of slavery (Patterson and Zhuo 2018). The new European slavery takes many different forms, from human trafficking and forced labour (Abellan Matamoros 2019) to the tens of thousands of modern slaves working in the south of Spain or Italy, picking food for privileged White Europeans under degrading and dehumanizing conditions (de Pablo et al. 2020). Finally, we see the ongoing strategies of *elimination* against Indigenous people in former settler-colonial societies such as Canada, where in recent years the human remains of Indigenous children have been discovered again and again in mass graves in Christian residential schools (Voce, Leyland, and Michael 2021). Then there is the murderous genocidal history of White Christian and liberal settler-colonial states that established settler democracies for the White occupiers, which even today still exclude the Indigenous population from citizenship rights and resources, threatening them with eliminatory politics (Wolfe 2006; Veracini 2013; Lloyd 2012). No different is what we see today unfolding in Israel's continuous strategies of annihilation of the Palestinian people that have developed into genocide since October 2023.

This list is only the tip of the iceberg, if we look at today's world. However, if my impression is correct, sociology unfortunately is not really interested in most of these global phenomena, but still seems concerned with problems within Western, 'modern', and 'developed' societies that scholars try to discuss as problems of inclusion/exclusion. I argue, though, that this strategy does not work for the manifold phenomena of exploitation and elimination within Western societies, and definitely not for most of the problems beyond the Western world, which, in a globalized world, are constitutively connected with one another.

Sociology needs new ways of theorizing and analysing the phenomena mentioned above. Yet, if sociology is interested in addressing them, it needs to do it in a fundamental way. In this book, I aim to present a fundamentally new approach to closure theory that enables us to fully grasp the range of all forms of closure. Analysing and explaining them, I argue, is only possible if one expands the understanding of *closure*, which is why my new approach is based on the distinction between three forms of social closure: exclusion, exploitation, and elimination. On this basis, I offer a new perspective, a new frame through which to analyse these phenomena, and a common explanatory logic of all strategies that promote them.

I.2 Social Closure: An Almost Forgotten Theoretical Concept and Analytical Idea

The younger generation of sociologists who grew up with the debate around *social exclusion*, who are familiar with the pair of terms *inclusion/exclusion*, and who work in both an academic and political environment focused on advancing inclusion into *society*, may no longer be aware of a much older tradition of sociological reasoning that originally referred to exclusion as a critical concept. What in the late 1970s and 1980s was called the *theory of social closure*, today, if at all, is mainly used in a metaphoric sense, referring to critical terms of this tradition, such as exclusion and usurpation, dual closure, or the social closure equation. However, this generation cannot be blamed for not considering the idea of social closure that can be traced back to Max Weber, since the potential it harbours has never been fully recognized or realized—neither by Weber himself nor by the tradition of the theory of social closure (Mackert 2004a). Of course, both approaches—social exclusion and closure theory—show some overlap, yet there are many more differences than similarities. Briefly juxtaposing contexts of origin, objects of interest, and approaches of both traditions will reveal their differences with respect to these basic aspects.

The so-called theory of social closure as it was developed by Frank Parkin and Raymond Murphy in the 1970s and 1980s actually started from rediscovering a basic sociological concept in Max Weber's (1978 [1922]) *Economy and Society*, namely *open* and *closed* social relationships. Widely neglected or simply taken for granted in the broad reception of and debate on Weber's work by generations of theoretical sociologists, it never received the interest that it deserves, as I show in this book.

The theory of social closure was developed in the social context of still-functioning Fordism, with stable welfare state institutions and the global historical context of the contradictory systems of capitalism and socialism that, however, dissolved only a year after Murphy's fully elaborated theoretical approach *Social Closure. The Theory of Monopolization and Exclusion* was published in 1988. At the same time, a core conflict in Western sociology that had been prominent and authoritative for quite a long time—the hiatus of conservative functionalist stratification theory on the one hand, progressive structural Marxism on the other—had already come to an end, with Talcott Parsons' *orthodox consensus* crumbling and Marxism paying the price for a political and economic system in Eastern Europe that had failed and disregarded its citizens' rights. While Parkin and Murphy both were looking to overcome this kind of theoretical standstill, they succeeded with Parsonian functionalism but, especially in Murphy's work, ideas of structural Marxism survived and remained as an ominous theoretical burden.

At the beginning of the 1990s, with the end of the Cold War and the dissolution of the Soviet Empire and state socialism, problems of exclusion seemed to be a thing of the past given the alleged dawn of a global democratic age with rising living standards for all people who now apparently lived in a 'global village'. In view of the neoliberal promises of a bright future, not only was Marxism suddenly a dead dog but the theory of social closure, still fraught with assumptions of structuralist Marxism, was consigned to oblivion.

However, it was not too long before the European Union and the individual Western European states, whose governments had to varying degrees already turned to neoliberal policies, were confronted with a harsh reality. Politicians, and above all the citizens of these societies, began to realize that the future was not as bright as neoliberal economists and ideologues had promised, except for the political elite and the wealthy. Yet, instead of setting up new welfare programmes to absorb the hardship for ever greater parts of the populations in the face of the cutting of social nets and the privatization of former public goods such as health, education, and pensions, the European Union launched the huge programme TSER (Targeted Socio-Economic Research) that included the section Social Integration and Social Exclusion to push social research on social exclusion and funded it with about 30 million ECU. One might have hoped that social scientists would have been more sceptical and reserved in the face of such generous funding, as the government of the United Kingdom, the most liberalized society in the European Union and still a member of it at the time, even established a so-called Social Exclusion Unit that then began to organize social policies from the perspective of avoiding *social exclusion* (see Steinert 2003, 275). Finally, about 1,000 social scientists all over Europe were busy delivering new insights, no longer doing research on poverty, despair, exploitation, homelessness, or social decline, but lumping their interests under the umbrella term of *social exclusion*. Suddenly, migrants were excluded, the homeless were excluded, poor people were excluded, and so forth. They were no longer poor, disenfranchised, or victims of a housing market that had already turned to speculation with real estate instead of providing affordable housing for all members of society and, of course, instead of attacking the causes of these transformations, social scientists were calling for those who were excluded to be included again. Ideology had trumped critical social science.

Today, social exclusion has widely infiltrated sociology's vocabulary and sociologists' minds. Yet, as a term and concept, it has remained somehow obscure and has not allowed for theorizing *processes* of exclusion or for problematizing its *methodological* base, if there is one, nor have its *dynamics* and *underlying causes* been made explicit. Rather, analyses of social exclusion have concentrated on the effects of neoliberal policies or the social consequences of exclusion and are aimed at developing indices to make exclusion measurable (see Silver 2007a; 2007b; 2019; Silver and Miller 2003). Studying *exclusion* has thus remained restricted to social phenomena that are related to a withering welfare state, while the debate has not found its way to general theorizing.

Not surprisingly, the study results of these myriads of social scientists allowed neoliberal politics to develop strategies to even intensify exclusion by putting even more pressure on clearly defined parts of the population, or to identify which vulnerable groups should still be supported if, and only if, they were ready to do even the worst of jobs offered in an attempt to demonstrate their employability. All these analyses also allowed policy makers to draw fine lines between the deserving and undeserving parts of the population, thereby exposing those defined as undeserving of social support to even greater risks, as we have seen in cases such as the Grenfell disaster in 2017 and the way it was dealt with (Preston 2019), in that the only people who were killed were of little or no value at all to neoliberal British society.

The debate around social exclusion is thus of little to no help at all when we want to know more about processes in today's world that deeply affect human beings' life chances or even their chances of survival. In view of the limited subject area with which this debate is concerned, namely its theoretical, methodological, and analytical ambiguities and shortcomings, its involvement in a politically desired preoccupation with something called *social exclusion*, and its West-centredness focusing on 'modern', 'developed' societies, this approach to examining phenomena of exclusion is of little help if we broaden the perspective and look also to other parts of the globe and their connectedness with the West. Indeed, the latter produces not simply exclusion at home—which for those who suffer from it is a political scandal and a human catastrophe—but also critical if not catastrophic consequences abroad.

However, there is no simple way back, if any, to what has been called the theory of social closure. While without any doubt closure theory has suffered from historical, political, and economic change as well as from neoliberal political (research) strategies, there are too many problems with how this theory has been modelled for it to be saved. We simply have to realize that Parkin's approach, but especially Murphy's theory of exclusion and monopolization, have led closure theory to a dead end. Yet, rejecting the theory of social closure does not mean that there will be a simple way back to Weber and the way in which he applied his concept of open and closed social relationships to empirical phenomena. Instead, we need to reconsider Weber's critical concept for an understanding of social life and begin anew with theorizing social closure. What I do here is thus return to these basic concepts to discuss the critical shortcomings of both Weber's own application of the concepts and those of the theory of social closure, and begin again to theorize social closure.

In this sense, the theoretical endeavour must view the meaning of social closure in a new light. While I start from Weber's concept, I depart from him not only in theoretical, methodological, and analytical terms but also with regard to the scope of application of closure analysis, thereby broadening the range of phenomena that sociology should examine from the perspective of social closure. At the same time, the intention is to overcome the West-centredness of closure theory and its self-imposed restriction of only analysing phenomena of exclusion, which, as I will conceptualize it, is one form of social closure but by no means the only one. Extending the scope of application thus turns social closure into a *general sociological tool* that allows researchers to analyse and explain processes of social closure, from the rather informal exclusion of women from higher positions in organizations through what is known as the *class ceiling* to fundamental social processes in the Middle East.

In such a new approach, the aim is to develop a viable concept and a general theoretical tool for analysing and explaining phenomena and manifestations of social closure in the world of today that fundamentally reorients closure theory and consequently goes far beyond what closure theory analyses have so far considered to be their subject area. This approach needs to be outlined briefly.

I.3 Critical Aspects of the New Approach to Social Closure

With the living and working conditions of billions of people around the world deteriorating at an unprecedented rate, the world of today, maybe more than ever in modern history, reveals that social life *is* struggle. Such struggles, I will claim, are about the realization of life chances and chances of survival that need to be theorized and analysed from the perspective of a new theory of social closure. The analysis of social closure, as I conceive it in this book, is the analysis of critical social relations in which powerful collective actors deploy strategies that are of a kind to reduce, minimize, or even destroy the life chances of the less powerful within these relations, at times turning their life chances into mere chances of survival.

My approach to social closure therefore neither restricts the analysis of closure to status struggles (as Weber did) nor to 'advanced' capitalist societies (as the theory of social closure did), but rather concentrates on social relations that result from what I define as the three major global dynamics. I argue that *neoliberalism*, *capitalism*, and *settler colonialism* have caused and continue to drive a disastrous development depriving most of humanity of their life chances, one that characterizes today's life in globalized modernity. In this sense, looking at neoliberalism, global capitalism, and settler colonialism from the perspective of a new theory of social closure shows today's world as what it is: a place of ongoing radical exclusion, exploitation, and elimination.

I am thus interested in developing a differentiated view of forms of closure and strategies that the powerful in social relations of closure can employ. To do so, my new approach concentrates on analysing and systematizing the strategies of the powerful side in social relations of exclusion, exploitation, and elimination and explaining how the strategies of the powerful side—the excluders, exploiters, and eliminators—trigger *social mechanisms* that operate in ways that restrict, if not destroy the *life chances / chances of survival* of the less-powerful side—the excluded, the exploited, and those threatened with elimination—in ongoing daily social closure struggles.[1]

In this sense, a new approach to social closure is part of a sociological counter-programme to hegemonic discourses that describe today's global situation as reasonable, rational, and without any alternative. It rejects static descriptions of *the world as it is* and its seeming *normality*. Instead, by taking seriously the three major historical dynamics and the fatal consequences for the very largest part of humanity that they have triggered, and continue to do so, I argue that a fundamentally revised and renewed closure theory can provide a common perspective, since social closure, as I conceive of it and develop in this book, is about the struggle for resources and rights, for opportunities to integrate into social institutions or networks, and, not least, to maintain control over one's own life. Thus, the distinct effects of all three dynamics can be seen as struggles for life chances / chances of survival.

I.4 Global Dynamics and Life Chances / Chances of Survival

As the social relations characterizing neoliberalism, capitalism, and settler colonialism are the core theoretical and methodological analytical units of the analysis of closure struggle, a brief look at these dynamics will clarify their crucial role in global struggles to redistribute life chances / chances of survival from the less powerful to the powerful.

Neoliberalism, the transformation of all social relations into markets, thereby conceiving of societies as self-regulating markets and ascribing a certain value to each and every thing and thus distinguishing human life on the planet according to economic and market criteria as either *valuable* or *valueless* life (Mavelli 2022), pushes ahead the comprehensive and radical *exclusion* of human beings declared to be worthless.

Around 2014, the European Union reorganized its migration policy in response to the increasing migration along the 'Balkan route' and the subsequent immigration of people fleeing mainly from Syria, Iraq, and Afghanistan, as well as the equally undesirable migration from sub-Saharan Africa across the Mediterranean. Not only did it manage to strike a deal with Turkish President Erdogan to keep Syrian refugees in particular away from European territory, but, already in 2014, in the face of the so-called migration crisis, the European Union discontinued its *Mare Nostrum* rescue mission in the Mediterranean and set up the *Triton* mission, which was not only much smaller than its predecessor but was also led by and subordinate to Frontex, the European Border Management

---

[1] Throughout the book I use the terms 'mechanism' and 'social mechanism' interchangeably.

Agency. Instead of rescuing migrants trying to cross the Mediterranean in their inflatable boats, as Mare Nostrum had done, this mission abandoned migrants and used drones to monitor how the Mediterranean Sea was turning into a mass grave (Ahmed, K. 2020). In 2023, the European Union decided and officially announced it would strengthen the protection of its external borders with watchtowers, thermal imaging cameras, electronic surveillance systems, and fortifications (Brey 2023). Already in 2015, however, it had installed a migration defence system that for good reasons was largely kept secret and shows the brutality of exclusion in neoliberalism:

> In the past six years, the European Union, weary of the financial and political costs of receiving migrants from sub-Saharan Africa, has created a shadow immigration system that stops them before they reach Europe. It has equipped and trained the Libyan Coast Guard, a quasi-military organization linked to militias in the country, to patrol the Mediterranean, sabotaging humanitarian rescue operations and capturing migrants. The migrants are then detained indefinitely in a network of profit-making prisons run by the militias. In September of this year, around six thousand migrants were being held, many of them in Al Mabani. International aid agencies have documented an array of abuses: detainees tortured with electric shocks, children raped by guards, families extorted for ransom, men and women sold into forced labor. 'The E.U. did something they carefully considered and planned for many years,' Salah Marghani, Libya's Minister of Justice from 2012 to 2014, told me. 'Create a hellhole in Libya, with the idea of deterring people from heading to Europe'. (Urbina 2021; see Plaut 2017)

Closely connected with neoliberalism's rise and developing hegemony since the late 1970s, the rise of *global capitalism* is the second major dynamic shaping the world of today. Following the demise of the Soviet Union and the end of State socialism, the reorganization of global capital along with neoliberal economic shock doctrines for formerly state socialist countries finally allowed capitalism to go global, offering an almost unlimited reservoir of human labour to be *exploited*.

The spread of global capitalism, which since the 1990s has been discussed in academia, politics, and the media under the ideologically trivializing term *globalization*, has not—as proclaimed in the Global North—produced a world in which all people everywhere are better off due to the blessings of capitalist production on a global scale, but rather the opposite. Global production today is characterized by *global value chains* (GVCs) (OECD n.d.-a), which are the central feature of the new global division of labour, with the implementation, organization, and control of global business relations in the hands of multinational corporations. The extreme asymmetry of power between these corporations and subcontractors, who compete fiercely with each other, makes those who work at the bottom of the value chain, producing both value and surplus value, vulnerable to paying for the *price squeeze* of global corporations (Anner 2020). They have few resources to protect themselves against the demands of subcontractors, ranging from low wages to increased, chronic, and forced overtime, harassment, wage theft, and so forth, which is nothing but a kind of resurrection of uncontrolled Manchester capitalism in the Global South, the disenfranchisement of and contempt for working people instead of the promised better life for humanity. Yet, while this is bad enough, at the end of the GVCs we do not only find hyper-exploitation of people in the Global South and Global North. Rather, in this brave new world of global capitalism, there has been a dramatic rise in recent years of multiple manifestations of modern slavery: out of a total of almost 50 million people worldwide, some 17 million women, children, and men are considered modern slaves in the private sector, and thus in global capitalist production (ILO, Walk Free, and IOM 2022). Just a brief look at the degree of profit maximization achieved by reducing—mainly female—workers' salaries in the garment industry shows the destruction of life chances:

> Our investigation also found the lowest wages the WRC has documented in any garment exporting country in recent years: wages as low as US$ 0.12 per hour, less than US$ 25 per month. The average wage at the factories the WRC investigated, exclusive of overtime hours, was US$ 0.18 an hour (US$ 38 per month). The Ethiopian garment sector's rapid growth has been fueled by these extraordinarily low labor costs. The Ethiopian Investment Commission, a government body charged with attracting foreign investment, has beckoned to potential investors with promises of '[c]heap and skilled labor' with wages that are '1/7 of China and 1/2 of Bangladesh'. These wages are possible, in part, because Ethiopia is unique among significant apparel exporting countries in the developing world in having no statutory minimum wage for workers in the private sector, including garment workers. Ultra-low wages, and the lack of any legal wage floor, have, unsurprisingly, been the source of significant worker unrest in the country' garment sector, as well as in other industries. (Worker Rights Consortium 2018)

While the idea that neoliberalism, which has been driving the commodification and marketization of social life for decades, and global capitalism— 'the most fateful power of modern life' (Max Weber)—have, as global dynamics, transformed the globe into a space of permanent social struggles seems to be fairly obvious, the new approach I present in this book argues that understanding the dynamics that cause today's global struggles in social life cannot be limited to these two dynamics but requires taking a longer historical perspective and must therefore necessarily include settler colonialism as the third major dynamic. While decades of postcolonial thinking have shown how Western-centred discourses have powerfully excluded the voices of the subaltern (Said 1992 [1979]; Spivak 2010 [1985]) and thus rightly criticized sociology for its Euro- or West-centric view of the world (Go 2016), I am concerned with the actual social struggles and facts on the ground as a result of violent Western intrusion into other parts of the world. With this focus, insights from the settler-colonial paradigm that coincide with those of postcolonial thinking are crucial. From 1492 onwards, White European settlers all over the world conquered Indigenous lands, first driven by Christian and later by liberal ideology, both promoting White supremacy (Losurdo 2014) that legitimized the destruction of existing forms of social organization and civilizations. White settlers from the West brought racism and ethnic cleansing to the Rest of the world, their strategies following the *logic of elimination* (Patrick Wolfe) of settler colonialism, which not infrequently resulted in genocide:

> In sum, for the entire present-day United States from 1492 to the present, the total number of Indigenous deaths includes the 12 million estimated by Thornton; the additional approximately 790,000 deaths that occurred in Hawaii, Alaska, in Puerto Rico; and about 200,000 excess deaths since 1900. Thus, the Indigenous Holocaust in this country appears to have taken around 13 million lives. Signally, this horrific number of deaths was only a very small portion of the mind-numbing Holocaust throughout the Western Hemisphere. When Thornton's estimated hemispheric population decline of 70 million is multiplied by 2.5, the total number of Indigenous deaths throughout the Western Hemisphere between 1492 and 1900 appears to be about 175 million. And the number of Indigenous people who have died in the hemisphere because of war, repression, racism, and harsh conditions of life since 1900 surely runs into the millions. By any reckoning, the Indigenous Holocaust in the Western Hemisphere was, as Stannard has pointed out, 'the worst human holocaust the world had ever witnessed.' No words or numbers can adequately convey the scale of the horror and tragedy involved in the greatest sustained loss of human life in history. (Smith 2017, 13)[2]

However, settler colonialism is far from just a historical event that is long gone: rather, it turned the world inside out (Veracini 2021) and, to this day, over 500 years of economic, political, social, and cultural oppression and Western hegemony still have profound implications for global economic and geopolitical

---

[2] For important work on this Indigenous holocaust caused by Western settler colonialism, see Thornton 1987; Stannard 1992; Smith 2023.

relations and international governance. As sociology continues to ignore these findings, it is still dealing with a halved modernity. Moreover, European settler colonialism not only continues to have long-term historical effects; rather, land grabs and ethnic cleansing are taking place today in Palestine (Mann 2005; Mbembe 2016; B'Tselem 2002; Zonszein 2014). Zionist fantasies of extermination are far from history. On 26 February 2023, after Israeli settlers protected by the Israeli military had carried out a pogrom in the Palestinian town of Huwwara in the occupied West Bank, killing at least one person and injuring almost 400 by burning houses and cars, Israeli Finance Minister Bezalel Smotrich supported the atrocity, saying that Huwwara should be 'wiped out' (Middle East Eye 2023a). Only three weeks later, on 19 March he denied the existence of the Palestinian people altogether, saying: 'There's no such thing as a Palestinian people' (Middle East Eye 2023b). In 2023, dehumanizing Palestinians during seventy-five years of occupation and seventeen years of the siege of Gaza has finally led to genocide of the Palestinians. Being a European settler-colonial state, Israel, like any of its historical predecessors, thus has employed strategies of *eliminating* the Indigenous. In Gaza they have turned into genocide.

This brief sketch of the phenomena that a new approach to social closure necessarily needs to capture makes immediately clear that it needs to go far beyond what the previous closure theory of the 1970s and 1980s wanted to and could capture and must avoid its critical problems and shortcomings.

I.5 Social Closure: Overcoming Conceptual, Theoretical, and Methodological Problems

In developing a new approach to social closure, I start from the assumption that the ways in that both Weber and the theory of social closure developed the basic sociological idea are conceptually, theoretically, and methodologically flawed. I show that, *conceptually*, this basic sociological idea has been insufficiently developed and thus remained rudimentary; *methodologically*, neither Weber's individualist nor Murphy's holist approach could deliver a convincing perspective; *theoretically*, especially with Murphy's work, the theory of closure, although labelled neo-Weberian, was forced into the structuralist corset. Against this background, it comes as no surprise that the notion of social closure was not developed to serve as a general sociological concept but was rather used in a narrow economic sense that robbed the idea of its potentially basic and general meaning. Weber did make closure processes explicit in various contexts—by analysing economic relations of communities, the distribution of power within communities, and relations between ethnic groups—but ultimately, in these brief analyses he reduced closure to the maximization of economic resources.

This limited understanding of closure was reproduced in the work of Parkin (1979) and Murphy (1988), both of whom tried to complement Marxist class analysis with the idea of closure while concentrating on processes of monopolization in an economic sense. This continuing self-imposed restriction was by no means necessary or inevitable. Yet, the theory of social closure showed no interest in developing a general sociological tool to analyse processes beyond economic ones, even though Parkin introduced educational qualifications as another critical aspect besides private property to understand the status structure of modern capitalist societies and the closure processes associated with it.

Not surprisingly, such severe shortcomings have meant that for more than three decades the concept of social closure has not been revisited, nor has the theoretical approach been further developed or revised, even though the problems that could and should be analysed from the perspective of closure theory have multiplied. Rather, conceptually, theoretically, and methodologically, the current state of closure theory is deeply unsatisfactory and of no help when it comes to addressing the kinds of problems outlined above. For good reason, in sociological analyses social closure has been used more metaphorically than as a distinct and elaborated concept. Yet, being interested in a generic concept of social closure that is both broad enough to capture the effects of social struggles unleashed by settler colonialism, global capitalism, and neoliberalism and specific enough to identify the social mechanisms at work to produce the specific effects they trigger, I start anew with closure theory by suggesting a new concept of closure that will be put in a methodologically relational perspective. Further, instead of trying to fit closure into any kind of theory, I begin by theorizing social closure to develop a sociological tool that can be used to analyse all kinds of processes of social closure. In doing so, I do not reject Weber's work on closure in its entirety; rather, my reconceptualization of social closure starts from some of his ideas that I will take up but develop further.

I use three critical aspects in Weber's work as the starting point for a new understanding and a general concept of closure. First, there is Weber's basic sociological term *struggle* and his ontological assumption that struggle cannot be evaded in social life. Looking at social life from the perspective of such a *struggle paradigm* necessarily implies taking a much broader view than looking at struggles over the monopolization of economic resources only. In my view, seeing social life *as* struggle is indispensable for a closure theory perspective, as it assigns closure struggles not a residual place amidst processes of social life, but rather a very critical one. Thus, I conceive of social life *as* struggles for social closure.

Second, the systematic proximity of struggle and Weber's basic concept of open and closed relationships in his systematics of basic sociological terms assigns to the latter a no-less-fundamental significance for understanding and analysing processes in social life. Not only has this significance gone unnoticed, but sociology has failed even more to recognize that closure is presumably one of the most fundamental processes in social life, if not the most fundamental one. Without processes of closure, no form of either communal or associational social relationships, from couples to families, social groups, and larger communities to social classes, markets, or nations, would be possible or imaginable. Without closure, there would be no collectivities, no solidarity, and no collective action. Thus, closure is fundamental in two ways: On the one hand, it is the indispensable precondition for any collectivity to organize, develop a political identity, draw boundaries, and organize around an interest (closure to the inside). On the other hand, collective actors who have managed to close their community and develop a high degree of organization will be able to realize their interests at the expense of the less powerful (closure to the outside).

Third, if closure struggles in which collective actors fight for their interests are indeed fundamental to social life, what is the *real goal* of these struggles that cannot be brought to a standstill? While Weber occasionally mentions that closure increases the *life chances* of status groups, he neither develops the concept further nor systematically determines its place within social closure analysis. A new approach to social closure assigns central importance to life chances, which I see as the *real goal* of closure struggles. Yet, not only in Weber but also in sociology in general, this concept has been left rudimentary and insufficiently and unsatisfactorily fleshed out. I therefore revise and recast it and offer a new and differentiated concept of what I call *life chances / chances of survival*, which is a concept that allows us to understand how diverse closure strategies are directed at the dimensions of life chances / chances of survival that I elaborate.

I.6 Key Issues of a New Theorizing of Closure

Apart from taking up Weber's critical yet undeveloped ideas, my new approach overcomes two important lacunae that have proven closure theory to be insufficiently developed. On the one hand, neither Weber nor the theorists behind the theory of social closure made their understanding of power explicit. While Weber thought power was sociologically amorphous, Parkin and Murphy seemed to take it for granted, and the way we should conceive of power in closure theory has remained unclear. Both positions are untenable. Rather, my approach develops a power-based concept of social closure, permitting an understanding of how powerful social actors employ strategies of exclusion, exploitation, and elimination. On the other hand, while it is obvious that social closure addresses collective struggles, in neither of the two approaches do we find an explanation of the preconditions for collective action and how people can *act in solidarity* (Mackert 2021). My approach conceptualizes the preconditions and ways to act in solidarity as an integral aspect of understanding processes of social closure, without which processes and dynamics of social closure cannot be understood.

This combination of taking up basic ideas of Weber, developing them further and bringing in new ideas allows me to develop a new way of theorizing social closure that proceeds as follows. First, as has already become clear, I start by defining three major *global dynamics* that have been operating as drivers of closure processes in a historical perspective. Neoliberalism, capitalism, and settler colonialism have not only shaped social relations from the local to the global and continue to do so but also 'invented' the most fundamental forms of social closure.

Second, I thus assign three *basic forms of closure* to these dynamics. Neoliberalism, which I conceive as mainly a political project, pushes ahead various processes such as marketization and privatization, the upward redistribution of wealth, the imposition of structural-adjustment programmes, and the politics of austerity, all of which promote one and the same basic form of closure, namely *exclusion*. Global capitalism, being quite self-explanatory, can operate only by imposing new forms of a global division of labour that, today, from a global perspective, has increased *exploitation* to an unprecedented degree. For the reasons mentioned earlier, I include into the analysis of global capitalism's basic form of closure manifestations of a *new slavery* as a critical dimension of exploitation, because from a historical perspective slavery has always been the cheapest labour power for capitalism—a fact that is true especially today. Settler colonialism, as the third critical dynamic, reveals that both the rise of the West, of capitalism, and of Western global hegemony and the way neoliberalism and capitalism operate today can be properly understood only if we take into consideration the eliminatory character of the West's occupation of the Rest of the world and thus take seriously both the historical and the ongoing *elimination*, at times genocidal annihilation, of millions of human beings.

Third, accordingly, I define distinct *basic forms of strategies* characterizing exclusion, exploitation, and elimination that must be analysed empirically in their various manifestations as to their consequences for human beings. The three basic forms of strategies have different characters and pursue different goals. Neo-liberal exclusionary strategies of *marginalization* aim at getting people out of the way, pushing them to the edges of society or another social entity; global capitalism's exploitative strategies of *extraction* use human beings for the sake of profit; settler-colonial eliminatory strategies of *annihilation* aim at destroying human beings.[3] These three distinct forms of closure strategies are constitutive and typical of 'global modernity' and characterize closure struggles from both historical and contemporary global perspectives.

---

[3] See Jan Philipp Reemtsma's 2012 [2009] distinction between forms of violence that proceeds similarly.

Fourth, all this also means that a methodological revision is indispensable and unavoidable. As I am interested in analysing how processes of social closure transform social relations among collective actors, neither an individualist nor a holist approach will do. As today's world is characterized by severe *exclusion*, extreme *exploitation*, and the ruthless *elimination* of Indigenous people in what have been or still are settler-colonial societies, I pursue a *methodologically relational perspective* for two reasons. On the one hand, in taking social relations as the basic methodological units of sociological analysis, I argue that to adequately analyse the diverse manifestations of the three basic forms of closure, we need to analyse the social relations of exclusion, exploitation, and elimination as the basic methodological units of the new approach. This means that strategies of marginalization unfold in social relations between the excluders and the excluded, strategies of extraction in social relations between the exploiters and the exploited, and strategies of annihilation in social relations between the eliminators and those threatened with being eliminated. These relations are characterized by (at times) extreme power asymmetries.

On the other hand, a relational methodology[4] also allows me to bring the relations between the Global North and the Global South into sociological theory and analysis and to understand how strategies of highly organized actors in the Global North have led to the destruction of life chances / chances of survival in the Global South for centuries. From a relational perspective, the constitutive relationship between the Global North and South that began with settler colonialism is critical, as the former did not simply develop on its own. Its development can only be sufficiently understood if we take into account the West's centuries-long hegemonic relationship with the Rest of the world in a systematic way.

These are the steps that a new approach to closure theory must take against the background of settler colonialism, capitalism, and neoliberalism that, over a long-term period (over 500 years of settler colonialism), a mid-term period (about 300 years of capitalism), and a short-term period (50 years of neoliberalism as a political and economic project), have shaped and continue to shape the Western-dominated world we live in today. While I suggest a common perspective from which to analyse their destructive effects, I do not claim that their effects are simply the same. Rather, while fundamentally interconnected, they are distinct dynamics that produce different effects for human beings. Nevertheless, as I show in the processes they trigger, not only are the same social mechanisms at work but they also all produce social struggles that unfold within social relations between more-powerful and less-powerful

---

[4] This resonates with Go's 2016 argument that only a relational methodology will allow social theory to bridge the gap to postcolonial theory by breaking with the former's Eurocentric view of modernity, modern society, or liberal democracy, as well as its Western-centred discourse of history and legacy of colonialism.

collective social actors fighting for the realization of their life chances / chances of survival. A new approach that takes these global dynamics into consideration allows me to analyse and explain the processes and manifold strategies that destroy the life chances / chances of survival of billions of people all over the globe. Pointing to this destructiveness that shapes the world today resonates with Achille Mbembe's characterization:

> The contemporary era is undoubtedly characterized by forms of exclusion, hostility, hate movements, and, above all, by the struggle against an enemy. As a result, liberal democracies—already considerably ground down by the forces of capital, technology and militarism—are now being drawn into a colossal process of inversion. (Mbembe 2016, 23)

In fact, in reconsidering and hopefully reviving closure theory, we must deal with the impact of settler colonialism, capitalism, and neoliberalism on social life in a global perspective. Each of these comes along with specific sets of social relations, typical processes, and characteristic strategies of social closure that make these closure forms distinct, yet distinguishing between them also makes it conceivable how they overlap and might interact and reinforce one another.

Of course, being subjugated under an eliminatory settler-colonial regime may come along with extreme exploitation for the Indigenous, if they are forced to sell their labour to simply survive. Marginalization under conditions of neoliberalism can easily merge into annihilation and be based on hyper-exploitation. Under conditions of extreme exploitation and slavery, the road to annihilation is very short. Making a distinction between different forms of closure allows to identify specific strategies of marginalization, extraction, and annihilation. All of them, as I show, are based on dominant structural elements of power. This does not mean, however, that 'in the last instance' one form of power alone ultimately determines all strategies of closure. To show how different forms of power interact, how forms of closure complement each other, and how closure strategies can mutually reinforce one another are the task of empirical analyses and cannot be determined theoretically from the outset.

At this point, I should also say what this book will *not* offer. The new approach to social closure presents neither full case studies of exclusion, exploitation, or elimination but makes plausible the logics of explanation in these cases. Nor does it offer an analysis of the strategies that the excluded, exploited, or those threatened with elimination can employ in daily closure struggles. While I refer to them during the analysis of the explanatory character of strategies of social closure, doing so would require to writing another book. However, the task for this new approach is first and foremost to deeply understand the strategies of the powerful in our world today.

I.7 Structure of the Book

Closure theory needs a completely new beginning. The task of the book is thus to develop a generic concept of social closure rather than a narrow one, to allow for analyses of all kinds of processes of social closure that originate in the dynamics of neoliberalism, capitalism, and settler colonialism.

Part I discusses in detail the state of development of closure theory to date. It is the merit of the theory of social closure that it has rediscovered Weber's basic concepts, if not their importance for the analysis of social life in general. However, the discussion shows that Parkin and Murphy did not see the idea of opening and closing social relationships as a general idea and tool for understanding and explaining the most critical processes in social life, nor did they adequately theorize it or put it into a reasonable methodological perspective. I discuss the approach and identify its critical deficiencies to prepare the ground for a fundamental reorientation of closure theory.

Part II brings together the concepts that are indispensable for a new theorizing of social closure. It starts from the statement that neither Weber himself nor the previous theory of social closure ever properly theorized the fundamental ideas of social closure. Revisiting Weber's work, I firstly suggest reconsidering his basic concepts of the opening and closing of social relationships as the ultimate starting point for any new theorizing of social closure and elaborate on them. Secondly, I bring in the concepts needed for a new approach: 1) As closure theory lacks a concept of *group formation* that would permit an understanding of collective social action in closure struggles, I outline a relational approach for how to conceive of closing social communities as a form of drawing boundaries that then allow them to develop a shared political identity as a precondition to *acting in solidarity* in social closure struggles. 2) I develop a relational concept of *power* that allows me to conceive of relations of exclusion, exploitation, and elimination as social relations of power. 3) I propose fundamentally revised concepts of both *life chances / chances of survival* and the *opportunity structure*. While the former are the actual goal of closure struggles, the latter denote the structural foundations needed to be able to realize these chances, which are themselves created and recreated in closure struggles.

Part III finally comes up with a new theorization of social closure. The core of the book, this part presents my outline of a new concept and approach to social closure by following three critical steps: conceptualization, typology, and explanation (Swedberg 2014). *Conceptualization* serves to define the three forms of closure that I distinguish, specifies the concepts of *power*, *group action / acting in solidarity*, and *life chances / chances of survival* and introduces the two crucial social mechanisms of social closure. These elements allow for a new and general conceptualization of closure. On this basis, for a *typology* of closure strategies,

I cross-tabulate basic strategies of closure (marginalization, extraction, and annihilation) with the critical dimensions of life chances / chances of survival (resources, rights, networks/institutions, and communities), which allows me to differentiate between four distinct strategies of closure for each form of closure, which makes twelve strategies of social closure as a whole. Proceeding this way, I develop a new and more complex sociological approach that finally moves social closure from a descriptive concept to an *explanatory* one. In accordance with theoretical and methodological developments in sociology taking place in the last decades, I come up with an explanation from a relational perspective, whose logic rests upon the identification of two critical *social mechanisms—denial of access* and *intervention into community closure*—that operate in all kinds of social closure struggles. Going beyond simply describing *exclusion*, as closure theory has been doing so far, I claim that closure struggles unfold within the social relations of exclusion, exploitation, and elimination in which powerful social groups develop strategies to realize their own life chances at the cost of the life chances / chances of survival of less-powerful groups, by 1) denying them access to resources, rights, and critical networks/institutions and 2) trying to exercise control to prevent the less powerful from closing their communities and acting in solidarity against the powerful, keeping these communities in a subordinate position. I then empirically lay out the logics of explanation for specific cases of each form of closure and reveal the plurality of processes and strategies of social closure and the destruction of life chances / chances of survival for an ever-increasing number of *The Wretched of the Earth* (Fanon 2004 [1961]), who shall not have a place in a world shaped by the historical legacy and dynamics of settler colonialism, global capitalism, and neoliberalism and the dynamics they unfold.

I
THE MISGUIDED PATH OF THE THEORY OF SOCIAL CLOSURE

Part I offers a comprehensive discussion of social closure theory as it was developed in the 1970s and 1980s. It analyses the contributions of Frank Parkin and Raymond Murphy, both of whom were crucial to the development of social closure theory, and identifies its theoretical and methodological problems. This discussion makes it clear why social closure theory has been forgotten and that it needs to be fundamentally rethought.

1
A Critical Discussion of the Theory of Social Closure

By the mid-1970s, the Parsonian *orthodox consensus* had finally lost its appeal for sociological theory, and structural Marxism had become a sterile and unsatisfactory theoretical project for analysing the class structure of the capitalist mode of production. During this time, the revival, or rather the (re)discovery, of Max Weber's concept of *open and closed social relationships*, conceptualized as social closure in the work of Frank Parkin (1974), attracted widespread interest as a new approach to sociological analysis.

In the late 1970s and 1980s, the concept of social closure was brought to the fore as a way of overcoming severe limitations of the class analysis of advanced capitalist societies. This approach reintroduced agency into sociology and introduced closure as a strategy of action. Following Parkin, Raymond Murphy (1984; 1985; 1986; 1988) developed a more systematic approach, culminating in his conceptual outline *Social Closure: The Theory of Monopolization and Exclusion* (1988). Despite being called a neo-Weberian theory, Murphy's work retained elements of structuralist Marxism, which limited its impact and relevance in concrete sociological analyses.

Other sociologists, such as Randall Collins and Pierre Bourdieu, also analysed exclusion processes in modern societies. Considerable overlap exists between Parkin and Murphy's theory of social closure and Collins's approach in *The Credential Society* (1979), which discusses how credentials exclude individuals from certain occupational positions. However, Collins (1971; 1975) did not consider himself as a closure theorist; instead, he focused on sociological conflicts in general and did not contribute theoretically or systematically to the theory of social closure.

Credentials also play a crucial role in Bourdieu's work, particularly in *Distinction* (1984 [1979]; see also Bourdieu 1986), where he discusses how they codify and validate institutionalized cultural capital. This cultural capital is acquired through educational institutions that enable individuals to outcompete others (via tests or examinations, diplomas or doctorates) for professional positions. Nevertheless, Bourdieu's analysis extends beyond the role of professions, perhaps because of his academic specialization or personal interest, given that social closure is a fundamental aspect of social life encompassing a broad range of processes, dimensions, and aspects. However, this may also be attributed to the theoretical and conceptual narrowness of the theory of social closure characteristic of academic debates at the time.[1]

The contributions of Parkin, and to some extent Murphy, sparked a lively debate which divided proponents into two camps. On one side were the Weberians, who supported using Weber's ideas to overcome the narrowness of structural Marxism. On the other side were the Marxists and neo-Marxists, who defended class analysis, either in its traditional form or through more developed concepts of class, class struggle, and class relations.

A Weberian like Günther Roth (1980) warmly welcomed Parkin's approach, while Marxist scholars criticized it defending concepts such as exploitation, the established models of analysis of class structure, and the dominance of the sphere of production (Barbalet 1982; MacKenzie 1980; Wrong 1981).[2]

While Parkin's approach generated lively interest and led to a fruitful debate on a Weberian approach to analysing the class and status structure of advanced capitalist societies, Murphy's approach faced strong criticism and even rejection on several critical fronts. David Swartz, among others, criticized the lack of clarity both in terms of conceptualization in general and in terms of the core of the theory, namely the distinction between structures, rules, and forms of closure, which in principle he saw as highly interesting (Swartz 1990). Jeff Manza (1992) further criticized the theory of social closure for lacking an explanatory approach, while Anne Witz (1988) argued that gender, along with ethnic, religious, and linguistic groups, was relegated to a secondary and less-significant position compared to social classes and class relations. Finally, Carl J. Cuneo (1989) contended that although the theory claimed relevance across all societies, Murphy's interest and analyses were predominantly limited to capitalist societies and their communist counterparts at that time.

Undoubtedly, the conceptual narrowness of the theory of social closure, its entanglement in another strange and unproductive Marx/Weber debate, and its systematic incoherencies have hindered closure analysis, preventing it from achieving its full analytical potential (Mackert 2004a). However, despite the limitations and shortcomings in its conceptual, theoretical, and analytical frameworks, scholars have continued to explore the intuitively intriguing phenomenon of social closure across various aspects of social life.

These highly interesting contributions have been explored in various fields, including the following:

---

[1] See Manza 1992, 176, who also refers to contributions to the general concept of closure and distinguishes other theoretical perspectives from the theory of social closure.

[2] Giddens 1980 engaged in a theoretical debate with Parkin 1980, who quite rightly pointed out most of Giddens's critique of his approach was missing the mark and in fact served to present his own theoretical ideas (Giddens 1976a; 1979) rather than taking Parkin's arguments seriously.

Closure debates of status positions and professional occupations with the Weberian tradition (MacDonald 1985)
Social inequality (Kreckel 1992; Sørensen 1996; Giesecke and Verwiebe 2009; Groß, 2009)
Gender and social inequality (Cyba 1985; Cyba and Balog 1989; Balog and Cyba 1990)
The labour market (van de Werfhorst 2011)
Gender and closure in the labour market processes (Wilz 2004)
Ethnic closure (Wimmer 2008; Hartmann 2011)
Political ethnicity (Neckel 1995)
Positional competition and globalization (Brown, P. 2000)
Age discrimination (Edmunds and Turner 2004; Roscigno et al. 2007)
The analysis of marginalization in advanced societies (Wacquant 1996)
Closure and educational attainment (Fasang, Mangino, and Brükner 2014)
Social closure as discrimination from a legal perspective (Albiston and Green 2018) or race/sex discrimination (Roscigno, Garcia, and Bobbitt-Zeher 2018)
Migration (Joppke 1999; Schmidtke and Ozcurumez 2008; Schmidt 2021)
Torture and terrorism (Mackert 2014; 2015)
Citizenship as an instrument of social closure (Brubaker 1992; Mackert 1999; Mackert and Turner 2017b)[3]

Although serious efforts have been made to address the general nature of the concept of social closure and to use elements of closure theory in a more theoretically sophisticated manner for sociological analyses (Mackert 2014; 2015; 2021; Hartmann 2011, Schmidt 2021), sociology still needs a radically new and fundamental approach that rethinks, critically discusses, and revises the current state of closure theory.

The approach to closure theory that I develop in this book addresses this challenge. I align with several critical perspectives on the theory of social closure, arguing that while it has been labelled neo-Weberian, it selectively incorporates Weber's ideas without fully realizing their potential as foundational concepts for sociological exploration of social closure. Currently, the theory primarily focuses on capitalist (and then communist) societies and on enriching the analysis of class structure. In doing so, it remains committed to structuralist Marxist ideas such as a teleological perspective of social development and a logic of derivation that assumes that capitalist class relations always have primacy for understanding social processes and social life.

---

[3] This list is by no means exhaustive. It simply shows the many different social fields in which closure analyses have been prominent.

All these justified criticisms make it clear that a new approach to closure theory must begin at a much more fundamental level, as these shortcomings cannot simply be remedied by minor changes. Instead, closure theory needs to be completely rethought in terms of its theory, methodology, and concepts. I begin this endeavour with a critical discussion of the theory of social closure.

2
Frank Parkin
Social Closure as Exclusion and Usurpation

Frank Parkin's (1974; 1979) initial involvement with Weber's sociological concept of closure stemmed from a strong interest in the analysis of both the class structure and the stratification order in advanced capitalist societies, as well as a deep dissatisfaction with the dominant structural Marxism at the time. Critical of the fact that Marxist analyses were based on a rigid dualist classification scheme that forced all kinds of social relations in society to be analysed according to its mutually exclusive categories of capital and labour, Parkin was convinced that this theoretical perspective could no longer provide satisfactory analyses of the complex structure of modern capitalist society.

In Parkin's view, Marxism only allowed the analysis of interclass relations, focusing solely on economic exploitation and political domination between the two main classes in capitalism. In contrast, he argued that Weber's concept of closure could provide a more satisfactory approach to analysing the stratification order of advanced modern societies, capturing its complex internal social structure. Far from simply rejecting the analysis of class relations, Parkin claimed that he was interested in an 'alternative approach to class analysis which preserves the traditional and necessary focus on dichotomy without its constrictive zero-sum accompaniments' (Parkin 1974, 3). Yet this required going beyond the strictures of structural Marxism for at least three reasons. First, Parkin advocated taking intraclass relations into account, which would make it possible to also consider differentiations and conflicts within social classes. Second, this would allow a focus on stratifications and tensions 'associated with membership in racial, ethnic, religious, and linguistic communities' (Parkin 1974, 2). Finally, by not restricting the analysis to structural features of capitalism, it would reintroduce the long-overlooked social action of individuals and social groups back into sociological analysis.

2.1 The Framework for an Analysis of Social Closure

To understand all forms of structured inequality in society by drawing upon the analysis of closure, Parkin advocates for several 'refinements and enlargements upon the original usage' (Parkin 1979, 44). In his view, four major aspects allow us to establish a framework for the analysis of all forms of closure in society: *first*, the concept of the social closure equation; *second*, the comprehension of exclusion and usurpation as strategies of social action; *third*, the inclusion of the state in the analysis of closure struggles; *fourth*, a broadening of the concept of closure.

2.1.1 The Social Closure Equation

While Weber focused on the social actions of individuals and groups driving the closure of social relationships, Parkin broadens the concept of *closure* to systematically consider the social activities of those who are excluded:

> An initial step in this direction is to extend the notion of closure to encompass other forms of collective social action designed to maximize claims to rewards and opportunities. Closure strategies would thus include not only those of an exclusionary kind, but also those adopted by the excluded themselves as a direct response to their status as outsiders. (Parkin 1979, 44–45)

Therefore, Parkin defines closure as involving two different reciprocal action strategies, namely strategies of exclusion and strategies of usurpation:

> The distinguishing feature of *exclusionary closure* is the attempt by one group to secure for itself a privileged position at the expense of some other group through a process of subordination. That is to say, it is a form of collective social action which, intentionally or otherwise, gives rise to a social category of ineligibles or outsiders. Expressed metaphorically, exclusionary closure represents the use of power in a 'downward' direction because it necessarily entails the creation of a group, class, or stratum of legally defined inferiors. (Parkin 1979: 45; emphasis added)

According to this view, usurpation can be understood conversely:

> Countervailing action by the 'negative privileged', on the other hand, represents the use of power in an upward direction in the sense that collective attempts by the excluded to win a greater share of resources always threaten to bite into the privileges of legally superior. It is in other words a form of action having *usurpation* as its goal. (Parkin 1979, 45; emphasis added)

On this basis of understanding *exclusion* and *usurpation* as strategies of social action that deploy power against one another in struggles for access to resources, goods, and opportunities, Parkin sees them 'as the two main generic types of social closure, the latter always being a consequence of, and collective response to the former' (Parkin 1979, 45). This refinement and expansion of the concept lead to a basic reconceptualization of social closure as a form of social struggle for the redistribution of monopolized resources and goods. This struggle finds its expression in the metaphorical notion of the *social closure equation*, implying exclusionary closure to represent one side, while the 'collective efforts to resist a pattern of dominance governed by exclusion principles can properly be regarded as the other half of the social closure equation' (Parkin 1979, 45). In social struggles over the monopolization of resources and goods, and demands for the redistribution of these, social actors oppose each other over struggles for certain social goods. Thus, social closure encompasses both exclusion and usurpation, requiring us to carefully conceptualize both sides of the closure equation as distinct yet interrelated processes.

2.1.2 Strategies of Social Action

We need to be more precise regarding these strategies. Contestations over the distribution of goods and resources in society can be understood as political struggles where both sides pursue reciprocal action strategies. Unlike Marxist positions, Parkin no longer views these strategies as simple expressions of actors' positions in the production process and, consequently, the class structure. Instead, he sees them as political strategies expressing struggles for social resources and goods, for which social actors are permanently competing.

Parkin highlights an important difference between the two reciprocal strategies of social action in closure struggles. First, strategies of exclusion that aim to monopolize resources, social goods, privileges, or opportunities typically have a *legalistic* character. They can rely on state support to legally legitimize and protect institutions of private property and on credential systems that guarantee exclusive access to resources and privileges. As exclusionary strategies of the dominant class that are backed by the state, these strategies are 'the predominant mode of closure in all stratified systems' (Parkin 1979, 45) that allow the powerful to monopolize goods and resources, effectively excluding outsiders.

Second, despite the dominant class's efforts to maintain the existing class structure and stratification order through exclusionary closure strategies, the main feature of usurpationary closure strategies is to assert new standards for the distribution of social goods and resources in society. By means of usurpation, subordinate social classes and groups aim to reduce the dominant class's share of resources to their credit. As the subordinate class cannot rely on the backing of the state in social closure struggles, their members are forced to rely on *solidaristic* strategies:

One of the important differences between usurpationary closure and exclusionary closure is that the former tends to rely heavily upon the public mobilization of members and supporters, as in the use of strikes, demonstrations, sit-ins, marches, picketing, symbolic vigils, and the like. As a result, usurpationary activities normally stand in an uncomfortable relationship to the legal order. The borderline between lawful and unlawful usurpationary acts is often rather finely drawn, and tends moreover continuously to be redrawn over time, as chequered history of the right to strike and to 'peaceful picketing' well illustrates. (Parkin 1979, 74–75)

2.1.3 Bringing the State into the Analysis of Social Closure

The fact that exclusionary strategies by social actors can be viewed as legalistic since they are usually backed up by the state draws attention to the role of the latter in closure struggles in general. Of course, here Parkin is referring to the state's clear role in codifying private property as capital and providing it legal protection. Yet there is a second important aspect in that the state comes into play as Parkin shows, thereby pointing to a critical weakness in Weber's claim. To reduce the number of competitors in a market, he argues that 'any externally identifiable characteristic of another group of those (currently or potentially) competing, such as race, language, and confession, local or social origin, descent, residence and so forth will be taken as a reason to attempt to exclude them from competition' (Weber 1985 [1922], 201; my own translation based on Weber 1978 [1922], 341–342).[1] Contrary to this, Parkin argues that any exclusion of social groups leverages these groups' legal subordination enacted by the state:

> In all known instances where racial, religious, linguistic, or sex characteristics have been seized upon for closure purposes the group in question has already at some time been defined as legally inferior by the state. Ethnic subordination, to take the commonest case, has normally occurred as a result of territorial conquest or the forced migration of populations creating a subcategory of second-class citizens within the nation-state. (Parkin 1979: 95-96)

In both regards, Parkin asserts that it becomes obvious that closure struggles cannot be analysed without also examining the state and its role in already

---

[1] Unfortunately, parts of the translation of Max Weber's *Economy and Society* are misleading, if not utterly wrong. Throughout my debate on Weber, I will stick only a few times to the English translation (Weber 1978 [1922]). In most cases, I will revise this translation or translate parts anew.

having legally defined categories of powerful and subordinated groups in society that are, by definition, easily exposed to the power strategies of superordinate actors. Thus, the state is a crucial player in closure struggles.

2.1.4 Closure and Exploitation

Intending to develop an instrument designed to analyse all power relations in society, Parkin reconceptualizes *exploitation* and redefines its correlation to social closure. According to his critique of Marxism, his main step to broaden the spectrum of social processes to be analysed as social closure is to redefine the Marxian concept of exploitation by including social relations of all social sides, including classes, groups, and so forth, in which one group monopolizes any given resource or good, thereby excluding the others. Referring to exploitation, Parkin argues: 'There is no compelling reason why the term should be restricted to its conventional Marxist usage, referring to the appropriation of surplus value on the part of capital, since this is itself but one important case of the more general phenomenon of exclusionary closure' (Parkin 1979, 46). Certainly, this generalization has consequences in terms of how to perceive exploitation in the face of strategies of action in both a downward and an upward perspective:

> In so far as exclusionary forms of power result in the downward use of power, hence creating subordinate social formations, they can be regarded by definition as exploitative. Exploitation here defines the nexus between classes or other collectivities that stand in relationship of dominance and subordination, on whatever social basis.... Collective efforts to restrict access to rewards and opportunities on the part of one social group against another, including one group of workers against another can be regarded as inherently exploitative even though the relationship is not one of surplus extraction deriving from property ownership. Relations of dominance and subordination between bourgeoisie and proletariat, Protestant and Catholic, whites and blacks, men and women, etc., can all be considered exploitative relationships in the non-Weberian sense. (Parkin 1979, 46)

Conversely, Manza rightly points out that 'clearly, a conception of exploitation in which *all* types of social domination through closure are defined as exploitative is not very helpful' (Manza 1992, 291). Yet, firstly, Parkin argues that all forms of exclusionary strategies are exploitative, while, secondly, he claims that closure is the more general concept and exploitation is only a special case of it. Thus, he attempts to reduce exploitation to a *moral* phenomenon (Parkin 1979, 47) that loses any specific meaning which would make it distinguishable from other forms of exclusionary closure. This certainly does not seem to be very helpful because neither different exclusionary processes nor the results they generate will be the same.

However, in Parkin's view, this broadening of the concept of exploitation opens the perspective for closure analysis to come to terms with intra-class relations that cannot be analysed on the grounds of a Marxist conception of exploitation. Rather, social closure is now thought to be an instrument that enables us to analyse all kinds of power relations in society in which individuals, communal groups, classes, and other social actors are excluded from life chances. The structure of society can thus no longer be simply understood as the result of exploitation in a Marxist sense but as the consequence of reciprocal strategies of exclusion and usurpation, which is a critical aspect of the distribution of power in society. Parkin calls for translating the vocabulary of closure 'into the language of power—not through the portrayal of power as a mysterious something extra whose uncertain location complicates the stratification system, but as a metaphor for describing the very operation of the system' (Parkin 1974, 15).

2.2 Social Closure as Exclusion

This broader concept of social closure enables us to take a closer look at exclusionary strategies allowing the dominant class and powerful groups in society to preserve their privileges, thereby defending the class structure and stratification order to safeguard their prerogatives in a system of structured inequality.

2.2.1 Private Property and Credentialism

Although, by reinterpreting the concept of closure, Parkin broadens the range of phenomena to be analysed as closure struggles, he does not abandon the critical role private property plays in modern capitalist societies. Rather, he argues that private property is of the utmost importance in order to understand closure struggles. Yet, following Weber's class analysis, Parkin deems credentials in modern societies, given both their educational and professional structure based on individually acquired certificates, to be equally important to exploitation based on private property. 'In modern capitalist society the two main exclusionary devices which the bourgeoisie constructs and maintains itself as a class are, first, those surrounding the institutions of property; and second, academic or professional qualifications and credentials' (Parkin 1979, 47–48).

Therefore, against the background of his conception of closure, Parkin is interested in the various ways the legal system of advanced capitalist society privileges different groups of society by excluding others from chances in life on the grounds of either property or credentials, thus pointing to the significant role of the state in closure struggles:

> Each represents a set of *legal arrangements* for restricting access to rewards and privileges: property ownership is a form of closure designed to prevent general access to the means of production and its fruits; credentialism is a form of closure designed to control and monitor entry to key positions in the division of labour. (Parkin 1979, 48; emphasis added)

This, of course, is nothing less than a double attack on Marxist positions: first, Parkin offers a specific revision of the concept of private property, while second, he attributes credentials to be of equal importance for understanding all forms of exclusionary closure in society. As Parkin sees both—property and credentialism—as 'state-enforced exclusionary practices' (Parkin 1979, 48), the state (more precisely, the legal system) plays a critical role here.

Private Property
In examining the role that private property ownership should play in a concept of social closure, Parkin critically discusses and rejects sociological strategies that attempt to reduce the significance of exploitation as resulting from private property ownership or simply abandon and consequently reduce private property to being merely a form of authority.[2] He argues that none of the sociologists in the 1970s distinguished between 'property as rights to personal possessions and property as capital' (Parkin 1979, 49). Yet the main criterion for properly understanding the meaning and significance of private property is how it is legally defined: 'What the sociological definition of property as possession interestingly fails to ask is why only certain limited forms of possession are legally admissible' (Parkin 1979, 50). Thus, Parkin not only exposes sociologists' confusion regarding rights to *personal possession* and *property as capital* but he also rejects proposals like Ralf Dahrendorf's to instead argue that property is only a historically specific and narrow form of authority which is the more general phenomenon (Parkin 1979, 51). This idea only shifts the general problem of the societal effects of private property to one of organizational settings, completely ignoring questions of exploitation, profit maximization, and the role of capital. Yet 'authority relations are inseparable from property rights.... Managerial command over labour takes place within a legal framework in which the inviolability

---

[2] Parkin does not adopt the neo-Marxist interpretations that attempt to include workplace control and authority as criteria to address the narrow understanding of private property as simply meaning exploitation of added value. See, for example, Wright 1985.

of property is already guaranteed' (Parkin 1979, 52). Both the critical role of the state and the fact that it legally guarantees private property as well as Parkin's reinterpretation of exploitation as exclusionary closure make it possible to redirect and relocate private property within the general understanding of power relations:

> The case for restoring the notion of private property into the centre of class analysis is that it is the most important single form of social closure common to industrial societies. That is to say, the right of ownership can be understood not so much as a special case of authority so much as a specific form of exclusion. (Parkin 1979, 53)

In distinguishing private possession and private property as capital, Parkin argues that both allow for strategies of exclusionary closure. Yet 'it is only the exclusionary rights embedded in the latter that have important consequences for the life-chances and social conditions of the excluded' (Parkin 1979, 53).[3] It is the state that confers these rights to some and excludes the rest from social goods and resources: 'If such exclusionary powers are legally guaranteed and enforced, an exploitative relationship prevails as a matter of definition' (Parkin 1979, 53).

Credentialism

In the face of capitalist society that had become more differentiated with a more diversified class structure, Weber referred to the critical role of education and, consequently, qualifications and the rise of professions. His introduction of the concept of *commercial classes* pointed to the positively privileged commercial classes, including among others 'f) professionals with sought-after expertise or privileged education (such as lawyers, physicians, artists), or g) workers with monopolistic qualifications and skills (natural or acquired through drill or training)' (Weber 1978 [1922], 304).

To understand class formation and the stratification order of modern society in the face of this transformation, Parkin declares credentialism to be as significant as private property. Starting from Max Weber's analysis and conceptualization of classes, he is interested in how credentials are used for closure purposes and argues that processes of professionalization, the emphasis on them being different from blue-collar work, or their insistence on technical competence

---

[3] Barbalet strongly criticized Parkin for allegedly conceiving life chances as only a phenomenon of distribution rather than one of exploitation in the sphere of production: 'Any explanation of social inequality which is predicated on the concept "life-chances" is positively inhibited from going beyond relations of unequal distribution and can therefore ignore entirely relations of production and exploitation' (Barbalet 1988, 491).

may well serve as ways to exercise control over the standards of the relevant professions. Yet, at the same time, he follows Weber's assessment:

> Normally this concern for efficient performance recedes behind the interest in limiting the supply of candidates for the benefices and honours of a given occupation... Such monopolistic tendencies and similar economic considerations have often played a significant role in *impeding* the expansion of a group. (Weber 1978 [1922], 344)

While credentialism may have this dual nature, Parkin makes further strong arguments to expose the side of it that is normally concealed. Increasing numbers of graduates who have the required qualification may lead to strategies of restricting their influx into the professions by introducing tests that may allow access only to those with the highest test scores. Although formal qualification and certificates would seem to *objectively* represent an individual's abilities, knowledge, and *cultural capital*, they were simply 'designed to measure certain class-related qualities and attributes rather than those practical skills and aptitudes that may not so easily be passed on through the family line' (Parkin 1979, 55). Certainly, credentialism also serves as a form of protection for those in professional positions from competition in the marketplace.

As in the case of private property, Parkin's argument again refers to the role of the state. Similar to strategies used in manual trades to reduce competition and exclude newcomers through systems such as closed shops or differentiating between skilled and unskilled work, 'those adopted by the professions is that the latter generally seek to establish a legal monopoly over the provision of services through licensure by the state' (Parkin 1979, 57).

Backed by the state, the privileged professions in modern society could enforce their position as *legally privileged groups* (Weber), in contrast to blue-collar workers. Parkin also points out that the restrictive practices of workers or trade unions are efforts to protect vulnerable subordinate groups in society from the dominant class, whereas credentialism serves fundamentally different purposes: 'The learned or free professions were never directly subordinate to an employing class during the period when they were effecting social closure' (Parkin 1979, 57). Having established monopolies of professions allowing their members to present themselves as guardians of exclusive knowledge, the state backs these exclusive professions because questioning their monopolies might backfire, given that today the professions are among the social groups most enthusiastically defending the (neo-)liberal order at the expense of the excluded and subordinate. Thus, to understand the processes that promote the specific class structure and stratification order of modern capitalist societies, Parkin argues that 'on all these grounds it is necessary to regard credentialism as a form of exclusionary social closure comparable in its importance for class formation to the institution of property' (Parkin 1979, 58).

2.2.2 Collectivist and Individualist Strategies of Exclusion

Based on the distinction between private property and credentialism that allows members of the bourgeoisie to benefit from state-backed exclusionary closure, we would expect a guaranteed reproduction of the class structure and stratification order no less reliable in capitalism than in premodern societies. Yet we must concede that the two 'exclusionary practices that secure the position of a given class do not always guarantee the safe transmission of advantage to family descendants' (Parkin 1979, 60). Neither private property nor credentials work as well as aristocratic descent and lineage did in the past to safeguard the reproduction of the capitalist class structure to protect the privileges of the dominant class. Rather, 'bourgeois forms of closure ... are not obviously perfected to bring about this result', as 'neither property nor credentials are altogether reliable as institutions for preserving family privileges intact over several generations' (Parkin 1979, 60).

Unlike lineage, for instance, both devices can make social climbing possible for individual members of the subordinate classes. Given that the foundations of gaining property are manifold—even more so in today's financial capitalism, where you might simply be lucky with speculation—on the one hand, people might make their fortune paving the way for new groups to become part of the privileged and owning class. On the other hand, intelligent and bright members of the subordinate class passing exams and acquiring certificates—despite these qualifications normally privileging middle and upper classes—may also enter high positions in the occupational structure.

In the face of such uncertainty, the strong desire of the bourgeoisie to reproduce and transfer privileges to their offspring obviously collides with the dominant liberal ideology in capitalist society and its strong commitment to the right to private property and individual performance, confirmed and officially legitimated by certificates. This obviously leads to some confusion about how to interpret liberal ideology:

> The classical liberal doctrine of individualism contains a powerful rejection of those principles and practices that evaluate men on the basis of group or collectivist criteria. The political driving force of individualist doctrines arose in part from the opposition of the emergent middle classes to aristocratic pretensions and exclusiveness centred around the notion of descent. (Parkin 1979, 64)

This debate is highly illuminating because it refers to the collectivist and individualist criteria that the dominant class deploys in capitalist society to reproduce the class structure and preserve privileges for themselves and their families. Parkin offers two interpretations of liberalism that the dominant class deploys to justify and legitimate processes of closure that do not coincide with liberalism's own individualist assertions and claims.

Liberalism's Alleged Rejection of Collectivist Criteria

The first strategy plainly shows a fundamental contradiction in liberal ideology of officially rejecting the evaluation of an individual as being a member of a social collectivity while propagating individualism. Parkin shows that, while previously having been a driving force in abolishing privileges of the few, individualist liberalism turns into a means of illegitimate justification of exclusion once it has become the legitimating ideology of preserving the class structure in capitalism.

The dominant class's lip service to the individualist ideology, officially rejecting collectivism, is at odds with its political praxis because individualism underhandedly allows officially individualist criteria to operate as a means of collectivist exclusion. As is already obvious from the writings of classic liberals such as Jeremy Bentham, James Mill, or John Stuart Mill, it was common practice for the bourgeoisie to keep the lower classes excluded from democratic processes (Macpherson 2012 [1977]). Thus, they made access to the ballot conditional on *individualist* criteria such as owning private property:

> Yet, the justice of such an arrangement was clearly dependent on the tacit disregard for the inequalities of condition that ensured that only a few would be in a position to meet the standards of political entry. The outcome would not have been dramatically different if workers had been excluded purely by virtue of their proletarian status. Individualist criteria could thus be employed to produce a form of closure similar to that brought about by the use of collectivist criteria. (Parkin 1979, 65)

We see a similar situation regarding the much-heralded ideal of individual merit in the field of education and the passing of exams. It is well documented that the standards in education systems in bourgeois society have clear middle-class biases. Yet this simply means that even above-average success of middle-class children would not discredit the system but simply be used to defend individual performance and skills. 'In this interpretation, working-class or black children would be excluded not because they were working class or black, but because of their genuinely lesser abilities as *individuals*' (Parkin 1979, 65; emphasis added).

What is the essence of this first constitutive contradiction within the liberal individualist ideology that Parkin discusses? Both criteria—private property and credentials—allegedly classical individualist criteria of possessive liberalism, can thus be seen as nothing but collectivist criteria in disguise that 'produce a pattern of social closure that quietly discriminates via the collectivist criterion of class or racial membership' (Parkin 1979, 65).

Liberalism's Problem with Inheritance

The second contradiction to liberalism's ideological self-conception of being constitutively individualist arises from the problem of property rights and inheritance:

> Whereas the ownership and acquisition of wealth resulting from a person's own exertions are deemed fully defensible, the inheritance of wealth is not because it rewards those who have demonstrated no ability other than in their judicious choice of parents. (Parkin 1979, 66)

Inheritance is intrinsically unfair because it advantages the dominant class's offspring while operating as an obstacle for those trying 'to make their own way to the ranks of ownership' (Parkin 1979, 66). Hereditary processes also play a crucial role in the education system that privileges children from families bequeathing high cultural capital to the next generation. There simply is no equality of opportunity in the education system. This claim is one of liberalism's biggest ideological chimeras (see Bourdieu 1984 [1979]; Bourdieu and Passeron 1977). Never has there been a real equality of opportunity for children from different social classes in the education systems of capitalist societies.

What is at the core of this second constitutive contradiction in the ideology of individualist liberalism? Here is what Parkin asserted:

> The essence of this version of liberal ideology is that social closure conforms to the standards of justice only in so far as it discriminates between individuals on the basis of their innate capacities and performances, and that these are not contaminated by the social inheritance of material or cultural goods. (Parkin 1979, 66)

Without any doubt, social closure on the grounds of radical individualist ideas would make the bourgeoisie suffer from the consequences of the ideology that justifies their privileges and legitimates their domination of capitalist society, as we would see this class only basally reproduced. As Parkin argues, it would be the duty of the state to guarantee precisely these conditions in order to have free competition for positions, rewards, and resources to make liberalism actually work and abolish all unfair political tactics of the dominant class: 'Liberalism finds nothing reprehensible in exclusionary closure *per se*, provided that it is grounded in a genuine and uncompromising individualism and not in the spurious version that masks the ignoble version purpose of class reproduction' (Parkin 1979, 66).

Against the background of these two constitutive contradictory aspects of liberal ideology and its political praxis, it is interesting to see that this ideology allows capitalist societies to present themselves as being open to individual success while at the same time securing the reproduction of the class structure. This leads to one last aspect regarding collectivist and individualist strategies of exclusion, namely the distinction between collectivist and individualist criteria of exclusionary closure and the question of how and with what consequences they combine in closure strategies.

Parkin offers a useful classification to help understand the reproduction of social classes always based on both collectivist and individualist criteria. First, exclusion based on purely collectivist criteria produces and reproduces *communal groups* according to criteria such as race, religion, language, etc., eventually leading to ghettos, segregated areas in cities, apartheid systems, and so forth. Merely being a member of these groups plays a role in the politics of exclusion. Second, exclusion based on purely individualist criteria (pure meritocracy) would produce and reproduce *segmental status groups* that would in a sense replace class by clearly segregated meritocratic social segments. Third, essentially as a mixed form, the relative interaction of both collectivist and individualist criteria of exclusion produces and reproduces *social classes* more to either one or the other pole of the pure cases. This happens according to the relative dominance of how and based on what criteria are used to exclude members of a subordinate class from civil society, political participation, and so forth.

Thus, looking behind the mask of liberal individualism reveals that the reproduction of the class structure always combines collectivist and individualist criteria of exclusion. As Parkin stresses, despite the ideological claim of liberal individualism, no simple juxtaposition of collectivist criteria of closure could be assigned to premodern societies based on kinship ties and lineage and individualist criteria of closure operating exclusively in liberal modern capitalist class societies.

2.3 Social Closure as Usurpation

Why does Parkin describe the counterstrategies used by the excluded as *usurpationary*? This somewhat awkward term draws attention to the critical role of the state in legitimizing and supporting exclusionary closure strategies used by the dominant class by declaring them to be in accordance with the law. Because of this, all strategies that call into question the class structure and stratification order that has been established and reproduced over the generations by means of exclusionary strategies obviously challenge and attempt to delegitimize what has so far been the legally backed order of unequal access to resources, goods, and opportunities. Thus, 'usurpation is that type of social closure mounted by a group in response to its outsider status and the collective experiences of exclusion' (Parkin 1979, 74).[4]

What the manifold strategies used by excluded groups fighting against their exclusion have in common is that they mobilize power against the group that dominates and excludes them from opportunities in society and that is supported by the state by organizing demonstrations and resistance through social mobilization of those excluded to unite them and gain social power.

In comparing exclusionary and usurpationary strategies of closure, Parkin notes that the latter are dangerous for the ideologically legitimized class structure and the accompanying distribution of resources, privileges, and social goods in society. The more successful usurpationary strategies become, the more they can potentially transform the social order itself. Ultimately, successful usurpationary strategies might threaten the class structure of society as such: 'Hence there can never really be the same degree of legal and institutional backing for usurpationary activities as for exclusionary ones' (Parkin 1979, 75).

In a first step, Parkin discusses the obviously growing power of trade unions in the United Kingdom in the 1970s, pointing to the reconstruction of capitalist companies or increasing international interdependence that made them more vulnerable to usurpationary activities of the working-class rejecting a given model of social justice by promoting a different one. This debate is, of course, linked to the class structure and its transformation in the post-war period and is an effort to capture economic and political class struggles within the vocabulary and framework of closure theory. Yet, interested not only in interclass but also intra-class conflicts as well as conflicts among communal groups, Parkin, in a second step, then turns to usurpationary forms of closure beyond interclass relations: 'The collective efforts of women or racial and ethnic groups to seek either full inclusion into civil society, or some degree of secession from the existing nation state are generically similar to the countervailing actions of a subordinate class' (Parkin 1979, 84–85).

---

[4] Weber introduced the term *usurpation* in *Economy and Society* 'to refer to the struggles of urban plebeians (the nascent bourgeoisie) against patrimonial rulers in the Middle Ages' (Wrong 1981, 36).

In fact, Parkin refers to two different arenas of usurpationary struggle. First, within the economy, in the workplace he sees the members of racial or ethnic groups or the female workforce as a whole to be too dispersed to organize and develop usurpationary strategies. Consequently, they are trapped in low positions, resulting in weak bargaining positions that make them vulnerable and barely allow for mobilization of their interests with regard to their demands for higher wages, better representation within the unions, or even a reorganization of the structure of distribution of power in the workplace.

The second arena then refers to the legal struggles of these groups in the wider society:

> Civil rights movements and feminist groups have tended to lay considerable store on the vulnerability of key sections of the exclusionary group to moral appeals that articulate the high ideals of the formal ideology—in particular those centred around the flexible notion of equality. (Parkin 1979, 85)

In these circumstances, it is not so much the power per se that these groups, especially ethnic groups, excluded from civil and/or political rights are able to mobilize, but rather their morally convincing state agents of the illegitimacy of their exclusion. 'In bourgeois society, at least, it would seem that the phenomenon of "white liberalism" has its analogue in all situations of collective exclusion, whatever their bases, so that usurpationary claims grounded in moral appeals are not wholly without effect' (Parkin 1979, 86).

In these cases, as in both liberalism's alleged rejection of collectivist criteria and its ignorance towards inheritance as forms of exclusionary closure, it is obvious how liberal ideology and its political practice are contradictory. Of course, the subordinate class cannot expect the dominant class to be insightful and recognize this betrayal of individualist ideals. Instead, this class, like communal groups, has to mobilize power in order to attack the illegitimate privileges of the powerful.

2.4 Dual Closure

Up to this point, Parkin has offered an approach that allows us to think about interclass conflicts in capitalist society not on the grounds of the classes' fixed positioning in the class structure but by referring to the collective strategies they pursue:

> For definitional purposes, then, the dominant class in society can be said to consist of those social groups whose share of resources is attained primarily

by exclusionary means; whereas the subordinate class consists of social groups whose primary strategy is one of usurpation, notwithstanding the occasional resort to exclusion as a supplementary strategy'. (Parkin 1979, 93)

Now Parkin turns his attention to the internal divisions of the subordinate class and conflicts within it, arguing that the collective actions of the groups within the working class or between these and communal groups cannot simply be understood by concentrating on usurpationary strategies. Rather, these groups adopt legalistic strategies as supplementary strategies to defend their position within the subordinate class—a concept he calls *dual closure*.

Parkin elaborates on this by referring to a number of social phenomena. He mentions, for instance, the coalition of the working class with labour parties to push legislation through; strategies used by the labour aristocracy to exclude newcomers; the relationship between Black and White workers under Apartheid in South Africa, or in the South of the United States, where the civil rights movement attempted to implement legislation to bring racial discrimination to an end; as well as the conflicts in Northern Ireland between Protestant and Catholic members of the workforce, and the feminization of semi-professions or the workforce in general. In all these cases, we see privileged strata or groups of the subordinate class fighting against others by deploying exclusionary strategies of a legalistic rather than a usurpationary character.

Yet Parkin argues that within the labour class, exclusionary struggles among different group of workers, such as the conflicts between of White and Black workers or men excluding women, are not forms of racist or misogynistic behaviour. He sees them instead as a mediated consequence of the policies of the state: 'Ethnic minorities, for example, that have at some time or other been deprived of political and civil rights by the state are the natural target for exclusionary moves by the lower strata of the dominant cultural or racial group' (Parkin 1979, 95). Moreover, referring to all these internal closure struggles, he argues:

> None of these possibilities could be realized because the dominant class and the state had not already paved the way by creating the appropriate legally and politically vulnerable category. There is thus nothing in the least arbitrary in the selection of exclusionary criteria. (Parkin 1979, 96)

Building on Parkin's theoretical and conceptual work on the idea of closure, Murphy contributed to the *theory of social closure* by introducing further differentiations.

3
Raymond Murphy
Rules, Structures, and Forms of Social Closure

Raymond Murphy's (1984; 1985; 1986; 1988)[1] critical elaboration of social closure can be seen as an 'attempt to develop a conceptualization of the rules of social closure and their transformation, an attempt which takes as its starting point the work of Weber and certain non-Weberians' (Murphy 1988, 4). Not only does Murphy's discussion concentrate on reconceptualizing and developing closure theory but, at the same time, it deals with the two dominant theoretical schools of the late 1970s and early 1980s—structural Marxism and Functionalism—and aims at transcending them with closure theory as the most promising theoretical perspective in sociology. To do so, he picks up critical 'elements for a unified "theory of social closure"' (Swartz 1990, 480) that he finds in Weber and, in particular, Parkin.

Murphy's main contribution to closure theory is his development of different rules of closure, its structures, and forms that make it possible to rank these rules conceptually (Swartz 1990, 480). He aims to overcome the crucial problem in neo-Weberian closure theory, which is 'the neglect of the relationships among the different rules of closure and hence the failure to analyse how the rules of closure are structured' (Murphy 1988, 65). As Murphy claims that analysing these specific relationships would make it possible to reveal the hidden *deep structure of domination* in capitalist society, he sets himself the task of developing such a theoretical and methodological approach.

3.1 Elaborating on (Neo-)Weberian Closure Theory

Throughout his *Theory of Monopolization and Exclusion*, Murphy discusses closure within the context of market relations, arguing as follows:

> Weber used the term 'closure' (see, in particular, Weber, 1978 [1922], 43–46, 302–307, 339–348, 635–640, 926–955) to refer to the process of subordination

---

[1] Murphy has published a number of critical articles. His 1988 book *Social Closure: The Theory of Monopolization and Exclusion* is mainly a collection of these earlier articles; for a review of this attempt, see Morrow 1990.

whereby one group monopolizes advantages by closing off opportunities to another group of outsiders beneath it which it defines as inferior and ineligible. Any convenient, visible characteristic, such as race, language, social origin, religion, or lack of a particular school diploma, can be used to declare competitors to be outsiders. (Murphy 1988, 8)

Following Weber's concentrating on processes of closure being motivated by instrumentally rational orientation and therefore confining the analysis of social closure from the outset to the analysis of opportunities in the market, Murphy discusses Parkin's development of the approach of closure theory, agreeing with most of his elaboration of Weber's basic ideas. *First*, he also advocates distinguishing between exclusion and usurpation as two reciprocal strategies of action in closure struggles. Yet, Murphy rejects abandoning the structural significance of the positioning of individuals in the class structure, which he believes Parkin has given up in favour of strategies of action. Rather, he insists on keeping in mind the concept of a dialectical relation of agency and structure and argues that thinking about strategies without having any idea about the positioning of individuals in the class structure would be counterproductive and too arbitrary. *Second*, against this background, Murphy concurs with Parkin and also believes closure theory makes it possible to analyse all forms of power relations and domination in society since any exclusion presupposes the exertion of power—with the dominant classes using power in a downward direction, and the subordinate classes, conversely, in an upward direction. *Third*, Murphy agrees that closure theory needs to develop a broader concept than the Marxian idea of exploitation in line with Weber's wider concept of closure. This concept also allows a discussion on exclusionary practices of a dominant social group increasing their gains at the expense of a subordinate one, irrespective of both the basis and legitimation that enables this, be it private property, credentials, race, ethnicity, religion, language, or gender:

> Closure theory does not reduce communal and sexual exclusion to exploitation in the Marxian sense nor does it merely add on factors exogenous to the Marxian conception of exploitation *ad hoc*. Instead it begins with a broader conception—exclusion, also expressed as closure or monopolization—which captures the common and essential feature of property, credential, knowledge, gender, Communist Party, and communal domination. It is this explicit concept that provides the basis for a coherent critical theory and seizes the *raison d'être* of struggle and conflict. At the root of Weberian closure theory is the perception of the parallel between processes of monopolization (and exclusion) based on capital in the market and those based on closed relationships between status groups. (Murphy 1988, 101–102)

Fourth, Murphy advocates taking into consideration the side of the excluded since they may not simply accept the exclusionary practices at play. Rather, all forms of exclusion must be seen as potentially triggering usurpationary reactions. At this point, Murphy introduces a distinction as he defines strategies of the excluded that claim the redistribution of resources within the existing system as *inclusionary*, while demands to reject a given structure of distribution and aiming at overthrowing this because it is perceived to be utterly unjust as *revolutionary*. This, of course, is significant as the two types of usurpationary strategies may also be seen as the extremes of the various options that excluded social actors may take.

Despite this overlap, Murphy has a different view of many things. His main criticism of neo-Weberian closure theory is that, so far, it has not succeeded in developing a frame of reference that would make it possible to differentiate between different rules of closure, the structures they have, the way they are related to one another, and their different levels of significance in changing social contexts:

> Closure theory has the value of making objective exclusion more transparent and of clarifying the nature, sources, and consequences of exclusion rules. It provides a conceptual framework which recognizes exclusion for what it is, rather than camouflaging it with euphemisms. (Murphy 1988, 48)

Reconstructing this framework will show not only how Murphy attempts to further elaborate on the theoretical framework for an analysis of all phenomena of social closure in society but also further ways in which he deviates from Parkin's ideas.

3.2 A Model for the Analysis of Social Closure

Three key aspects characterize Murphy's approach: first, developing a comprehensive conception of different rules of closure; second, clarifying how these rules correspond with one another; third, defining the priority of a specific rule of closure within a given type of society. Furthermore, a framework for analysing the structure of these rules of closure has to be developed that can be used to explain what Murphy calls the *deep structure of domination* in society. For this, Murphy proposes taking four methodological steps. Of course, when looking at the empirical examples (see figure 3.1), we must remember that this approach was developed in the 1980s.

The *first methodological step* required for a reconceptualization of closure analysis in Murphy's view is to differentiate between *principal*, *derivative*, and

Closure Structures*	Forms of Closure		
	Principal (P)	Derivative (D)	Contingent (C)
Tandem 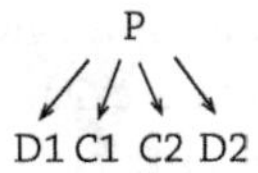 P ╱│╲╲ D1 C1 C2 D2	Lineage (Aristocratic Society) Private Property (Capitalist Society) Communist Party (State-Socialist Society)	---- Credentials[+] ---- ---- Gender[+] ---- ---- Race[+] ---- ---- Ethnicity[+] ---- ---- Language[+] ---- ---- Religion[+] ----	
Paired 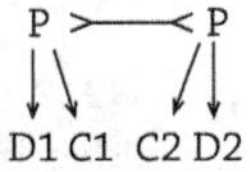 P >——< P │╲ ╱│ D1 C1 C2 D2	Property – Apartheid (South Africa) Property – Citizenship (World Capitalist System)		
Polar 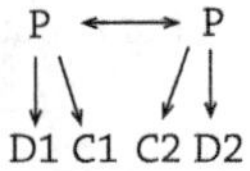 P ←——→ P │╲ ╱│ D1 C1 C2 D2	Property vs. Communist Party (World System)		

* ↓ Indicates dominance-dependence relationship
>——< Indicates complementary relationship
←——→ Indicates oppositional relationship
[+] ---- Indicates that these rules of closure have both derivative and contingent forms, with the importance of one form or the other varying from society to society and historically. Under the South African system of apartheid race constitutes one of the principal forms of exclusion

Figure 3.1 The structure of social closure
Source: Murphy 1988, 76

contingent forms of exclusion. Furthermore, it is important to specify the principal form of exclusion that is not only decisive for the specific distribution of resources in society but also determines the entire closure process and the relationship between the lower-ranking forms of exclusion. 'The principal form of exclusion refers to the set of exclusion rules, backed by the legal (and hence ultimately the military) apparatus of the state, which is the main determinant of access to, or exclusion from, power, resources and opportunities in society' (Murphy 1988, 70). Contrary to Parkin, who claims credentials are just as important as private property for pursuing strategies of exclusionary closure in capitalist societies, Murphy defines the legally supported possession of private property as the only *principal* form of exclusion in capitalism. Derivative and contingent forms of exclusion that are also associated with rules for monopolizing opportunities can then be distinguished from this principal form.

Derivative forms of exclusion 'are rules for the monopolization of opportunities in society derived directly from the principal form of exclusion, yet not identical to it' (Murphy 1988, 70). This first step of reconceptualizing the closure perspective already shows how strongly Murphy remains committed to structural Marxism even while allegedly developing a neo-Weberian approach. Not only does he stick to his conviction that it is precisely private property that has *ultimate primacy* with regard to the structure of distribution of resources, goods, and positions in the class structure, but he also argues in favour of a *logic of derivation* by conceptualizing derivative and contingent forms of exclusion as always being dependent on private property without having independent effects on the exclusion of individuals, social groups, or classes. Consequently, Murphy discusses all the following rules of derivative and contingent forms of exclusion exclusively within a framework of the class structure in capitalist society.[2]

For both sets of rules, Murphy gives an identical list of criteria that might work as either derivative or contingent forms. Credentials qualifying individuals for specific positions in the occupation structure 'as well as mechanisms that tend to exclude racial, ethnic, religious groups, or the sexes' can be deemed to be directly *derived* from the principal form only if they 'derive their force from the state-backed legal structures of private property in capitalist society and the Communist Party in state-socialist societies' (Murphy 1988, 71). Hence, if credentials, race, ethnicity, religion, language, or gender are to operate as *contingent* rules, this only happens in social fields not directly linked to the productive sector (i.e., not in capitalist enterprises). What Murphy has in mind are credentials for doctors or the nursing staff in hospitals, any form of work in research facilities, in education, public services, catering, journalism, freelancing in general, and so forth:

> Although not directly derived from the principal exclusionary form, the very nature of these rules of exclusion depends on the principal exclusionary form in society and their very existence is contingent on the principal form. These contingent forms of exclusion are often, but not necessarily, directly backed by the legal apparatus of the state. (Murphy 1988, 72)

---

[2] It seems clear that Murphy's central idea for closure theory—the derivative logic of rules of exclusion—has at once been its Achilles heel and partially responsible for the theory of social closure being ignored over the past few years or even decades. Why should women, people of colour, certain groups (ethnic, religious, or language), members of the LGBTQI community, and many more be interested in a theoretical approach that perceives their struggles to be simply derivative—if not contingent—phenomena? Who, being part of these struggles, would turn to a theory that from the outset claims they are of minor significance instead of going directly to the heart of these problems without ignoring class struggle in the twenty-first century?

The *second methodological step* Murphy proposes is to clarify empirically the boundary between derivative and contingent forms of exclusion as well as their precise relationship to the principal form in a given case.

Then, the *third methodological step* consists in analysing the entire structure of exclusion. Murphy believes that we must distinguish between three types of exclusion structures. First, there are societies characterized by a *tandem structure of exclusion* based on one principal form of exclusion with subordinate derivative and contingent forms. The principal form of exclusion in feudal society, for example, is lineage. In capitalist class society, it is private property. In state socialist society, it is the nomenklatura of the Communist Party. Second, there are societies with a *dual structure of exclusion* characterized by two complementary principal forms of exclusion. Derivative and contingent forms of exclusion can be derived from each of these. On the level of the capitalist world system, these two principal forms of exclusion are private property and citizenship, both enabling the distributive structure of resources and rights. Murphy does not delve deeply into how we can understand derivative and contingent structures deriving from citizenship. He limits himself to discussing the legal backing of these structures, even though the concept of citizenship extends beyond production relations. Finally, the third type of society is characterized by a *polar structure of exclusion*. Here, we can distinguish between two principal but opposing structures. Again, on the level of the world system—another historical example— Murphy views capitalist and socialist societies as representing opposing principal structures: private property in capitalist society and the Communist Party in socialist society, along with their respective derivative and contingent forms.

Finally, the *fourth methodological step* takes into consideration the excluded themselves and their strategies that Murphy divides, as we have seen, into *inclusionary* and *revolutionary forms of usurpation*. While suppressed groups pursuing inclusive strategies aim at being included into the existing stratification order and the system of distribution, in the latter case, they endeavour to fundamentally transform the underlying structure. At this point, it should be mentioned that Murphy offers a different conceptualization of usurpation than Parkin's conception, which he finds unsatisfactory and inherently unclear. Admittedly, he also argues that usurpation is a potential threat to the existing stratification order and that it implies demands made on the grounds of different standards of social justice for the excluded, yet his doubts concern 'Parkin's conception of usurpation as the polar-opposite mode of closure to exclusion, a conception which obscures the fact that exclusion is involved in usurpation' (Murphy 1988, 52). He also argues that a subordinated racially defined group that fights against its racial exclusion necessarily excludes other groups within the subordinate class belonging to other races, 'and especially to the dominant race' (Murphy 1988, 52). Thus, by fighting against its exclusion, an excluded racial group in turn excludes other racial groups in the dominant class. This appears to be extremely obscure, yet Murphy argues it is that way for all 'minority-group movements along ethnic, religious, linguistic, and gender lines' (Murphy 1988, 52–53). Consequently, he deems usurpation to be a 'special type of exclusion which creates a group of excluded ineligibles' (Murphy 1988, 53).

3.3 A Conceptual Framework for Closure Theory

Following this methodological analysis of forms of exclusion, Murphy offers a four-step *conceptual framework for closure theory*. First, it has to follow Weber's concept of class that encompasses all 'structural relationships of domination and exclusion (based on property, credentials, race, ethnicity, gender, etc.)' (Murphy 1988, 124). Second, following this path means understanding the composition of class and the relations between the relevant sides that enact strategies of exclusion. Third, it includes doing the same on behalf of the excluded who react to these strategies, which means understanding their interests in usurpationary struggles. Finally, this analysis involves examining 'the mediating elements of organization, consciousness (and underlying ideological struggle), and the conjuncture' (Murphy 1988, 124).

Surprisingly, we would expect all this to have been made plausible in Murphy's own book, but that is not the case. To date, this framework only helps us understand that exclusionary strategies should be viewed as based on class action, while the subordinate side has been almost completely neglected. Although by referring to race, ethnicity, language, or religion, Murphy introduces Weber's concept of *communal* and *associational* relationships that, in conjunction with *status*, makes it possible to differentiate between various *social aggregates* (Murphy 1988, 124), he does not offer an analysis of these aggregates but instead treats them as being derivative or contingent phenomena. Consequently, Murphy assumes that dominant class strategies may have the effect that the subordinated are 'virtually isolated from one another and disorganized, forming little more than an amorphous plurality' (Murphy 1988, 126). Finally, such disorganizing effects of exclusionary strategies may be directed against racial, ethnic, language, or religious groups and, in turn, trigger usurpationary reactions yielding 'shared qualities of the plurality and their specific usurpationary interests or cause' (Murphy 1988, 126).

This is not convincing at all, as Murphy does not come up with any kind of action theory that might help fully understand why and how social actors take up certain strategies in closure struggles. There is no elaboration on the idea of social actors developing a sense of community, creating an identity that could enable them to take joint action, making decisions, and acting against their exclusion. Like Parkin, Murphy concentrates on constructing a *structural frame* within which contestations among social actors might be analysed. However, the actual strategies of action are not explained.

3.4 The Rationalization of Closure

Finally, Murphy aims to contextualize closure theory within Weber's concept of rationalization. Referring to Weber's famous remark that 'not ideas, but material interests, directly govern men's conduct. Yet very frequently the "world images" that have been created by "ideas" have, like switchmen, determined the tracks along which action has been pushed by the dynamic of interest' (Weber 1946, 169–170), Murphy intends to extend Weber's claim by asking what the tracks were and how, based on ideas, such material and ideal interests have been pushed in society. His conclusion puts social closure at centre stage: 'I would argue that they are none other than codes of social closure: formal or informal, overt or covert rules governing the practices of monopolization and exclusion' (Murphy 1988, 1).

Murphy argues that certain world images based on specific ideas are responsible for specific conditions of exclusion, such as a set of laws backing private property. In this vein, other world images would be based on meritocratic ideas, on racism, or on patriarchal domination, promoting systems that allow the monopolization of the credentialed at the expense of the uncredentialed, the White at the expense of the Black, or men at the expense of women. Looking back at history, Murphy also argues that rules of exclusion such as heritage, aristocracy, bloodline, and so forth that had been dominant in premodern societies had then lost their power and almost disappeared. Yet, in a way, they are still powerful but mainly working beneath the surface:

> Formal rules, and indeed laws, regarding the exclusion of women (for example from medical schools, from employment after marriage) are disappearing in confrontation with the changing world images of the relation between the sexes, but deeply embedded gender rules in terms of informal customs still constitute tracks which lead directly to male monopolization and the exclusion of women. (Murphy 1988, 2)

Here the basic argument is as follows: world views are based on certain ideas. These world views are responsible for laws and rules governing sets of exclusionary practices that allow certain groups to push their interests along these lines, thereby monopolizing resources and goods at the expense of excluding others; the established exclusionary codes are not permanent and unchangeable—as history has shown. Yet, previously dominant forms of closure can survive, operating beneath the surface, working as informal codes of monopolization and exclusion; the ideas that create world images in turn emerge from closure struggles in society, 'particularly from the contradictions that build up as exclusionary codes are elaborated, and hence ultimately form the creative reactions of the excluded' (Murphy 1988, 4).

Murphy considers this idea at the end of his book, where he discusses in detail Weber's *great unifying theme* of rationalization and attempts to relate his concept of closure theory to rationalization. Here he makes a 'rather strong claim by arguing that "the most important thing that is being rationalized is the process of exclusion itself" (Murphy 1988, 219), as exclusionary rules shift *'from collectivist to increasingly individualist criteria'* (Witz 1988, 661; emphasis added).[3] Of course, while teleological in a certain way, given today's reality with regard to processes of social closure this understanding of a rationalization of closure is at the least highly questionable.

---

[3] A detailed discussion of Murphy's debate of rationalization is beyond the scope of the present book.

4
Critical Shortcomings of the Theory of Social Closure

There can be no doubt that, in developing the theory of social closure, both Parkin and Murphy have contributed immensely to bringing Weber's basic concept of processes of closure to the forefront of sociological reasoning. Social closure has been discussed in a wide range of fields of social analysis and shed a light on the production and reproduction of social inequalities, power relations, and strategies of social action by putting processes of exclusion centre stage.

However, serious problems exist with their approach. Taking up the threads of Parkin's elaboration of Weber's concept of closure, Murphy (1988, 10) denies that Parkin has developed a coherent theory—something Parkin in fact never claimed to have done. Yet this finding also applies to Murphy's own work, despite asserting he has presented a *theory of exclusion and monopolization*. The theory of social closure as it stands—which is the status quo of 1988—is not a *theory* but offers interesting sensitizing concepts and ideas that shed light on important phenomena and processes in the social world such as closure, monopolization, exclusion, usurpation, power, domination, and strategies of social action (cf. Cuneo 1989, 305). We should not consider this finding to be a disadvantage, since concept building is always an interesting step of theorizing. However, the theory of social closure not only falls short of offering more than this conceptual step but is also fraught with problems and pitfalls that make it impossible to simply revise them and use the conceptual and methodological apparatus for a new approach to closure theory. I discuss these problems to show why we have to leave the theory of social closure behind and start anew with theorizing closure.

4.1 Closure: A Concept in a Procrustean Bed

Although one might expect them to pick up the threads of the concept of social closure right from the very beginning, neither Parkin nor Murphy seriously deals with Max Weber's basic concepts of *open* and *closed* social relationships. From the outset, they both contextualize the concept of closure within Weber's debate on class and status groups. Thus, they discuss closure in a systematically narrowed perspective that focuses almost exclusively on closure through market processes. Neither of them is interested in further developing Weber's basic concept of closure. Rather, they attempt to find an instrument that enables them to overcome the deadlock in the then confrontation of class analysis and the functionalist analysis of the stratification order as well as the unsatisfactory condition of the analysis of the class structure. Murphy argues that Weber's introducing the concept of closure 'enabled him to analyse the monopolization of opportunities in the market by property classes as well as other forms of monopolization by status groups, in terms of one coherent overall problematic' (Murphy 1988, 9). This may be true to a certain extent, yet it remains only part of the story of what a theory of social closure might have been able to analyse if it had started from the outset with engaging in a critical debate of Weber's basic concepts. Thus, the way the theory of social closure has taken up the idea of social closure has led to severe consequences of a much-too-narrow and much-too-specific concept of closure.

4.1.1 Closure as an Economically Restricted Concept

The theory of social closure has always been labelled as neo-Weberian. There are good reasons to argue this, particularly with Parkin bringing in credentials as being critical for processes of exclusion, emphasizing the social actions of (communal) groups or a rethinking of the concept of exploitation. Ironically, Murphy, who—even more so than Parkin—claims to further elaborate on closure theory in a neo-Weberian sense, actually attempts to preserve one of the most questionable aspects of structural Marxism. His model describes a *logic of derivation* that defines possession of private property in capitalist society to be the only dominant feature in capitalist society from which all the other critical criteria relevant for struggles of social closure—race, ethnicity, religion, language, credentials, and gender—can be *derived*. In cases not directly linked to the production process, they are even simply *contingent*.

The irritating consequences of such a position become obvious in a highly questionable assessment: 'Racial exclusion, for example, does *not just mean exclusion from beaches*, but more importantly from access to the means of production and the distribution of its fruits' (Murphy 1988, 68; emphasis added). Of course, in recent decades, due to social and academic struggles, issues of race, gender, ethnicity, religion, and so on have become more prominent than they were in the 1980s, but economic determinism was a problem even then. Manza points to this problem, arguing, 'Murphy fails to *justify* the claim—either theoretically or empirically—that, for example cultural capital, credentials or being a white male cannot be as important an asset in actually existing capitalism as ownership of economic capital' (Manza 1992, 293).

Indeed, why should we give ultimate primacy to capitalist relations of production in any process of closure? By deemphasizing race, ethnicity, nationality, gender, religion, or language in social closure theory, it fails to do justice to its importance in terms of very different processes of social closure. Certainly, class relations remain significant for the analysis of closure, but the simple notion that all forms of exclusion should and can be derived from access to and ownership of the means of production must be rejected, as it gives more weight to abstract class theory than to empirical reality and the daily experience of humiliation and degradation of people. In particular, Murphy's elaboration on social closure—which to this day represents the *state of the art* of closure theory—is simply outdated. In times of Black Lives Matter, Palestinian Lives Matter, #Me Too, and other social movements, who would be content, in the face of the resurgence of White supremacism, fierce misogyny, the discovery of settler-colonial atrocities, and so forth, that these struggles for the *right to have rights* (Hannah Arendt 2017 [1951]) and the right to earn a living in actual equality are reduced to secondary contradictions of relations in the production process? This position is not only theoretically unconvincing but has certainly contributed to the fact that social closure theory has fallen out of focus in recent years, if not decades, and makes it understandable why closure theory in its present form plays hardly any role in sociological work.

4.1.2 The Two Sides of the Social Closure Equation

According to Parkin's concept of the social closure equation, social closure consists of two reciprocal strategies of social action: exclusion and usurpation. While this interesting intention was to take into account the strategies of excluded groups to define closure as both exclusion *and* usurpation, there are two critical weaknesses. First, to reduce and classify the huge variety of closure strategies in today's world simply to *strategies of exclusion* and *strategies of usurpation* does not do justice to a complexity that needs to be elaborated conceptually. Second, declaring an analysis of social closure only to be complete if both sides have been analysed is neither satisfactory nor useful. Instead, I follow Weber's remark that group action that excludes others, grants limited admission, or defines access according to certain conditions '*may* provoke a corresponding reaction on the part of those against whom it is directed' (Weber 1978 [1922], 342; emphasis added).

There is no sine qua non. Not all excluded persons or groups will or can react. We do not know whether the excluded will respond, nor can we simply assume that they will. It may be that the excluding side has put insurmountable obstacles in the way of the excluded, or it may be that the excluded are not organized enough or have not been able to develop a collective political identity. Either way, we need to explain what is actually happening instead of simply arguing that social closure means exclusion *and* usurpation. Naming strategies does not mean explaining them. So, we have to ask what enables people to act in struggles for closure. And conversely, we need to ask how others act, what enables them to act, or why they might not act at all, as there will also be groups that simply practice *self-exclusion* (Mackert 1999) as a form of collective action against a social order that is fundamentally unjust, racist, misogynist, exploitative or eliminatory and do not develop *counterstrategies* (Hartmann 2011).

4.1.3 Closure as Teleological: Towards an Iron Cage of Closure

At the end of his book, Murphy puts closure analysis into the Procrustes bed of what he calls Weber's *unifying theme* of rationalization. Weber's understanding of the interaction between interests and ideas has been widely recognized as the 'starting point and vanishing point for the analysis of processes of social and cultural change' (Sigmund 2014, 66; my own translation; see also Tenbruck 1975; Lepsius 1990; Schluchter 2005; 2008; Kalberg 1980), triggering a broad debate on how to view this interaction and their respective significance when they are combined in processes of change. Of course, there have been proponents who have argued in favour of either interests or ideas being the more significant. Yet there is strong evidence to support the position that interests and ideas are equally relevant factors in causal explanations of social facts in processes of change in which only one of them may be effective. The interactions of both may therefore be understood as a diachronic interaction (*diachrone Wechselwirkung*), a situation that according to a given constellation of action might turn into its opposite (see Sigmund 2014, 68). In any case, in a Weberian perspective, we should see the interaction of interests and ideas to be a flexible one with complementary factors of explanation.

However, Murphy takes a different perspective. Asking about the tracks 'that are determined by world images' based on ideas, 'and along which action is pushed by the dynamic interest', he concludes: 'I would argue that they are none other than codes of social closure: formal or informal, overt or covert rules governing practices of monopolization and exclusion' (Murphy 1988, 1). Unceremoniously, Murphy declares the very complex correlation in Weber's work to be a 'Weberian dialectic of material interests and ideas, the dialectic of constraint and creativity. Certain ideas create particular world images which in turn determine specific rules of exclusion' (Murphy 1988, 4). Closure struggles between the excluding and the excluded are the driving force in this process. 'New ideas and new world images are formed as a product of this reaction and struggle' (Murphy 1988, 4). In this process, an exclusionary code may be replaced by a new one.

This is too simplistic a perspective on Weber's conceptualization of how to analyse social and cultural processes of transformation, turning a flexible explanatory instrument into a relatively mechanistic, supposedly dialectical one. Although Murphy argues that he does not see any predestination in Weber's approach (Murphy 1988, 4), which indicates a teleological perspective in his interpretation, this assertion becomes more than dubious at the end of the book when Murphy takes up the process of rationalization, arguing again that closure is being continually rationalized, an assumption that simply inoculates a teleological principle into the dynamic struggles of social closure that, in fact, should be conceptualized as open—even in the face of persisting asymmetric power relations in society. I agree that, as Murphy argues, there is a substantive end to the process of rationalization that may be 'control (over nature, economic competitors, ideological adversaries, political opponents, and military enemies)' (Murphy 1988, 218). Yet I do not agree with the thesis that 'the reorganization of exclusionary codes is at the heart of the historic process of formal rationalization. In fact, the most important thing that is being rationalized in this process is exclusion itself' (Murphy 1988, 219).

In contrast to Parkin's rather open debate about collectivist and individualist criteria of closure, particularly his reflections on how liberalism's high ideals of individualism are strategically used to enforce collectivist exclusion, pointing to contradictory processes of closure, Murphy offers an interpretation of rationalization that assumes a specific direction in which codes of collectivist exclusion are transformed into individual codes in processes of rationalization. While collectivist exclusion has triggered powerful collective movements of counterstrategies, like the feminist movement, the civil rights movement, or the anti-Apartheid movement, Murphy assumes that growing formal rationalization resulted in collectivist criteria of exclusion becoming illegitimate, the consequence being a rise of individualist criteria:

> The resulting rationalization of exclusion led to exclusionary criteria being no longer explicitly or directly founded on the collectivity within which one was born, but rather on the capacity to convince others that one had the means to accomplish valued goal. (Murphy 1988, 220)

This is a rather interesting interpretation as it suggests that the processes of both formal rationalization, in general, and the development of exclusionary criteria, in particular, follow a clear direction. It also disregards the fact that collectivist criteria—whether officially illegitimate or not—continue even today to underly the most severe and violent processes of social closure.[1] In general, Murphy

---

[1] One might ask whether this interpretation does justice to Weber's conceptualization of rationalization that actually referred to the level of organizations and specific orders. The term itself is

offers a somewhat static model that does not explain processes of social closure and the ways in which social actors may produce and reproduce closure structures. Following Weber, he assumes an inevitable process of ever more control through an ongoing rationalization of instruments of social closure creating an *iron cage of closure*.

4.2 The Lack of Group Action

When it comes to collective actors, we encounter one of the biggest problems with both Weber and the theory of social closure. Although collective strategies are discussed, we learn nothing about the collective actors and how they become capable of acting. Heinz Steinert (2004) has therefore rightly attributed a fundamental problem to closure theory in relation to *group action*. Referring to the theory of collective action (Olson 1965; Jordan 1996), which describes the formation of clubs to assert certain interests, Steinert argues that closure presupposes the process of organizing an interest. This process of joining a club or other organization generates solidarity as a prerequisite for conflict capacity—that is, the possibility of plausibly threatening to deny access to a necessary service or good (cf. Steinert 2004, 199).

Thus, it is not monopolization but solidarization that is crucial if we want to understand how collective action becomes possible. Referring to Weber's historical examples, Steinert argues that he overlooks the categorical difference between monopolization and solidarization. 'Land is a resource that exists independently of closure—professional licences only become a resource through the formation of associations (and protection by the state). In one case, a resource is monopolised through appropriation; in the other, the resource is only created through solidarity' (Steinert 2004, 199; my own translation). However, we have to go beyond this statement, because what must necessarily be included in closure theory is to clarify the preconditions and conditions for the agency of social actors. And with this, a new approach to social closure goes beyond its current state. This means that to deal with closure we need to determine exactly how social actors get into a position that enables them to exercise powerful strategies of

---

ambiguous and dazzling (Müller 2014, 110), and it is not convincing that the rationalization of exclusion should be its most important aspect. It should at least be taken into consideration what this would mean for Weber's concept of value spheres and orders of life that do not develop in a unitary sense or a unitary logic. All this is critical in Weber's conceptualization, but it is brought into one direction by reducing plural processes that may even be contradictory into the single concept of closure. However, Murphy does not argue that collectivist exclusionary criteria no longer play a role in modern societies. Instead, he suggests that because these criteria have become 'illegitimate' in his concept, they are now merely derived from or contingent on the principal form of social closure, which is private property.

closure in the first place and to analyse which consequences this generates for the less powerful.

This critical aspect of *organizing an interest* is also missing in Parkin's and Murphy's work, as their conceptual elaborations on Weber's approach to closure remain in a strictly hierarchical frame of reference in which class relations are foregrounded for the analysis of social closure or the question of the organizational capacity of social groups is not raised at all. Strangely enough, collective action seems to exist solely because of the actors' position in the class structure. While Weber's individualist perspective assumed that a certain social status leads to shared ideas, beliefs, and interests among its members, who then act in a certain way, Murphy's structuralist assumptions almost completely neglect collective social actors, making their strategies a simple reflection of their position in the class structure. Neither of these approaches is satisfying.

4.3 Power: A Missing Concept

Although *power* lies at the core of the theory of social closure, there is an odd inadequacy with regard to its apparent significance in Parkin's and Murphy's approaches and an almost non-existent conceptual debate on it. Parkin uses the term in many different senses: strategies of social closure are an expression of the distribution of power, whereas exclusion is the use of power in a *downward* direction, usurpation is using power in an *upward* direction, and thus *exclusion* and *usurpation* are strategies of social action that deploy power against one another. For Parkin, closure analysis means revealing all kinds of power relations in society: exclusionary power is legally backed by the state, usurpation strategies are enacted to mobilize power to gain social power, and exploitation should be seen as resulting from all kinds of power relations in society. Parkin ultimately indicates how he thinks the use of power in closure theory may be handled, but his approach is of limited usefulness:

> To conceive of power as a built-in attribute of closure is at the very best to dispense with those fruitless searches for its 'location' inspired by Weber's more familiar but *completely unhelpful definition in terms of the ubiquitous struggle* between contending wills. (Parkin 1979, 46; emphasis added)

Rather, 'to speak of power in the light of closure principles is quite consistent with the analysis of class relations' (Parkin 1979, 46), the only difference being not to conceive it as 'conflict between classes defined not specifically in relation to their place in the productive process but in relation to their prevalent modes of closure, exclusion and usurpation, respectively' (Parkin 1979, 46).

Murphy follows Parkin in focusing on power and power relations, seeing exclusion as a strategy to keep others away from access to power, or by mentioning that premodern exclusion rules almost lost their power in modern society. He believes 'the principal cleavage in the social order is seen as the line where power undergoes a modification of its organizing principles and directional flows' (Murphy 1988,11) or views usurpation as 'the biting into the power and advantages of the dominant group' (Murphy 1988, 54).

All these different uses of *power* are unsatisfactory, somehow metaphorical and provoking confusion. Do Parkin and Murphy see power as a resource? Is it institutionalized in social positions? Is it a means to an end or an end in itself? Admittedly, Murphy devotes an entire chapter to an analysis of the Weberian concept of power, yet this debate neither stands in any relation to his model of social closure nor does it help us understand exclusionary strategies. Strangely enough, Murphy argues that although power is critical in sociology it is one of the most ill-defined concepts. However, this strange statement simply contradicts the fact that after the end of the Parsonian *orthodox consensus* in the 1970s and 1980s there was widespread interest in theorizing on power, with quite a number of very interesting conceptualizations.[2]

Although Murphy begins his chapter 'Elaboration and Application of the Weberian Concept of Power' (Murphy 1988, 132–160) by asserting that 'power has typically been used as if it were an unproblematic concept which may be taken for granted' (Murphy 1988, 132), he does not—as he claims—explicitly examine Weber's concept. Instead, Murphy distinguishes between three different capacities that constitute power. The first is the power to command, which, following Weber, Murphy defines 'as "the probability that a command with a given specific content will be obeyed by a given group of persons"' (Weber 1978 [1922], 53). It is the capacity to elicit obedience to a command, no matter what the basis for that obedience' (Murphy 1988, 135). The second subcategory of power is 'the capacity of a unit to constrain the action of others while pursuing its own interests without having to command the action of others' (Murphy 1988, 135). The third subcategory of power, in Murphy's view, is the power to profit from, which he defines 'as the capacity of a unit to profit, in order to realize its goals, from the autonomous actions of others, which the unit did not itself initiate and which may be oriented to goals other than its own' (Murphy 1988, 136).

What we get from Murphy is thus not a concept of power but three aspects of power: the power to command, the power to constrain, and the power to profit from. These are not linked in any way to his conceptual framework for closure analysis to allow for analysing the deep structure of domination in society. This

---

[2] See among many others the conceptualizations by Offe 1972; Giddens 1973; Lukes 1974; Mann 1986.

is simply insufficient. A new approach to closure theory thus needs a concept of power to make comprehensible how collective social actors are able to mobilize power in closure struggles.

4.4 Methodology: A Dead End

The discussion in this first part of the book has made clear that the theory of social closure, despite its characterization as *neo-Weberian*, adheres to a version of structuralist Marxism that was prominent in the early 1980s. In methodological terms, therefore, a holistic view is prevalent in Murphy's work. Structuralist/systemic explanations start from a given and fixed social unit, be it a system, a society, a family, or an economic structure, which produces certain effects, and thus 'explain events within that unit by their location within the unit as a whole' (Tilly 2005a, 18). Such ways of explaining social closure are obvious in the tradition of the theory of social closure, as I have shown in particular in the discussion of Murphy's contributions. His explanation of social closure reduces it to a structural effect of capitalism's mode of production. Social classes as a whole are the focus of interest whether in capitalism or in state socialism, and they are treated as if they were coherent entities. The same applies to all groups that Murphy claims are at best of secondary interest, such as gender, ethnic, religious, and linguistic groups.[3] In this sense, Murphy views the system of class structure as the larger social system in which classes appear to explain processes of social closure according to the self-generating process of *rationalization*. However, such a holistic or systemic view is fraught with at least three critical problems. First, there is no real explanation of how rationalization actually works in particular events of social closure. Second, Murphy introduces a kind of functional explanation by describing closure processes as existing because they serve to drive rationalization as a precondition of the class structure (cf. Tilly 1999, 264). Third, a holistic view dispenses with a theory of action, because the classes as main actors merely fulfil the imperatives or functions of the system. Thus, Murphy's holistic approach necessarily dispenses with an actual explanation, since structuralist or systemic approaches either refer to functionalist explanations (cf. Giddens 1976a) or dispense entirely with an explanation of the processes in the social world.

Given these serious objections to holistic methodology in general, and with regard to understanding and explaining social closure in particular, we must inevitably leave this perspective behind and methodologically reorient closure itself.

---

[3] For a detailed critique of elements of holism see Bunge 1996, 260.

5
Going Beyond the Theory of Social Closure

Without doubt, the theory of social closure has successfully focused the attention of sociological work on the idea of social closure and has led to some interesting concepts and ideas that can shed light on important phenomena and processes in the social world. However, as I have shown, there are good reasons why closure theory in its current state is relatively meaningless when it comes to theorizing and analysing some of the most challenging and important processes in our world today. Serious theoretical, methodological, and conceptual problems make a simple revision of theory of social closure impossible, necessitating a new approach to closure theory:

1. Two strategic theoretical choices in the theory of social closure are fundamentally problematic. First, social closure is seen to be limited to (1) analyse processes of exclusion and monopolization; and (2) exploitation is subsumed under the term/concept of *exclusion*. Neither of these steps is convincing or helpful, as they both limit the scope of the concept of closure and prevent closure from referring to all forms of structured inequality. Second, although the theory of social closure refers to the then-still-existing communist part of the world and the Third World, its interest is almost entirely limited to the class and status structure of advanced Western capitalist societies. This too is insufficient, not only because it limits the analysis of social closure to interclass and intra-class relations within the capitalist core but also because it ignores historical long-term developments and ongoing settler-colonial and colonial dependencies of the Global South from the hegemonic Global North, which are highly relevant to closure relations.
2. The introduction of the concept of the *social closure equation* is an interesting step, but I disagree with two consequences it entails for Parkin and Murphy. *First*, I disagree with the assumption, already discussed, that closure always promotes a reaction of the excluded and that closure struggles must be analysed according to an action-reaction scheme (Parkin). In contrast, I claim that a new theorizing of social closure must concentrate on the strategies of the powerful side in closure struggles. I will thus concentrate

on this task, since I also claim that only what might be called *theorizing counterstrategies* can do justice to the agency and options of the less fortunate.[1] Second, I argue that merely distinguishing possible strategies of the excluded as inclusionary or revolutionary (Murphy) does not do justice to the complexity of strategies of action in closure struggles. Furthermore, it does not make sense to distinguish between strategies based on their respective assumed goals.

3. Parkin's emphasis on the role of the state in relation to social closure is an important aspect that must continue to be taken seriously—not only because of the insight that people or social groups affected by exclusion have been stigmatized in advance by the state but also because of the constitutive role of the state as an actor in closure struggles itself. In my approach, the state thus plays a central role because it is not only inextricably intertwined with the economy in the neoliberal rationality we are dealing with today but is also an actor that exercises violence and control.

4. It is crucial to conceptualize social closure as social processes and strategies, as Parkin suggested. Unfortunately, he neither elaborated on that nor did he address the far-reaching consequences such a move might have for the impact of closure theory as an important tool of critical sociology. Only by reformulating closure in terms of strategies of action will it be possible to understand closure as an expression of power struggles and to distinguish and systematize the strategies of powerful actors in closure struggles. This does not mean that we abandon a constitutive relationship between the agency of social actors and a conception of structure that enables them to exercise these strategies in the first place, as Murphy argues in his defence of the importance of class structure—quite the contrary. It does mean, however, that we need a non-reductionist approach that does not view the relationship between structure and agency as a dualism, but rather as a theoretical approach that reconstructs the relationship between structure and agency as a duality in order to properly conceptualize and explain closure strategies.

5. While I agree with Murphy that we need a differentiated view of social closure, I reject his emphasis on structures of closure that ultimately understand closure as effects of an economic structure in capitalist societies. In contrast, I argue that a new approach to the theory of closure needs to distinguish forms of closure that allow us to identify differentiated strategies of closure that make their various and specific dynamics conceivable.

---

[1] Consequently, I neither deal with Parkin's ideas of strategies of the excluded as *usurpationary* nor with the idea of *dual closure*, which to my mind is simply referring to what Weber called *closure within*.

The discussion has shown that a new approach to closure theory can only tie in to a very limited extent with the theory of social closure. While there are interesting suggestions, I will take a different conceptual, theoretical, and methodological path and thus unlock more analytical potential in the idea of social closure.

PART II
BASIC TERMS, CONCEPTS, AND METHODOLOGY FOR CLOSURE THEORY

Part II serves to overcome all critical lacunae in closure theory. First, it revisits Max Weber's approach by putting his basic concepts *open* and *closed social relationships* in context with concepts he postulates and which stand in close proximity with them. This part therefore starts with a discussion of Weber's idea of the meaning of *struggle* in social life and the significance of *communal and associative social relationships*, which allows for a deeper understanding of what social closure actually is about and defines opening and closing of social relationships as the most fundamental process in social life. Against this background it critically analyses Weber's own making empirically plausible his approach and rejects this way of analysing closure.

Against the background of this deeper understanding of closure from discussing and revisiting Weber's work, the part introduces, elaborates and fleshes out the critical concepts that have been missing in closure theory so far—*group action and acting in solidarity*, *power*, and *life chances / chances of survival*—that are all defined as core concepts of the new approach to closure theory.

6
Reconsidering, Problematizing, and Introducing Critical Concepts for Closure Theory

To be sure, Parkin's and Murphy's work have left closure theory in an unsatisfactory state from a theoretical, conceptual, and methodological point of view, yet the problems with it begin earlier, as Jeff Manza pointed out in the early 1990s:

> Despite the apparent centrality of the concept of 'closure' in *Economy and Society*... it remains one of the obscure and least well-developed of the theoretical concepts presented by Weber. Closure is never systematically defined or clarified in that text, and it has not generally been included in the bundle of theoretical tools contemporary sociology has inherited from Weber. (Manza 1992, 277)

Indeed, the idea of closure as a basic sociological concept, and its relation to other basic concepts in close proximity, has remained unexplained by Weber himself and has been disregarded both by the *theory of social closure* and by the general sociological debate on Weber's broad work.

A new approach to social closure cannot follow this path. Instead, it must start from these two specific problems: on the one hand, it must precisely analyse the concept of *open* and closed *social* relationships, and on the other hand, it must clarify the systematic references to other Weberian concepts. Thus, revisiting Weber's basic concepts will reveal how conceptual shortcomings have obscured important aspects of social closure and created confusion about its nature. Additionally, these shortcomings have hindered the development of a convincing approach to analysing social closure, which must address four critical problems: First, it has to bring in group action into closure theory. Second, a concept of power must be developed that can ground social closure theory. Third, the actual goal of closure theory must be defined, which surprisingly has not been done so far. Fourth, just as the methodological holism of the *theory of social closure* had to be rejected, so too must we reject Weber's individualistic approach. It is no less unconvincing and does not help to understand social closure, which, as I argue, must be discussed in a methodologically relational perspective. We need to expose and overcome these deficits to prepare the ground for a new approach to closure theory.

On Social Closure. Jürgen Mackert, Oxford University Press. © Oxford University Press 2024.
DOI: 10.1093/oso/9780197781685.003.0007

RECONSIDERING MAX WEBER'S APPROACH

This sub-part engages with a critical analysis of Max Weber's work on the idea of social closure. It argues that to properly understand what social closure actually is, we need to discuss Weber's basic term in relation to other basic terms that stand in close proximity to *open and closed social relationships*. Looking more closely at the terms *struggle* and *communal and associational social relationships*, we can draw the conclusion that first, closure is a critical element of an understanding of the ontological perspective that social life *is* social struggle, and second, that social closure is the most basic process in social life. On this background the discussion of Weber's own brief empirical closure analysis shows that his own conceptualization of closure leads to utterly unsatisfactory results and has thus to be fundamentally revised.

7
Max Weber's Critical Basic Terms for Theorizing Social Closure Reconsidered

Returning to Weber's discussion of the basic concept of *open* and *closed* relationships in *Economy and Society* (Weber 1978 [1922], Vol. 1, part 1, 10) acknowledges the fact that it is the inescapable point of reference for any sociological debate on social closure. I argue, however, *not* to detach the term from its context, as is usually the case, but to take into account that it stands in close proximity to two other basic terms that help to define its status and meaning: *struggle* (Weber 1978 [1922], Vol. 1, part 1, 8) and *communal* and *associative relationships* (Weber 1978 [1922], Vol. 1, part 1, 9). Proceeding in this way will give us a better understanding of the meaning of open and closed relationships, of the significance of their opening and closing, and consequently of the meaning of *social closure* itself.

In discussing the three basic concepts, I briefly argue that (1) Weber's understanding of social life as a struggle helps us understand social closure as ongoing struggles in the social world; (2) the distinction between communal and associative relationships—two ideal types—shows what brings about such struggles and what they are based on; (3) the introduction of open and closed relationships (whether associative or communal) points to the crucial way in which such struggles take place, thus making opening and closing the two fundamental social processes in social life, because without them neither type of social relation would be possible. Considering these connections could have underscored the significance of the concept of social closure from the very beginning, establishing its *centrality* (Manza), because its processes—and thus *closure struggles*—are central to an understanding of how the social world functions. However, Weber did not achieve this, either conceptually or methodologically.

7.1 The Ontological Idea: Social Life as Struggle

Weber's ontological view of *struggle* as a fundamental aspect of social life provides the perspective for a new approach to understanding social closure, emphasizing its critical role in the social world. In *The Meaning of 'Value Freedom' in the Sociological and Economic Sciences*, Weber asserted 'that struggle[1] is an ineradicable element of all cultural life' (Weber 2012 [1922], 320; correction of translation by J.M.). In *Economy and Society*, Weber defined *struggle* accordingly:

> A social relationship will be referred to as a *'struggle'* (*Kampf*) insofar as action is oriented intentionally to carrying out the actor's own will against the resistance of the other party or partners. *'Peaceful means'* of struggle refers to those that do not consist of actual physical violence. The peaceful struggle shall be called 'competition' insofar as it consists in a formally peaceful attempt to attain power of disposition over chances which are also desired by others. A competitive process is called 'regulated competition' insofar as its ends and means are oriented towards an order. The (latent) struggle for existence between human individuals or types for life chances or chances of survival that takes place without a meaningful orientation in terms of fighting against each other, shall be called 'selection'. Insofar as it is about chances of the living in life, it is 'social selection'; insofar as it concerns chances of survival of hereditary characteristics, it shall be called 'biological selection'. (Weber 1985 [1922], 20; my own translation based on Weber 1978 [1922], 38)

The notion of struggle as the very basis of social life naturally shows quite a broad spectrum of influences on Weber's thinking. While Weber, like Friedrich Nietzsche, assumes that man is driven by the *will to power* (Schmidt-Wellenburg 2020, 97; Hennis 1987, 167), he also takes up Charles Darwin's evolutionary perspective in a specific sense by alluding to the *struggle of the fittest* and arguing with processes of *selection* of social relations, a highly problematic approach that easily turns into social Darwinism, which is well known in sociology and has been widely discussed.[2] Many sociologists follow Weber's argument that the logic and dynamics of society are characterized by social struggles (Müller 2007, 119), ranging from peaceful negotiations to violent confrontations for survival. What sociology has largely neglected in such debates, however, is to consider the world-historical context of imperialism and colonialism, in which sociology as a scientific discipline emerged and that necessarily had a decisive influence on Weber's sociology as the

---

[1] Unfortunately, as in the translation of *Economy and Society*, we have the same problem here with the absolutely misleading translation of the original German term *Kampf* as *conflict*. I will stick with *struggle* throughout the rest of this book.

[2] See, for example, Raymond Aron 1964; the debate between John Langton 1982, 1984 and Valerie H. Haines 1984; W. G. Runciman 2001.

unleashing of violent power as nations like England, France, Germany, the United States, Belgium, Italy and others mounted new territorial assaults upon Africa and Asia. By 1900, the new empires were ruling 90 per cent of Africa, 56 per cent of Asia, and 99 per cent of the Pacific. By the First World War, imperial powers occupied 90 per cent of the entire surface of the globe. (Anderson 2013; Young 2001, 2). (Go 2016, 3)

Larry Siedentop has correctly argued that 'the dynamics of empire have not been incorporated into the basic categories, explanatory models and narratives of social development of classical sociologists' (Siedentop 2015, 314). However, concepts such as *struggle* and its constitutive connection with such fundamental ideas such as *chances of survival* or *selection* for understanding social life have obviously found their way into the basic concepts of sociology in Weber. Recognizing the colonial and imperial context is crucial for rethinking social closure.[3] Because in their daily life social actors are confronted with opponents, competitors, or even enemies in social struggles that cannot be terminated, we inevitably must extend the concept of social closure and go beyond discussing processes of *exclusion* and *exploitation* in this framework—as the theory of social closure did. A new and generic concept of social closure—one that avoids critical shortcomings such as not taking historic and ongoing colonial and settler-colonial processes into consideration—necessarily must include the critical aspect of *elimination*. This view encompasses all kinds of struggles, from peaceful competition to fierce and violent clashes; the processes preventing others from obtaining scarce resources, rights, and positions or from becoming part of any form of social association are the driving forces of social life. However, such a view cannot be restricted to analysing processes within Western societies. Rather, it has to consider the colonial, postcolonial, and settler-colonial relations of the Global North and Global South as social relations of closure and take seriously the effects that result from these relations for the latter.

Against this background, it is important to note that in elaborating on *struggle* as a basic term, Weber introduces the differentiation of the struggle of individuals for personal gain and survival from the *conflict* and the *selection* of social relationships (cf. Weber 1978 [1922], 39). Regarding the latter, Weber remarks that this kind of conflict and selection may be a consciously intended or even an unintended consequence of social behaviour. Looking at the former, Weber argues that

---

[3] See especially George Steinmetz 2008a, 2023, who is revealing the imperial and colonial roots of sociology as a discipline.

human action can a) be consciously directed towards disturbing or preventing the emergence or continuation of certain concrete or generally ordered social relationships, i.e. actions that correspond to their meaning (a 'state' can be deliberately influenced by war or revolution, a 'conspiracy' by bloody repression, 'concubinage' by police measures, or 'usurious' business relations by denial of legal protection and punishment) —or it may premise the existence of one category to the disadvantage of the other. (Weber 1985 [1922], 21; my own translation; emphasis added)

Yet, looking at the strategy pursued in social struggles, the resulting consequences may be a mere by-product. Human action may then be

b) the unintended side effect of the course of social action and the conditions of all kinds that determine it. Namely, that certain concrete or specific relationships (i.e., always: the action in question) have a decreasing chance of continuing or emerging. All natural and cultural conditions of any kind, in the event of change, act in some way to shift such opportunities for the most diverse kinds of social relations. (Weber 1985 [1922], 21; my own translation)

With regard to these processes, Weber argues that although we can speak about selection, we should keep in mind that

in every single case we have to enquire about the reason behind the alteration of chances for the one or other form of social action and the social relationships, behind the breakdown of a social relationship, or which permitted it to continue at the expense of other competing forms, and that the causes may be so manifold that a uniform expression seems to be inappropriate. (Weber 1985 [1922], 21; my own translation based on Weber 1978 [1922], 40)

Weber's basic sociological concept of struggle provides a perspective on social closure as ongoing struggles in the social world. Incorporating the significance of colonialism and settler colonialism and their ongoing effects in today's world, the range from peaceful means to the use of violence in relations of social closure, and the consideration of intentional strategies as well as their unintended consequences allows us to understand social closure as struggle—as a dynamic process unfolding in social relations, which then offers a new perspective for theorizing social closure. This leads us to the second basic concept that can help clarify what closure actually means.

7.2 Communal and Associative Relationships

Weber distinguishes *communal* and *associative* as two ideal types of social relationships based on his types of social action:

> A social relationship will be called 'communal' (*Vergemeinschaftung*) if and so far as the orientation of social action—whether in the individual case, on the average, or in the pure type—is based on a subjective feeling of the parties, whether affectual or traditional, that they belong together. A social relationship will be called 'associative' (*Vergesellschaftung*) if and insofar as the orientation of social action rests on a rational (instrumentally rational or value-rational) motivation to either balancing or combining interests. (Weber 1985 [1922], 21; my own translation based on Weber 1978 [1922], 40–41)

The purest cases of *associative relationships* include market exchange and voluntary goal-oriented association to pursue objective (economic or other) interests or voluntary value-oriented association. The purest cases of *communal relationships* include religious groups, comradeship, and the family, all acting affectual or traditionally motivated. Of course, being ideal types, none of these types will be found in its purest sense in empirical reality; instead, they incorporate traits of both.

We should not assume that communal relationships are harmonious and inclusive while associative relationships are marked by enduring struggle. Instead, being the characteristic trait of social life, although communal relationships and struggle seem to be radically opposed:

> Any kind of violating the mentally more yielding person even within the most intimate communal relationships is absolutely normal. In this sense, as anywhere else, there is a 'selection' of types within the community that promotes difference in the life chances and chances of survival it has created. (Weber 1985 [1922], 22; my own translation based on Weber 1978 [1922], 42)

Thus, imposing one's will on others is typical even in the most intimate relationships. Further, associative relationships 'are very often only a compromise of opposed interests that only eliminate part of the object of the struggle or of the means of struggle (or at least try to do so) while incidentally retaining the opposition of interests and the competition for chances' Weber 1985 [1922], 22; my own translation based on Weber 1978 [1922], 42).

Thus, Weber's two ideal types allow us to understand the different kinds of social relationships that struggles in social life can target. This differentiation highlights the very varied processes within communal and associative relationships and the broad range of forms these struggles can take:

> Struggle and community are relative terms. Struggle varies enormously according to the means (violent or 'peaceful') and how ruthlessly they are employed. And any kind of order of social action, as has already been pointed out, in some way allows the pure actual selection in the competition of different types of people for life chances to persist. (Weber 1985 [1922], 22; my own translation based on Weber 1978 [1922], 42)

Understanding social life as struggle, Weber's distinction between two ideal types of social relations enables us to understand all types of social relations—communal and associative—as constitutively linked to and arising from social struggles. However, this dynamic perspective needs to be clarified in terms of how the social world emerges from changing, contested, and reorganized (sometimes dissolved or destroyed) social relations. This leads us to Weber's basic concept of *open* and *closed relationships*.

7.3 Open and Closed Relationships

The third and, of course, crucial basic concept that we must deal with is Weber's notion of open and closed relationships:

> A social relationship (irrespective of whether communal relationship or associative relationship) will be spoken of as 'open' to the outside if and insofar as on the basis of their current orders no one who is both able and competent to do so is rejected from participating in the mutual social action that is oriented at a specific meaning. In contrast however, a relationship will be called 'closed' insofar as and to the extent that either their meaning or their current social orders exclude, limit, or attach conditions to participation. (Weber 1985 [1922], 23; my own translation based on Weber 1978 [1922], 43)

According to Weber's types of social action, openness and closeness of social relations may be motivated traditionally, affectually, value-rationally, or by instrumental rationality:

> a) Closure of communities where belonging is based on family relations is usually motivated traditionally; b) closure of strong personal emotional relations (such as erotic relations or often those based on piety) is usually motivated affectually; c) (relative) closure of strict belief communities is usually motivated

value-rationally; d) closure of economic association with a monopolistic or plutocratic character is usually motivated by instrumental rationality. (Weber 1985 [1922], 23–24; my own translation based on Weber 1978 [1922], 43–44)

On the basis of distinguishing forms of closure by means of actors' motivations, Weber introduces a final significant aspect of closure by differentiating *closure within* a social relationship and *closure to the outside* and introducing the sociologically highly interesting idea of degrees to which social relationships can be closed. On the one hand, 'both the degree and the means of regulation and closure to the outside can vary, so that the transition from openness to being regulated and being closed is fluid' (Weber 1985 [1922], 24; my own translation based on Weber 1978 [1922], 45). There is a huge variety of criteria that account for regulating access or completely closing social relationships, such as passing exams or a novitiate, buying shares in a cooperative, proving descent from a certain family, paying a huge amount of money to become a member of a prestigious club, and so forth. Because in all these cases the degrees of regulation and closure to the outside may vary, Weber argues that both are *relative terms* (Weber 1985 [1922], 24; my own translation based on Weber 1978 [1922], 45).

On the other hand, *closure within* (i.e., closure among a certain group's members) may also take many forms. Any kind of closed relationship can guarantee monopolized chances to its members in different ways. This may be 'a) free competition among the members; b) in a regulated or rationed way; or c) appropriated by individuals or subgroups on a permanent basis and relatively or completely inalienable' (Weber 1985 [1922], 23; my own translation based on Weber 1978 [1922], 44). Here, too, we find a variety of criteria allowing for degrees of enacting closure within, such as within castes or guilds, in chances within a family obtained by inheritance, competition for customers within a closed market, free or limited usage of soil within an agricultural community, and so forth.

Because social action to impose different degrees of *closure within* social relationships and *closure to the outside* can be motivated in different ways with regard to the critical motive for closure, Weber distinguishes three aspects: first, the maintenance of quality and consequently prestige and, related to this, opportunities for honour and profit; second, a shortage of opportunities related to consumer needs; third, a shortage of commercial opportunities. Normally, the first motive is combined with the second or third (see Weber 1985 [1922], 24–25; my own translation based on Weber 1978 [1922], 46).

The differentiation between *closure to the outside* and *closure within* is critical because both processes point to the two basic aspects of closure that Weber distinguishes. While *closure to the outside* refers to a social site's *monopolization* of goods or resources, thereby keeping other groups from enjoying them fully, *closure within* refers to processes of creating and acting in solidarity.

These definitions of open and closed relations and the important sociological concept emphasizing degrees of closure, as well as the distinction between closure within and closure to the outside, provide a basic explanation of what social closure is and how it works. Building on the discussion of the three basic concepts, I will now examine Weber's brief analyses of social closure.

8
Max Weber's Closure Analyses
Three Contexts

In three short chapters in *Economy and Society*— 'Open and Closed Economic Relationships', 'The Distribution of Power within the Community', and 'Relations between Ethnic Groups'—Weber outlines analyses of social closure in three different contexts. A brief explanation of these will help to understand the processes of supra- and subordination that Weber saw as resulting from processes of social closure.

8.1 The Economic Relationships of Communities

In his discussion of *open and closed economic relationships*, Weber references a classical distributional problem: the number of competitors in a market is rising in relation to what can be earned or from which profit can be made. Consequently, the intention here is to reduce this number of competitors. To do so, 'any externally identifiable characteristic of a part of those (currently or potentially) competing, such as race, language, and confession, local or social origin, descent, residence, and so forth will be taken as a reason to attempt to exclude them from competition' (Weber 1985 [1922], 201; my own translation based on Weber 1978 [1922], 342).

Interestingly, Weber claims that it does not matter in the slightest which characteristic is used to exclude competitors. Instead, whatever characteristic seems appropriate is all it takes. However, as Parkin has made clear, this randomness is obviously misleading because the state plays a critical role in these processes insofar as powerful groups in the market may well be able to draw upon previous subordination of the less-powerful groups by the state. Yet, for Weber, seizing upon any such characteristic constitutes a *group action* that 'may provoke a corresponding reaction on the part of those against whom it is directed' (Weber 1978 [1922], 342).

Weber refers here to a tendency in existing groups 'to set up a kind of association with rational regulations.' Processes of further institutionalization eventually promote the establishing of 'a legal order that limits competition through formal monopolies', allowing members of the community to protect monopolistic practices. Strategies of closure in this case establish a '*"legally privileged group*" (*Rechtsgemeinschaft*) and the participants have become *"privileged members"* (*Rechtsgenossen*). This type of closure, as I refer to it, is an ever-recurring process; it is the source of property in land as well as of all guild and other group monopolies' (Weber 1978 [1922], 342). With regard to these processes, Weber conceives 'the tendency towards monopolization of specific, normally economic chances, as the specific driving force in such cases as: "cooperative organization", which always means closed monopolistic groups' (Weber 1978 [1922], 342). Concerning closure of a community, he refers to such different phenomena as property in land, guild, monopolies, or:

> Fishermen taking their name from a certain fishing area; the establishment of an association of engineering graduates, which seeks to secure a legal, or at least a factual, monopoly over certain positions; the exclusion of outsiders from sharing in the fields and commons of a village; 'patriotic' associations of shop clerks ... all these groups first engage in some joint action (*Gemeinschaftshandeln*) and later perhaps an explicit association. This monopolization is directed against competitors who share some positive or negative characteristics; its purpose is always the closure of social and economic opportunities against *outsiders*. (Weber 1978 [1922], 342)

In the brief paragraph on *open and closed economic relationships*, Weber points to three critical aspects in social closure struggles: first, collective action of those pursuing strategies of closure; second, the monopolization of goods and resources through strategies that lead to the emergence of positively and negatively privileged groups that, third, turn the latter into outsiders in struggles for the distribution of goods, resources, and options of any type.

However, this approach has some serious problems. While collective action seems self-evident and remains unexplained, community building itself is an essential precondition for collective action and indispensable for a community's ability to act in solidarity. Although it is right to mention the effects of monopolization, the various processes that enable monopolization in the first place remain unmentioned and the concept under-complex.

8.2 The Distribution of Power within the Community

Weber's second analysis applies the idea of closure to his debate of power with regard to classes and status groups and departs from defining power as 'the chance of a human being or a number of human beings to realize their own will in a collective social action (*Gemeinschaftshandeln*) also against the resistance of others who are also participating' (Weber 1985 [1922], 531; my own translation based on Weber 1978 [1922], 926). In Weber's view, phenomena of this *distribution of power within the community* are class, status, and party. While his discussion of closure focuses on statuses (*Stände*) and status situation (*ständische Lage*), we find at least a few references to the role of closure concerning *class* and *party*.

With regard to the distribution of power within classes, *monopolization* plays a crucial role given the market situation that determines class situation, which according to Weber means that:

(1) A number of people have in common a specific causal component of their life chances insofar as (2) this component is represented exclusively by economic interests in the possession of goods and opportunities for income, and (3) is represented under the condition of the commodity of labor markets. (Weber 1978 [1922], 927)

As possession and disposition of material property are critical in terms of class situation, excluding groups from their processes of distribution means that the propertied class monopolizes the goods, thereby increasing its own chances of profits:

Other things being equal, the mode of distribution monopolizes the opportunities for profitable deals for all those who, provided with goods, do not necessarily have to exchange them. It increases, at least generally, their power in the price struggle with those who, being propertyless, have nothing to offer but their labor or the resulting products, and who are compelled to get rid of these products in order to subsist at all. (Weber 1978 [1922], 927)

As *property* and *lack of property* are 'the basic categories of all class situations' (Weber 1978 [1922], 926) that have to be conceived of as pure market situations, closure as monopolization of a good plays a crucial role in blocking access to valued goods and options, thereby excluding the propertyless class(es) from enjoying them.

In class situations that refer to the economic determination of life conditions on the basis of the distribution of material property between the classes, Weber negates a collective social action to be necessarily promoted. This occurs, however, in a *status situation*—the second phenomenon of the distribution of power—which refers to 'every typical component of human beings' fate in life that is determined by a specific, positive or negative, social estimation of the "honor" that is tied to any common trait among them' (Weber 1985 [1922], 534; my own translation based on Weber 1978 [1922], 932). In both cases, closure creates a status order with *positively* and *negatively privileged*.[1] However, unlike

---

[1] We have to bear in mind that this subordination is also based on a previous subordination of the less-powerful groups by the state.

pure market relations, the critical aspect of a *status situation* is status honour. This 'is normally expressed by the fact that above all else a specific style of life is expected from all those who wish to belong to the circle' (Weber 1978 [1922], 932; cf. Müller 2007, 233).

This expectation also serves as the lynchpin for processes of closure since social actors in privileged status situations tend to close their social circles to restrict social intercourse, *connubium*, and *commensality* to a high degree or even completely. In doing so, they are keeping chances for employment in high and prestigious positions in business, politics, science, and so forth exclusive for themselves and their offspring, while expressing an exclusive style of life.[2] Closure thus creates a system of social stratification:

> For all practical purposes ... stratification by status goes hand in hand with a monopolization of goods or opportunities, in a manner we have come to know as typical. Besides the specific status honor, which always rests upon distance and exclusiveness ... material monopolies provide the most effective motives for the exclusiveness of a status group. (Weber 1978 [1922], 935)

The emerging status order that arises from status groups' monopolization has a critical consequence: 'As to the general *effect* of the status order, only one consequence can be stated, but it is a very important one: the hindrance of the free development of the market' (Weber 1978 [1922], 937). In this sense, class situation and status situation combine to create a common status order of the positively and negatively privileged: 'With some over-simplification, one might thus say that classes are stratified according to their relations to the production and acquisition of goods; whereas status groups are stratified according to the principles of their *consumption* of goods as represented by special styles of life' (Weber 1978 [1922], 937).

In a brief concluding paragraph on *parties*—the third phenomenon of a distribution of power—Weber mentions that while class is an aspect of the *economic order* and status is an aspect of the *social order* (i.e., the sphere of honour), 'parties reside in the sphere of power. Their action is oriented toward the acquisition of social power, that is to say, toward influencing social action no matter what its content may be' (Weber 1978 [1922], 938). There are no additional specific details about aspects of closure as parties mobilize power to influence *social action no matter what its content may be*. However, this vague and ambiguous statement is a simply a result of Weber's unclear and unsatisfactory treatment of power.

---

[2] Usurpation practices by members of subordinated status situations attempt to take a share of these privileges, or, in the case of wealthy groups, declare different variations of status honour by drawing on any criterion possible.

8.3 Relations between Ethnic Groups

In the paragraphs on race, membership, and the emergence of the belief in common ethnicity in economy and society, we find Weber's third analysis of social closure processes. He elaborates on these processes in analogy to those closure processes promoted by status situations. Introducing this debate, Weber makes an important remark about the seemingly specific problem of closure in relations between ethnic groups that is worth quoting at length because it is critical for a comprehensive and general understanding of processes and the dynamics of social closure:

> A much more problematic source of a community's social action as discussed so far is 'race membership', common inherited and inheritable traits that are really based on common descent. Of course, this kind of membership creates a 'community' if and only if it is perceived individually as a common trait. This only happens when a local neighbourhood or attachment of racially different people are linked to a joint (mostly political) action, or, conversely, when some common fates of members of the same race are linked to any antagonism against members of a *noticeably* different community. In general, the social action of the members of the community that then comes into being expresses itself only negatively: against those who are strikingly different; they separate themselves from them or despise them, or, on the contrary, they express superstitious awe towards them. (Weber 1985 [1922], 234; my own translation based on Weber 1978 [1922], 385)

Weber points out that what is at stake here is not a biological but a social phenomenon. It is a person's *habitus* that drives groups to seclude themselves from others, either by condemning those who are members of subordinated communities or by superstitiously admiring those who are socially superior. To Weber, being repelled from a different outer habitus is a *primary* and *normal* reaction. Yet this is in no way a specific reaction among ethnic groups but rather a general social process of closure:

> However, 1) neither is this kind of 'repulsion' only a typical trait of those sharing anthropological commonalities against outsiders, nor does the degree of their anthropological relationship determine its degree. 2) Also, this 'repulsion' does not—by any means—only draw upon inherited differences but no less upon striking differences of the outer habitus. (Weber 1985 [1922], 234; my own translation based on Weber 1978 [1922], 385)

Thus, as Gertrude Neuwirth has remarked, 'Weber's analogy between ethnic and status communities is explicitly drawn in terms of life styles' (Neuwirth 1968, 151), as he assumes that status communities, like ethnic communities, can monopolize economic and occupational resources or chances, allowing for a striking difference in the lifestyle of certain communities. These different styles may cause others to be repelled, and neither *tradition* nor *inheritance* plays any specific role in these processes. Weber even goes one step further, arguing that that monopolistic exclusion can draw upon 'any externally identifiable characteristic' (Weber 1985 [1922], 236; my own translation based on Weber 1978 [1922], 387).[3]

These characteristics may, however, generate a consciousness of commonality among those who feel they are of the same kind. This commonality may serve as the basis for a communal association which will then promote common mores. Weber points out that almost any form of commonality or difference in the habitus of various communities can lead to a *subjective belief* among members of attracting and repelling groups that there might be a kind of affinity or alienness of tribes. An ethnic group can thus be defined as a group of people sharing a similar outer habitus or mores, and whose belief in a commonality of descent is based on memories of colonization and migration. This, however, is only a *commonality* in which people believe; it is *not* a community: 'The difference between a "kinship group" and an "ethnic commonality" lies in the fact that the latter is only (imagined) "commonality" and not "community" like the former. The nature of kinship groups is, *inter alia*, essentially characterized by specific common social action' (Weber 1985 [1922], 237; my own translation based on Weber 1978 [1922], 389). Thus, while ethnic commonality, without being a community itself, might allow for community building and serve as a basis for political action, it might also simply be an effect of the political community (cf. Weber 1978 [1922], 389).

Weber thus refers to the *artificial character* of the emergence of the belief in common ethnicity that nevertheless has social consequences. This belief quite often—though not always—represents a *boundary* that delimits contacts with certain social circles, as it is constitutively linked to an *ethnic honour* that operates similarly to a *status honour* as a means of repelling others and excluding them from any form of social intercourse.

Weber's debate on ethnic groups and their relations is problematic and misleading. Not only is the essentialist definition of *racial* membership unconvincing and problematic, but also the notion of how a community, and thus a collective actor that can engage in closure struggles, comes into being. Weber claims that 'all history shows how easily political action can produce a belief in

---

[3] This is, of course, a much more fundamental argument than Parkin's. Before Syrian refugees were degraded in EU member states, they were of course victims of EU policies.

consanguinity, unless gross differences of an anthropological nature stand in its way' (Weber 1978 [1922], 393). Yet, this turns the problem on its head. Neither is the process of acting in solidarity a simple one nor does Weber take seriously that strategic action establishes boundaries and a political identity in relation to others and that this identity does not simply arise from consanguinity. Of course, Weber does not seriously develop this relational idea. Instead, he sticks to subjective beliefs, an emphasis on external habitus, the strained analogy of ethnicities and status groups, and the emphasis on the relevance of lifestyles rather than relations with other communities that are crucial in this process. None of this helps to deal with today's processes of closure based on race or ethnicity or the settler-colonial distinction of *civilization* and *barbarism*. Processes of identity and consequently community formation, which are unalterable prerequisites for the exercise of social closure strategies by collective actors, cannot be reduced to questions of status, mores, honour, or lifestyles. In this sense, Weber's notion of race and ethnic groups is not only misleading but also historically and sociologically outdated and simply obsolete.

9
Beyond Max Weber
Towards a New Idea of Social Closure

It is to Weber's credit that he pointed out the importance of closure processes for understanding how the social world works. The idea of *struggle*, and thus Weber's *paradigm of struggle*, from which perspective he views the social world, is of central importance—especially if we take it seriously and consider today's ongoing struggles, including colonial and settler-colonial struggles—to develop a general concept of closure to reorient the theory and analysis of closure. Since Weber's concept of struggle is linked to those of *associative* and *communal* relationships, the conceptual pair of *open* and *closed* relationships enables a specific perspective on social life with regard to any form of social relation. The opening and closing of social relations thus become the two fundamental social processes in the social world. They make possible various degrees of closure of social relations, ranging from the complete exclusion of others to the restriction of access or the enabling of participation under certain conditions, without which a conception of social life would not be possible. But each of the three basic concepts has serious problems, as the preceding discussion has shown. This is more than evident in Weber's analyses of social closure, which suffer from an inadequate conception of power, a narrow conception of closure that he sees as critical for the construction of an economically determined status order, and an unsatisfactory conception of collective action and community formation. His conception of race and ethnic relations fails to explain how these groups also create a political identity that cannot be equated with economic or social status but which relates to honour and lifestyles.

Despite these issues, Weber's conceptual approach and his empirical analyses are helpful for an initial idea of what a new concept of social closure that fits into the *struggle paradigm* must offer, or for how to conceptualize closure as ongoing processes in the social world. However, while all that must be reconstructed, like with the methodological dead end of structuralist Marxism in the theory of social closure, I also reject Weber's individualistic approach because it does not allow for an adequate conceptualization of either social closure or closure processes.

In rejecting methodological individualism, I follow Mario Bunge's view that collective actors are not simply aggregates of persons or aggregates of properties of their individual members since the interaction of these actors does not simply consist of 'the totality of interactions between their individual members' (Bunge 1996, 245). However, Weber's conceptual engagement with struggle, his distinction between associative and communal social relationships, between open and closed social relationships, and his analyses of closure—be it closure in market relations, power relations, or ethnic relations—reveal a characteristic feature that is also at the heart of the critique of the individualist approach, as Charles Tilly and Robert E. Goodin have made clear: 'In every such analysis, a market-like allocative structure emerges that operates outside the choosing individual—but it is surprising how rarely methodological individualists examine the means by which these allocative structures do their work' (Tilly and Goodin 2006, 10).

In fact, it is hard to see how we explain closure struggles if we start from a status group, a social class, or an ethnic group where homogenized actors share the same ideas, convictions, motivations, and so forth solely because of their shared status. It is also unconvincing to see all these shared ideas, convictions, or motivations as sufficient causes for explaining why these actors employ strategies of social closure. We simply have to assume that the external allocative structures of status groups, classes, or ethnic groups produce the kind of monopolizing strategies that Weber refers to. Methodological individualism does not offer a satisfying explanation of social closure—neither in its instrumentally rational (Elster 1996) nor its value rational (Boudon 1996a; 1996b) variant, which both define social actors

> as independent choice-making persons (that are treated) as the fundamental units and starting points of sociological analysis. Its explanations pivot on mental events—choices or decisions. People make choices that forward their interests, preferences, or utilities within constraints set by personal resources and environmental settings. What causes those choices? Other mental events in the form of calculating concerning the likely outcomes of different actions. (Tilly 1999, 263)

This is precisely what we find in Weber's closure analyses. Regardless of different contexts, 'humans acquire beliefs, concepts, rules, goals, and values from their environments, reshape their own (and each other's) impulses in conformity with such ideas, and act out their socially acquired ideas' (Tilly 2003b, 5). Closure is always to be understood as an effect of individual calculations; a common external structure such as status group, class, or ethnic group promotes mental processes that—presumably among a large number of individuals in the same socio-political, socio-economic, or socio-cultural situation—lead to the decision to strategically exclude others. Surprisingly, these *others* neither play a role in the decision or choice to monopolize resources nor affect the strategies taken. Additionally, the three different contexts seem insignificant in this regard:

> The consistent individualist overlooks the fact that individual intentions and expectations, hence choices, are largely shaped by social circumstances: that few individuals are free to choose the social rank they wish to belong to. Such oversight of the social context of agency is bound to lead to utterly false models of social facts. (Bunge 1997, 440)

Therefore, to avoid false models of closure struggles that ignore how social closure and related struggles emerge from established social relations and are fought by collective actors who neither automatically exist because of a shared class position, status, honour, or lifestyle nor *establish themselves* through their collective action alone without taking into account the relations with those they strategically act against, I reject methodological individualism as the basis of a new theory of social closure. Instead, I argue for a methodologically relational approach in which processes, dynamics, and contexts play a central role. In newly theorizing social closure, I will therefore argue that a relational perspective is the only convincing methodological basis to lead social closure theory out of its current impasse.

To newly theorize social closure, we need further steps guided by a relational perspective. *First*, although Weber acknowledges the emergence of group formation, he does not conceptualize it. *Second*, there is no concept of power to explain how social actors can develop strategies and processes of social closure and implement them. *Third*, closure theory has surprisingly failed to make explicit the very goal of social closure. The relational perspective that I employ will now guide the discussion of these three critical lacunae in Weber's theory of social closure: group action / acting in solidarity, power, and life chances / chances of survival in the opportunity structure.

NEW CONCEPTS
FOR CLOSURE THEORY

This sub-part develops the essential concepts for a new theorizing of social closure that have been missing so far in closure theory. It discusses the relevance of three concepts—*group action and acting in solidarity, power,* and *life chances / chances of survival*—and outlines them in a methodologically relational perspective. This step of concept building is a crucial step in theorizing social closure and is inevitable to solve the problems and overcome the shortcomings of traditional closure theory.

10
Group Action and Acting in Solidarity

In contrast to Weber's assumption of a seemingly unproblematic and self-generating solidarity between members of the same social situation due to their individualistic choices, solidarism is a highly presuppositional social process. While it is obvious that Weber and the *theory of social closure* focus on collective actors, in an illuminating analysis Heinz Steinert (2004) attributed a general problem to both approaches concerning *group action*. Referring to specific aspects of both Mancur Olson's (1965) and Bill Jordan's (1996) approaches to a theory of collective action, Steinert points to the important fact that 'closure means the procedure of *organizing* an interest as the very precondition of conflict ability, i.e., the possibility of plausibly threatening to refuse a necessary service or good' (cf. Steinert, 2004, 199; my own translation). Yet, Steinert shows that Weber neglected processes of group formation.

This crucial aspect of organizing points to 'processes of solidarism in order to develop a position in collective bargaining' (Steinert 2004, 200; my own translation).[1] What is at stake here is the simple fact that to be able to fight in closure struggles of daily life, social groups first of all must be able to draw boundaries, thereby developing a political identity and closing their community. This aspect addresses two critical questions. First, how can we properly understand these processes that allow for social groups to develop a political identity that is the precondition for their conflict ability? Second, how can we understand, in a closure perspective, why these processes fail, and social groups fail in doing so? The answer to these questions not only reveals a fundamental weakness of closure theory but also broadens the perspective to better understand and adequately conceive of closure in a new way.

To understand how collective political identities form, a relational methodological perspective is recommended. This approach aligns with the methodological ideas developed by anthropologist Frederik Barth (1969), who was the first to propose a different perspective about the creation of collective identities. He suggested a constructivist approach that rejected an essential understanding of groups or collectivities, who could be conceived of being in opposition because of certain inherent traits. Instead of assuming existing boundaries that

---

[1] I developed the following arguments in Mackert 2021 and take parts from it.

separate groups from the very beginning, it is the construction of their respective identities that create and re-create boundaries in relation with one another in situations of exchange, conflict, or struggle, or simply by coexistence.

Adopting such a relational and at the same time constructivist methodological perspective on social closure enables us to ask a new set of questions: In closure struggles, who are those in powerful positions, able to enact closure strategies that inevitably compromise the life chances of those affected by them? Who are those in weaker positions, confronted with the impact of that social closure (i.e., being excluded, exploited, or threatened with elimination)? In closure struggles, social actors simply ask, 'Who are we?' and 'Who are they?', which means that by drawing a line between *us* and *them* (Tilly 2003a), social actors become capable of developing a conception of themselves that allows them to act collectively. As Barth argued, rather than assuming already existing collective social actors that in social closure struggles start to interact, as both Weber and the theory of social closure for methodological reasons did, following Charles Tilly's (2003a; 2003b; 2005a; 2005b) relational view allows for understanding how, in permanent social interaction of both parties, collective identities emerge that become critical in closure struggles:

> Identities belong to that potent set of social arrangements in which people construct shared stories about who they are, how they are connected, and what has happened to them. Such stories range from the small-scale production of excuses, explanations, and apologies when something goes wrong to the large-scale production of peace-settlements and national histories. (Tilly 2003a, 608)

Between the extremes of these small-scale and historical, large-scale events, we can locate the process of creation of collective identities in closure struggles that we can define as *political* identities, given that in all closure struggles, as discussed earlier, governments play a critical role (Tilly 2003a, 609). More precisely, from this perspective, we can distinguish four aspects of identities: '1) a boundary separating me from you or us from them; 2) a set of relations within the boundary; 3) a set of relations across the boundary; 4) a set of stories about the boundary and the relations' (Tilly 2003a, 608).[2]

---

[2] Tilly's approach is highly informative as it offers a unique way to understanding the processes in question in the tradition of Barth. Looking at how collective identities arise from this constructivist perspective has also been stressed by Andrew Abbott 1995 in his *Things of Boundaries*, while single aspects of Tilly's approach have been prominent in various debates. Regarding boundaries, see Lamont and Molnár 2002; regarding symbolic struggles, see Bourdieu 1984 [1979]; regarding questions of identity in processes of exclusion, see Elias and Scotson 1994, Alexander and Smith 1993; for various aspects and forms of community building, see Somers 2008, Brubaker 2006, and Wimmer 2008.

That collective identities are constructed by social actors on both sides of the boundary becomes obvious if we take seriously that both parties in closure struggles ask the critical question of who they are in relation to the others. From this methodological perspective, the plurality of social relations is expressed in various stories—about the boundary, about one's own group ('Who are we?'), about the other group ('Who are they?'), and common stories told about the relations of both sides. From this perspective, we can understand how by drawing boundaries social actors develop their collective identities, because 'identities reside in relations' (Tilly 2005b, 8). It is this process of identity construction that allows them to turn to *group action*.

Such a relational approach also helps explain why not all social groups are able to develop a collective identity and turn to group action. Social groups may be unable to draw boundaries to develop a sense of who they are, the consequence being that they are unable to succeed in closing their community and therefore remain vulnerable to closure attacks. Neither Weber nor the theory of social closure has paid attention to this critical aspect of social closure, which is why the equally important aspect of the less-powerful sides' efforts to close their own community went unnoticed. Taking this aspect seriously, it becomes clear that social closure is not just about the powerful side in closure struggles denying the less-powerful side access to resources, goods, or rights.

While this aspect is of course crucial, it is pivotal in my newly theorizing of social closure that a second and equally important dimension of closure inevitably needs attention and systematic consideration. This is the strategy of the powerful, within social relations of closure, to prevent the less powerful from drawing boundaries and developing a collective political identity that would enable them to participate successfully in closure struggles. This dimension, as I show in Part III of this book in detail, is about maintaining control over the less powerful and keeping them in a subordinate position.

The relational perspective thus not only helps to overcome a critical gap in closure theory but also allows a much more accurate understanding of what is actually meant by processes of social closure. In newly theorizing and analysing social closure, I will systematically take into consideration that closure is not only about monopolization and denial of access but also about strategies of the powerful to prevent the less powerful from closing their own community, either by trying to prevent the development of their shared political identity that would enable acting in solidarity or by destroying them.

The creation of a collective political identity is an essential prerequisite for what Steinert has called *organizing an interest* and *acting in solidarity* and makes it possible to understand the development of common goals and strategies. However, to understand the diversity of strategies in closure struggles, we also need to take seriously, as a further step, that all these strategies depend on the ability of social actors to mobilize *power*. This fundamental concept, as I have shown, is made explicit neither by Weber nor by the theory of social closure. Yet, because my relational approach to social closure is essentially power-based and conceives of closure struggles as power struggles, I now turn to the development of a relational concept of power that will serve as a basis for both social closure theory and the analysis of struggles for social closure.

11
Power in Closure Analysis

To argue that power has until now been actually absent from closure theory may be surprising and irritating. However, to conceive of closure struggles as power struggles and to ask how social actors can participate in closure struggles makes this lack of a concept of power immediately obvious. Arguing along relational lines inevitably calls for a concept of power that must meet two conditions. First, it needs to conceive of power as a fundamental aspect of social life and thus as characterizing any kind of social relation. Relations of social closure have thus to be conceptualized as being based on power. Second, a relational concept of power needs to draw attention to the ways structural aspects of power are linked to the agency of social actors. In this sense, all aspects of social closure refer to social relations that are intrinsically and constitutively linked to a concept of power that makes conceivable how social actors can exercise power by drawing upon structurally given elements of power. Conceiving of social life *as* struggle, and having defined the *opening* and *closing* of social relationships as the *most fundamental processes in social life*, makes closure struggles a matter of strategic human conduct, an exercising of power in social relations, and a dynamic social process.

Proceeding from the assumption that power is the ultimate basis of closure struggles enabling social actors to get involved in them, in this chapter I discuss the sociological approaches to power of Heinrich Popitz, Anthony Giddens, and Michael Mann. Although their concepts of power are distinct, their ideas about the role power in social life, the way it operates, and how it can be analysed are compatible and can be combined into a relational concept of power. This combination allows for theoretically reconceptualizing and empirically reorienting social closure analysis. While Popitz starts from the thesis 'that power constitutes a universal element of the human condition, fundamentally affecting the very essence of human sociability' (Popitz 2017 [1986], 1), his 'anthropologically determined forms of power ... can be read as an answer to Max Weber's observation that the concept of power is amorphous' (Göttlich and Dreher 2017, xvi). In contrast to Weber's neglecting power, Popitz's conception, as it were, gives shape to a presumably shapeless phenomenon—hence the talk of *forms* instead of *ideal types* of power (Göttlich and Dreher 2017, xvi) and his being mainly interested in power formation, its stabilization, and the institutionalization of power that he discusses within three distinct contexts of social relations that serve as the base for three fundamental contexts of social closure that I define in Part III of this book. In analysing social struggles in these contexts, Popitz stresses the critical role of *organizing* as essential for participation in these struggles, which brings us back to the importance of developing political identities in closure struggles.

Giddens criticizes Weber's definition of power as 'the chance of a human being or a number of human beings to realize their own will in a collective social action (*Gemeinschaftshandeln*) also against the resistance of others who are also participating' (Weber 1985 [1922], 531; my own translation based on Weber 1978 [1922], 926) for two reasons:

> On the one hand, it reflects Weber's subjectivist methodological position, and leads to the dualism of action and structure that I have insisted to overcome; on the other, considered solely from the point of view of the connection between power and agency, it does not bite deeply enough. For the notion of human action logically implies that of power, understood as transformative capacity. (Giddens 1979, 256)

Arguing for a duality instead of a dualism of action and structure, Giddens not only rejects methodological individualism but elaborates on a socio-theoretical perspective on power that is relational in the sense that it clarifies how power as both structure and agency are related to one another. By defining empirically identifiable structural elements of *resources* of power, Giddens bridges the gap between socio-theoretical reflection and empirical analysis.

Mann, in a neo-Weberian approach, also goes beyond Weber defining power as 'the ability to pursue and attain goals through mastery of one's environment' (Mann 2006, 6). His approach treats power as being of fundamental significance for understanding social relations. By placing power at the centre of the analysis of human history, like Popitz, Mann stresses processes of organization to explain how social struggles unfold. Like Giddens, Mann further rejects the idea of *society*, which allows for closure analyses to stretch beyond national boundaries. Finally, by defining distinct *sources* of social power, we can expand and complement Giddens's concept of resources of power. Bringing sources (Mann) and resources (Giddens) together, I use the latter term and conceive of them as four critical *resources* of power when theorizing social closure and analysing closure strategies.

Having referred to the common starting point, mentioned the differing approaches, and highlighted how they relate to each other, I now take a closer look at each of these theoretical approaches to power to carve out their critical aspects, which will allow for a relational concept of power for social closure.

11.1 Heinrich Popitz: Processes and Mechanisms of Organizing Power

Heinrich Popitz's (2017 [1986]) *Phenomena of Power*, an outstanding and pivotal discussion on the role of power in social life he began in his *Prozesse der Machtbildung* (1968) and finally developed into *Phänomene der Macht* (1986) offers a unique perspective on how power in its various guises is inextricably linked to human conduct. Being an anthropologist, a philosopher, and a sociologist, Popitz is essentially interested in creating a research programme 'which can be labelled "anthropological sociology". His central concern is to develop a general sociological theory that characterizes the cross-cultural fundamental structures of human sociation and that conceives the human as social being' (Göttlich and Dreher 2017, xiii).

In Popitz's view, power is an essential phenomenon of human conduct and any form of human sociation.[1] Although he does not make this explicit, referring to human sociations that are all characterized by *power relations* makes the approach an explicit relational one, based on a dynamic concept of social life in which *processes* are critical. The forms of power that Popitz differentiates pave the way for understanding power relations against the background of his anthropological reasoning. His assumption that forms of power and their respective organizational forms can operate separately but also interact and reinforce each other makes this approach exceptionally interesting for coming to terms with the dynamics of both social life in general and social closure struggles in particular that, as I will argue, operate in this way.

11.1.1 Premises of Conceptualizing Power

Popitz starts from three assumptions: First, he understands 'the nature of power-based orders as humanly *produced* realities' (Popitz 2017 [1986], 2). As human beings intentionally intervene in the ongoing processes in the world, power relations have to be conceived as being constructed by human beings: 'One of the taken-for-granted premises of our understanding of power is the conviction that power is "made" and can be remade otherwise than is now the case' (Popitz 2017 [1986], 4). Second, Popitz assumes that power is omnipresent as we can find power at work in any kind of social relations from revolutions to the most intimate relations:

---

[1] Besides power, Popitz also conceives of norms, techniques, and creativity as such essential phenomena.

Power lurks behind everything—all one needs to do is to see it. It does not matter whether this view is advanced as a theoretical claim or is only emotionally supposed in the form of a generalized suspicion of power: power is assumed a component of all social processes. It is ubiquitous. (Popitz 2017 [1986], 5)

Third, he argues that 'all exercise of power is a limitation of freedom. On this account, all power needs justification' (Popitz 2017 [1986], 6). As exercising power limits the freedom of others, power and freedom are always in conflict.

Arguing from a historical perspective, Popitz does not see these premises as specific to a certain kind of society but believes power to be of fundamental significance for any kind of society or social relation, which means that, seen anthropologically, power is a capability of human beings: they are capable of winning out over external forces. This assertiveness leads Popitz to two critical and interrelated sets of questions. The first concerns the *capability* of human beings to exert power, its presence in all social relations, and its actual basis. The second set examines the *limitation of freedom* that power causes. Thus, what makes people suffer from power? In Popitz's words, 'Power as ability and power as suffering—only if we pose questions of such general nature can we hope to attain understandings whose scope matches the premises of our historical consciousness of power' (Popitz 2017 [1986], 9).

These two fundamental perspectives provide the foundation for Popitz to develop a systematic approach towards the exertion of power and the suffering it can cause, given that social actors' ability of self-assertion points to specific *human capabilities* while the susceptibility of human beings to suffer from power points to their *vital dependencies*. However, to develop a systematization of power based on this differentiation, Popitz introduces distinct forms of power instead of ideal types, as he is in fact interested in its various empirical manifestations.

11.1.2 The Concept of Power

At the heart of Popitz's outline of the concept of power that provides anthropological and philosophical considerations of the critical and indispensable role of power in social life is a differentiation of distinct forms of social power that he sees as the basic and ineluctable forms of power: the power of action, instrumental power, authoritative power, and the power of data constitution.

1. Power of action. Arguing in an anthropological vein, Popitz starts from the human capability to inflict harm on all other organisms as well as other human beings, even up to the point of killing them. Here, power is unequally distributed, as human beings differ in terms of physical strength, speed, and so forth, as well in terms of access to weapons. As weapons increase the pure power of action and because this process of increasing efficiency is virtually unlimited, Popitz argues that the potential danger for human beings simultaneously becomes unlimited. At the same time, the human being 'is exposed to being harmed in multiple and subtle ways' (Popitz 2017 [1986], 11), as three forms potentially threaten her/his existence. First, human beings can be killed as their exposure corresponds to fantasies of inflicting harm, such as torture, or a death sentence. Second, in addition to this creatural dimension, there is an economic one making it impossible for a human being to reproduce. Third, denying human beings the possibility of social participation can also threaten their very existence: 'This then is the first root of power: humans can exercise power over other humans because they can do harm to them' (Popitz 2017 [1986], 12).

2. *Instrumental power.* Unlike power of action, instrumental power perpetuates power in order to control and influence the behaviour of those who are subject to this power being exerted: 'Power is rendered durable to the extent that certain acts—punishments or rewards—can be turned respectively into threats and promises, extending across time and space the effect of the mere power to do harm' (Popitz 2017 [1986], 12).

Popitz argues that the basis of instrumental power is being in a position to make decisions about *give and take*. Therefore, the strategy of enacting instrumental power becomes visible insofar as—for all those affected by it—punishments *and* rewards are possible, the consequence being that their conduct is divided into the two categories of *conformity* and *insubordination*. This alternative promotes fear and hope on the part of the subordinated, and it only works because human beings' social conduct is oriented towards the expectable conduct of others, and, as a result, the subordinates' hopes can be exploited by a power that creates fear. In the case of instrumental power, human beings are made an instrument of someone's will: 'The instrumental power to threaten and to promise is the typical power of everyday life ... Every long-lasting power relationship *also* rests on instrumental power' (Popitz 2017 [1986], 14).

3. *Authoritative power.* With regard to this third form of power, Popitz makes an important differentiation by contrasting '"external power" (as that manifesting itself in threats and promises) with "internal power". The latter does not need to operate by means of extrinsic advantages and disadvantages: it produces a willing, compliant disposition to obey' (Popitz 2017 [1986], 14). This internal power then promotes conformity even if conduct is not controlled; further, it does not only control behaviour but, no less, attitudes, dispositions, perspectives, or criteria of human beings as well as the way they are judged—which are all aspects of internalized control.

Why is this kind of internal power effective? Popitz, again in an anthropological sense, refers to a human need for orientation in the form of a need for standards as the self-esteem of human beings depends on recognition by others; they are looking for certainty, or signs that show that they have been able to prove themselves. Of course, this use of internal power establishes a relationship of authority in the sense of a dual process of recognition: on the one hand, those in subordinate positions accept others being superior, which allows them to set obligatory standards; on the other hand, these people strive for subordinates' recognition and them giving signs of approval. This again shows a dichotomous structure, namely 'the alternative between hoped-for recognition and dreaded withdrawal of it. Whoever can and does intentionally establish such alternatives in order to guide the conduct and attitude of others exercises authoritative power' (Popitz 2017 [1986], 15).

4. *Power of data constitution.* Popitz's fourth form of power highlights that human beings not only exert power over other human beings but also use technical knowledge to impinge on nature, reconstructing it and thereby triggering consequences for themselves and perhaps all of humanity. Popitz mentions several intrusions, such as urban planners' creating new settlements that impact the living conditions of other people. In doing so, urban planners also make decisions about spaces of freedom and constraints for people living in these areas. Moreover, building bridges, streets, fences, or walls separates people from one another by creating distinct areas that specific people may not be allowed to enter. 'The power to constitute data is a power mediated by objects . . . On this account it is by no means a power of things over men . . . but a power of producing and of the producer, built by the latter into things, which often remains long latent, but can manifest itself at any time' (Popitz 2017 [1986], 16). When this kind of power is exerted, decisions are made concerning the living conditions of human beings.

The discussion of Popitz's analysis so far has revealed four forms of power, the constitutive capabilities and vital dependencies of humans that allow us to define distinct forms of power relations that arise in social life, as shown in table 11.1.

Each form of power creates power relations independently. First, the capability to inflict harm, combined with human vulnerability to various forms of harm, results in *sheer violence*. Second, the capability to issue threats and promises, in the context of humans' expectations about the future, leads to *outright blackmail*. Third, the capability to set standards, paired with the need for standards and recognition, leads to *unquestioned dignity*. Fourth, the capacity for technical action, along with people's dependence on artefacts, enhances the *sheer effectiveness of technical action* (see Popitz 2017 [1986], 20).

However, this is only the first step towards fully understanding emerging power relations. After all, they can also interact in manifold ways, thus creating

Table 11.1 Forms of Power

	Constitutive Capabilities	Vital Dependencies	Power Relations
Power of Action	Capability to inflict harm	Being exposed to being armed in multiple and subtle ways	Sheer violence
Instrumental Power	Capability to formulate threats and promises	Expectations relating to the future	Outright blackmail
Authoritative Power	Capability to set standards	Need for standards and recognition	Unquestioned dignity
Power to Constitute Data	Capability for technical action	Being dependent on artefacts	Effectiveness of technical action

more complex forms. First, the individual forms of power may either combine and promote *bipolar forms of power*, or *external* and *internal* alternatives may combine, thereby promoting *forms of power that are difficult to decipher*. In either case, we then observe forms of power accumulation. One form of power might simply increase, or it is conceivable that the opportunities each form of power offers is used to transform one form of power into another. Second, there may also be different types of interplay between the different forms of power. On the one hand, it may work like a *coalition of powers* of assertiveness. On the other hand, the different forms may *complement each other* in such a way that all exit options that might exist for the subordinate are blocked simultaneously.

Against the background of anthropological assumptions and philosophical considerations, Popitz's approach to phenomena of power has a strong relational character in terms of methodology. In his view, power relations arise because 'human beings can *directly do something* to other human beings, furthermore they can modify *expectations, standards, and artifacts* that exercise effects upon others' (Popitz 2017 [1986], 18). It is all about the different and specific ways in which power helps create, transform, and solidify human social relations. Power is an inevitable aspect of human life that characterizes any form of social relations and the conduct of human beings. Yet Popitz considers all these power relations as always transformable and—particularly with regard to extremely asymmetrical and violent power relations—in the long term as unstable: 'Power in general may be the unavoidable fate of every form of sociation, yet any concrete power structure is not' (Göttlich and Dreher 2017, xviii).

11.1.3 Power Formation

By conceiving of power as fundamental for all processes in social life, Popitz's insightful discussion on the formation of power becomes critically important. It provides both a conceptual framework for a new understanding of closure and critical aspects for a relational methodological perspective.

Based on his differentiation between various forms of power and referring to the roles of sheer violence, outright blackmail, unquestioned dignity, and the effectiveness of technical action in processes of power formation, in a second step Popitz asks the following questions: 'How does it happen that few gain power over many? That a small advantage gained by some can be transformed into power over other human beings? That some power becomes more power and from more power arises much power?' (Popitz 2017 [1986], 131). By way of example, Popitz discusses these basic questions of power formation within three distinct social contexts and

> without saying so at the outset, Popitz intentionally gives the reader to understand gradually that at stake in these examples is power by means of, respectively, (i) ownership and rent, (ii) control over means of production, and (iii) currency and taxation. (Harrington 2018)

These contexts, established by three specific sets of social relations, are such that participants cannot simply leave. Because Popitz is interested in the definitive starting point of processes of power formation, he assumes that in these contexts all participants start from the same situation. This approach allows him to identify the processes through which a minority gains power and exerts it over the majority.

Just as the nature of the contexts becomes clear, so does the *relational, processual*, and *mechanismic* perspective of Popitz's account. First, in his examples of power formation, Popitz focuses on the *reorganization* of the social *relations* and how this transformation reinforces processes of an increase of power. Second, he identifies the *processes* of the social puzzle: why, over time, a minority ends up in a position to exert power over the majority and control them. Third, looking at how these processes unfold, Popitz is interested in the operation of *social mechanisms*, meaning specific small-scale processes—social and psychological—that unfold and concatenate into larger processes. Finally, as in all cases of social change, the newly emerging order resulting from the transformation of social relations has to be *stabilized*.

This account, which emphasizes contexts, relationships, processes, and mechanisms, serves as a kind of model for a new theory of social closure that will proceed along the same lines of reasoning. As an explicitly power-based approach, it will set the general perspective for a new theory of social closure. The three contexts of *currency and taxation, control over means of production*, and *property and rent* represent what I will discuss as the three contexts of social closure: *exclusion, exploitation*, and *elimination*. The social relations established within these contexts are those of the *excluders and the excluded*, the *exploiters and the exploited*, and the *eliminators and those threatened with elimination*. Since contexts and the processes of social closure within them are critical for my new approach, I follow Popitz's discussion of the formation of power within the three different contexts.

1. Power Formation on the Mediterranean Cruise Ship
On the ship, we see a basic social order of deck chairs that are available for everyone. Upon the arrival of a new group of people, this social order collapses as the newcomers declare all deck chairs to be occupied and in their possession. Threatening the others with violence was part of the groups' imposing of a new order:

> After the assertion by one partial group of exclusive faculties of disposition over a consumer good desired by all, the previously formless ensemble of passengers acquired a structure. Two classes had established themselves—possessors and not-possessors, those positively privileged and those negatively privileged. (Popitz 2017 [1986], 133–134)

Violently enforcing a new social order results in newly established social relations of the two groups where the privileged group gains use of deck chairs, the good previously available to everyone. Those who were there before and resisted the new arrangement had their demands rejected. Popitz claims that the value of occupying the chairs lies in the fact that this new order could be developed further, perhaps into a fundamental denial of access to the chairs, a renting system, or even the introduction of the function of guardians from the group of the negatively privileged (Harrington 2018). Of course, such a strategy weakens the less-powerful group even more, as privileging some of them is going to divide it. 'With this, an essential clarification takes place: from now on, the not-possessors find themselves in the worst position voluntarily and because of their own fault' (Popitz 2017 [1986], 134). Here, the critical question arises: how could a minority group overthrow an established social order against the will of the majority and successfully establish a new one?

In explaining the *formation of power* in this case, Popitz argues that the majority relations do not play a critical role here. Rather, the minority is 'more capable of undergoing organization' (Popitz 2017 [1986], 135). Organizing turns out to be crucial, and it is the minority group that can do so because it has a common interest, which is not necessarily so in the majority group. Cooperation by organizing interests on the part of the minority group and claiming possession of the chairs becomes critical, as 'the possessors *immediately have something to offer* one another—being represented, being protected, receiving confirmation' (Popitz 2017 [1986], 136). Thus, the superior ability to organize gives the minority an opportunity to claim possession, to defend it, to redistribute the good, eventually with the aid of guards they select, and to generate a consensus about the newly established order. From this starting point, a power relation is established that will be reproduced over time and eventually increase the power of the minority. With regard to processes of *group action*, we may also say that this group has been able to create a collective identity and to close their community, which enabled them to organize an interest at the cost of the majority:

> The new group at first possessed only the momentary opportunity of having de facto at their disposal a good of general use and advanced the claim to an exclusive and lasting power of disposal: this apparently very small advantage sufficed for the formation of superior organizational capacity—and thus for the beginning of a process of power accumulation in opposition to the interests of the majority. (Popitz 2017 [1986], 139)

The main *process of stabilization* of this newly established order is one of a further expansion of power, Popitz argues, one that he calls 'the generatio equivoca of the achievement of valid legitimacy' (Popitz 2017 [1986], 140). Contrary to Weber's conceptualization of the belief in legitimacy of authority among the subordinates that is critical for the legitimation of any kind of domination, Popitz maintains that the newly created order first appears to be legitimate to the privileged themselves, not to the subordinated majority. According to a principle of reciprocity, the members of the small group mutually attest to each other the legitimate claim they make: 'because the other recognizes me, as I recognize him, and I him, as he me, our claims are based on our right' (Popitz 2017 [1986], 140).

With this, Popitz highlights an extremely significant aspect of the belief in legitimacy of social relations. The subordinate do not, initially, have to consent to being suppressed or—as I will show later—being the target of processes of social closure in the face of extremely asymmetrical power relations. The oppressors can—and do—assure themselves their claims are legitimate. This assurance increases security among the group's members and functions as a suggestive force as a result of their cooperation.

2. Power Formation in a Prisoner Camp

In his second example, Popitz discusses the situation in a prison camp. A social order of 'each man for himself' (Popitz 2017 [1986], 142) was reorganized by a small group of four prisoners who managed to build a stove to prepare some food made of the raw ingredients prisoners received. The men pooled their talents, and all 'this resulted in an exceptionally productive cooperation, thanks to which the group soon became the prosperous aristocracy of the camp' (Popitz 2017 [1986], 143). This transformation of an existing social order was possible because the group could prevent others from also making a stove. This allowed them to 'gradually gain monopoly over food production by drawing all other inmates into relations of dependency in services of supply, preparation, distribution and sabotage of attempts at rival stoves' (Harrington 2018). The creation of a means of production and thus the establishing of new social relations enabled a group of four to dominate the whole camp.

This process of power formation, Popitz argues, was possible thanks to the productive superiority of a nucleus of solidarity that allows organized action among the inmates who had been prepared not simply to cooperate. Rather, what they did was 'an act of daring disproportionate and ungrounded given the circumstances—a conduct that simply presupposed the reciprocity of solidarity, a "leap into trust"' (Popitz 2017 [1986], 145). It is precisely this creation of a bond of solidarity that allowed the small group an enormous range of performances that Popitz calls 'helping and dividing' (Popitz 2017 [1986], 145) as the basis for all this, and that cannot be captured using the usual sociological tools such as *division of labour, specialization*, or *cooperation*. Within the process of establishing a new social order and new social relations, *helping and dividing* denotes a kind of process that comprises various mechanisms that strengthen the power of the nucleus of inmates. These include 'coordinated collective activity', 'temporal sequencing of similar activities', 'spatial separation of similar activities', 'representing each other', a 'consciously constructed subdivision of the general task', and, of course, 'the effects of an established division of labour' (All quotations Popitz 2017 [1986], 146). Not only do all these mechanisms have external effects linked to the tasks to be solved but they also, simultaneously, reinforced internal solidarity of the nucleus group. Insofar as both effects have critical consequences for the group's relation to outsiders, they already point to the *stabilization* of this emerging power relation, the new social order, and the character of social relations:

> Power relations began to develop only with the increasing dependency of outsiders—with their having to rely on the group's favour—and were reinforced when the monopoly over production became accepted. (Popitz 2017 [1986], 148)

As the group had established a monopoly of means of production with the stove being the only one in the camp, the group had to ensure individual dependencies on the stove by all inmates in order to stabilize the power relations, the most important point being to avoid the 'formation of anticoalitions' (Popitz 2017 [1986], 149). To do so, the nucleus group initiated the 'policy of dividing... as an attempt to differentiate outsiders *in their relationship to the power center*, ranking them and thus generating different interests by dividing them in this fashion. We shall call this the creation of *echelons*' (Popitz 2017 [1986], 149–150).

Such groups or echelons are arranged like concentric circles around the power centre. The first is a group Popitz characterizes as *part owners, kinsmen, staff,* or *clientele* that is closest to the nucleus of power, though without its members actually being part of this. Rather, they may be assigned certain functions and tasks on behalf of this nucleus. Second, there are the *neutrals, spectators,* or the *non-involved,* forming a kind of a public that is not involved and 'to whom it can be suggested that it has nothing to do with the whole process of power extension, with conflicts that may arise' (Popitz 2017 [1986], 151). Third, we have the group of the underprivileged, the *pariah, shirtless,* or *serfs*. Excluding a group of underprivileged will have the effect of the other two echelons supporting the decision and strategies of the power centre, thus enabling it to simply argue it is 'carrying out the *volonté générale*' (Popitz 2017 [1986], 152). This *divide and rule game,* of course, plays the groups off against one another, allowing the power centre not only to further strengthen solidarity among its members but also to treat each of the echelons in specific ways so as to alienate them from one another.

3. Power Formation in a Boarding School

In the third example, a group of young cadets in a boarding school were granted a huge degree of autonomy to trust 'the blessings of self-administration and in the salutary effect of education by comradeship' (Popitz 2017 [1986], 153). After some of the boys had developed a way of conserving the two biscuits each cadet received for breakfast, a power centre emerged as the *chief,* and three boys formed an auxiliary team to ensure that 'other cadets render a portion of their biscuits to the ring-leaders via a class of collectors acting as tribute enforcers' (Harrington 2018). By establishing such a system of redistribution and profiting from it, this newly established social order transformed a group of equals into a stratified system by creating echelons. In the face of such a stratified system, Popitz argues that it is not the question of how such a group could develop that is of interest 'but rather the processes that continue to take place within the system', as

> we cannot assume that the processes of power formation had come, so to speak, to a standstill as its 'final result'. All power orders must be considered as systems in which the power that ordains the order continually reproduces itself. If there is a relatively stable power gradient, this means only that a given power distribution also reproduces itself in those processes. (Popitz 2017 [1986], 154–155)

Popitz here takes an explicit processual perspective on the establishment of a system of redistribution that in the beginning might have to be secured by violence to stabilize it (Popitz 2017 [1986], 155).Yet, once established, such a power structure, or a specific power relation, is reproduced by the workings of the system of redistribution itself by the operation of two processes: *keeping* and *taking and giving*. Keeping the confiscated bread is the first step, making it possible to accumulate it; taking and giving are then critical 'as part of the system of planned redistribution, they constitute suitable methods for producing power and the existing power distribution' (Popitz 2017 [1986], 155). This process, however, is not just one of allocating a good but also a process in which both subordinated groups become part of the system of redistribution that reinforces the power system as members of both groups, through their participation, 'place themselves at his or her service. In this way they also give him or her the means for collecting bread, thus by the same token for controlling the behaviour of *others*' (Popitz 2017 [1986], 156). As both groups in this process are under subjection, observing and controlling each other, they keep each other in the system, while the power centre only needs to continue modifying the pressure on them at times and playing them off against each other. In this game, Popitz points to a crucial factor concerning both subordinated groups; it is the weakness of their ability to organize that keeps them dependent on the power centre, albeit in a different way: 'Orders of this kind resemble machines, power machines whose driving energy is supplied by the dominated themselves. Such systems can no longer be "spontaneously broken up from inside"' (Popitz 2017 [1986], 157).

The stabilization of such an asymmetric social relation thus begins with members of the subordinated groups accepting this newly established order beginning to 'not merely comply, but serve; that they not only are in fear of the norms of this order, but internalize them; that they do their part, not just as a matter of solid habit but dutifully in terms of willingness and as followers' (Popitz 2017 [1986], 158).

This process, however, is a complicated and complex one. First, as Popitz shows again, we must take into account the reciprocal recognition among the members of the power centre, creating a certainty among them, but that does *not* in itself create a belief in legitimacy among the subordinated. Rather, second, the power centre must create and guarantee a form of social order to shape a consciousness among the disprivileged to push them to actually accept the order. To do so, a *security of order* must be established that is not arbitrary but according to which members can develop mutual expectations of conduct. This is not a specific aspect of any kind of democratic order; it also works in despotic and oppressive regimes. In some way, the established order must have a *value* to the subordinated in the sense that the order persists over a longer period, which allows them to develop mutual expectations, thus giving them reliability and orientation. These preconditions allow individuals to somehow *invest* in the future by attempting to become indispensable, which in turn strengthens the bonds that tie them to the existing order, because 'just as everyone is interested in not losing what one's activities can gain him or her, one also becomes interested in the persistence of the order into which one has deposited those activities. One's investments accrue from the sheer duration of this order' (Popitz 2017 [1986], 159–160), which finally leads to an increase in the *investment value* of the existing order.

All three aspects—security of order, value of order, and investment value—have critical effects by (1) rendering oppression systemic; (2) the power centre attempting to attribute a certain value to their investments; (3) the power centre succeeding in sustaining the existing order (see Popitz 2017 [1986], 160–161). If the power centre succeeds with respect to them, Popitz argues that the everyday experience of the subjugated will create a *basic legitimacy* that goes well beyond Max Weber's conception of a belief of legitimacy in authority.

11.1.4 Discussion

Within each of the contexts in which Popitz discusses processes of power formation, he starts from the assumption that all participants start from the same situation. Assuming that neither power asymmetries nor systems of domination have been established, Popitz is interested in the processes that allow for a minority to gain power and exert it over the majority. Power formation is made possible by the fact that the minority groups for different reasons—according to context—are able to organize. Accordingly, the 'deficit of organization among the "others"' (Popitz 2017 [1986], 162) has serious consequences. These include a matter-of-fact allocation on the cruiser, the power of productive superiority of nuclei of solidarity, and the reproduction of power in the redistribution system. As power formation establishes specific social relations among the minority and majority, this emerging order needs to be stabilized. In processual perspective, Popitz points to further processes: the emergence of legitimacy from the principle of reciprocity among the members of the minority group, an extension of newly established power relations by creating echelons that establish a kind of stratified order, and the creation of a consciousness of supposed profits among the dominated majority that renders the newly established power arrangement systemic. Popitz repeatedly emphasizes that while power in social conduct is unavoidable and an anthropological feature of human life, this does not apply to any given institutionalized power relation that may be transformed, rebuilt, or demolished at a certain time. Yet, in his analyses, Popitz exhibits in brilliant detail the ability of minority holders of power to entrench, augment and transform an initially relatively marginal and contingent situation of advantage into complexly evolving systems of functional relations of interdependence and mutual interest of affected parties. Resistance or overthrow of the system is always possible in theory but in practice invariably undermined by an inability of dominated groups to escape immediate exigencies of collaboration in barest vital self-interest. (Harrington 2018)

The discussion of Popitz's analyses of power relations is critical for obtaining a better idea of social closure struggles. Making power the inescapable basis to understand processes in social life allows for defining contexts of power formation that correspond to the three fundamental contexts of social closure. The formation of power and the stabilization of newly established social relations are of fundamental significance for the analysis of social closure and will be critical in my analysis in Part III of this book.

However, we must also take a slightly different approach with regard to two aspects in Popitz's approach. First, thinking about processes of social closure cannot begin from the premise that all social actors start from the same conditions. Rather, we start from a given social order, in that established social relations are reorganized by means of strategies of social closure. Second, as this reorganization can and does not play a role in Popitz's analyses, as he assumes a kind of social order to be newly established by processes of power formation, I argue that such *processes of reorganizing established social relations are a matter of processes of social closure*. In this sense, I will show that we can use Popitz's analyses also in contexts of already established social orders that are transformed by processes of power, since he repeatedly mentions that processes of power are leading to more power and a consolidation of power in emerging social orders. Thus, from the perspective of social closure, it will be of interest to see how the dominant minority can mobilize power to increase the power gap and reorganize social relations between the powerful and the less powerful in contexts of social closure. In the classic two-step of *reorganization* and *stabilization* (Mackert 2004b) in theories of social change following Émile Durkheim's (1992 [1950]) analyses in his *Professional Ethics and Civic Morals*, I thus argue that social closure comes in if we want to know in detail how, in which ways, and with what consequences a social order is reorganized on the base of power relations. In this sense, I will argue in favour of making a new approach to social closure an instrument of analysing in detail the *reorganization* of established social relations in contexts of exclusion, exploitation, and elimination. These processes will be the focus of the analysis.

Assuming that in such analyses we do not start from a situation where all actors start from the same conditions but rather from already established power relations, we need to go one step beyond Popitz's anthropological sociology with regard to understanding power. Theorizing and analysing power processes in different contexts requires a concept of power that encompasses various forms of power that must be mobilized to reorganize social relations. To overcome these problems and to further develop the relational concept of power for a new theorizing of closure, I turn to Anthony Giddens' social theory, which discusses power in a central place.

11.2 Anthony Giddens: Socio-Theoretical Considerations of Power

Anthony Giddens' *theory of structuration* that he outlined in *The Constitution of Society* (Giddens 1984) is a socio-theoretical approach that seeks to overcome critical dualisms in social theory and to transform them into a duality. In this approach, the idea of power can be seen as the lynchpin of theorizing and analysing that not only sees the agency of human actors constitutively linked with power but also conceptualizes the exercise of power always within a duality that links action to given structural preconditions that simultaneously constrain and enable human agency. This relational idea of power allows us to elaborate on Popitz's conceptualization of power and to expand it with a structural foundation. Thus, to further develop a concept of power for theorizing social closure and empirically analysing processes of social closure, I discuss some of Giddens' critical concepts, such as agency and structure as well as the way they are related in the duality of agency and structure, the concept of power, and the critical role it plays in social life, and finally the praxeological and processual perspective of this socio-theoretical approach.

11.2.1 Agency

Instead of assuming an initial point at which social actors start to act in order to form power, in Giddens' theory we start from ongoing processes of the production and reproduction of the social world in which power relations that, at times, can be extremely asymmetrical play a critical role. How can we make sense of human beings exerting power when acting in the social world? What are the structural preconditions of this ability of social actors in any kind of social relation? What exactly allows social actors to mobilize power? What are social actors' capabilities to do so?

Questions of this kind lead us to Giddens' approach to human agency, which he describes using two critical concepts: the *knowledgeability* and *capability* of social actors. Viewing human beings as *knowledgeable* actors means recognizing that they possess extensive knowledge of human behaviour, including why human beings behave the way they do, how they do so, and of the conventions that shape their conduct.[2] This kind of knowledge corresponds to what Giddens calls the *rationalization of human conduct*,[3] which means 'that human agents chronically, but for the most part tacitly "keep in touch" with the grounds of their activity, as a routine element of that activity' (Giddens 1982, 30). Being an integral part of all human conduct, this type of reflexivity does not mean that actors can discursively give reasons for the motives behind their conduct at any time. Rather, *keeping in touch* means that human actors can give reasons for why they act as they do and that they know *how to go on* in their daily life. As Giddens defines this kind of knowledge as *practical consciousness*, asking powerful actors in closure struggles why they exclude, exploit, or eliminate others, we would certainly receive answers in which social actors would give reasons—without stating that the reasons given are fundamentally true or correct.

To ascribe *capability* to social actors indicates a praxeological perspective that views

> action or agency as *the stream of actual or contemplated causal interventions of corporeal beings in the ongoing process of events-in-the-world*. The notion of agency connects directly with that of *Praxis*, and when speaking of regularized types of act I shall talk of human *practices*, as an ongoing series of 'practical activities'. (Giddens 1976b, 81; see also Giddens 1984, 55–56)

This idea implies a specific 'freedom of the acting subject' (Giddens 1976b, 103) that is determined neither by human nature nor by structural imperatives or system needs. At any point in time, the actor 'could have done otherwise' (see Giddens 1979, 56) in both a positive sense by intervening in the stream of social events or in a negative sense by refraining from it. Against this background, Giddens argues that 'the world as constituted by a stream of events-in-process independent of the agent does not hold out a predetermined future' (Giddens 1976b, 81).

A social actor's capacity to either intervene in the ongoing events in the social world or to refrain from doing so is the very capacity that makes her/him an actor in Giddens' view. Much as in Popitz's anthropological perspective, for Giddens this capacity is based on the fact that social actors have power in the

---

[2] I will discuss the different aspects of Giddens' theory only insofar as I need them for the purpose of the argument. Because this chapter is about power, I do not elaborate on the aspect of social actors' knowledgeability in detail.

[3] This idea departs distinctively from Weber's or Sigmund Freud's use of the term.

sense of a *transformative capacity*—an assessment that logically links human conduct to a concept of power:

> Action depends upon the capability of the individual to 'make a difference' to a pre-existing state of affairs or course of events.... In this sense, the most all-embracing meaning of 'power', power is logically prior to subjectivity, to the constitution of the reflexive monitoring of conduct. (Giddens 1984, 14–15)

Giddens rejects sociological concepts of power 'as the capability of an actor to achieve desired ends or goals' as he sees it most prominently in Weber's influential definition in 'various notions of power which regard power above all as a property of collectivities: modern versions of this sort of standpoint include those developed by Parsons or Foucault' (Giddens 1981, 49). However, conceptualizing social actors as knowledgeable and capable has further consequences, as 'we have to acknowledge that the knowledgeability/capability of human agents is always *bounded*, or constrained by elements of the institutional contexts in which their action takes place' (Giddens 1982, 30). Although social actors can be seen as intentional and purposive—whatever they do unfolds under conditions of *bounded rationality* and will therefore promote unintended consequences which can in turn become unrecognized conditions of further social action.

However, the structures in institutional contexts are not simply constraining human agency; at the same time, they are enabling it, because actors have to draw upon structural aspects of the institutional contexts in which they are acting. Therefore, Giddens defines structures as *rules* and *resources* that actors necessarily must draw upon in their conduct.

11.2.2 Structure: Rules and Resources

To conceptualize *structure as rules*, following Wittgenstein, Giddens conceives human conduct as acting according to rules in the sense that actors cannot discursively explicate these rules but they know how to continue with their conduct according to these rules by using their practical knowledge. This dynamic concept of structure allows us to understand how rules are shaped by human conduct while simultaneously enabling and constraining it. Giddens distinguishes between these rules as *rules of signification*, referring to processes of the constitution of meaning, and *rules of legitimation*, referring to processes of enforcing obligatory rights and duties and the sanctions for their violation.

Conceptualizing *structure as resources* means to conceive of structures as referring to social power and domination. To be able to understand what allows human actors to exercise power to make a difference in the ongoing processes in the social world and to intervene in it, Giddens makes an important distinction.

By differentiating between *authoritative* and *allocative resources,* he points to the two critical structural dimensions that clarify precisely what the idea of humans' capabilities to practically intervening in the social world means:

> Allocation refers to man's capabilities of controlling not just 'objects' but the object-world. Domination from this aspect refers to human domination over nature. Authorization refers to man's capabilities of controlling the humanly created world of society itself. (Giddens 1981, 51)

This argument highlights the most basic resources that actors need to utilize if they want to intervene in the social world. It also allows to make comprehensible social closure struggles, which are an important aspect of everyday life and a critical aspect of human *praxis* that unfolds in a relational setting. First, the structural elements of allocative resources that we can find in any society are as follows:

(a) Material features of the environment (raw materials, material power sources).
(b) Means of material production/reproduction (instruments of production, technology).
(c) Produced goods (artefacts created by the interaction of (a) and (b)) (Giddens 1981, 51)

In contrast to these structural elements, which pertain to human interaction with nature and highlight the economic institutions made up of them, in every society there are authoritative resources. These denote the coordination of social actors and relate to political institutions. Here, with regard to authoritative resources, we also can define their structural elements:

(a) The organization of social time-space (i.e. the temporal-spatial organization of social interaction such as the workplace and working hours.
(b) The production and reproduction of the human body, such as the organization and relations of human beings in society like class relations.
(c) The organization of social actors' life chances, meaning the distribution of chances of social actors to attain specific lifestyles or forms of self-realization. (Giddens 1981, 51–52)

The most critical aspect here is Giddens' rejection of the idea that power is a resource that social actors possess. Rather

> like other structural characteristics of social systems, however, the forms of authoritative resources, like allocative resources are not 'possessed' by individual

social actors but are features of the social totality . . . They only exist as resources in and through the very structuration of society which they facilitate or help to make possible. Taken together, the allocative and authoritative resources . . . are constitutive of the societal totality as a structured system of domination. (Giddens 1981, 52)

Against the background of this perception of resources and power, we can finally see the general implications of the logical relationship between human conduct and power in structured contexts. Given that agency means that social actors are able to *make a difference in the world*, any human conduct is logically linked to power as a *transformative capacity*. As social actors do not simply *possess* a certain amount of power in any kind of social relation, even those who appear to be completely powerless in extremely *asymmetric power relations* have to be seen as able to *mobilize* resources that allow them to make an impact. As asymmetrical as social relations may be, these actors will be able to defend the scope of action in their everyday life against more-powerful actors to a certain degree. No actor, as asymmetrical as his or her relationship towards other actors may be, is ever completely powerless. Therefore, social actors in social relations of super- and subordination are never simply the *victims of a system*. Rather, under conditions of asymmetrical power relations, a *dialectic of control* unfolds:

> Anyone who participates in a social relationship, forming part of a social system produced and reproduced by its constituent actors over time, *necessarily sustains some control over the character of that relationship or system. Power relations in social systems can be regarded as relations of autonomy and dependence*; but no matter how imbalanced they may be in terms of power, actors in subordinate positions are never wholly dependent, and are often very adept at converting whatever resources they possess into some degree of control over the conditions of reproduction of the system. In all systems there is a *dialectic of control*, such that there are normally continually shifting balances of resources altering the overall distribution of power. (Giddens 1982, 32; emphasis added)

Seen from this explicitly relational perspective, within a social system, human agency and power are related to a degree 'that an agent who does not participate in the dialectic of control ipso facto ceases to be an agent' (Giddens 1982, 32). This conduct does not necessarily have to be in opposition to those exerting power, but, of course, it includes the different ways of complying with a power centre or the participation in a social order that is characterized by asymmetrical power relations, by investing in it and attempting to extract some advantages, as Popitz has discussed in detail.

Against this background, in Giddens' view *any kind of a social relation is a power relation* because we simply cannot properly understand human relations if we refrain from taking power into account. This relational view of power relations in social systems—relations of autonomy and dependence—naturally brings closure struggles into focus. By definition, closure relationships are asymmetrical power relations within these relationships of autonomy and dependence.

11.2.3 Duality of Structure

Having discussed both agency and structure, we now need to know how exactly these two poles of social theory can be related as the 'constitution of agents and structures are not two independently given sets of phenomena, a dualism, but represent a duality' (Giddens 1984, 25). In other words: 'The concept of structuration involves that of the duality of structure, which relates to the *fundamentally recursive character of social life, and expresses the mutual dependence of structure and agency*' (Giddens 1979, 69). The duality of structure, which transforms the traditional dualism of structure and agency into a duality can be illustrated as shown in figure 11.1.

This figure shows that agents and structures are no longer conceptualized independently of one another. Instead, both the knowledgeability of agents and their capability are intrinsically linked to their respective structural properties. Referring to these properties enables agents to act and intervene in social life—of course, to different degrees, which might, in Popitz's view, be a consequence of their different degrees of being organized—while, at the same time, their agency reproduces these structural properties. Structuration theory thus proposes a model of the reproduction of given social systems through the agency of human beings. Reproduction implies that knowledgeable social agents depend on rules of signification (i.e., language) in order to communicate by drawing on

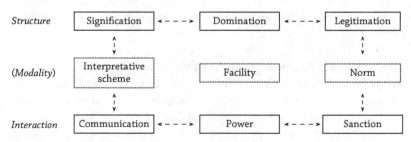

Figure 11.1 The duality of structure
Source: Giddens 1984, 29

interpretative schemes. As knowledgeable social agents, they also rely on rules of legitimation, such as laws or normative prescriptions, to sanction the behaviour of others by referencing norms in everyday encounters. As capable human agents, they can exercise power to either transform nature or to (re-)order social life by drawing on certain elements of structural properties. In Giddens' view, the dimensions of communication, power, and sanction (on the part of human actors)—and signification, legitimation, and domination (on the part of structure)—are only analytically separable and intrinsically entwined in the everyday production and reproduction of social life. Emphasizing the centrality of power in these processes, Giddens argues:

> The concept of power both as transformative capacity (the characteristic view held by those treating power in terms of the conduct of agents) and as domination (the main focus of those concentrating upon power as a structural quality), depends upon the utilization of resources. I regard each view as implying the other, however. Resources are the media whereby transformative capacity is employed as power in the routine course of social interaction; but they are at the same time structural elements of social systems as systems, reconstituted through their utilization in social interaction. This is therefore the correlate, in respect of power, of the duality of structure in respect of the communication of meaning and of normative sanctions: resources are not just additional elements to these, but include the means whereby the meaningful and the normative content of interaction is actualised. (Giddens 1979, 91–92)

As discussed, in Giddens' conceptualization, the critical resources in social life are of an allocative and authoritative nature, encompassing both the exploitation and reorganization of nature and the socio-spatial coordination of social actors. These are the structural principles that operate as the media allowing social actors to enact power. In this vein, Giddens still argues on a socio-theoretical level, proposing how to overcome the dualism of agency and structure. However, by examining his idea of structure more closely, we also move a step closer to empirical reality:

> The most important aspects of structure are rules and resources recursively involved in institutions. *Institutions* by definition are the *more enduring features of social life*. In speaking of the structural properties of social systems I mean their institutionalized features, giving 'solidity' across time and space. I use the concept of 'structures' to get at relations of transformation and mediation which are the 'circuit switches' underlying observed conditions of system reproduction. (Giddens 1984, 24; emphasis added)

On the basis of the distinction between rules of meaning and legitimation on the one hand and authoritative and allocative resources of domination on the other, Giddens finally develops a systematics of the basic institutional order in social systems (Giddens 1984, 31–33). What is critical here is that he does not simply assign one of these rules or resources to an institution. Rather, he argues that these basic institutions are characterized by the dominance of one of the rules or resources, while the others always play a role as well. In this sense, economic institutions, for example, are primarily characterized by allocative resources, while authoritative ones, as well as rules of signification and legitimation, are also important in understanding the way they operate in social orders. This pivotal insight of a weighting of importance will be crucial for my reconceptualization of closure theory and the different forms of power on which it is based. Like Giddens, I will argue that in terms of social closure relations we can identify structural resources of power that dominate in them, while all other forms of power also play a crucial role.

11.2.4 Discussion

The main building blocks of Giddens' structuration theory offer a sophisticated socio-theoretical approach to social life. The elements of his social theory discussed earlier complement some aspects of Popitz's groundwork on power while also further developing others, thus enriching the conception of power essential to the new approach to social closure.

First, by agreeing with Popitz on power being an integral part of social life, we can enhance the understanding of power by incorporating structural elements. This approach allows us to view closure as a powerful strategy employed by social actors. The social actors exercise their power by utilizing structural resources, which they must draw upon. This critical idea is elaborated through the concept of the *duality of structure.*

Second, taking a praxeological and relational view of social life enables us to view closure struggles as struggles unfolding in asymmetrical relations of power between powerful and less-powerful social actors. This relation finds expression in the theorem of the *dialectic of control* that leaves no actor powerless but always situated within relations of autonomy and dependence. Additionally, within contexts of exclusion, exploitation, and elimination, this means that we have to assume that social actors in closure struggles always preserve a certain degree of ability that—at least in principle—will allow them to organize and fight back against any strategy of social closure.

Third, however, the relational perspective of structuration theory goes beyond just explaining closure as actors restricting access to resources for others.

Structuration theory, as I will show, explains how powerful actors succeed in intervening in the creation of collective identity on the side of the less powerful, preventing them from closing their community and developing a political identity that would make them capable of fighting back in closure struggles.

In complementing and theoretically underpinning some of Popitz's critical ideas, Giddens elaborates in detail on a concept of power that serves as a foundation when it comes to explaining strategies, processes, and struggles of social closure. Yet, I argue that we must elaborate on Giddens' concept of the structural dimension of power, his distinguishing between allocative and authoritative resources, and add further dimensions to have a more comprehensive list of structural elements that social actors are able and forced to utilize in social closure struggles.

11.3 Michael Mann: The Social Sources of Power

In the course of several decades from 1986 to 2013, Michael Mann developed an impressive four-volume oeuvre: *The Social Sources of Power*. In these analyses, he argues that he is 'concerned with the same kind of things as Marx and Weber, which is the basic transformations of our times and how we understand those' (Mann in Lawson 2006, 495)[4]. His analyses offer a comparative historical sociology of power that aims to provide 'a history and theory of power relations in human history' (Mann 1986, 1) by analysing 'the sources of social power from the beginnings of human history to the present' (Hutchinson 2008, 87).[5] Like Giddens and other sociologists, Mann rejects the idea of a concept of *society*. Instead, he believes societies not to be bounded and distinct social entities throughout human history but 'overlapping and intersecting power networks' (Mann 1986, 2):

> A general account of societies, their structure, and their history can best be given in terms of the interrelations of what I will call the four sources of social power: ideological, economic, military, and political (IEMP) relationships. (Mann 1986, 2)

---

[4] Being mainly interested in the ways power is exercised in various forms of sociation, Mann has been criticized as being mainly a *top-down historian of power* (Go 2013, 1476) who does not pay enough attention to bottom-up processes in social struggles. While this may be the case, it is important to note that Mann simply is aware of extreme power asymmetries and sceptical with regard to analyses too confident about the possibilities of social movements, classes, or other collective actors to successfully fight against organized power.

[5] Mann is interested in trans-historical processes in a comparative perspective of historical sociology and not in case studies. Yet, in his latest books, although not giving up the comparative perspective, Mann has delivered detailed case studies of ethnic cleansing and fascism. I do not think this adulterates his conceptualization of power if it plays a critical role in analysing cases of social closure.

These four sources of power are at the same time overlapping networks, none of which can claim to have ultimate primacy over the others; they are also 'organizations, institutional means of attaining human goals' (Mann 1986, 2). Mann rejects the view that the significance of these four sources comes from human desire or any need for specific forms of satisfaction 'but from the particular *organizational means* each possesses to attain human goals, whatever these may be' (Mann 1986, 2), thereby not only loosely following Weber's idea of *spheres of value* but also Popitz' stressing of the fundamental significance of organizing for understanding power processes in social relations. While Mann also follows Weber in aiming to construct *ideal types of power* (Mann 1986, 4), as far as empirical historical work is concerned, he is interested in

> a more concrete *sociospatial* and *organizational* level of analysis. The central problems concern organization, control, logistics, communication—the capacity to organize and control people, materials, and territories, and the development of this capacity throughout history. The four sources of social power offer alternative organizational means of social control. (Mann 1986, 2–3)

Although Mann declares himself a methodological individualist, this characterization does not hold true on closer inspection[6], because to develop an alternative perspective on power as Weber's, he interestingly agrees with three critical aspects of Giddens' non-individualist but relational socio-theoretical approach. First, he argues, 'Like Giddens (1979, 91) I do not treat "power itself as a resource. Resources are the media through which power is exercised"' (Mann 1986, 6).[7] Further, Mann does not see power as a goal in itself that humans strive for or as an end in itself but rather as a means for human beings to accomplish their goals: 'A form of power may not be an original human goal at all. If it is a powerful *means* to other goals, it will be sought for itself. It is an *emergent* need. It emerges in the course of need satisfaction' (Mann 1986, 6). Power, in this sense, is a medium rather than a resource.

Second, Mann's perspective resonates with the core idea of the *theory of structuration* to transfer the dualism of structure and agency into the *duality of structure*: 'my model abandons the distinction between ideas and materiality in favour of one between "ideas-and-practices combined" (or "action

---

[6] As shown by Kiser 2006, Mann is not a rational-choice theorist either. In in his more recent analyses, Mann (2004; 2005) has included value rationality and even emotions in his explanatory armature. See Boudon 1996a, 1996b for this specific form of methodological individualism. Yet, I stress the relational aspect of his approach to power.

[7] Mann argues, 'I do not focus on power resources held by individuals—unlike Bourdieu's model of economic, cultural, political and social forms of power' (Mann 2006, 343).

and structure combined") in each of four power networks' (Mann 2006, 346; emphasis added).[8]

Third, and based on both these aspects, Mann explicitly refers to the institutional conceptualization of society in the theory of structuration, arguing that Giddens 'also distinguishes four types of power institution: symbolic orders/ modes of discourse, economic institutions, law/modes of sanction/repression, and political institutions' (Mann 1986, 11).

Mann, however, departs from Giddens' differentiating rules of signification and legitimation and resources, as he is interested only in the role and the actual sources of power in relation to human agency in all social contexts. In his view, not only *political* and *economic* power, as in Giddens' approach, but also *ideology* and *military* power serve as the sources for the structural foundation of power as distinct sources of power.

Expanding sources of power in this way is decisive for a broader and more convincing base of structural resources for closure theory. A brief analysis of Mann's IEMP model (i.e., the four power sources: ideological, economic, military, and political) will prepare the ground for it.

11.3.1 Ideological Power

Mann claims that sociological debates on ideological power come from three traditions: first, the idea that human beings need concepts and categories of meaning in order to orient themselves in the social world; second, conceptions of a shared norm, giving people an understanding of how to behave properly in social relations; third, aesthetic and ritual practices that human beings follow (see Mann 1986, 22). In general, Mann rejects the use of ideology as being a form of false consciousness used to dominate parts of a population or a class. Although he admits that ideological movements transcend individual experience, he also rejects a critical and frequent assumption in debates on ideology: 'people are not manipulated fools' (Mann 1986, 23). In particular, however, on this point he clearly departs from Giddens' rejection of ideology as a distinct source of power that has its own structural elements on which social actors can and have to draw to exercise power. In his discussion on structural resources, Giddens argues that 'in the theory of structuration ideology is not a particular "type" of symbolic order or form of discourse. One cannot separate off "ideological discourse" from "science", for example. "Ideology" refers only to those asymmetries of

---

[8] It is somewhat strange that Mann nowhere refers to Popitz's approach, although it is, in many respects, very close to his own (for instance, the fundamental meaning of power in social life and of it being organized).

domination which connect signification to the legitimation of sectional interests' (Giddens 1984, 33).

Certainly, Mann concedes that ideologies always contain legitimations of private interests and material domination. If that were all, however, they would not have such a tight grip on people. Rather, they appear to have a kind of a plausibility or to be convincing, as far as these people are concerned, as long as they exert power over them. Thus, in Mann's view, rather than referring to a symbolic order or a form of discourse, he sees ideologies as sources of power in their own right, with the three principal functions that allow him to go one step further to explain how ideologies are having an impact on social life by being organized, as 'ideas can't *do* anything unless they are organized' (Schroeder 2006, 6). Arguing that 'by ideology I mean only a broad-ranging meaning system which "surpasses experience"', Mann (2006, 345) offers an ideal-typical systematization that allows us to differentiate between organizational types of ideology.

First are *transcendent ideologies* that 'transcend existing institutions of ideological, economic, military and political power' (Mann 1986, 23)[9] and are the most powerful ideologies with a universal appeal. Of course, world religions are extremely important here, but Mann also includes socialism, fascism, nationalism, and religious fundamentalism, which in his view 'have also claimed transcendent visions and have drawn into an emergent collective network people from across the boundaries of different institutionalized power networks' (Mann 2006, 347).

Second, *immanent ideologies* are morales 'intensifying the cohesion, the confidence and, therefore, the power of an already established group' (Mann 1986, 24). While initially Mann (1986) had distinguished between these two main types of ideological organization, more recently he added a *third* type, which is of a more residual character: *institutionalized ideologies*, which he characterises as 'conservative and pragmatic, endorsing ideas, values, norms and rituals which serve to preserve present social order' (Mann 2006, 348). Examples of this type of ideology include Thatcherism and Social Democracy, each reflecting varying degrees of readiness to compromise and pragmatism in in pursuit of their visions for a better society (Mann 2006, 348). Especially in consideration of this third aspect, it is not convincing to claim that ideology should not be socio-spatially dual (i.e., having specific consequences within any form of territorially organized social entity that may differ enormously from the effects on a regional or global scale). We see the same argument with regard to economic power.

---

[9] This is one example of Mann's functionalism as he follows Durkheim, arguing 'religion arises out of the usefulness of normative integration (and of meaning and aesthetics and ritual), and it is "sacred", set apart from secular power relations' (Mann 1986, 23). In contrast, Giddens conceives his theory of structuration as 'a non-functionalist manifesto' (Giddens 1979, 7). I will follow the latter and avoid functionalist arguments.

11.3.2 Economic Power

To define *economic power*, Mann argues that it 'derives from the satisfaction of subsistence needs through the social organization of the extraction, transformation, distribution, and consumption of the objects of nature' (Mann 1986, 24). He also follows the Marxian claim that a class—in Mann's sense a grouping organized around the tasks that satisfy human needs—is a purely economic social phenomenon and that classes play a major role in social relations of super- and subordination with regard to the stratification order in a society. Yet Mann agrees neither with the Marxian nor the Weberian tradition; he assigns neither production relations nor market relations greater significance in this structuring of social stratification, insofar as classes have to be understood as 'groups of differential power over the social organization of the extraction, transformation, distribution, and consumption of the objects of nature' (Mann 1986, 25).

Against this background, we need to ask how economic power is becoming organized in order to become productive. Again, in the same vein as Marx, Mann argues that economic organization 'comprises circuits of production, distribution, exchange, and consumption', referring to them as 'circuits of praxis' (Mann 1986, 25). Yet, again diverting from Marx, he does not assign to production any primacy over the other aspects, declaring a mode of production to be merely 'shorthand for "mode of production, distribution, exchange and consumption"' (Mann 1986, 25). As with ideology, it seems strange not to distinguish between all these economic processes that unfold within a *society* as a bounded territorial entity and beyond and simply to assume that all forms of economic relations are de-territorialized. This is all somewhat surprising, especially given Mann's reference to this significant problem of socio-spatiality with regard to military and political power.

11.3.3 Military Power

As the differentiation between ideology (culture), economy, and politics is interpreted broadly in the social sciences, Mann has argued that his 'model is not particularly original. The tripartite scheme is very common ... So my separation of the military is the main addition I have made, and I do it for both empirical and analytical reasons' (Mann in Lawson 2006, 490). Separating military power from political power and revising an earlier definition of it, Mann now defines *military power* as 'the social organization of concentrated lethal violence', thus perceiving military force as 'focused, physical, furious, lethal violence' (Mann 2006, 351).

Interestingly again, there is an obvious link to Giddens' ideas. In both *The Nation State and Violence* (1985) and *The Consequences of Modernity* (1990), Giddens claimed that military power was one of four institutional dimensions of modernity and the globalized world system, while military power does not play a role in *The Constitution of Society* (Giddens 1984). Yet, in the context of Mann's debate in general and with regard to social closure in particular military power is critical. Of course, in closure struggles, the state's organized means of violence often serve as the ultimate means it can deploy, sometimes playing a key role. Regarding social closure, Mann's concept becomes crucial because it emphasizes the role of power in the sense of organized and systematically deployed power— the centralized and monopolized means of violence—in social life, particularly with regard to his claim that military power 'is not confined to armies. Lesser organized, lethal violence comes from gangs of paramilitaries, criminals or youths' (Mann 2006, 352).

Other candidates might also come to mind here, but it should be emphasized that lethal violence is not confined to official organizations of a state's military and that the exertion of lethal violence is governed by very few rules. Thus, 'military power wielded over *outsiders* is the most despotic and arbitrary power imaginable' (Mann 2006, 352). This, of course, depends largely on what is meant by *outsiders*. Looking at settler societies as contexts of elimination, closure strategies follow a *logic of elimination* (Wolfe 2006; Pappe 2006; Veracini 2015). This despotic and arbitrary power is yielded within the territory, particularly against Indigenous peoples who are deemed outsiders within the borders and vulnerable to the threat of elimination.

As far as military organization is concerned, Mann distinguishes between an internal and an external aspect. With regard to the former, he points to its distinctive internal organization that allows social control to be highly concentrated (Mann 1986, 26) because it 'combines the apparent opposites of hierarchy and comradeship, intense physical discipline and *esprit de corps*' (Mann 2006, 352). The last aspect highlights that 'military power also has a more extensive reach, of a negative, terroristic form' (Mann 1986, 26), involving the subjugation, oppression, enslavement, or killing of people. However, these actions may be difficult to be controlled in everyday life:

> Thus military power is sociospatially dual: a concentrated core in which positive, coerced controls can be exercised, surrounded by an extensive penumbra in which terrorized populations will not normally step beyond certain niceties of compliance but whose behavior cannot be positively controlled. (Mann 1986, 26)

11.3.4 Political Power

Finally, Mann turns to *political power*, defining it as 'centralized, territorial regulation of social life' (Mann 2006, 352). This is, of course, only significant for the modern state and not for other forms of exerting political power, such as in feudalism. Mann therefore uses the term *political* exclusively for the state and its different levels, ranging from national to regional to local (Mann 2006, 352), distinguishing between two main contributions of the state to social life relative to the other three sources of social power. First, 'political power heightens boundaries, where the other power sources may transcend them. Second, military, economic, and ideological power can be involved in any social relationship, wherever located'. This means that political power is 'necessarily centralized and territorial, and in these respects differs from the other power sources' (Mann 1986, 27).

However, this appears to be too narrow a model of political power to fully encompass all the political processes relevant for analysing social closure. Undoubtedly, the centralized power of the state plays a key role when it comes to exclusion on the grounds of citizenship, as does the state's legal definition of *private property* when it comes to exploitation, or a states' strategies and decisions in accordance with the military or para-military groups in the case of elimination. Yet these are critical aspects of highly formalized processes of closure, ignoring more informal processes, or, at least, less-formalized political processes such as those defined by Giddens within his conceptualization of authoritative resources that allow organized socio-spatial coordination of social actors.

Of course, this does not detract from Mann's claim that in much the same way as military power, political power is also *sociospatially dual* (Mann 1986, 27), leading to a distinction between domestic and international forms. While the domestic organization refers to a territorial centralization and boundedness that allows for growing and more autonomous power of *centralized territorial states*, the state is also part of a *geopolitical-diplomatic* interconnectedness with other states. Mann admits that this latter aspect is different from all the other power organizations discussed so far, yet 'it is an essential part of social life and is not reducible to the "internal" power configurations of its component states' (Mann 1986, 27).

11.3.5 Discussion

The IEMP model argues that the four sources of social power constitute the most important networks that human beings construct in social life to achieve their goals. They effectively structure the socio-spatial organization of social life in multiple ways: 'transcendent or immanent (from ideological power), circuits of praxis (economic), concentrated-coercive (military), and centralized-territorial and geopolitical diplomatic (political) organization' (Mann 1986, 28). Methodologically, Mann points out that these sources have to be understood as ideal types that temporarily concretize in specific organizations shaping social life (see Mann 1986, 28). In this process, the organizational means to shape and reshape social life will interact, and new means will emerge in between these means (*interstitially*, in Mann's words).

With regard to a new theorizing of social closure, Mann's conception of power allows for a nondeterministic and non-teleological perspective that overcomes two of the major shortcomings in the theory of social closure. First, while Mann, like Murphy, takes up Weber's idea of the switchmen, he does not interpret them as determining social processes in a teleological way. Rather, conceiving of the four sources of social power as *tracklaying vehicles* (Mann 1986, 28), he argues that they push social life ahead in specific directions, yet without predetermining the direction social life will take. They simply 'are "the generalized means" through which human beings make their own history' (Mann 1986, 28). Second, the four sources of social power allow us to overcome Murphy's rigid and static claim of class relations always being the dominant form of closure in capitalist societies, joined only by citizenship if we take the world system of nation states into account. Thus, instead of sticking to the claim that the economic structure will always have the ultimate primacy, the four sources of social power actually allow us to analyse empirically which type of social power is decisive in a specific case of social closure (see Manza 1992, 293).

11.4 Elements of a New Concept of Power for Social Closure

The discussion of the three conceptions of power has produced important elements of a concept of power that can serve as a foundation for a new theorizing of social closure. Pulling the threads of the analyses together will prepare the ground for a relational, processual, and context-sensitive approach to social closure.

First, Popitz's discussion of power formation begins with an initial situation where all actors find the same conditions, and from there, a social order is created by processes of power formation. This differs from the context of social closure, where established social actors participate in closure struggles to gain more power, albeit to vastly asymmetric degrees. Popitz's theoretical framework assumes that no social order has been established yet, and thus is not concerned with analysing how an already existing order is going to be transformed. Yet, such *processes of reorganization are what social closure is about*. How, in which dimensions, and with what consequences these processes of reorganization take place will be the core of both a new theorizing of social closure and the empirical analysis of processes of closure struggles.

Second, following Popitz, we can understand closure struggles as unfolding in distinct contexts in which various forms of power can be exerted: power of action, instrumental power, authoritative power, and the power of data constitution. This arrangement of forms of power implies a continuum of manifestations of power, ranging from the immediate impact of sheer violence to the exercise of power by the transformation of nature and the created environment. Closure can therefore be exercised through an enormous range of power-based strategies that may directly affect the body of the less-powerful actors, control and influence their expectations of the future, act on less-powerful actors' need for standards and recognition they have internalized, or transform the natural and created environments that these actors depend on and in which they orient themselves.

Third, defining specific and distinct contexts where power forms and newly established social orders are stabilized allows for systematizing social closure struggles, as elaborated in Part III of this book. Harrington categorizes Popitz's contexts of power formation as contexts of *ownership and rent*, *control over means of production*, and *currency and taxation*. This contextual differentiation broadens closure theory from a narrow economic focus to include closure in contexts of exclusion, exploitation, and elimination. Moreover, Giddens and Mann further expand this by acknowledging the critical role of the structural elements of ideology, economic, military, and political powers that social actors draw upon in their daily closure struggles. In this sense, a new approach to theorizing social closure will not argue in favour of an ultimate primacy of one of the sources in shaping social life. Rather, processes of closure may show *temporary primacy* of one of the sources, changing dominance, and what Mann calls their *promiscuity*, which is their being intrinsically linked in pushing ahead social life.

Fourth, given these distinct contexts of closure, a clear understanding of the character of the social relations within them becomes possible by taking into consideration Giddens' conception of agency and power being constitutively linked. His explicitly praxeological and relational perspective on the social world situates social actors within social settings of power and *relations of autonomy and dependence*. The *dialectic of control* ensures that no actor is ever devoid at least minimal power. This is the most accurate and convincing expression of the relations of social actors in closure struggles. In this relational view, power functions as the fundamental medium of social relations. It establishes asymmetric power relations where certain social actors possess greater ability to organize and to build nuclei of solidarity, or by establishing systems of redistribution to restabilize a newly created order, thereby creating structures of power that others have to suffer from.

Fifth, within the contexts of closure and in the face of social relations of autonomy and control, Giddens' concept of power gives Popitz's anthropological-sociological idea of power a socio-theoretical foundation. Relationality is crucial here, as it elucidates how human capabilities are related to structural resources that people leverage to exert power. This approach clarifies how social actors mobilize structural resources of power to enact power across different social closure contexts, highlighting the transformative capacity of power.

Sixth, Giddens' differentiation of authoritative and allocative structural resources of power can and needs to be supplemented by Mann's emphasis on ideology and the military as significant sources of power. Integrating both frameworks, we need to note two qualifications. On the one hand, while Giddens refers to economic resources as allocative ones, I will stick to his characterization but call these resources *economic*. On the other hand, while Giddens discusses political resources as authoritative ones, and Mann makes a convincing argument as to why to treat legal resources also as an aspect of power, I stick to Giddens' characterization but will call the resources *politico-legal*. Further, as Mann makes the point that violence is not only exerted by the military but also by other groups, such as militias and others, I will take this into account and express it by calling this power resource *military/violence*.

As will become obvious in Part III of this book, these four resources of power—ideological, economic, military/violence, and politico-legal—are essential for understanding the logics and dynamics of closure struggles across various contexts and for identifying the respective structural elements of each of these resources for the empirical analysis of closure struggles (see figure 11.2).

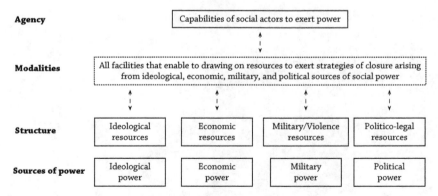

Figure 11.2 Resources of power for closure theory
Source: Own conceptualization based on Giddens 1984, 29, and Mann 1986

Given that social life inherently involves struggles that cannot be halted, humans are compelled to engage in these struggles by organizing and mobilizing ideological, economic, military/violence, and politico-legal resources to make an impact on the ongoing events in the social world. The question then arises: what are the ultimate goals for which social actors fight in these struggles, which I conceptualize as closure struggles. Closure theory has not yet clearly articulated the *real goal of closure struggles* and why social actors engage in them. To address this gap, I propose integrating the concept of life chances / chances of survival into closure theory. This concept will provide the foundation for a fresh approach to theorizing social closure.

12
Life Chances / Chances of Survival: The Real Goal of Closure Struggles

Although in his discussion of open and closed social relationships Weber repeatedly referred to *life chances*, his understanding of the concept has remained obscure and blurred. Because of their narrowed economic conception of closure, the goal of closure struggles in Weber and the *theory of social closure* has consequently been reduced to making economic gains, which has led to characterizing closure theory as simply representing an economic *paradigm of monopolization* (Silver 1994).

Such a reductionist and narrow understanding of life chances will not do for a new theory of closure. While I argue that life chances / chances of survival must be seen as the real goal of closure struggles, to be meaningful for a new closure theory this idea must be developed into a sociological concept that can be considered the vanishing point of all closure struggles. In Part III, 'Theorizing Social Closure', I introduce this concept. However, to do so, we must first consider, how sociological theory has previously addressed this idea to see whether we can build on some aspects of this existing work.

12.1 A Critical Idea but Rudimentary Concept

Weber used the terms *life chances* and *chances of survival* repeatedly, but he did not flesh them out to a proper concept. However, as he used both in the context of his debate of basic sociological concepts critical for closure theory, revisiting their rudimentary status gives us clues as to how these terms can be developed further to a critical concept for closure theory. Given the ontological status of *struggle*, Weber puts the idea of life chances / chances of survival at the centre of this conceptual debate, attributing to it an outstanding importance:

> The (latent) struggle for existence between either individuals or social types for *life chances* or *chances of survival* without a meaningful mutual intention of struggling against one another will be termed selection: social selection insofar as it is about the chances of the living in life, biological selection insofar as it is about the chances of survival of a genotype. (Weber 1985 [1922], 20; my own translation; emphasis added)

On this broad and general foundation, understanding social closure in the face of severe social struggles in today's world, struggles for life chances / chances of survival range from having a bit more or a bit less to all or nothing, threatening the survival of individual/collective social actors. In Weber's words, *struggle* and *selection* among social relationships means 'that a specific kind of social action is ousted by another, be it the same or other people' (Weber 1985 [1922], 21; my own translation based on Weber 1978 [1922], 39). This correspondingly broad perspective is crucial because it makes explicit the spectrum of *struggles* that we need to consider when we assume that social struggle cannot be avoided in social life. Struggle refers from every human being necessarily participating in daily struggles to earn a living to the existential dimension of a specific social relationship, be it associative or communal, to be wiped out in these struggles. Weber also refers to (violent) struggles characterizing these processes of *ousting*, a term that is open to interpretation and allows for various possibilities that go as far as elimination. Thus, in newly theorizing social closure, we cannot simply refer to life chances but necessarily need to add the idea of chances of survival for such a concept to be useful for a new and generic concept of social closure that claims to address struggles of exclusion, exploitation, and elimination in today's world.

In defining *communal* and *associative* relationships, Weber claims that processes of closure unfold in any conceivable kind of social relationship. There are no intrinsically and exclusively harmonious social relationships, which points to the manifold empirical manifestations of closure struggles within social relationships. Because social life develops in struggles, life chances / chances of survival are central to it. Thus, Weber argues, 'It has already been pointed out that any type of order of social action somehow leaves room for a process of *selection* in the competition between different types of people for life chances' (Weber 1985 [1922], 22; my own translation based on Weber 1978 [1922], 42).

In discussing processes of *opening* and *closing* social relationships, Weber not only shows, substantiates, and justifies his ontological stipulation of social life as struggle but also unveils its characteristics, since individuals and collective actors are involved in permanently fighting for life chances / chances of survival that produce and reproduce a social formation by mechanisms of social closure.

12.1.1 Life Chances and Chances of Survival in Weber's Closure Analyses

There is a strange incoherence, if not a contradiction, in the way Weber refers to the idea of life chances / chances of survival in his brief closure analyses. Whereas he attaches fundamental importance to the idea, in his empirical analyses he only discusses distributional conflicts of goods and resources in society that unfold according to the hierarchical status of social groups and refers to the economic fact that different life chances arise from the distribution of private property in society or relate to membership of a status group. As has become clear in this discussion, the exclusivity of certain statuses, the honour associated with them, or the specific way of life result exclusively from a basic distribution of resources and goods, which Weber also assumes in discussing the relations of ethnic groups: 'All differences of "mores" can sustain specific feelings of "honor" and "dignity" among its practitioners ... that may ultimately have effects on highly differentiated life chances, chances of survival, and chances of reproduction' (Weber 1985 [1922], 236; my own translation based on Weber 1978 [1922], 387).

As Weber analyses social closure in purely economic terms, the concept of life chances / chances of survival is also limited to an economic understanding, in that individual actors make choices to obtain more resources or rights. Whether economic situations, contexts of power distribution, or conditions of ethnic relations, closure struggles are all explained through an economic model and individual choices that limit the concept of life chances / chances of survival to merely an effect of a given and stable distribution of resources, goods, and rights.

By referring to different contexts, Weber tried to show that people make decisions in an individualistic way despite different circumstances and contexts. In all contexts, different opportunities for life chances / chances of survival arise from competition for and ultimately the 'successful monopolization of economic and social power by groups at different levels of the social opportunity structure' (Neuwirth 1968, 150). As the discussion of Weber's basic concepts has made clear, such an individualistic perspective, which models all social processes according to market processes, leads to false models of social facts. This becomes even clearer if we look at the sociological debate on Weber's idea of life chances.

12.2 Life Chances / Chances of Survival and the Opportunity Structure

Robert K. Merton and Ralf Dahrendorf, who both followed Weber's idea, discussed the idea of life chances, yet while Dahrendorf used it for an apologetic defence of the alleged achievements and promises of a liberal order, Merton (1968 ([1957])) is credited with taking up the idea for theoretical sociological reasoning and to linking it to the idea of the opportunity structure. In analysing deviant behaviour in the context of his anomie theory, Merton initially used the idea of life chances to understand the interplay of actors' decision-making in the face of extremely different structural conditions with regard to their positioning in the social structure that promotes deviant behaviour. In his early application of Weber's discussion of life chances, Merton rightly referred to it as the 'still loosely utilized but important concept of what Weber called "life chances" in the opportunity structure' (Merton [1957] 1968, 230).[1] However, almost four decades later, in 1995, Merton advocated using this concept not as a specific and limited one but as a general one that would allow the development of an explanatory approach to social life in general:

> That concept, I had begun to realize, should apply in principle to every kind of socially patterned choice. It should find empirical expression in aggregative social patterns of choices and outcomes while allowing for individuality by being coupled with the concept of a distribution of choices among individuals similarly situated in the social structure. (Merton 1995, 29)

Merton rightly points out the constitutive complementarity of the two concepts, emphasizing the importance of establishing the *opportunity structure* as a generic sociological concept. This step is critical. However, while I consider this suggestion crucial for evolving social closure from a still rather descriptive to an explanatory concept (Manza 1992, 287–288; Mackenzie 1980, 583), I will neither simply follow Merton's conception of opportunity structures nor the explanatory logic he associates with it. This is no less true of Dahrendorf's (1979) contribution, who follows Merton to some extent in attempting to flesh out the concept of life chances for his political intentions. In my opinion, both approaches are unsatisfactory and do not help. Before I propose new concepts for life chances / chances of survival and the opportunity structure, as well as how to conceive of them as interrelated, a closer examination of both ideas is necessary. This will allow us to further develop them and demonstrate the insufficiencies of Merton's and Dahrendorf's elaborations that we must reject and move beyond.

12.2.1 Life Chances as Related to the Opportunity Structure

Merton's formulation of *life chances in the opportunity structure* succinctly expresses his idea of *structural explanation*, which argues for explaining social life as a consequence of structural constraints on action. This explanatory programme states that the position of social actors in the social structure does not completely determine their access to life chances, but it does strongly influence them. In other words, in social life, individual actors make socially structured choices to achieve their goals. Individual choices are constrained by a given and relatively stable opportunity structure (structural aspect), which limits the number of options for individual actors to realize their life chances (individual

---

[1] Merton's reference to Weber is misleading, however, as the latter did not use the term *opportunity structure*.

action). By emphasizing the interplay between structural context and individual choices (Merton 1995, 26), Merton argues that the term *life chances* refers to the structurally variable access to opportunities, while the term *opportunity structures* refers to a structurally given *degree* and *distribution* of opportunities (Merton 1995, 27; emphasis added). Linking macro and micro levels in this way reveals Merton's fundamentally individualistic approach, despite his plea for what he called *structural explanation*—that is, the basic assumption that with regard to the decisions of social actors, the 'objective situation of action ... is decisive for the success of their actions' (Schmid 1998, 75; my own translation). From this perspective, to understand the meaning of life chances, we must systematically refer to individuals' social positions (macro conditions), which define their opportunity structure. The importance of the structural aspect—the *degree* and *distribution* of opportunities according to a social actor's position in the hierarchical social structure—is to explain why the possibilities for these actors to realize life chances vary accordingly. In this way, the hierarchical social structure and individuals' positioning in it is conceived of as their opportunity structure, and in this sense, they fall in one. If this were the case, what would be the theoretical value added by the term and concept of the opportunity structure?

Furthermore, both Weber and Merton, in their use of the concept of life chances, emphasize structural conditions—a *context* (Weber) or the *opportunity structure* (Merton)—as a given objective distribution, especially of resources (but also of rights in Weber's case), while highlighting how life chances are constrained in terms of the ability of social actors to dispose of scarce resources. In this sense, they explicitly offer a concept of life chances that is reduced to actors having different amounts of resources at their disposal. Again, we are confronted with an individualistic perspective and the corresponding economic model of human actors as decision-makers, which resonates with a reductionist economic understanding of the social world. As this idea corresponds to the narrow worldview of the liberal tradition in social and political theory, Dahrendorf (1979) sought a definition of *life chances* by conceptualizing resources *as* life chances, thereby following Weber and Merton.[2] At the same time, however, he claimed that life chances cannot be limited to resources but must be understood more broadly, as they include *options* and *ligatures* (Dahrendorf 1979, 30-34).[3] While options referred to rights and resources, Dahrendorf's

---

[2] For a detailed discussion on the conceptions of life chances and opportunity structures in Weber, Merton, and Dahrendorf, see Mackert 2010.

[3] Dahrendorf has more or less ignored Merton's early theoretical and explanatory elaboration on life chances. Mentioning the context of 'anomie theory' in which Merton had introduced the idea of 'life chances in the opportunity structure', Dahrendorf does not engage in a sociological debate but simply argues that *anomie* was a false term that should be replaced by *deviance*, dismissing Merton's approach altogether. Yet this is not the place to discuss in detail why and how Dahrendorf misunderstood and misinterpreted Merton's sociological approach and explanatory ideas.

introduction of ligatures pointed to important *social ties* that give meaning and significance to an individual's life, such as family ties and relationships to the home, the village, or the church. While one may argue about the concrete meaning of all these seemingly crucial ties, the basic idea of thinking about the importance of social relations for a concept of life chances / chances of survival is crucial and will play an important role in my new approach to social closure. Yet unfortunately, Dahrendorf did not elaborate on his idea of ligatures in a concept of life chances / chances of survival but seemed to take them for granted. Instead, following Weber and Merton in focusing on the importance of rights and resources in a liberal society, he outlined a normative social theoretical approach by arguing that the realization of life chances—in the sense of access to rights and resources—serves as an indicator for the realization of any form of the *liberal realm of freedom* (Dahrendorf). Such a teleological liberal ideology is contraproductive for proper sociological reasoning and must be rejected.

This critical debate on life chances in the opportunity structure reveals at least three problems. First, neither Merton nor Dahrendorf actually succeed in overcoming a rudimentary idea of the concept and stick to an understanding of life chances as making choices. Second, their individualistic perspectives of the concept of life chances prevents its actual potential from being developed. Third, both approaches neglect the significant aspect of chances of survival, focusing the sociological debate only on Western *liberal* societies, but it must be reintroduced to address serious impairments of individual or collective life in closure struggles in today's world that takes into consideration that life chances in the *West* may and do decisively depend on chances of survival in the *Rest* (Stuart Hall).

However, the debate also leads to important results that need to be considered in a new conceptualization: First, the idea of *opportunity structure* is crucial in its relation to the concept of life chances / chances of survival. Second, the opportunity structure cannot be equated with the hierarchical social structure of a society. Third, the concretization and extension of the idea of ligatures in a new concept of life chances / chances of survival is crucial, even if not in the outdated and seemingly self-evident way proposed by Dahrendorf. Given all that, a new approach to closure theory must develop a new understanding of life chances / chances of survival and opportunity structure and recast the relationship between them.

13
Discussion

This part of the book discussed critical terms and concepts that need to be revised, recast, or introduced in the first place to lay the groundwork for a new theorizing of social closure. To address the vagueness of the concept of closure, Weber's basic concepts of *open* and *closed* relationships were contextualized in relation to other basic concepts of his. The critical step was to link processes of social closure constitutively with Weber's notion of social life as a continuous *struggle*. Since social relationships, whether *communal* or *associative*, inherently involve processes of social closure, their opening and closing are the most fundamental processes of social life. Given the significance of social closure for understanding social life, I have argued that the ambiguity in Weber's concept of closure—and consequently in his closure analyses—is due both to his methodological individualism and to three conceptual lacunae: a lack of concepts of *group action* and *power*, and a blurred idea of *life chances* that are the real goal of closure.

To reorient closure theory in the face of these serious problems, I have argued as a first step that we must abandon the perspective of methodological individualism that characterizes Weber's approach to social closure. I have explained in detail how the shortcomings of an individualist approach have led closure theory to a dead end in theoretical, analytical, and empirical terms. My approach to placing closure theory on a new footing, therefore, assumes that closure is a fundamentally relational concept consisting of three forms of closure: in social relations of exclusion, of exploitation, and of elimination. This perspective places social closure within the tradition of both classical relational thought in sociology, such as that of Karl Marx, Norbert Elias, and Gregor Simmel, and that of the younger generation, such as Charles Tilly, Mustafa Emirbayer, and Andrew Abbott.

With regard to the three crucial gaps in closure theory discussed at length in this part of the book, I have proposed three steps to overcome them. *First*, instead of just assuming immediate collective action by classes, status groups, or other collectivities, we need to clarify the conditions under which actors are able to participate in closure struggles in the first place. Following Steinert's critique of closure theory for not having developed an idea and concept of *group action* and *acting in solidarity*, we cannot assume that common interests of social groups are simply given. Rather, a group's possibilities to act are highly presuppositional and rest upon a common identity that must be developed first. A relational perspective allows to understand that political identities can only be developed within a social relationship. In terms of social closure, this means that political identities emerge in the social relations of the excluders and the excluded, the exploited and the exploited, and the eliminators and those threatened with elimination. Only such an identity makes *acting in solidarity* possible. Bringing this idea into social closure theory is particularly important because it allows us to understand the efforts of powerful actors to either prevent the less powerful from creating such a political identity or to attack and destroy an emerging or existing identity as one of their critical strategies in struggles for social closure.

Second, to understand what enables social actors to participate in closure struggles and to develop strategies in closure struggles, closure theory needs a clearly defined concept of power. Weber's characterization of power as *sociologically amorphous* (Weber 1978 [1922], 53) is well known but useless, but the *theory of social closure* also lacks a clearly defined concept of power. A new approach to closure theory must necessarily fill this gap. To this end, I have proposed a concept of power based on the relational approaches of Popitz, Giddens, and Mann that will inform the new social closure theory and allow for empirical analyses of exclusion, exploitation, and elimination.

Third, to clarify the actual goal of social closure, I have argued that actors in closure struggles are fighting for the realization of *life chances / chances of survival.* These chances are neither accidental nor strictly determined by the positions of individual actors in the hierarchical structure of society, as traditional individualist theories suggest (e.g., Weber, Merton, and Dahrendorf).This deficient view results from the fact that both concepts are conceived of in individualistic terms and thus stand unmediated next to each other, which is not very helpful but rather an obstacle to enhancing closure theory. I therefore hold that it is essential that the relationship between *life chances / chances of survival* and *opportunity structures* must be reconceptualized from a relational perspective.

Based on the methodological critique and conceptual work in this part of the book, I now turn to a new theorizing of social closure. This new theorizing draws on these revised and newly introduced concepts for the theory of closure to propose a new and general concept of closure, develop a typology of closure, and provide an explanation of the processes involved in the reorganization of social relations through exclusion, exploitation, and elimination in social closure struggles.

PART III
THEORIZING SOCIAL CLOSURE

Part III is the core of the book as it presents the core of a new theorizing of social closure by presenting its *conceptualization, typology, and explanation*.

Chapter 14 introduces and outlines the steps that need to be taken. Chapter 15 defines the three forms of closure that must be distinguished in the new approach to social closure: *exclusion, exploitation,* and *elimination*. Chapter 16 brings together closure and the newly developed concept of *power* that forms the basis of the new understanding of closure; it further defines the contexts of closure struggles, puts the conceptualization in relational perspective, and defines the critical structural elements of power that social actors have to draw in closure struggles. Chapter 17 outlines the new concept of *life chances / chances of survival in the opportunity structure* and elaborates on how we have to conceive of it as the real goal of closure struggles, while at the same time dynamizing the concept of the opportunity structure and defining the critical dimensions of life chances / chances of survival. Chapter 18 introduces and outlines the core of the *explanatory approach* in a new approach to the theory and analysis of closure by defining the two critical social mechanisms *denying access* and *intervention into community closure*. Chapter 19 brings all these elements together by outlining and defining a *new concept of social closure*.

By cross tabulating dimensions of closure with dimensions of life chances / chances of survival, Chapter 20 presents a *typology* of strategies of social closure. Defining twelve distinct strategies offers a new and encompassing way to analyse all kinds of social closure.

Chapter 21 begins with the explanation of social closure by introducing the critical role of events into the explanatory frame and by outlining the basic logics of social closure. Chapter 22 finally outlines the explanatory logics of exclusion, exploitation, and elimination. Chapter 22.1 explains the logics of *exclusion* by analysing how the four dimensions of the strategy of *marginalization—commodification/financialization, shifting, de-universalization,* and *de-solidarization*—operate in the context of neoliberalism as a politics of austerity. Chapter 22.2 explains the logics of *exploitation* by analysing how the four dimensions of the strategy of *extraction—deprivation, undermining, suppression,* and *subjugation*—operate in the context of a historically ongoing capitalism/slavery nexus as a politics of *developing and implementing global chains*. Chapter 22.3 explains the logics of *elimination* by analysing how the four dimensions of the strategy of *elimination—letting die, disenfranchising, segregation,* and *extermination* operate in a *politics of annihilation*—operate in the context of settler colonialism in the case of Palestine under Israeli occupation as a politics of erasure. Chapter 23 concludes Part III by discussing the prowess of the new relational and explanatory approach to social closure and how it allows for a fundamentally new and encompassing understanding of the crucial role of social closure in social life.

14
A New Approach to Social Closure

The discussion so far has laid the groundwork for a new theorizing of social closure by concentrating mainly on two critical aspects: First, against the background of a detailed critique of both Weber's individualist account of social closure and the rather structuralist one of the *theory of social closure*, I have addressed their shortcomings and will propose a new approach to social closure theory that follows a relational perspective. Second, by rethinking old concepts, elaborating on and specifying them, and by introducing previously missing critical concepts we are now equipped with all the necessary and indispensable concepts for a new theorizing of social closure. This groundwork allows me to present a new approach to social closure.

Following Marx's general claim that society does not 'consist of individuals, but expresses the sum of interrelations, the relations within which these individuals stand' (Marx 1977 [1939–1941], 193), this relational perspective also applies to social closure, in which collective social actors take part in permanent interactions or transactions that make up the core of closure struggles, which, as I argue following Weber are an ineradicable element of all social life. Within the framework of this *struggle paradigm*, I thus conceive of closure struggles as ongoing processes in the social world that cannot be stopped. Such a relational perspective takes a fundamentally different approach to closure than either Weber's individualistic or the structuralist account of closure theory:

> Rational-actor and norm-based models, diverse holisms and structuralisms, and statistical 'variable' analyses—all of them beholden to the idea that it is entities that come first and relations among them only subsequently—hold sway throughout much of the discipline. But increasingly, researchers are searching for viable analytic alternatives, approaches that reverse these basic assumptions and depict social reality instead in *dynamic, continuous*, and *processual* terms. (Emirbayer 1997, 281; emphasis added)

Dynamic, continuous, and *processual*—these terms qualify as the characteristics typical of the relational approach that inspires my new theorizing of social closure. Emphasizing this approach and thinking about social closure struggles in terms of strategies that reorganize established social relations, analysing them as conversations, interactions, or transactions means conceiving of these 'relations between terms or units as pre-eminently dynamic in nature, as unfolding, ongoing processes rather than as static ties among inert substances' (Emirbayer 1997, 289). Thus, they are neither effects of individual ideas, thoughts, or convictions, nor expressions of structural conditions. In this sense, I also follow Tilly, who has repeatedly stressed that sociological analysis needs to look at *bonds not essences* (Tilly 1998; 2005b) if the aim is to explain social processes. Approaching social closure from this methodological perspective, therefore, not only emphasizes relationality but agrees that from a relational perspective the primacy of *contextuality* and *processes* is critical (cf. Emirbayer 1997, 290).

As a general perspective on social closure, the relational approach also informs the three essential steps of this new theorizing of social closure: conceptualization, typology, and explanation (see Swedberg 2014). *Conceptualization* brings together the concepts revisited, revised, or newly introduced to synthesize a new concept of social closure. As the general perspective conceives of social closure in all its forms as a social relation among collective actors, it can be said that group action and acting in solidarity—so far absent from closure theory—play a critical role. Throughout the analysis, I focus on how interactions or transactions between opposing actors aim at reorganizing these relations in the form of closure struggles. To do this, collective actors need to mobilize power. Thus, the concept of power that I have developed is relational in the sense that it relates agency and structure, which makes conceivable the structural elements of power on which collective actors must draw to be able to exert power in closure struggles. Further, collective actors must inevitably engage in ongoing closure struggles since they are struggles for individuals' life chances or even chances of survival. They can do so only to the extent that their opportunity structures allow them to mobilize power. Relationality thus comes into play here as I relate the fundamentally revised concepts of life chances / chances of survival and opportunity structures, allowing for a dynamic understanding of how and why closure struggles unfold. Finally, I suggest two relational social mechanisms—processes that operate within interactions or transactions between parts of society (see Tilly 2003b, 7)—that make the concept of closure an explanatory one. Having argued that closure theory has so far equated the idea of *monopolization* with closure, I claim that monopolization points to only one of two critical mechanisms, which is first, the denial of access. This mechanism in my approach replaces monopolization while at the same time I am going beyond it by introducing a second mechanism, which is the *intervention into community closure*. This mechanism brings into closure analysis the manifold ways in which powerful collective actors in closure struggles exert forms of control over the less powerful to prevent them from organizing, developing a collective identity, and collectively acting in solidarity.

Based on these conceptual specifications and this relational understanding, I suggest a new concept of closure that differs fundamentally from those on which closure theory has drawn so far. This concept is *relational* rather than individualistic or structuralist/systemic. I start from the conviction that the social world is characterized by ongoing struggles, closure struggles being one pivotal form, and that their analysis tries to understand how classes, groups, or communities emerge as collective actors in these struggles. From there, I will analyse what creates the dynamics of closure struggles and how we can conceive of them as a permanent and continuous aspect of social life.

Following Emirbayer's emphasis on contextuality and processes in a relational approach, the new concept of social closure must be *generic* rather than specific to ensure the *contextuality* of closure analyses. Depending on the nature of the social relations at play in closure struggles, closure refers to different collective actors and/or dimensions of life chances / chances of survival for which collective actors fight. This means that *processuality* is crucial, which is why the concept of closure must also be *dynamic* rather than static. All these aspects allow for a new approach to social closure that does not describe states of closure but rather conceives of them as temporary states embedded within processes of reorganizing social relations.

By developing a *typology*, I go one step further in this new theorizing of social closure by systematically relating critical aspects of closure—distinct forms, defined strategies, and the two mechanisms—with elements of the new concept of life chances / chances of survival I suggest. By cross-tabulating these two dimensions, I propose a typology of social closure that allows us to identify distinct closure strategies and understand the goals toward which certain strategies of social closure are directed.

Explanation, finally, follows along relational lines, suggesting the context-specificity of an explanatory approach based on the two relational mechanisms: *denial of access* and *intervention into community closure*. I will outline the logics of explaining social closure and make this logic plausible with regard to forms of closure and dimensions of life chances / chances of survival.

CONCEPTUALIZATION

15
Three Forms of Social Closure

A new conceptualization of social closure must capture the fundamental importance of closure for the functioning of society, which I argue lies at the core of Weber's basic terms of *open* and *closed* social relationships. However, this potential has not been realized by either Weber himself or by the *theory of social closure*, both of which have focused on only specific aspects of what is in fact a much more comprehensive social idea. This comprehensive approach is based on two premises that elaborate on two of Weber's critical ideas. The first premise is that closure is ubiquitous. No form of associational or communal social relations would be possible without processes of opening and closing them. These most basic processes of social life are fundamental to the social world. A new conceptualization of social closure focuses on processes of closing rather than opening social relations. The second premise is that social life is inherently filled with persistent and unresolvable conflicts, directly linked to closure struggles for the realization of life chances / chances of survival.

Based on these premises, which assign processes of social closure a fundamental role in social life, I distinguish between three forms of closure: *exclusion*, *exploitation*, and *elimination*. These forms are based on certain dynamics with a global reach and establish different types of social relations. Within these relations, closure struggles that shape contemporary social life take place and unfold. While these struggles employ different strategies, follow various logics, and lead in different directions, the three forms of closure are not reducible to one another, but they can and often do interact.

Exclusion in today's world is driven by the dynamics of neoliberalism as a political, economic, social, and cultural/ideological project. This project has established social relations between the excluders and the excluded, marked by significant power asymmetries. The excluders are highly organized and powerful collective actors, while the excluded are less so. As a form of social closure, exclusion involves powerful groups employing strategies to *marginalize* social groups—removing people from their path—to enhance their own life chances at the expense of the less powerful by reorganizing existing social relations.

Exploitation in today's world is driven by the dynamics of global capitalism, which have established social relations between exploiters and the exploited that are characterized by extreme power asymmetries. The exploiters are highly organized and powerful collective actors, whereas the exploited are less powerful.

As a form of social closure, exploitation involves the powerful using strategies of *extraction*—drawing profit out of human beings—to enhance their own life chances at the expense of the less powerful by reorganizing the existing social relation.

Elimination in today's world is rooted in the ongoing dynamics of settler colonialism, which have established social relations between eliminators and those under threat of elimination. This social relation is characterized by extreme power asymmetries, with highly organized and powerful collective actors on one side and the less powerful living in fear of extinction on the other side. As a form of social closure, elimination involves the powerful employing strategies of *annihilation*—erasing human beings and ethnic communities—to maximize their own life chances by destroying the survival chances of the less powerful, continually dismantling existing social relations.

Against the background of distinguishing between these three different forms of social closure, my theory of closure will, throughout this part of the book, elaborate on and progressively clarify these forms to arrive at a generic concept of social closure.[1]

---

[1] In his highly interesting book *Violence and Representation in the Arab Uprisings*, Benoit Challand (2023) presents an analytical framework that distinguishes three forms of encroachments: capitalist, colonial, and imperial. This framework is particularly pertinent to my own analytical approach in the new theory of social closure that I develop here.

16
Power and Social Closure

The concept of power that emerged from the discussion of Popitz, Giddens, and Mann can now be adapted and employed as a fundamental element of a new power-based and relational conceptualization of social closure. The relational idea of power should consequently enable us to theorize and analyse social relations of closure—exclusion, exploitation, and elimination—as power lies at the core of all of them. Power then operates as a medium that enables social actors to establish the power asymmetries that characterize any kind of social relation. To adopt this concept and adapt it to relations of social closure, I start with a definition of *power*.

> Power is a constitutive and unavoidable aspect of social life and a fundamental trait and capability of human beings. It is a medium that operates in all kinds of social relations, not a resource of individual and collective agents or an inherent aspect of social structures. To be able to intervene in the ongoing events of social life, actors have to draw upon the structural elements of the four resources of social power—ideological, economic, military/violence, and politico/legal—that operate in institutional settings, thus allowing social actors to reorganize to varying degrees the social relations of an existing social order in the process of social closure struggles and stabilize newly established ones.

Based on this understanding, the critical ideas of the relational power concept can be adapted to a new theorizing of social closure. First, I use Popitz's differentiation between contexts and social relations of power and adapt them to social closure, which allows me to both distinguish different contexts of social closure and specify the kinds of social relations that unfold within them. Second, I adapt the idea of the duality of structure and specify the relationality of the structural foundations of power and the capability of social actors to play a role in closure struggles. Both steps serve to concretize the idea of a power-based approach to social closure that takes *relationality*, *processuality*, and *contextuality* seriously.

16.1 Power, Contexts, and Social Relations

Popitz's conception of power relations is pivotal for a new power-based conceptualization of social closure. His differentiation between the contexts of power formation as *essential* contexts of social closure—because in all three settings a powerful side pursues strategies of social closure against a weaker side—is also helpful in bringing together critical elements of a generic concept of closure. Following Harrington's (2018) interpretation of Popitz's analysis yet going one step further, it becomes clear that in the three contexts we can identify three different forms of social closure:

> *Power formation in a boarding school*: In contexts characterized by processes of *currency and taxation*, those who cannot claim to be included in a *system of redistribution* are confronted with *exclusion*.
> *Power formation in a prisoners' camp*: In contexts characterized by *control over means of production*, those who do not possess private property in a *system of profit maximization* face *exploitation*.
> *Power formation on the Mediterranean cruise ship*: In contexts characterized by *ownership and rent*, those who are not part of a *system of imagined purity* are threatened with sheer violence that can culminate in *elimination*.

This basic understanding of how to conceive of the settings of social relations as representing forms of social closure allows us to specify the different types of strategies that powerful social actors can deploy. Strategies of *marginalization* aim at pushing less-powerful actors/sides to the fringe of the social unit in question. Strategies of *extraction* aim at squeezing out labour from the less powerful and keeping them in a dependent and subordinate position. Strategies of *annihilation* point to the potential or actual wiping out of the less powerful.

Popitz's differentiation according to identifiable contexts of closure struggles is important because it allows us to understand the different forms and dynamics of closure struggles. However, following both Giddens's and Mann's critiques of the concept of *society* or closed social units in general, exclusion, exploitation, and elimination are not confined to modern society, but can be observed and analysed beyond its boundaries, on the basis of the four resources of power and how they are mobilized by social actors by drawing on their structural elements (see table 16.1).

Assuming the same initial conditions for all social groups in specified contexts, Popitz has argued that what enables one group to exert power over another is its members' superior ability to organize, which allows for their initial power formation. Yet, this superior ability to organize is crucial for an approach that views closure struggles as processes that do not begin from equal conditions for all actors but are instead permanently ongoing in the social world. Following Popitz and Mann, it is thus obvious that on the side of the powerful—such as neoliberal elites, multinational corporations, or the state of a settler-colonial society—we are dealing with actors, already highly organized, who were able to close their

Table 16.1 The Contextual Framework

Forms of Closure	Forms of Strategies	Characteristics of Social Relations/ Contexts of Social Closure	Social Relations
Exclusion	Marginalization	Currency and taxation	Neoliberal elites and the superfluous
		System of redistribution	The excluders and the excluded
Exploitation	Extraction	Control over means of production	Capital and labour
		System of profit maximization	The exploiters and the exploited
Elimination	Annihilation	Ownership and rent	The colonizer and the colonized
		System of imagined purity	The eliminators and those threatened with elimination

boundaries and develop a distinct political identity that makes them powerful collective actors in closure struggles. In the context of closure theory, however, the significance of these processes of organizing becomes more apparent when we turn to the opposite side—that of the excluded, the exploited, and those threatened with elimination. Their inferiority in terms of their ability to mobilize power consists, on the one hand, in their lack of a political identity and thus their inability to organize. On the other hand, this shows at the same time that closure struggles are not only about monopolizing goods or resources but also about the extent to which strategies of the excluders, exploiters, and eliminators can either prevent or—if they already exist—destroy precisely these processes of community closure and development of a political identity, leaving the less powerful in relations of autonomy and dependence that, at times, can be extremely asymmetrical. Therefore, while in all three contexts power is mobilized to monopolize a good or resource by denying another group access to it, in closure struggles the powerful also mobilize power to exert strategies that impinge on the weaker side's efforts to close its community and develop a political identity.

These insights from Popitz's approach help to lay the foundation for a new power-based approach to social closure. His contexts of power relations allow us to specify the logics of exclusion, exploitation, and elimination, their respective basic strategies, corresponding forms of closure, and the characterizing social relationships in each case: the excluders and the excluded, the exploiters and the exploited, and the eliminators and those threatened with elimination. On this basis, in a second step, we now have to elaborate on this concept of power and show how social actors can actually mobilize power. Turning to Giddens' and Mann's relational ideas of identifying the structural resources of power that social actors have to draw upon to act in the social world, we now need to clarify which structural elements of power are crucial to mobilize to reorganize established social relations in closure struggles.

16.2 Structural Elements of Resources of Power in Closure Struggles

Giddens' approach to power is critical in the sense that power is conceived as a medium relating agency and structure. His examination of the structural aspect of this duality as being made up of authoritative and allocative power resources, thus pertaining to political and economic aspects, is supplemented by Mann's critical elements of ideology and military/violence as resources of power to make the concept comprehensive. As a result, the structural dimension of power that we can now adapt to the new conceptualization of social closure comprises four dimensions that I define as ideological, economic, military/violence, and politico-legal resources of power.

Elaborating the concept in this way allows for *variability* in theorizing and empirically analysing social closure. Following Giddens' systematization of basic institutions in a societal order, discussed above, this variability stems from the fact that while all four resources of power are critical when analysing processes of exclusion, exploitation, and elimination, they are so to varying degrees with respect to each of the forms of social closure. I will argue later that exclusion rests *predominantly* on politico-legal resources of power, exploitation on *predominantly* economic resources of power, and elimination *predominantly* on ideological and military/violence resources of power. Of course, in each case the other resources play a critical role as well, but their importance is secondary.

Further, this differentiation detaches closure theory from the idea that either in general or ultimately it is always economic power that determines the processes and dynamics of social closure—although of course it always plays a role. At the same time, this variety of resources of power takes into account what Mann calls the *promiscuity* of power. While we can distinguish both analytically and empirically different resources of power, we have to consider and empirically investigate how at a certain point in time one of them becomes dominant, how this dominance passes to another, and how they may mutually reinforce each other.

Finally, releasing closure theory from its economic constraints by taking into consideration these four distinct resources of power also means opening it up to perceiving other differences and making them accessible to analysis. All critical dimensions—race, ethnicity, gender, religion, language, and so forth—that in the previous theory of social closure had been conceived of as *derived* and thus subordinate to class (or, in Weber's handling of ethnicity, as simply a question of status, honour, or lifestyle), can be analysed now in their own right. I will address these aspects in more detail when outlining the empirical plausibility of the explanatory logics of this new approach to social closure.

However, defining these four resources is only the first step. To understand how organized social actors can actually utilize them, we have to further outline and differentiate what Giddens calls the critical *structural elements of power* as the very elements upon which social actors can and must draw to be capable of making an impact on the ongoing processes of social closure and employing strategies that reorganize social relations of exclusion, exploitation, or elimination. As drawing upon these structural elements allows them to exert strategies of *marginalization*, *extraction*, and *annihilation*, we need to specify them.

Structural Elements of Ideological Power

Structural elements of legitimation stem from ideological power resources that can be distinguished with regard to their level of abstractness, from more informal to rather formal forms of closure. Asymmetric relationships with regard to superiority and subordination, benefitting from the production of material wealth and added value, as well as socio-spatial aspects of positioning and the threat of sheer violence, all demand legitimation. On the most general level, *transcendent visions* or world religions as ideologies that allow for a general and fundamental legitimation/justification of systems of closure are critical, legitimizing to various degrees systems of exclusion, exploitation, and elimination. The Old Testament, Western enlightenment, humanism, and liberalism are critical, but no less neoliberalism and settler colonialism belong in this category—all of them legitimizing a specific order or, in our case, a form of closure on a world scale by creating us-them boundaries. Examples include beliefs about being a civilized people in contrast to a non-civilized one, to see oneself as enlightened in contrast to the barbarian other, Christian in contrast to heathen, Jewish or Christian in contrast to Muslim, or European in contrast to Arab.

Such basic systems of legitimation are of a highly general nature and are more concretized in what Mann calls *institutionalized ideologies*, which more concretely justify and legitimize an existing order or the reorganization of established social relations of exclusion, exploitation, and elimination, such as neoliberal, capitalist, or settler-colonial legitimation strategies of unequally distributed life chances / chances of survival in contexts of social closure.

Finally, the most concrete systems of legitimation are *immanent ideologies*, which operate to justify existing social relations of domination constituting a specific order. This type of ideology coincides with what Heinrich Popitz defined as *morales*, which

> appeared legitimate in the first place to the privileged themselves. Yet not simply in the sense that each of them believed in himself, in his own claims and properly acquired rights. The recognition took place much more according to the *reciprocity principle* within an *exchange process* of the privileged with one another. This is decisive. As they out of evident interest assisted in the defense of their claims, they assisted themselves reciprocally in building up their convincingly good conscience: I do not recognize only my claim, but also the claim of the other who recognizes mine. Because I recognize the other, I am in the right; because the other recognizes me, he is in the right. Because the other recognizes me, as I recognize him, and I him, as he me, our claims are based on *our* right. (Popitz 2017 [1986], 140)

In contexts of social closure, this is true for powerful actors, who are 'intensifying the cohesion, the confidence and, therefore, the power of an already established group' (Mann 1986, 24). Rather than depending on a specific sense of solidarity between the chief and his staff or a belief in the legitimacy of those subject to authority, Popitz has made the critical point that legitimacy in concrete processes of reorganizing established social relations arises from the mutual recognition of the powerful that confirms that their claims are justified.

Structural Elements of Economic Power

Structural elements of allocation denote critical aspects of economic power resources that help sustain and reproduce global capitalism and secure or transform its accumulation regime. Private property and shareholder capitalism are critical here. The state of being either in possession of the means of production or authorized to dispose of them has a deep impact in closure struggles, as it allows individuals or groups to make use of natural resources *and* human beings. Thus, in capitalist relations, powerful social actors draw upon structural elements of economic resources. Three aspects are of utmost importance here: First, it is necessary to make use of individuals' labour force on the one hand, while extracting, acquiring, and using material features of the environment on the other hand. Second, the holder of power must be able to make use of the means of material production/reproduction, (i.e., instruments of production, ranging from human labour to capital and financial capital, technology for processing raw materials, and computerized technology and artificial intelligence). This is critical within a given society, within regional economic blocs, within the global capitalist system. Third, combining raw materials and human labour power, making use of the body in the production process of global capitalism, is another important structural element of allocation.

Structural Elements of Military/Violence Power

Powerful actors mobilize structural elements of military/violence to make systematic or sporadic use of means of violence. First, these actors draw upon them to establish, defend, or reorganize social relations among groups of people through war, invasion, occupation, or sieges. Second, they mobilize them to defend established relations of domination, social control, and relations of exclusion, exploitation, and elimination. Third, these structural elements of military/violence are mobilized to uphold or transform social relations, mainly used against outsiders. It is obvious that Mann here points to processes in which social relations are reorganized and justified that usually cannot be achieved peacefully, because the excluded, exploited, or those threatened with elimination may defend themselves. Of course, employing means of violence then usually requires some form of recourse to politico-legal or ideological structural elements of power.

Structural Elements of Politico-Legal Power

Structural elements of authoritative (i.e., politico-legal) resources refer to decisions made regarding the specific administrative ordering of human beings in time and space. Giddens here refers to specific structural elements that enable this ordering. First, the organization of social time-space, the temporal-spatial organization of social interaction in such forms as the workplace and work time, which ultimately refers back to class relations. Here, we should add the ordering of workplaces according to gender, ethnicity, or religion in specific contexts.[1] Second, we have to consider the production and reproduction of the human body, such as the organization of and relationships among human beings in class relations. The same should be added here with regard to exclusionary or exploitative relations between men and women, ethnic groups, and so forth. Third, the

---

[1] The Covid-19 pandemic seems to have fundamentally reordered the temporal-spatial aspects of these relationships, given the new options for employees to work from home, separated from one another and fully individualized according to the neoliberal logic.

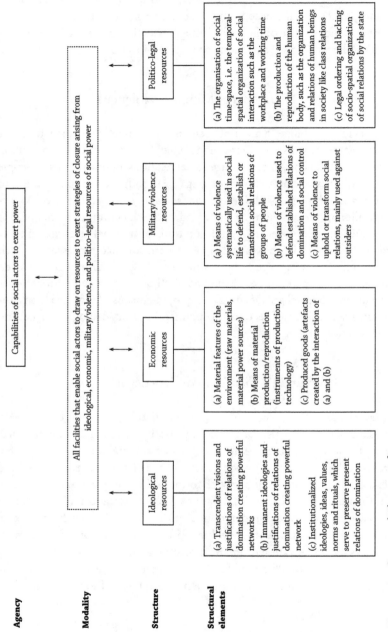

Figure 16.1 Structural Elements of Power

Source: Own conceptualization based on Giddens 1984, 29 and Mann 1986

legal ordering and backing of the socio-spatial organization of social relations by the state, which can include, for example, turning the city into a market and transforming living spaces and areas of political participation into a space of investment that consequently will exclude the less powerful and oust the poor from their homes, while the powerful and wealthy re-create the city according to their taste. Of course, what we see here are the preconditions, the structural elements that reorganize relations of social closure that are backed by the state, as Frank Parkin has already so insightfully pointed out (see figure 16.1).

On the basis of this concept of power that serves as the foundation of a relational theorizing of social closure, we can go on to ask some critical questions. From the perspective I develop here, given that social life must be understood *as* ongoing closure struggles that cannot be stopped, social actors need to develop strategies to maintain their power within closure struggles. They can do so by *organizing* and *drawing upon the structural elements of power* in a social entity, which will be possible to (extremely) varying degrees depending on the situation.

This asymmetry brings us back to the opportunity structure and life chances / chances of survival as the two inevitable concepts for closure theory that are constitutively related to one another. On the basis of the relational concept of power, they have to be revised and adapted as basic concepts necessary for theorizing and analysing social closure. While the former concept will explain why social actors can mobilize power only to varying degrees, the latter will allow us to define the real goal of social closure and the struggles being waged over it.

17
A New Concept of Life Chances / Chances of Survival in the Opportunity Structure

Suggesting a new concept of life chances / chances of survival within the opportunity structure requires constitutively relating the two concepts—opportunity structure and life chances / chances of survival—as aspects of structure and agency. To do so, we must revise both concepts, detaching them from their individualistic contexts, putting them into a relational perspective, and conceptualize them as dynamic ones. Just as we cannot conceive of the opportunity structure as simply a given and static structural distribution of goods and resources, nor are life chances / chances of survival just the outcome of social actors making choices regarding goods and resources according to their position in the hierarchical structure of society. Thus, reconceptualizing the concepts means putting them in the context of closure struggles and actors' varying ability to mobilize power.

17.1 The Dynamics of the Opportunity Structure

A new conception of the opportunity structure first and foremost needs to overcome its thus far static and individualistic character and link it to the dynamics of closure struggles. Based on the concept of power I developed in the previous chapter, social actors' opportunity structure is not simply structurally given but reflects their ability to draw upon structural elements of ideological, economic, military/violence, and politico-legal resources of power.

Given the powerful side's superior ability to organize in contexts of exclusion, exploitation, and elimination, and thus create and exacerbate power differentials compared to the less powerful, they are in a position to progressively expand their own opportunity structure—mobilizing structural elements of power—at the cost of the less powerful, whose opportunity structure as a result is restricted by the successful implementation of the powerful side's closure strategies. Consequently, the possibilities of social actors to realize their life chances / chances of survival do not rest on a given distribution structure of goods and resources, but rather on how and to what extent they are able to mobilize structural elements of power and thus shift the balance of power between the excluders and the excluded, the exploiters and the exploited, and the eliminators and those threatened with elimination. Conceived in this way, the idea of the opportunity structure can be conceptualized in a new way:

> Opportunity structures denote the unequally given possibilities of collective social actors to organize and draw upon structural elements of ideological, economic, military/violence, and politico-legal resources of power to reorganize existing balances of power between the powerful and the less powerful. As this asymmetry is always a temporary outcome of ongoing closure struggles, the asymmetry of being able to mobilize power to pursue strategies in closure struggles can be permanently reorganized and exacerbated. The more powerful actors can expand their opportunity structure the more they are able to narrow the one of the less powerful side.

In this sense, looking at the critical social relations of exclusion, exploitation, and elimination, the new concept of the opportunity structure stresses the fact that the ability of collective actors to draw upon the structural elements of power within the institutional make-up of any kind of social entity—be it a nation-state or the global economy—depends on their being organized. Conceptualizing the opportunity structure in this way transforms it from an individualist into a relational concept and emphasizes collective actors' ability to close communities, create political identities that allow them to organize their interests, and act in solidarity. Opportunity structures are thus the outcome of closure struggles.

To the degree that powerful actors are able to expand their own opportunity structures at the cost of the less powerful, they are able to mobilize structural elements of power that enable them to pursue closure strategies that will make it difficult if not impossible for the less powerful to realize their life chances / chances of survival. As I argue that the concepts of opportunity structure and life chances / chances of survival are complementary in the sense of Giddens' duality of structure and agency, the next step is to reconceptualize the concept of life chances / chances of survival.

17.2 Dimensions of Life Chances / Chances of Survival

Having identified the realization of life chances / chances of survival as the real goal of closure struggles, we now need to reconsider, elaborate, and adapt the rudimentary concept to overcome its individualist and static understanding that does not help and is an obstacle to recognition. Thus, like the opportunity structure, this concept needs to be both dynamized by putting it into the context of social closure struggles and expanded by differentiating and defining its critical dimensions that make comprehensible the targets of closure struggles.

This new concept of life chances / chances of survival comprises four critical dimensions: *resources* (socio-economic), *rights* (politico-legal), *networks/institutions* (socio-structural), and *communities* (socio-cultural). While I agree with Weber, Merton, and Dahrendorf that resources and rights are the critical socio-economic and politico-legal dimensions of life chances / chances of survival, I also agree in principle with Dahrendorf's argument that options (resources and rights) alone are not sufficient for a meaningful concept of life chances / chances of survival but need to be complemented by social ties, as these are necessary for human beings to find recognition, respect, dignity, and appreciation in their lives and to develop self-esteem.

Yet, the ties that Dahrendorf had in mind and that he called ligatures—the church, the village, the family—make only little sense now for a new concept of life chances / chances of survival, not only because they are historically rather outdated, but mainly because Dahrendorf interprets them as individualistic choices of isolated human beings. Therefore, to develop an adequate conception of such ties, I take up Weber's basic distinction between *associative social relationships* and *communal social relationships* and introduce *networks/institutions* and *communities* into a new concept of life chances / chances of survival. They both stress the collective nature of social closure—and thus the need to think about the communities involved in closure struggles rather than about individuals—and address the neglected aspects of political identity and group formation in closure struggles, which has critical consequences. First, adding networks/institutions to the concept introduces a *socio-structural* dimension of social ties that is critical, as it allows social actors to develop ties that will allow them to structurally integrate into existing networks/institutions of a given society or other social entity. Access to the health system, the education system, or the job market is vital in this regard. Such processes of structural integration increase life chances / chances of survival in a socio-structural sense. In an explicitly relational approach, Tilly has analysed the significance of strategic networks that allow individuals to gain access to mutual aid support that benefits them by monopolizing resources, distributing them within the network, and closing it off to the outside and thereby allowing for socio-economic integration (Tilly 1998).

Second, in addition to the socio-structural aspect of social ties, I add a *socio-cultural* dimension to the concept of life chances / chances of survival. This dimension includes *belonging to a community* as another crucial aspect. We must systematically introduce the critical relations among members of social groups (such as gender, religious, and language groups), Black people and people of colour, as well as the poor, single mothers, the elderly, underqualified persons, the disabled, foreigners, refugees, asylum seekers, and so forth within relations of exclusion, exploitation, and elimination. These relations should be treated as a vital and distinct dimension of the concept of life chances / chances of survival.

Both newly conceptualized and added dimensions—*networks/institutions* and *communities*—allow for a reconceptualization of the concept of life chances / chances of survival. Making choices to develop strategies is certainly important, but the choices made are created and re-created within social relations, highlighting the fact that social closure is of a fundamentally collective and relational character. Against the background of this revision and reconceptualization of the idea of life chances, I newly define the concept of *life chances / chances of survival*:

> The concept of life chances / chances of survival denotes the entirety of options available to and ties between individuals as members of a social collective, allowing them to earn a living or survive in a given society or different social entity relative to others, depending on power asymmetries between them. This entirety can be differentiated into
> Options: (1) participation in using resources to secure self-preservation (socio-economic dimension), (2) membership in a legal community through a full set of rights defining a legal status (politico-legal dimension).
> Ties: (3) integration in strategic networks/institutions (socio-structural dimension) in order to realize given socially organized options, and (4) belonging to communities (socio-cultural dimension) that secure the recognition of one's identities.

Conceptualized this way, the idea of life chances / chances of survival within the opportunity structure means that life chances / chances of survival can now be properly understood as the *real goal of social closure and thus of closure struggles*. By drawing upon structural elements of power, in closure struggles powerful organized actors expand their opportunity structures by exercising power in order to realize their life chances / chances of survival at the cost of others. These struggles are therefore a pivotal part of the ongoing struggles in social life, as the powerful involved in them are fighting for an enormously wide range of opportunities. As they may fight for more resources or an even more luxurious life at the expense of the less powerful, the struggles of those whose opportunity structures are restricted by the strategies of the powerful may unfold under extreme conditions. For them, the struggles may simply be about defending their existence or *bare life* (Agamben 1998 [1995]). This brings us to the core of our new understanding of social closure.

18

Reorganizing Relations of Social Closure

The Two Critical Mechanisms: *Denial of Access* and *Intervention into Community Closure*

The new approach to social closure conceives of the critical process of reorganizing social relations of exclusion, exploitation, and elimination as a process in which strategies of the powerful side aim at expanding their life chances / chances of survival at the cost those of the less-powerful by either denying them (1) access to valued *resources*, *rights*, and *networks/institutions* and (2) by inhibiting them from closing their own *community*, which would enable less-powerful actors to develop a political identity and thus to act in solidarity (Mackert 2021).

Instead of continuing to equate social closure with monopolization, I argue that two relational mechanisms are operating in closure struggles that explain how closure strategies of the powerful reorganize existing social relations of exclusion, exploitation, and elimination. Proceeding this way, I follow Tilly's understanding of social mechanisms as small-scale processes that 'produce identical immediate effects in many different circumstances yet combine variously to generate very different outcomes on the large scale' (Tilly 2003b, 20). In the case of closure, this means that we will see the same mechanisms at work but producing different effects with regard to different contexts of exclusion, exploitation, and elimination and strategies relative to dimensions of life chances / chances of survival.

First, denial of access is the mechanism that explains processes of monopolizing resources and rights that Weber called *closure to the outside* and the *theory of social closure* referred to as *exclusionary closure*. Yet, my new theorizing of social closure adds *networks* as a critical dimension of life chances / chances of survival from which social actors can be kept away. I thus define this first critical social mechanism that is familiar in closure theory:

> *Denial of access* operates when powerful social actors in social relations of exclusion, exploitation, or elimination increase their life chances / chances of survival at the cost of less-powerful social actors by preventing or even blocking them from utilizing resources and rights and from integrating into critical social networks/institutions.

By conceiving of denial of access as a mechanism that operates in various settings and is triggered by different strategies, this relational social mechanism causes 'major variations among times, places, and social circumstances in the character' (Tilly 2003b, 20) of social relations of exclusion, exploitation, and elimination.

Second, introducing *intervention into community closure* as the second critical mechanism of a new explanatory approach to social closure allows us to overcome the blind spot of *group action* and *acting in solidarity* in closure theory. Having shown that closing a community is an inevitable precondition for communities' participation in closure struggles, the powerful side's strategies to prevent less-powerful social groups from doing so turns out to be crucial in closure struggles. This mechanism can be defined in the following way:

> *Intervention into community closure* operates when powerful social actors are in a position to exercise control over less-powerful groups and make it difficult or even impossible for them to close their community to establish a political identity that would allow them to act in solidarity and mobilize structural elements of power to fight back in closure struggles.

Introducing this new mechanism into closure theory builds on Gertrude Neuwirth's (1969) critical idea that she presented in 'A Weberian Outline of a Theory of Community: Its Application to the "Dark Ghetto"'. In this article, she made explicit the consequences for a less-powerful social group if its attempts to close the community fails due to interventions from a more-powerful actor. Her lucid analysis highlights the consequences of political, economic, or cultural strategies of the White community that make it impossible for the Black community to actually achieve community closure, which effectively prevents them from overcoming their subordinated position (Neuwirth 1969, 151). However, the mechanism triggering these effects can be generalized as critical for all contexts of social closure, because it draws attention to the severe problems social groups face when they do not succeed in closing their community and develop a political identity, which leaves them unable to develop solidarity and thus actually to act in solidarity against the strategies of the powerful.

Neuwirth's analysis is instructive in that it allows us to understand the decisive importance of *control* in closure struggles, because it explains how the powerful are able to reorganize social relationships of exclusion, exploitation, or elimination by intervening into the latter's efforts to achieve community closure. Such processes inevitably have an impact on the less-powerful community's sense of dignity, self-worth, and self-esteem, as they enable more-powerful social actors to make decisions that have a significant impact on their lives, leaving them vulnerable. It is obvious from Neuwirth's analysis that she focuses on the consequences of the powerful and the less powerful being able to achieve community closure to extremely varying degrees. This asymmetry of well-organized, powerful social actors on the one hand and less-organized or not-yet-organized social actors on the other hand helps reveal not only why social actors are powerful while others are not but also what allows the former to employ strategies that trigger both social mechanisms. In fact, closing the community allows a group's members to act in solidarity, enabling the powerful side to deny the less powerful access to resources, rights, and networks/institutions and to intervene into the community closure efforts of the less powerful (see figure 18.1).

The time lag in organizing between powerful and less-powerful social actors highlights that *only by closing their community and creating a political identity can groups become capable collective actors in closure struggles*. This important aspect resonates with Popitz's and Mann's views that group action or acting in solidarity is neither easy to achieve nor a matter of course but rather a consequence of *organizing*. The organizing time lag allows the powerful to retain and stabilize their dominant position and then use it to successfully intervene in the less-powerful side's closure of its community. Neuwirth points to the facts

> suggesting that urban Negroes not only are unable to bring about community closure, but also that in reality *they are prevented from achieving it by the white community*. Establishing support for both of these assertions involves a functionally related point of view: the inability to effect closure is not only the result of certain historical and contemporary conditions concerning the Negroes' position within the larger society, but also in turn *facilitates attempts by others to prevent such community closure*. (Neuwirth 1969, 153–154; emphasis added)

And further, Neuwirth argues that

> the economic and social controls which representatives of society exert directly upon residents of the Dark Ghetto are further means to prevent community closure. They are forced to pay high rents for substandard housing; they are frequently over-charged for food and other household items; lacking knowledge and other opportunities, they may be charged with fraudulent interest rates for credit purchases. In their dealings with agencies of social control, such as the police, Negroes are exposed to different and discriminatory standards than are whites. These examples reflect rather obvious and deliberate attempts at preventing community closure. The white community also introduces other, more subtle attempts, which officially, are designed to alleviate problems of the ghetto but which actually tend to perpetuate the Negroes' powerlessness. This applies particularly to the programmes initiated by the War Against Poverty. (Neuwirth 1969, 157)

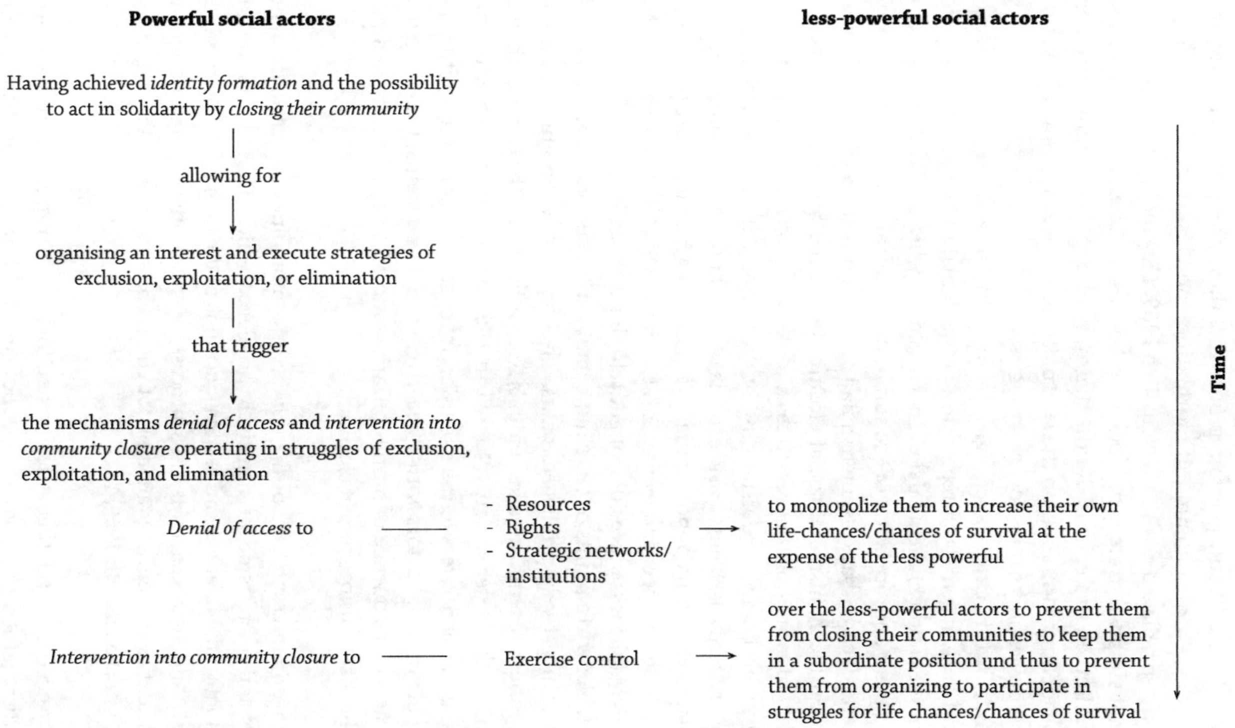

Powerful social actors   **less-powerful social actors**

                                                                          Time →

Having achieved *identity formation* and the possibility
to act in solidarity by *closing their community*

                    allowing for

organising an interest and execute strategies of
exclusion, exploitation, or elimination

                    that trigger

the mechanisms *denial of access* and *intervention into
community closure* operating in struggles of exclusion,
exploitation, and elimination

   Denial of access to   — Resources   → to monopolize them to increase their own
                                   — Rights   life-chances/chances of survival at the
                                   — Strategic networks/   expense of the less powerful
                                     institutions

   Intervention into community closure to Exercise control → over the less-powerful actors to prevent them
                                                                  from closing their communities to keep them
                                                                  in a subordinate position und thus to prevent
                                                                  them from organizing to participate in
                                                                  struggles for life chances/chances of survival

Figure 18.1 Strategic advantages of the powerful in closure struggles

From this analysis, we can draw some general conclusions for a new theorizing of social closure. First, arguing that 'closure by dominant communities may be so effectively directed against certain groups that these group members are unable to resort to their own community formation and closure in order to improve their under-privileged position' (Neuwirth 1969, 151) makes it obvious that closure is not simply a strategy of blocking others from access to a certain good or resource. Rather, strategies of dominant groups also prevent community closure and thus identity formation on the side of the less powerful, which leaves them unable to powerfully act in closure struggles.

Second, in this case a social group's 'inability to achieve closure leaves it "negatively privileged" with regard to (1) the denial of economic and political opportunities and (2) the denial of social esteem, which, as Weber argues, rests upon the prior appropriation of economic and political power' (Neuwirth 1969, 152). Here, decades back, Neuwirth had already pointed to what I call now the two critical mechanisms of social closure. While the first aspect refers to the possibility of monopolizing resources and blocking access to them, the second brings human beings' understanding of dignity and esteem as critical aspects into closure analysis. These basic aspects of social life do not simply depend on political and economic opportunities. Rather, they are much more profound for individuals' self-respect and feelings of self-worth, which the powerful systematically prevent the less powerful from developing and realizing.

Third, Neuwirth points out two important consequences of the 'vulnerability implicit in negatively privileged status. The denial of economic and political opportunities prevents these individuals from influencing the terms of their participation in the larger society' (Neuwirth 1969, 152). This first consequence is obvious, because it refers to the exclusion from social, economic, cultural, and political life of social actors with a negatively privileged status, which again can be seen as a consequence of monopolization and exclusion. Yet, the second aspect radicalizes this process of closure:

> Moreover, representatives of the dominant communities will *regulate* those affairs and interests of the negatively privileged which, if left uncontrolled, might affect the interests and relative positions of the dominant communities within the larger society. By this process, representatives of the dominant communities prevent any attempts of community closure by the negatively privileged. (Neuwirth 1969, 152)

While conceptual and theoretical reflections on closure theory have so far mostly disregarded this pivotal aspect of social closure, it is absolutely central to the relational approach I am suggesting here. Bringing it into closure theory, this aspect focuses on the heretofore unfortunately neglected but critical aspect of the social relations between the excluders and the excluded, the exploiters and the exploited, and the eliminators and those threatened with elimination. This aspect stresses how the more powerful side directly impinges upon the life and community of the less powerful. This, in fact, expands the perspective to a new and broader conception of closure theory. Emphasizing social actors' sense of self-esteem, self-worth, belonging, and dignity that results from closure struggles makes clear that social closure does, in fact, have to do with social actors' life chances / chances of survival in a more encompassing sense.

19
A New Concept of Social Closure

To suggest a generic concept of social closure, I start by defining *social closure* as a relational process and a strategy:

> Social closure is one of the most basic processes in social life that produces and continually reproduces social relations of exclusion, exploitation, and elimination. In these social relations, the powerful are opposed to the less powerful—the excluders versus the excluded, the exploiters versus the exploited, and the eliminators versus those threatened with elimination, while both sides are fighting for the realization of their life chances / chances of survival. In everyday closure struggles that cannot be brought to a halt, the powerful employ two kinds of strategies: first, strategies that increase their life chances / chances of survival at the cost of the less powerful by preventing the latter from using resources, exercising rights, or integrating into critical networks/institutions of the wider society. Second, strategies that exert control over the community life and the possibilities of individuals to develop a political identity and act in solidarity. Both strategies impinge on the opportunity structures of less-powerful social communities or social groups in ways that prevent them or even render them unable to participate in struggles life chances / chances of survival and to take advantage of them.

Based on this definition and the preceding discussion, the most important aspects of a new concept of social closure can be summarized as follows:

> First, collective action is critical because a new concept of closure allows for discussing and analysing the processes and dynamics of closure in which powerful collective actors employ various strategies to reorganize existing social relations of exclusion, exploitation, and elimination. The concept thus replaces the idea of closure as merely restricted to economic strategies stemming from a shared mentality of the powerful or simply as an effect of economic structures. Instead, it stresses the importance of organization leading to collective action and acting in solidarity.
> Second, social closure is a power-based concept. Collective actors must draw upon structural elements of power to pursue their strategies. In struggles involving exclusion, exploitation, and elimination, all forms of

power—ideological, economic, military/violence, and politico-legal—are relevant, but to varying degrees:

Exclusion is a form of social closure that mainly relies on the mobilization of structural elements of *politico-legal* power within systems of *currency and taxation*. In such contexts, the powerful side's strategies of *marginalization* push less-powerful social groups to the fringes of a society, a supranational entity, or the global system.

Exploitation is a form of social closure that primarily depends on the mobilization of structural elements of *economic* power within *systems of control over the means of production*. In such capitalist contexts, the powerful side's strategies of *extraction* reduce human beings to labour power that can be extracted, keeping them in their dependent position, be it in a national community or a supranational entity or globally.

Elimination is a form of social closure that mainly uses the structural elements of *ideological* and *military/violence* power within systems of *ownership and rent*. In such settler-colonial contexts, the powerful side's strategies of *annihilation* follow an idea of *purity*, imposing a new order that poses a severe threat to the survival of the less powerful.

Third, because realizing life chances / chances of survival—enjoying resources and rights, integrating into networks/institutions, as well as experiencing dignity, respect, self-esteem, and recognition—is the real goal of social closure, the generic concept assumes that the ability to realize this goal depends on social actors' different opportunity structures. The generic concept of closure conceives of these opportunity structures as an outcome of collective actors' varying ability to mobilize power—to organize, create a political identity, and act in solidarity, allowing powerful actors to exert strategies that narrow the opportunity structure of the less powerful to a degree that eventually may leave them unable to organize. Neither life chances / chances of survival nor opportunity structures are simply given but are rather a temporary outcome of the reproduction of social relations within closure struggles.

Fourth, the generic concept of social closure is an *explanatory* one. Explanation is based on strategies of the powerful that trigger two relational mechanisms of reorganizing the social relations of exclusion, exploitation, and elimination: (a) *denial of access*, which operates through processes that prevent less-powerful social groups from enjoying rights and resources or integrating into critical networks/institutions, and (b) *intervention into community closure*, which operates through processes that either prevent the less-powerful side from closing their own communities or that damage or destroy communities that have managed to close themselves off to the outside and are therefore able to organize and act collectively in solidarity within closure struggles. Both effects of this mechanism are expressions of exercising control over the less-powerful side in closure struggles.

Fifth, such a new and generic concept overcomes previous conceptual restrictions and gaps in closure theory in at least four ways: (1) It does not assume a fundamental dominance of economic processes in all kinds of closure struggles; instead, it conceives of 'race', gender, ethnicity, religion, and language —according to context—as equally important and thus allows us to analyse them in their own right. (2) It allows to analyse both highly formalized and informal processes of closure. Whether we analyse highly formalized closure processes of an organization or the *informal* glass ceiling that prevents women from moving to top positions in such organizations, closure analysis needs to analyse the unequal opportunities in such struggles to organize and mobilize structural elements of politico-legal and ideological resources of power in order to succeed. (3) Elaborating dimensions of life chances / chances of survival allows for a much more nuanced view of which aspects of life chances are actually targeted by the powerful side's specific closure strategies. (4) Although closure strategies are mainly intentional, the new conceptual approach also allows us to identify processes of closure that may be the unintended consequences of specific strategies.

This new concept of closure meets the requirements of a relational approach, understanding social closure as dynamic, continuous, processual, and context-specific (cf. Emirbayer 1997). Conceiving social closure within the sociological struggle paradigm makes closure a highly dynamic aspect of social life. Exclusion, exploitation, and elimination are seen as social relations in which social actors are situated in characteristic power asymmetries. These relations are the very starting point and the methodological reference point that allows us to analyse strategic reorganizations by powerful collective actors. Bringing in the *mechanismic* explanation by identifying relational social mechanisms directs the attention to those social processes that actually explain how and in which dimensions of life chances / chances of survival social relations between the excluders and the excluded, the exploiters and the exploited, and the eliminators and those threatened with elimination are reorganized, usually in favour of the more powerful. All these strategies, the resulting dynamics and processes, and the explanations are highly context specific and need to be clarified in the analysis.

TYPOLOGY

This chapter presents the second step of a new theorizing of social closure. By cross-tabulating forms and strategies of social closure with dimensions of life chances / chances of survival, it develops a typology that produces twelve distinct strategies of social closure that will inform the empirical part of the book.

20
A Typology of Social Closure

A typology of this new approach to social closure cross-tabulates forms of closure and their characteristic strategies with the four dimensions of life chances / chances of survival: resources, rights, networks/institutions, and communities. The resulting twelve-field framework analytically differentiates between strategies of closure that variously impact the less powerful in closure struggles, aiming to prevent them from realizing their life chances / chances of survival (see figure 20.1).

The typology's logic reveals that social closure is not a uniform process but a highly variable one, depending on the contexts of exclusion, exploitation, or elimination. In these contexts, the strategies of the powerful side are directed towards the four dimensions of life chances / chances of survival. This variability will be briefly characterized with regard to strategies and processes and discussed in detail in the empirical analyses of exclusion, exploitation, and elimination.

Resources

Strategies of social closure aim to deny the less powerful vital resources, cutting them off from participation in the wider society and compromising their possibilities of self-preservation in various ways and to different degrees.

In neoliberal systems, the *exclusionary* logic of redistribution involves strategies that denounce existing social contracts or ideas of a common 'social good', such as a redistributive welfare state system. In this sense, neoliberal policies, from tax cuts for the wealthy to the destruction of public services, act as strategies of *commodification/financialization* by the affluent towards the rest of society. In capitalist contexts, the *exploitative* logic of *deprivation* strategies has historically included 'original accumulation' and continues today by skimming off added value from human labour. In settler-colonial contexts, the powerful employ *eliminatory* strategies of *letting die* to deprive Indigenous group from as many vital resources as possible, making their survival impossible.

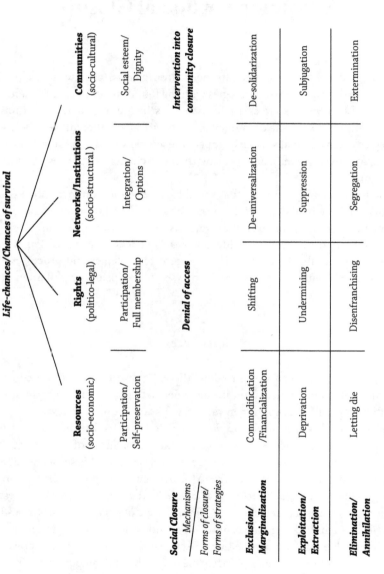

Figure 20.1 A typology of social closure

Rights

Strategies of social closure are intended to deny the less powerful access to rights, blocking them from enjoying their human rights and citizenship rights, thereby hindering their full participation in society.

While the *exclusionary* logic implies a *shifting* of social and political rights in neoliberalized societies, thus limiting citizens' options to assert claims on grounds of social and political citizenship rights, in global capitalism the *exploitative* logic of closure *undermines* rights with regard to production and labour processes in the Global North and Global South. In settler-colonial contexts, the *eliminatory* logic implies an outright *disenfranchising of the occupied*, reducing them to residents, subjects, or stateless persons.

Networks/Institutions

This dimension, networks/institutions, refers to ways in which the powerful hinder or prevent the less powerful from integrating into structures that guarantee security in their lives and offer them further options to make a living.

The *exclusionary* logic in the face of a neoliberal flexibilization of labour markets and privatization of health and education reveals the *de-universalization* of access to support, safety, and security to the detriment of the less powerful, exposing them to precarious living conditions. In global capitalist contexts, *exploitative* strategies of *suppression* point to processes that destroy the networks of the exploited, exposing them to radicalized exploitation. In settler-colonial contexts, the *eliminatory* logic of strategies of *segregation* completely prevents Indigenous people from accessing labour markets, health systems, or education systems, thereby rendering them vulnerable to elimination.

Communities

Communities, as a dimension of life chances / chances of survival, highlight how powerful groups' closure strategies directly impact less-powerful groups' ability to establish boundaries, develop political identities, and act in solidarity. These strategies lower social esteem of these communities and their members and deny their recognition as human beings.

The exclusionary logic of strategies of *de-solidarization* weakens many social groups, leaving them unable to fight and making their members feel responsible for their situation. This strategy suggests to them that they are unworthy of participating in redistributive systems. In global capitalism, exploitation strategies *subjugate* the global workforce through outright abuse that is destructive to individuals and communities and makes them powerless in closure struggles. In settler-colonial contexts, *eliminatory* strategies of *extermination* include politicide, memoricide, ethnic cleansing and at times genocide, and the destruction of Indigenous culture and civil society organizations. These strategies leave these groups exposed to the risk of elimination.

Based on this typology of social closure, its basic strategies, and the differentiation between dimensions of life chances / chances of survival, I will now elaborate on the explanatory programme of this new approach to social closure.

EXPLANATION

This sub-part presents the third major step in the new theorizing of social closure. Against the background of concept formation and the typology of a new approach to closure theory and analysis, it offers an *explanation* of processes of social closure. Chapter 21 not only introduces the sociological idea of *events* that is used as a methodological tool to interrupt the ongoing processes in the social world and allows to define a starting point for empirical analyses that is not chosen at random and can methodologically be justified. Further, it presents the *general explanatory model* and clearly defines and outlines what an empirical analysis of social closure struggles must do.

The three sub-chapters of chapter 22 finally offer *empirical analyses* to make the *explanatory logic* plausible for exclusion, exploitation, and elimination. For each of these forms of closure a specific context is chosen, a critical event defined, and the predominant resource of power in these specific closure struggles determined. In each of the cases analysed, the explanatory logic is reconstructed by analysing the way the *denial of access* and *intervention into community closure mechanisms* are operating. Thus, we see how closure struggles in neoliberalism (exclusion), global capitalism (exploitation), and settler colonialism (elimination) unfold by *reorganizing* social relations that then are *stabilized* and *legitimized*.

Chapter 23 discusses the strengths of the new relational and explanatory approach to social closure and how, in contrast to the traditional view of social closure, it reveals the dynamics of social life as social closure.

21
Towards an Explanation of Social Closure

Suggesting an explanation of social closure points to the critical fact that we must explain how the social relations between the excluders and the excluded, the exploiters and the exploited, and the eliminators and those threatened with elimination are reorganized in ways that allow the more powerful to improve their life chances / chances of survival at the expense of the less powerful. This means that we are interested in processes that *change connections among social units* (Tilly 2003b, 20–21), which in the case of social closure means that we have to explain how the same causal mechanisms operate in different contexts and forms of social closure and how the employed strategies of social closure trigger the *denial of access* and *intervention into community closure* mechanisms with the same immediate effect—barring access to resources, rights, and networks/ institutions, or having an impact on a community—but producing various and variable results in different contexts of exclusion, exploitation, and elimination. Thus, what we are going to explain is the *variability of social closure*.

As we assume the continuous and ongoing production and reproduction of social relations of closure, there is neither a hypothetical beginning of closure struggles nor a simple end to them after social relations have been reorganized and a new arrangement stabilized. Instead, we must conceive of them as struggles that cannot be terminated, and so we need a kind of methodological bracketing (Giddens 1976) or interrupting of these ongoing processes to convincingly explain processes of closure struggles that reorganize existing relations of exclusion, exploitation, or elimination. Such a methodological step becomes possible by joining the recent debate about *events* in sociology in a specific sense (Berezin 2012; Sewell 2005; Patterson 2007; Steinmetz 2008b).

21.1 The Critical Role of Events

The processual perspective that conceives of social life as a continuous process of making and remaking is prominent already in Giddens, who stresses that social life is an '*ongoing process of events-in-the world*' or a '*stream of events-in-process*' (Giddens 1976b, 81).[1] While a relational methodology focuses on social

---

[1] Here I refer only to the processual perspective, but do not claim that Giddens conceives of events in the way I understand them here, following Mabel Berezin's conception.

processes and their explanatory logic, it does not ignore social actors and the strategies they use to intervene in ongoing events in the social world. In contrast, with these strategies, they can '"make a difference" to a pre-existing state of affairs or course of events' (Giddens 1984, 14).[2]

Further, seeing social life simply as a *stream of events-in-process* (Giddens) or as a 'vast chaotic stream of events, which flows away through time' (Weber 1949, 111) does not help pinpoint where to start with empirically analysing strategies of social closure. Instead, such a methodological interruption of ongoing processes becomes possible by following the more recent debate about the crucial importance of *events* for analysing processes in the social world.[3] In a historical perspective, William Sewell (1996) emphasizes the *radical contingency*, which refers to the effect some events have on social change and transformation. In Sewell's sense, an event is '(1) a ramified sequence of occurrences that (2) is recognized as notable by contemporaries, and that (3) results in a durable transformation of structures' (Sewell 1996, 844).

While Sewell is without doubt the most important theorist of events in historical sociology, his approach nevertheless has rightly been criticized for abstaining from any kind of causal explanations (Patterson 2007) and for making clear that what counts as an event depends on public recognition of it (Steinmetz 2008b). Mabel Berezin (2012, 617) has referred to both of these critiques and presented a sociologically more convincing understanding of events as 'templates of possibility that collectivities experience as political facts' (Berezin 2012, 620), in the sense that they allow us to see where and when the ongoing processes in the social world take another direction, are interrupted, or actually break down while something new begins:

> *Events* are sociologically and politically important because they permit us to see relations and interconnections that speak to broader macro- and micro-level social processes. *Events* speak to collective resonance, present possibilities, and offer visions of possible paths—even if those paths are *not* pursued. *Events* make manifest what *might* happen, rather than predict what *will* happen. (Berezin 2012, 620)

---

[2] I am stressing this point because I do not follow Andrew Abbott's radical processualism, which 'begins by theorizing the making and unmaking of all these things—individuals, social entities, cultural structures, patterns of conflict—instant by instant as the social process unfolds in time. The world of the processual approach is a world of events' (Abbott 2016, ix). Further, 'the processual ontology... starts with events. Social entities and individuals are made out of that ongoing flow of events' (Abbott 2016, 200). This approach clearly reduces the social world and actors into events. I widely agree with Wilterdink's (2018) fundamental critique of this position.

[3] The strategy of analysing events in historical processes (Sewell 2005; Berezin 2012) has become one of the most fruitful in social research. It builds on and expands on a research tradition of historical sociology by social scientists such as Reinhard Bendix, Barrington Moore, Charles Tilly, Theda Skocpol, and Margaret R. Somers, among many others.

While presenting a tool for methodologically interrupting the ongoing processes in the social world, Berezin also points to the critical aspect that not everything can count as an event. Rather, 'events worthy of study force changes in collective perception. They fracture or affirm community' (Berezin 2012, 622). Referring to 9/11, she argues that this event not only altered the collective perception of security in the United States but also moved security to the centre of political debates.

In addition to claiming that *events* refer to macro- and micro-level processes and change public perception, Berezin further argues:

> Events focus our analytic attention. Events as objects of study offer methodological as well as theoretical advantages ... Events are embedded in social and political relations. Events incorporate structure and culture, institutions and actors. Events permit us to hear the voices of multiple subjects at the same time ... Political analysts must treat events *as if* they were fixed—with the full understanding that different agents might assign different possibilities to them'. (Berezin 2012, 629)

In this perspective, events can serve as tools for a methodological bracketing of the ongoing processes in the social world. However, to convincingly apply events to the new framework of closure theory, three qualifications have to be made.

First, I argue that from Berezin's conceptualization of events, no causal argument can be derived. In my view, events allow us to methodologically interrupt ongoing processes in the social world, and although they are points of reorientation or offer new perspectives, they cannot serve as the starting point of causal explanations. Such a causal argument is possible only with regard to historical processes that may have led making an event possible.

Second, while I agree with the claim that events in the historical process are templates of possibility, I argue that in social closure struggles, critical events can also be intentionally produced and set in motion by the powerful side and then be used *as if* they had simply happened.

Third, I agree with Berezin, who correctly argues that with regard to events 'different agents might assign different possibilities to them' (Berezin 2012, 629). However, we should not overlook that the way events alter public perception, the possibilities envisioned, or which interpretations of an event become dominant in the public discourse is influenced by the power asymmetries between collective actors in social closure struggles. In this context, there is no power balance.

Against the background of these qualifications, events play a critical role in the analysis of social closure, allowing us to begin the empirical analysis of relations of social closure from a starting point that can convincingly be defined as an event.

21.2 The Explanatory Model: Strategies, Mechanisms, Outcomes

A basic model of explaining social phenomena follows the sequence *strategies—mechanisms—outcomes*. This sequence allows researchers to explain how established social relations are reorganized by looking at the effects closure strategies have on dimensions of life chances / chances of survival. Reorganizing access to life chances / chances of survival as the real goal of struggles of social closure means reorganizing established social relations of exclusion, exploitation, and elimination. This is the basic model of the explanatory logic of social closure (see figure 21.1).

Figure 21.1 The explanatory logic of social closure

Following this explanatory logic in different contexts of social closure and starting from an event, the analysis of social closure follows several important steps.

First, taking *social relations* of closure as the fundamental methodological unit means that we are interested in the variety and variability of processes that reorganize relations between the excluders and the excluded, the exploiters and the exploited, and the eliminators and those threatened with elimination.

Second, we need to consider all three forms of closure as general processes rather than specific ones. Processes of exclusion, exploitation, and elimination will look different according to the social contexts in which they unfold. Specifying these *contexts* in which closure struggles unfold is critical.

Third, as contexts change, so do the critical *actors* in closure struggles—that is, the main coalitions and supporters that need to be defined to understand the critical relations from which closure strategies emerge. An empirical investigation of social closure in all three social relations of closure must specify who the powerful actors are, as well as their allies, strategic partners, collaborators, and internal/external supporters.

Fourth, to understand the variability of strategies of marginalization, extraction, and annihilation, empirical analysis needs to identify the predominant resource of power and the critical structural elements of power that social actors have to draw upon and mobilize.

Fifth, empirical analysis needs to look at variety of specific closure *strategies* that are pursued in closure struggles, as we want to explain the variability of closure. A relational explanation breaks down exclusion, exploitation, and elimination into specific strategies, mechanisms, and processes.[4]

Sixth, we must describe how the triggered *mechanisms* operate with regard to dimensions of life chances / chances of survival. Looking at the mechanism *denial of access*, this means describing how specific strategies reorganize access to resources, rights, and networks/institutions in closure struggles of exclusion, exploitation, and elimination. With respect to *intervention into community closure*, this means describing how closure strategies interrupt or prevent specific groups from closing their community, developing a political identity, and organizing to enable them to fight back in closure struggles against such strategies of exercising control (or to show how such strategies destroy existing communities). Following Neuwirth's critical arguments, closure analysis needs to show that (1) strategies of dominant communities effectively prevent the underprivileged from forming and closing their community, that (2) the denial of economic, political, and social opportunities *and* the denial of dignity and social esteem are both critical strategies to keep the less powerful in a subordinate social position, and that (3) this social status implies vulnerability, which may lead to the fact that dominant groups will regulate the affairs of the negatively privileged.

Seventh, we must keep in mind the specific interactions of the two critical mechanisms. Denying access to resources, rights, or networks/institutions necessarily already deeply impacts the dignity and self-esteem of both the individuals and social communities they target. Yet, there are also specific strategies of interfering directly in these communities to prevent them from closing their boundaries and creating solidarity, and thus exercise control over them.

Eighth, the analysis must describe *newly established arrangements of social relations* as new temporary outcomes in ongoing closure struggles of social life with regard to how the socio-economic, politico-legal, socio-structural, and socio-cultural dimensions of life chances / chances of survival are stabilized. Following Popitz, in contexts of exclusion, exploitation, and elimination we will find different processes of legitimation. In general, as Popitz has made clear, the further expansion of power is 'the generatio equivoca of the achievement of valid legitimacy' (Popitz 2017 [1986], 140), which means that this process of expanding power to achieve legitimacy is critical in social relations of exclusion, exploitation, and elimination. Yet, while these processes may be predominant, I argue that his ideas of *reciprocal recognition* and *horizontal legitimacy* among the powerful, instead of the belief in that legitimacy held by those subjected to authority, have to be seen as absolutely critical for legitimizing all forms of social closure, while the latter are reinforced by other processes.

---

[4] The logic of a relational approach to the explanation of political processes means the 'reduction of complex episodes, or certain features of those episodes, to their component mechanisms and processes' (Tilly 2008, 8).

22
Explaining Social Closure

This chapter does not offer a detailed and encompassing empirical analysis of social closure in the contexts of exclusion, exploitation, and elimination. Rather, I try to make plausible the logic of a new, explanatory analysis of social closure within specific contexts. This means that I show how the logic of explaining closure processes may be employed in empirical analyses and thus highlight strategies that can, could, or might be analysed from the perspective of my new approach to closure theory. Having outlined the critical steps of such an analysis, I discuss exclusion in the general context of neoliberalism, in particular the *politics of austerity*. I analyse *exploitation* in the general context of global capitalism, in particular within *global labour value chains*. Then I discuss *elimination* in the general context of settler colonialism, in particular the Israeli settler-colonial regime's *politics of erasure* against the Palestinian people.

22.1 Analysing and Explaining the Reorganization of Social Relations of Exclusion

Analysing exclusion as the first form of social closure addresses the strategies of highly organized and connected powerful neoliberal actors who push forward global marketization, thereby creating conditions in which the powerful have the 'freedom of the stronger to do down the weaker by following market rules' (Macpherson 2012 [1977], 1). The communication, interactions, and transactions among states, the wealthy, neoliberal think tanks (such as the Mont Pèlerin Society, the Cato Institute, the Atlas Network), and institutions of financial capital, as well as neoliberal institutions such as the World Trade Forum (WTF), International Monetary Fund (IMF), central banks, World Bank, Organization for Economic Co-operation and Development (OECD), G7, and G20 bodies have created conditions of deep inequality within and between societies. Neoliberal reorganization has caused rising rates of poverty, and, by destroying the environment and pushing for the militarization of foreign politics and geopolitics, leads to migration movements all over the world, pushing human beings into inhumane living conditions.

In pursuing strategies of *marginalization*—the basic form of exclusionary strategies—powerful neoliberal actors target social groups or communities such as social classes, women, various groups (e.g., religious, language, cultural, and ethnic), single parents, the disabled, and the chronically ill, as well as refugees, asylum seekers, and working migrants to reorganize social relations in *systems of redistribution*.

Marginalization occurs in a variety of empirical manifestations in all kinds of social arenas. Social groups are excluded from professions when their foreign degrees or diplomas are not recognized, because of their use of any kind of religious symbols or rather informal clothing habits, all the way to the formal legal decision to reduce public services and the de facto abolishment of the right to asylum in the European Union to keep asylum seekers out of the continent. In this sense, strategies of exclusion are pushing human beings to the brink.

22.1.1 Context: Neoliberalism and Marketization

Neoliberalism can be conceived of as an economic theory, a political ideology, a policy paradigm, and a social imaginary (Evans and Sewell 2013, 36; see also Centeno and Cohen 2012, 318) that has gained global dominance and hegemony as both '"a prescriptive concept that articulates a normative vision of the proper relationship between the state, capital, property and individuals" (Ganti 2014, 93) as well as "a class project, masked by a neoliberal rhetoric about individual freedom, liberty, responsibility, privatization and the free market" (Harvey 2005, 1)' (Di Feliciantonio and Aalbers 2018, 138). Following David Harvey, at the heart of neoliberalism lies *marketization* as an economic idea, an ideological project, and a political programme that pushes to transform all kinds of social relations *into* market relations. Marketization thus points to the neoliberal conviction that markets are superior—more effective and efficient—for organizing social life, allocating goods and resources, and ensuring better outcomes:

> Markets, the argument goes, are better at allocating resources and producing wealth than bureaucracies, cartels or governments. Furthermore, the global diffusion of marketization has had an impact well beyond the traditional boundaries of the economy. Marketization implies a redefinition of economic rules of the game but also a transformed perspective on states, regulation and their role. Marketization is questioning all forms of protective boundaries and barriers and having an impact, as a consequence, on social and also cultural and legal policies. (Djelic 2006, 53)

The *broad trend of marketization* (Rodrik 1996, 85) as the decisive characteristic of neoliberal globalization ranges from demands to conceive of an entire society as a system of self-regulating markets (Polanyi 2001 [1944]) to the introduction of markets or pseudo-markets into public services such as education (Crouch 2001), all the way to ideological invocations to individuals to see themselves as human capital:

> For themselves, for a business, and for a national or postnational economic constellation such as the European Union. Consumption, education, training, mate selection and more are configured as practices of self-investment where the self *is* an individual firm. (Brown, W. 2016).

Thus, in its global outreach, neoliberalism as marketization has a deep impact on every aspect of social life (Caliskan and Callon 2009). While economics claims that markets are a power-free sphere in which the *natural laws* of supply and demand, or pricing, and the same chances for everybody in the market guarantee a smoothly operating society, from the perspective of closure theory, marketization is the critical context for processes of exclusion and, consequently, for the reorganization of the social relations between the excluders and the excluded under neoliberal conditions.

The fierce struggles of exclusion that a marketization of all spheres of social life unleashes today have a historic predecessor dating back to the period before World War I, when radical liberal ideas were transformed into an ideological-political programme that pushed for the market to be seen as the organizing principle of society and consequently to transform societies into market societies. In the face of the disastrous consequences this programme had—the global economic crisis of the 1920s, political radicalism, and two World Wars—in his critique of this programme that he saw as barren of any realism, economic historian Karl Polanyi (2001 [1944]) argued in *The Great Transformation* that conceiving of societies as *self-regulating markets* necessarily neglects the character of both markets and societies. As Fred Block and Margaret R. Somers (2014, 8–11) have shown, Polanyi's analysis is based on three fundamental ideas. First, while markets are necessary, they at once pose a threat to social life and a democratic ideal. Second, the market is not an independent sphere—as liberals and neoliberals claim—but for Polanyi:

> The human economy is always and everywhere embedded in society.... By this he means that even 'free market' economies consist of cultural understandings, shared values, legal rules, and a wide range of governmental actions that make exchange possible. (Block and Somers 2014, 9)

Third, Polanyi assumes that the persistent ideology of the free market stems from the promise to roll back the influence and control of politics and the state over the lives and choices of individuals.

On this basis, Polanyi convincingly shows that experiments with free markets are extremely destructive for the social fabric of societies, as they treat land, labour, and money as commodities even though—contrary to real commodities—they have not been produced. Thus, he argues that these three factors are *fictitious commodities*:

> In other words, according to the empirical definition of a commodity they are not commodities. Labor is only another name for human activity which goes with life itself, which in its turn is not produced for sale but for entirely different reasons, nor can that activity be detached from the rest of life, be stored or mobilized; land is only another name for nature, which is not produced by man; actual money, finally, is merely a token of purchasing power which, as a rule, is not produced at all, but comes into being through the mechanism of banking or state finance. None of them is produced for sale. The commodity description of labor, land, and money is entirely fictitious. (Polanyi, 2001 [1944], 75–76)

During the last decades, neoliberalism has carried the commodification of these factors, essential for the reproduction of both social relations and societies, to the extreme. With regard to land, large-scale processes of *land grabbing* (Liberti 2013) and the transformation of the city into neoliberal spaces of speculation (Brenner and Theodore 2002; Theodore, Peck, and Brenner 2011; Wolf and Mackert 2020) are critical. With regard to labour, as will become clear in the following sub-chapter on exploitation, similar processes are at work because global capital has generated a new global division of labour with extreme exploitation and conditions of slavery mainly, but not exclusively, in the Global South. Finally, there is financialization. Without doubt, the ever-expanding liberalization of the financial sector since the 1980s is the most important aspect of these profound constructions of fictitious commodities. The willingness of states to free up money and liberalize capital controls (Helleiner 1994) profoundly transformed the global economy in such a way that ultimately led to the global economic crisis in 2008 at the expense of nation-states and their citizens. Strangely enough, even after the dot-com crisis in March 2000 and, more importantly, after the global banking crisis of September 2008, neoliberalism is still with us; it has survived (Crouch 2011; Mirowski 2013; Streeck 2014).

Although Polanyi delivered this highly sophisticated and convincing analysis of both the development and the consequences of free market strategies for modern societies with great conviction, his prediction that global economic crises, two World Wars, and the experience of fascist regimes would end all further experiments with free and unregulated markets unfortunately did not hold true. After four decades of intensified marketization, which began in the

1980s with the erosion of the Keynesian post–World War model of organizing and regulating national economies, we now see the repercussions of attempts to turn societies into self-regulating markets—today in their *neo*liberal form. These repercussions include deep global economic crises, extreme social inequalities, and right-wing, populist, and outright fascist movements.[1]

After decades of pushing the neoliberalization of the social forward, we again face the scenario of *market fundamentalism* (Block and Somers 2014). What began in Great Britain and the United States in the 1970s has developed into a global political-economic regime: 'When the Reagan administration took control of Washington, it quickly tried to fashion the IMF and the World Bank into what Joseph Stiglitz has called "missionary institutions" for neo-liberalism' (Evans and Sewell Jr., 2013, 45). In 1989, the deployment of these two international institutions led to what has been called the *Washington Consensus*, namely an orthodox neoliberal programme that completely reorganized financial aid for developing countries or countries in need of credit. Any support now depended on programmes of *structural adjustments* in these countries that included strict neoliberal political measures, such as the following:

> Fiscal discipline; a redirection of public expenditure, priorities toward fields offering both high economic returns and the potential to improve income distribution such as primary health care, primary education, and infrastructure; tax reform (to lower marginal rates and broaden the tax base); interest rate liberalisation; a competitive exchange rate; trade liberalisation; liberalisation of inflows of foreign direct investment; privatisation; deregulation (to abolish barriers to entry and exit); and finally, secure property rights.
> (Williamson, 1999)

While all such policy prescriptions indeed seem to propagate a complete renunciation of regulations to *deregulate* and *set free* the economy, this is not what is really meant. What neoliberal apologists of the market actually want to see deregulated are established social arrangements of citizenship, relations, and contracts in the economy, democratic accountability in politics, or security for

---

[1] Radical marketization has further brought forth what Polanyi called a *countermovement*: that is, measures taken by society to protect itself from the disastrous consequences of the free market dystopia. On the one hand, such movements may be progressive in counteracting economic disasters with inclusive politics, but on the other hand, they can also be regressive, as was the case in Europe in the 1930s when it drowned in fascism and National Socialism as political and social catastrophes. Experiments with free markets are thus not only out of touch with reality, but such attempts negate the essence of the social and are the greatest risk to a functioning democratic society and the survival of humanity. This important aspect of Polanyi's analysis cannot be developed here. However, the rise of fascist movements and neofascist political parties in Europe proves that he was correct in his analysis of the destructiveness of societies as self-regulating markets and the possibility of reactionary and fascist countermovements.

citizens in the social sphere, which are all achievements of Keynesian *embedded liberalism* (Ruggie 1982). Thus, they denounce government involvement in taxes and the regulation of labour relations, governments forcing enterprises to contribute to health insurance schemes, and costly welfare programmes. Ordinary citizens should no longer be protected against risks in social life, unacceptable working conditions, old-age poverty, environmental pollution, and so forth. Yet, while citizens in fact should be exposed to market dynamics without any protective regulations, the demands of neoliberals for the corporate sector look very different. Especially for financial capital that since the 1990s has risen to become the most important element of neoliberalism's global marketization, 'politicians established a new set of rules that provided government protection for the financial sector' (Block and Somers 2014, 9–10). Instead of using the term *de*regulation, marketization is thus better described as what Block and Somers call *re*regulation:

> By the term *reregulation* ... we aim to push back against the belief that the success of neoliberal ideology since the mid-1970s has been matched by markets being increasingly freed from regulations and government management. On the contrary, regulations did not go away; they simply changed. Those that had previously been written to protect employees or consumers were systematically rewritten to support business interests and reduce previous restrictions on business practices. (Block and Somers 2014, 20; emphasis added)

Rather than arguing for a retreat of the state,[2] in neoliberalism the economy and the state have become ever more intertwined, the state protecting the *free* economy with rules, regulations, protective tariffs, subsidies, and so on. Against all neoliberal *free market propaganda*, there is no longer such a market for corporate business. Fred Block and Matthew R. Keller (2011) coined the term *state of innovation* to capture this neoliberal reality and argued that many industrial sectors do not show Adam Smith's *invisible hand* of the market, but instead the *invisible hand of government* (Block 2011, 1). It is not a free market but state subsidies, state investments, and taxes and tariffs on competing industries from abroad that have always been part of neoliberal politics—even under the signpost of *free trade* areas.

Thus, lifting the ideological veil of neoliberalism just a little reveals what lies behind the claims of marketization in all social spheres and its aggressive promotion. This closer examination shows an extreme power asymmetry in a field

---

[2] In the 1990s, scholars of international political economy and international relations were at the forefront in arguing that the state was and should be in retreat. See Strange 1995, 1996; Stopford and Strange 1991; Cox 1986; Cable 1995; Del Rosso Jr. 1995; Deudney 1995; Schmidt 1995.

where power is supposedly irrelevant. As highly organized neoliberal social actors have succeeded in making the state an instrument for their advantage (see Harvey 2005), this neoliberal politico-economic elite has created protections for *free markets* and *free enterprise* that guarantee their wealth, while ordinary citizens face increasing risks as they are exposed to market forces due to marketization and privatization in critical fields such as education, health, housing, insurance, and pensions. Thus, marketization describes the context in which various processes and strategies reorganize the social relations of exclusion. The highly organized and state-protected wealthy and politico-economic elites are on the side of the excluders, while ordinary citizens and non-citizens are on the side of the excluded.

22.1.2 Event and Principal Strategy

Exclusion in neoliberalism is a consequence of an ongoing process of marketization of all kinds of social relations. While this process has been underway for decades, it was radicalized in the period following the *banking crisis* in 2008/2009, which I take as the *event* that served as a *template of possibility* (Berezin) for highly organized neoliberal elites to envisage new options for themselves. In the crisis, they aimed for an intensified reorganization of the social relations of the excluders and the excluded, privileging the powerful, who could further reorganize an already marketized social life, shift state-society relations, reinforce neoliberal governance, and increase competition in society in coordinated action against the less powerful, who found themselves even more excluded.

While this is not the place to discuss in detail the reasons for the banking crisis in 2008/2009, it makes sense to take a brief look at its historical, institutional, and actor-centred causes. From a historical perspective, Block has applied a neo-Polanyian framework, arguing that, as in the 1930s, the 2008/2009 crisis 'can only be understood as the confluence of three distinct factors—longstanding global imbalances, a disruptive financial mechanism, and deep structural problems in the world's largest economy—the United States' (Block 2015, 366). Yet, Block also argues that this time policymakers 'were able to halt the economic downturn by aggressive policies of economic stimulus including flooding the global economy with liquidity' (Block, 2015, 376), a policy they themselves abandoned by taking up politics of austerity. With regard to the medium-term, rather institutional perspective, James Crotty has added that 'although problems in the US subprime mortgage market triggered the current financial crisis, its deep cause on the financial side is to be found in the flawed institutions and practices of the current financial regime, often referred to as the New Financial Architecture (NFA)' (Crotty 2009, 564), arguing that the 'deregulation and the globalisation of financial markets, combined with the rapid pace of financial innovation and the moral hazard caused by frequent government bailouts helped to create conditions that led to this devastating financial crisis' (Crotty 2009, 575).

Finally, in an immediate, rather actor-centred perspective, John Coffee Jr. (2009) has identified three critical aspects that led to the bursting of market bubbles and consequently to a major financial crisis. Besides investors recognizing a systematic failure by a critical institutional actor—in the case of the 2008 crisis, credit rating agencies—and fundamental managerial failures, a third critical aspect

> is a significant regulatory failure. This is virtually definitional, because if regulators had performed adequately the crisis would have been averted or contained. In the case of the current crisis, a critical deregulatory step was taken in 2004 when the Securities and Exchange Commission (SEC) relaxed its rules, possibly unintentionally, so as to largely eliminate the ceiling on the maximum leverage that major investment banks could utilize. This relaxation was quickly exploited by the subject firms, who had lobbied for this change and who uniformly increased their leverage in its wake. As a direct result, three of the largest US investment banks—Bear Stearns, Merrill Lynch & Co, and Lehman Brothers—became effectively insolvent in 2008. (Coffee Jr. 2009, 3)

What followed was a wave of bank nationalizations in North America and Europe (Barrell and Davis 2008), bailouts of these banks, and the shifting of private debts to societies, leading to a sovereign debt crisis by turning 'a lending crisis into a spending crisis' (Blyth 2014). With these decisions, amid the deepest crisis of the neoliberal model, its politico-economic-financial elites proved powerful enough to even radicalize their politics in their own favour at the cost of ordinary people—citizens and non-citizens.

In the European Union (EU), the so-called rescue programmes for the banks were implemented by the infamous Troika—the International Monetary Fund (IMF), the EU Commission, and the European Central Bank—a new body that was neither democratically elected nor legitimized. Rather, in a coup-like move this body demanded from European states that they radically reduce public spending by cutting down on employment, salaries, and pensions in the public sector and marketize them for financial actors such as hedge funds or financial investors, or even banks themselves again. Consequently, many goods and resources have become the subject of closure struggles leading to an extreme redistribution of wealth in these societies. Thus, the decision to implement *politics of austerity*—a radical programme of marketization—emerged as the most important strategy with which to forge ahead with the reorganization of the social relations between the excluders and the excluded. Yet, why is austerity so critical from the perspective of analysing and explaining processes of exclusion?

Austerity can be defined as 'a form of voluntary deflation in which the economy adjusts through the reduction of wages, prices and public spending to restore competitiveness, which is (supposedly) best achieved by cutting the state's budgets, debts and deficits' (Blyth 2013a, 2; Hayes 2017, 21). Given the dramatic results of the failure of financial capitalism and the irresponsible behaviour of the banking sector, neoliberal elites and governments were quick to deliberately transform private debts into public ones (Crouch 2011; Blyth 2013a; Mirowski 2013; Gualerzi 2017) to rescue those who had failed in the market. The proponents and advocates of this policy then imposed the harshest possible neoliberal austerity against citizens, which, according to Richard Seymour, can be characterized by seven aspects: first, a rebalancing of the economy from wage-led to finance-led growth; second, a redistribution of income from wage earners to capital; third, a promotion of *precarity* in all areas of life as a disciplinary mechanism and a means to reinforce the financialization of everyday life; fourth, a recomposition of social classes featuring increasing inequality in income and wealth and greater stratification within classes; fifth, a facilitation of the penetration of the state by corporations; sixth, an acceleration of the turn from a Keynesian welfare state based in shared citizenship rights to a workfare regime that relies on coercion, casual sadism, and, especially in the United States, penalties; and seventh, a promotion of the values of hierarchy and competition (see Seymour 2014, 2–4).[3]

As sceptical scholars such as Marc Blyth (2013a; 2013b) have shown, such *politics of austerity* are contra-productive and of a sort to further aggravate the situation rather than solve the crisis. According to Isabel Ortiz et al. (2015, 18), 'Numerous studies highlight the fallacious basis of austerity programs' (Center for Social and Economic Rights 2012; ILO 2012; 2014a; Krugman 2012; Stiglitz 2014; UNCTAD 2011; United Nations 2013; OHCHR 2013; Weisbrot and Jorgensen 2013; Salmon 2017). 'In the short term, austerity depresses incomes and hinders domestic demand, harming economic activity and employment and ultimately undermining recovery efforts. In the long term, as unemployment

---

[3] 'In other words, austerity demands the cutting or capping of the wage bill, rationalizing and/or further targeting social safety nets, reforming old-age pensions, labour flexibilization reforms, increasing consumption taxes on goods and services, privatization of public assets and services, and finally healthcare system reforms' (Ortiz et al. 2015, 12–13).

and excess capacity persist, potential output may decrease' Ortiz et al. (2015, 18). Thus, austerity is unmasked as simply being a highly ideological tool that does not operate in ways that solve the crisis as neoliberal elites 'explained' to their citizens. Nevertheless, their core argument described all these measures as *inevitable* and *without any alternative* (Callinicos 2012; Farnsworth and Irving 2018; Clark and Newman 2012). In this sense

> in the period since the Wall Street crash, the refurbished rationale for austerity measures is that the imposition of strict fiscal discipline and government spending cuts is the (only) way to restore budgetary integrity—thereby securing the confidence of the investor class, appeasing the jittery markets and paving the way to growth. The critical test case that is Europe, of course, shows no signs of working. (Peck 2012, 626)

Against this background, I argue that austerity is a package of strategies of marginalization by the powerful in daily closure struggles. Of course, while global neoliberal elites used the event itself—the breakdown of the neoliberal banking and credit system—to implement these strategies of marketization, the elites' *politics of austerity,* far from solving the global economic crisis, imposed various measures on citizens and non-citizens in Western liberal welfare states and put millions of human beings into misery. Thus, instead of being an unavoidable cure of the misery, the *politics of austerity*, from the perspective of closure theory, are nothing but a radical reorganization of the social relations between the excluders and the excluded that pushes the latter to the fringes.[4] Global neoliberal actors' ability to impose these strategies of marketization upon ordinary citizens and non-citizens makes explicit that their high degree of organization is critical for their creation of highly favourable opportunity structures for themselves by drawing upon the relevant structural elements of power and mobilizing them to safeguard their own life chances / chances of survival at the expense of the less organized and thus less powerful.

---

[4] Since the 1970s, in order to 'fight' the debt crisis of countries in the Global South and later reinforced by the Washington Consensus, both the IMF and World Bank demanded in return for granting loans to countries in financial need the implementation of so-called 'structural adjustment programmes' that have simply been a strategy to push through processes of marketization in these countries. As is well known, while these demands to open these countries' markets served the interests of powerful economic actors in the Global North to make profits, within those countries they created processes of radical marginalization by destroying local markets, pushing ordinary people to the edges and triggering extreme poverty. Against this experience, we know today that the Troika's 'rescue programmes' after the banking crisis in 2008/2009 simply imposed this destructive programme of marginalization on so-called developed countries of the Global North—under the label of austerity.

22.1.3 Mobilizing Predominantly Politico-Legal Structural Elements of Power

Strategies of global neoliberal politico-economic elites to reorganize social relations of exclusion are based predominantly on their ability to mobilize structural elements of politico-legal power: (1) the temporal-spatial organization of social interaction, (2) the organization and relations of human beings in society-like class relations, and (3) the states' or, for example, the European Union's legal ordering and backing of these strategies.

These highly abstract notions of structural elements need to be clarified and made plausible for the purpose of analysing marginalization in the context of austerity politics. First, the reorganization of the temporal-spatial organization of social interaction in contexts of austerity politics actually refers to any kind of social relations, due to efforts to marketize all spheres of society. This ranges from the reordering of job and workplace conditions by creating huge numbers of atypical occupations and part-time jobs and demanding flexible working times, to prioritizing the city as a place of investment and speculation, triggering processes such as gentrification that leads to the displacement of local residents, as well as the reorganization of private lives, demanding ever more flexibility from people as a precondition of realizing themselves as human capital, thereby reorganizing if not destroying social interactions within families, social groups, and communities.

Second, the reorganization of the production and reproduction of the human body refers to the dominant relations of exclusion in society, such as class relations; the relations between insiders and outsiders linked to gender, race, religion, or ethnicity; or between the rich and the poor. These aspects are critical, since the neoliberal reorganization of societies has radically increased the gap between the wealthy and the poor on national, regional, and global levels; it is forcing people into precariousness, marginalizing them.

Third, the role of the neoliberal state is critical—even more than in the time of the Fordist regime, because in neoliberalism, a reorganized neoliberal elite is able to issue new directives and introduce a new model of redistribution and consequently hegemonic ideas of *valuable* and *valueless* human beings (Mavelli 2022), as became obvious following events such as the 2008/2009 banking crisis and the Covid pandemic. Intertwined neoliberal politico-economic-financial elites' decisions were simply put into law and codified, thereby turning their interests into authoritative rules of society (Vogl 2015), strengthening the rights of the powerful to possess property and invest, or turning social life into markets—all liberal values advantaging the powerful while the rest is marginalized in temporal and spatial terms.

Of course, in struggles of exclusion, besides these most critical politico-legal structural elements of power, all other structural elements play a role as well. As will become clear, the ideological element of neoliberalism plays a vital role in pushing ahead and legitimizing these processes of reorganization. Of course, military and police power is also essential, as we witnessed in the crackdown on demonstrations against the European Union's austerity dictate in the case of Greece, which has impoverished large parts of the Greek population, and in the violent protection of banks' property in Spain and in the United States (Eviction Lab 2022) when police evicted residents from their homes.

22.1.4 The *Politics of Austerity* as a Strategy of Social Closure: Processes and Mechanisms

Turning to the core of explanation and conceiving of the neoliberal *politics of austerity* as a strategy of *marginalization*, we now need to look more closely at its various dimensions and aspects by analysing how strategies of *commodification/financialization, shifting, de-universalization,* and *de-solidarization* operate, triggering the mechanisms *denial of access* and *intervention into community closure* with regard to the different dimensions of life chances / chances of survival.

Neoliberal elites' efforts to advance marketization in all areas of social life should not obscure the fact that none of these strategies would be possible without the state, or in the case of Europe, states together with the European Union, in the driver's seat. Only the mobilization of politico-legal structural elements of power enables the strategies of marginalization to be pushed through. Closure analyses, therefore, need to concentrate on either the state's or the European Union's critical role in reorganizing the social relations of the excluders and the excluded under conditions of neoliberalism in general, austerity in particular. It is *state-led* strategies that are important here, with serious consequences regarding any of the four dimensions of life chances / chances of survival for ordinary citizens and non-citizens. With regard to (1) *resources,* marginalization results from turning resources into commodities that can be financialized to make a profit, while at the same time denying the excluded access to vital resources; (2) with regard to *rights,* political decision-making is shifted from citizens as voters to the market and thus to powerful oligarchic actors; (3) with regard to *networks/institutions,* the de-universalizing of the access to public services and critical structures for integration is essential; (4) with regard to targeted *communities,* who shall be prevented from developing a common identity that would allow them to act in solidarity, marketization's desolidarizing of social communities, replacing collective relations with radically individualized market relations that allow individuals to be made responsible for social risks, is crucial.

In contrast to neoliberal politico-economic elites' ideological claim of austerity being without any alternative and thus unavoidable, from the perspective of closure theory, the *politics of austerity* are a state-led programme of favouring the wealthy while destroying the social fabric of societies. Warren Buffett has put it very bluntly: 'There's class warfare, all right ... but it's my class, the rich class, that's making war, and we're winning' (Stein 2006). *Explaining* the strategies of this war of exclusion is the task of closure analysis, and they all must be analysed according to the same explanatory logic (see figure 22.1).

Commodification/Financialization

Commodification/Financialization, the first aspect of a politics of austerity as a strategy of marginalization, refers to the fundamental aspect of marketization that turns resources into commodities that can be financialized and traded on markets to make a profit. Closure theory is interested in the dynamics of marketization in the form of a politics of austerity that, by pushing ahead the commodification of critical resources, has stressed the dual character of use value/ exchange value as the critical process triggering the mechanisms *denial of access* and *intervention into community closure* so as to marginalize ordinary people.

Given that housing is a vital and indispensable resource for human beings to earn a living and is thus a basis for actually participating in social struggles of daily life, I look closer at this resource to understand how neoliberal elites' strategies trigger the mechanism *denial of access*, preventing ordinary citizens and non-citizens from making use of it. The commodification of housing has turned it into a *central aspect of financialization* (Aalbers, 2017, 542; Schönig and Schipper 2016) that plays a crucial role in the global neoliberal political economy—without losing its significance for ordinary citizens and non-citizens as a vital resource in daily life. This fundamental contradiction that lies at the heart of the reorganization of the social relations between the excluders and the excluded in closure struggles stems from the *dual nature* of housing as a commodity as well as a resource. While as a resource housing has thus a *use value* for ordinary citizens and non-citizens as either house or flat owners or tenants of public homes or privately rented flats and houses, it is a financialized commodity at the same time and thus simply has *exchange value* for the neoliberal elite (Alexandri and Janoschka 2018; Christophers 2010). The dominance of housing as exchange value in financialized neoliberal capitalism means that ordinary citizens and non-citizens face powerful neoliberal actors whose strategies of marginalization trigger the mechanism *denial of access*, which operates in a way that deprives the people of a basic resource, turning housing and the urban space as a whole into spaces of investment and return via a kind of *winner-take-all*

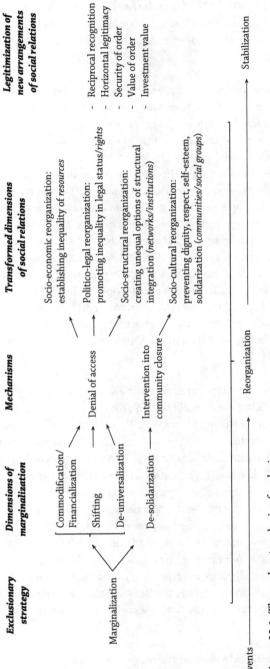

Figure 22.1 The explanatory logic of exclusion

urbanism (Florida 2017, 13).[5] From the perspective of closure theory, this direct connection is decisive, as it allows us to explain how financialization as a strategy of marginalization leads to homelessness, housing evictions, a socio-spatial division of cities, and poverty:

> Across the globe, the greatest challenge to the realization of the right to housing by 2030 [i.e., a guaranteed access to this basic resource—J.M.] is posed by the unprecedented dominance of financial corporations in the housing sector ... Historic, structural changes in housing and financial markets and global investment have occurred in recent years. Rather than being valued as a place to live in a community, *housing has become a commodity to be bought and sold for profit, valued as security for financial instruments that are traded in global markets and treated as a means to accumulate massive wealth for a few, while rendering housing unaffordable for others.* These global challenges to the human right to housing are generally referred to as the 'financialization of housing'. The term refers to the way capital investment in housing increasingly disconnects housing from its social function of providing a place to live, to the way housing and financial markets are oblivious to the role housing plays in the well-being of people and communities. In short, the financialization of housing stands in direct opposition to the idea that housing, as a human right, is linked to personal dignity, security and the ability to thrive in communities. (Farha and Porter 2017)

While neoliberal elites' strategies of financializing housing were causally responsible for the banking crisis in 2008/2009, they were powerful enough not to *let a serious crisis go to waste* (Mirowski 2013). After they had created a housing bubble that led to the indebtedness of millions of people, plunging them into misery and destroying their life chances / chances of survival for the elites' own profit, their high degree of organization allowed them to use the banking crisis as a *template of possibility* and finally even claim repossession (Cano Fuentes et al. 2013). As a highly organized and dense network in the global political economy, global financial institutions, hedge funds, banks, private equity firms, rating institutions, nation-states, the European Union and the European Central Bank, and international neoliberal organizations such as the IMF, the World Bank, and the OECD pushed through the *politics of austerity*, imposing a 'solution' on ordinary citizens and non-citizens that was simply more of what had caused the disaster, thus adding fuel to the fire. Valesca Lima has shown that

---

[5] See di Feliciantonio and Aalbers 2018 for an interesting analysis of the prehistories of neoliberal housing policies in Italy and Spain; see also HRW (Human Rights Watch) 2014 for an analysis of the impact of the housing crisis on vulnerable groups in Spain.

the responses to the crisis were focused on trends of privatization of public spaces and the process of financialization of housing, shaped by a for-profit logic, with weakened rental protections, shortage of affordable housing and the transformation of housing into a financial asset (Fields and Uffer 2016). Housing as a commodity reflects a new paradigm based on the retreat of the state from direct housing provision and the enactment of policies the (sic!) creates strong ties between governments and market-based models of finance (Rolnik 2013; Kitchin et al. 2012; Alexandri and Janoschka 2018; Norris and Fahey 2011). The growing influence of financial actors in government policies has led to deep transformations in the economy, where housing finance systems have important complementarities with the large economy (Schwartz and Seabrooke 2009). This linkage was previously facilitated by access to credit for home purchase but currently it is the financial market who occupy an increasingly dominant position in the economy (Aalbers 2008). (Lima 2020, 2–3)[6]

The critical role of the financialization of housing in the global economy becomes obvious when looking at the huge sums involved. According to the Savills World Research Forum (2016), 'Worldwide real estate assets comprise nearly 60% of the value of all global assets, including equities, bonds and gold'. Amounting to about US $217 trillion, it is obvious that 'housing is at the centre of an historic structural transformation in global investment and the economies of the industrialized world with profound consequences for those in need for adequate housing' (United Nations 2017) (see table 22.1).

This financial power shows not only that the financialization of housing has become a dominant profit-generating strategy in global financial neoliberalism, but no less that this ongoing and radicalized process of making the exchange value of housing dominant is a critical element of the politics of austerity that needs to be protected at any price. Thus, state- and EU-backed profit-protecting and -guaranteeing measures allowed global financial actors to profit from the crisis, which had

> created *unprecedented opportunities* for buying distressed housing and real estate debt, which was sold off at fire sale prices in countries such as Ireland, Spain, the United Kingdom of Great Britain and Northern Ireland and the United States of America. The Blackstone Group, the world's largest real estate private equity firm, managing $102 billion worth of property, spent $10 billion to purchase repossessed properties in the United States of America at courthouses and in online auctions following the 2008 financial crisis,

---

[6] For similar proposals in the EU Commission paper *Rental Market Regulation in the European Union*, see Cuerpo, Kalantaryan, and Pontuch 2014, 17.

Table 22.1 Real Estate Assets

Asset (values in US$ trillions – rounded)	Investable (trillions)	Non-investable (trillions)	All (trillions)
All Real Estate	$81	$136	$217
Residential	$54	$108	$162
High Quality, Global, Commercial	$19	$10	$29
Agricultural Land	$8	$18	$26
Other Investments			$155
Equities	$55		$55
Outstanding Securitised Debts	$94		$94
All Gold Ever Mined			$6
Global Mainstream Asset Universe			$372

Source: Savills World Research Forum (2016) referring to Savills World Research, Bank for International Settlements, Dow Jones Total Stock Market Index, Oxford Economics

emerging as the largest rental landlord in the country (Beswick et al. 2016, 323–325). Other major institutional players invested $20 billion to purchase approximately 200,000 single-family homes in the United States between 2012 and mid-2013 (Right to the City Alliance 2014). With the recovery of the United States housing market, Blackstone and other private equity firms have sought to take advantage of other buying opportunities in Europe and Asia. Cushman and Wakefield estimated that there was over €541 billion of distressed real estate debt in Europe in 2015, much of it held by public asset management companies such as the National Asset Management Agency in Ireland and the Sociedad de Gestión de Activos Procedentes de la Reestructuración Bancaria (company for the management of assets proceeding from the restructuring of the banking system) in Spain. The vast majority of that debt is being purchased by giant private equity firms. (Debt and Development Coalition Ireland 2017, 9; UN 2017, 8–9; emphasis added and references inserted)

From the perspective of social closure, commodification in general, and specifically neoliberal elites' strategy of financialization, reveals that the 'main substantive achievement of neoliberalization . . . has been to redistribute, rather than to generate, wealth and income' (Harvey 2005, 159). In particular, 'paradigmatic changes in housing (Rolnik 2013) are tantamount to a redistribution of wealth and debt' (Cooper and Paton 2018, 75) as the financialization of housing connects directly growing wealth on the side of the excluders with growing marginalization, misery, and poverty on the side of the excluded—moderate- or low-income households and the poor (Desmond 2016).

Financialization is a strategy of marginalization, since 'with an increased exposure to the financial market, austerity-driven welfare reforms have resulted in the transference of debt to the individual' (Cooper and Paton 2021, 588) and led to millions of ordinary people who either cannot pay their rent or cannot service their loans and are therefore threatened by foreclosures or evictions (see Toussaint and Betavatzi 2021). Financialization thus created a situation that prolongs, intensifies, and radicalizes our *age of evictions and expulsions* (see Sassen 2014a).

Evictions are the immediate effect of the financialization of housing as a strategy of marginalization, as it triggers the mechanism *denial of access* to housing as a resource, destroying ordinary peoples' life chances / chances of survival. As a matter of fact, in recent years evictions have become one of the most pressing social issues in contemporary capitalism, with rising numbers in the global North and global South (Soederberg 2018, 286).[7] Household evictions in Europe among both homeowners and tenants have become a social epidemic, having an enormous impact on ordinary citizens and non-citizens:

> Eviction is one of the worst forms of violence that can afflict someone. It is not one of life's ups and downs; it is a mark of infamy inflicted by society through institutions such as the police force and the legal system. Eviction is not only a punishment, it is a collective abandonment of other people; *prioritising one individual's right to own property over another individual's most basic needs.* (FEANTSA & Abbé Pierre Foundation 2017, 82; emphasis added)[8]

The intrinsic link between the exchange value *and* use value of housing and thus the immediate consequences of the financialization of housing becomes obvious here. In a situation of global economic crisis with stagnating incomes and high rates of unemployment in which huge numbers of citizens and non-citizens could not and cannot pay mortgages and rents, evictions and dispossessions have risen dramatically (Cooper and Paton 2021).[9] The state's role is critical here, in this closure struggle, as allowing the financialization of housing, establishing various legal repossession frameworks that prioritise ownership (Paton and Cooper

---

[7] Of course, evictions are not simply a problem of Western societies resulting from measures taken after the banking crisis of 2008/2009.

[8] See UN HABITAT & OHCHR 2014 for a critical view of forced evictions from the perspective of international law and human rights.

[9] While Hartman and Robinson already in 2003 had addressed the problem of housing evictions after the imposition of the politics of austerity, Desmond argued that 'eviction is perhaps the most understudied process effecting the lives of the urban poor' (Desmond 2012, 90). Yet, still in 2021, Cooper and Paton (2021) expressed their surprise when they noticed an ongoing lack of academic interest in this critical development.

2016), backing strategies of financial capital, selling publicly owned housing to funds, and, finally, violently evicting people from their homes with the help of the police all show that we are dealing with state-led evictions (Cooper and Paton 2018) dependent on the mobilization of structural elements of politico-legal power, yet also of structural elements of military/violence. At the same time, we see that this state-backed and state-protected finance-led capitalism in the context of a politics of austerity has led to new urban displacements (Walks and Soederberg 2021). The intimate relation between the state (or the EU) and (financial) capital thus creates a dynamic that fundamentally reorganizes the social relations of exclusion. It does so by a fundamental shift that, by protecting private property at the expense of ordinary citizens and non-citizens, not only exposes the latter to the threat of being evicted but also leaves them indebted. Meanwhile, neoliberal elites profit from what has been called *accumulation by dispossession* (Harvey 2003), a process that has become virulent in Europe but also around the world. Looking at both sides of the effects of evictions, Vickie Cooper and Kristeen Paton have argued that they are critical 'not only due to how prolific and everyday evictions are, but also because of their centrality in the functioning of the contemporary global political economy. The growth in evictions through the marketization of housing, rent and debt has seen them become a key site of capital accumulation and profit' (Cooper and Paton 2021, 597).

Thus, the Human Rights Council in the United Nations General Assembly has made clear looking at Western societies that in

> "hedge cities" housing prices have increased to levels that most residents cannot afford, creating huge increases in wealth for property owners in prime locations while excluding moderate- and low-income households from access to homeownership or rentals due to unaffordability. Those households are pushed to peri-urban areas with scant employment and services... Elsewhere financialization is linked to expanded credit and debt taken on by individual households made vulnerable to predatory lending practices and the volatility of markets, the result of which is unprecedented housing precarity. Financialized housing markets have caused displacement and evictions at an unparalleled scale: in the United States of America over the course of 5 years, over 13 million foreclosures resulted in more than 9 million households being evicted (Sassen 2014b, 5–6)... There were almost 1 million foreclosures between 2009 and 2012 in Hungary (Sassen 2014a, 48). (United Nations 2017, 3–4; references inserted)

These numbers of evictions vary according to the respective welfare state system, policies pursued, or resistance organized, but they are rising everywhere. From 2000 to 2018, in the United States an average of 3.6 million eviction cases were filed each year (Garnham, Gershenson, and Desmond 2022; The Eviction Lab 2022; Gromis et al. 2022; National Low Income Housing Commission 2022). In England, 'new government figures released today reveal that as the cost-of-living crisis bites, 3,405 households in the private rented sector were evicted by bailiffs in England between April and June 2022—up 39% on the previous quarter' (Shelter 2022), while governmental figures also 'show that during April–June, there were 5,788 accelerated claims made as a result of a Section 21 "no fault eviction". This led to 1,651 no fault evictions—a 52% increase in just three months—and continues to highlight the growing turbulence for renters in the private sector' (Crisis 2022).

In EU countries, official, reliable, and comparable data on household evictions is rarely available. However, there are hints and figures of similar processes triggering the mechanism *denial of access* to housing. In France, we can observe a decades-long rise in evictions of more than 123,000 in 2016, mainly caused by rising rents. 'The number of forced evictions (actual evictions, with the police in attendance) has also risen, now standing at more than 13,000 a year' (European Action Coalition for the Right to Housing and to the City 2016, 45–46). Homeowners are less threatened, as they are better protected legally than tenants.

In Germany, on 22 November 2022, public and private broadcasters[10] announced the collapse of social housing construction in Germany, with almost 70% of planned projects put into question because of inflation and rising interest rates and energy costs in the face of indebted public budgets. A further rise in evictions will therefore not be compensated by social housing and access to this vital resource. This is only bad news for the rising numbers of people and families who have faced evictions or been threatened with eviction in recent years. However, although Germany is still considered a functioning welfare state:

> There are no official numbers on evictions nor on eviction notices for the entirety of Germany. Estimates are 33,000 cases of forced eviction annually, and 53,000 households moving before the actual eviction takes place. In Berlin, around 10,000 new court cases are started annually, and between 5000 and 7000 eviction notices are sent out. (European Action Coalition for the Right to Housing and to the City 2016, 46)

In Greece, up to 30% of the people are living in conditions of extreme poverty, as 'housing costs have risen from 67% [of an earner's income] in 2009 to 95% in 2013', exposing them to the threat of being evicted and becoming homeless (European Action Coalition for the Right to Housing and to the City 2016, 46). The millionfold destruction of the life chances / chances of survival of ordinary

---

[10] Among them ARD, ZDF, Bayrischer Rundfunk, Pro 7, and Deutsche Welle.

citizens and non-citizens caused by the Troika-imposed politics of austerity—under the guidance of Germany and France—becomes particularly obvious, as the Troika was powerful enough to

> demand legislative changes to benefit the banks, notably changes in the Katseli law (which was put in place to limit the eviction of insolvent households by seizing their main residence for unpaid debts) (Gotev 2019). In February 2019, for example, the Eurogroup had openly threatened Greece with no interest payments on its ECB-held debt in exchange for a tough reform of the Katseli law. It eventually underwent numerous reforms to the benefit of the banks, facilitating foreclosures. (Toussaint and Betavatzi 2021)

In Ireland, in the first six months of 2022, the 'number of termination notices issued by landlords to tenants, as notified to the Residential Tenancies Board, rose by 58 per cent . . . compared to the previous six months' (Wilson 2022). In response to the Irish rental crisis, the Irish cabinet approved a temporary eviction ban for six months lasting until the end of April 2023 (Phelan 2022), which protected residential tenants from receiving eviction notices through the winter. However, 'there are some exceptions regarding tenants who damage properties or who fail to pay agreed rent. In cases where the tenant is at fault, the tenancy can be terminated during the winter, subject to the usual notice periods to be given' (Heaney 2022). This policy was simply a temporary political measure, but it revealed fundamental problems. After the banking crisis, the subsequent economic crisis, and the imposition of ruinous politics of austerity in recent years, these problems have become more apparent:

> 24% of owner-occupier mortgages have been defaulted on, rising to 36% for buy-to-let mortgages. This includes both mortgages in arrears and those that have since been restructured, often in an unsustainable short-term fashion. Evictions have so far been kept low, partially as a result of these restructurings, but there has been a significant increase in the amount of legal proceedings in the last two years, rising from approximately 300 a quarter in 2012 to over 3000 a quarter in 2014. (European Action Coalition for the Right to Housing and to the City 2016, 47)

In Portugal, in '2011 and 2012, around 12,500 homes were seized by banks, leading to widespread evictions. In the rental market in the first 4 months of 2013 there were 1,289 procedures for eviction. There is a shift to withdraw from the jurisdiction of the courts by assigning more power to new administrative entities; in 2014 the fiscal arm of the state auctioned 5,849 family homes' (European Action Coalition for the Right to Housing and to the City 2016, 49–50). Although the United Nations welcomed Portugal's new basic housing law that entered into force on 1 October 2019, celebrating it as a milestone for the implementation of the right to housing in the country (OHCHR 2019), there is much reason to be sceptical, as House Rights Watch in an assessment of the law concluded:

> At this stage, then, on the one hand the Law can hardly be effectively mobilised in legal proceedings to defend individual, families' or groups' right to housing. On the other, the provisions on the protection of vulnerable households would only become effective with significant reform and reinvestment in social services—considering the concrete state of said services, a stronger protection *from* eviction seems to be urgently necessary. (House Rights Watch 2019)

In Spain, more than half a million foreclosures between 2008 and 2013 resulted in over 300,000 evictions (Observatory of Economic, Social and Cultural Rights and Platform of Mortgage Victims 2013, 12). Moreover, until '2015 over 600,000 foreclosures took place and more than 400,000 home evictions, along with mass, unaccounted forced migrations and ongoing gentrification' (European Action Coalition for the Right to Housing and to the City 2016, 52). With regard to Spain, one has to bear in mind that since the Franco era it has pushed for people to buy homes, while only 2.5% of homes are social housing (Madrid No Frills 2021), which has the immediate effect of 'around 10 million owner-occupiers with a mortgage in this country' (Cano Fuentes et al. 2013, 1198). This has led to extremely high numbers of evictions compared to other countries in Western Europe. This historical and traditional pattern is intensified by a neoliberal strategy of austerity, which has led to more than 2.5 million people who have been evicted from their homes across Spain, while the then-governing Partido Popular sold thousands of council homes to vulture funds (Madrid No Frills 2021). The inevitable consequence of such strategies of exclusion, marginalizing ordinary people even under conditions of the pandemic, were that 'one in five people live under the poverty line in Spain, and 29,406 evictions took place in 2020 while people struggled to make ends meet as COVID took over their lives. Simultaneously, 3.4 million apartments remain empty in Spain, which are often owned by banks and investment funds' (Redfish 2021; Centre for Social and Economic Rights 2012; 2018).

Because of evictions, the numbers of homeless people are skyrocketing. In their report *Third Overview of Housing Exclusion*, the Abbé Pierre Foundation & FEANTSA made explicit the high and rising figures of homelessness in European countries[11] (see table 22.2).

---

[11] The sixth *Overview of Housing Exclusion* of FANTSA and Abbé Pierre Foundation 2021 confirms trends of their former reports and sheds a light especially on the situation of young people.

Table 22.2 Evictions in Europe

Country	Numbers of Homeless and Conditions	Percentage Increase in Time Periods
Austria	15,090 statutory homeless people 2016	+32%; 2006–2016
Belgium (Brussels)	3,386 homeless on one night in November 2016	+96%; 2008–2016
Denmark	6,635 homeless in one week in 2017	+8%; 2015–2017
England	4,751 homeless sleeping rough on one night in 2017	+169%; 2010–2017
France	20,845 people called the 115 homeless helpline requesting accommodation (one month June 2017)	+17%; 2016–2017
Germany	860,000 homeless in 2016	+150%; 2014–2016
Ireland	8,857 people in emergency accommodation (November 2017)	+145%; 2014–2017
Lithuania	4,569 people in temporary accommodation (one night in 2016)	+16,2%; (n.d.)
Spain	16,437 people per day on average in emergency shelters in 2016	+20,5%; 2014–2016
The Netherlands	60,120 people in homeless accommodation services in 2016	+11%; 2011–2016

Source: FEANTSA and Abbé Pierre Foundation 2018, 11

While evictions make people homeless, denying them access to housing, we can understand this process of wealth transfer as one of *accumulation by dispossession* (Harvey 2003), pointing to the fact that banks, moneylenders in general, corporate landlords, and real estate firms benefit from the increasing numbers of evictions (Cooper and Paton 2021, 584). This shows that dispossessing people through forced evictions is a way to capitalize on denying access to housing and at the same time indebt ordinary citizens and non-citizens:

> In 2021, the total volume of outstanding mortgage loans in the EU27 reached EUR 6.5 tn. Adding the UK, Norway and Iceland to the European stock, the figure reached EUR 8.7 tn outstanding, a new all-time high. In the meantime, total gross lending reached EUR 1.2 tn in the EU27 in 2021, above 2020's record-breaking mark. (European Mortgage Federation 2022)

A deeply indebted citizenry also results in a redistribution of wealth under neoliberalism. The state has actively promoted the financialization of housing and secured the right to property, thereby redefining the dominance of housing as an exchange value. In addition, the state plays another crucial role in creating the legal preconditions for an eviction industry to emerge (Paton and Cooper 2016):

> The money spent by the UK tax authority on private debt collectors has quadrupled in the past five years, suggesting an increasingly 'aggressive' approach to collecting unpaid tax, accountants have warned. HM Revenue & Customs spent £26.3m on private debt collectors in 2018, up from just £6.2m in 2014. It is part of an increase in the amount handed to private sector debt agencies by HMRC, which has spent more than £140m on their services since 2011. (Agyemang 2019)

Such processes also become obvious with regard to the European Union, as it is creating markets for non-performing loans (NPLs). Without going into the details of the European Union's pushing 'the financialization and marketisation of distressed debts in Europe' (Metz 2020):

> The Commission is known for promoting financial markets—most recently, capital markets (Thiemann 2016) —and the marketisation of debt claims (Metz 2016). The NPL regulation indicates a step further in this direction. The current situation is testimony to certain limits of financialisation (Montgomery and Tepe-Belfrage 2016) whereby financialised households are no longer able to 'make good' on their debts. The promotion of distressed debt markets reveals a willingness to *marketise* and *capitalise on* these very limits. (Metz 2020; references inserted)

This brief outline of a critical aspect of *the housing question* (Friedrich Engels) in the twenty-first century can only make plausible the logics of closure analysis regarding the reorganization of the social relations between the excluders and the excluded in the declared *war of the rich class against the poor class*. Detailed empirical investigations need to look more closely not only at the legal frameworks and policies that allegedly show how the state cares for its citizens and non-citizens by issuing temporary eviction bans and the like. In contrast, closure analyses also need to take particularly seriously the idea of *social life as struggle* and thus concentrate on daily closure struggles, analysing severe problems such as *The hypocrisy of Europe's big corporate landlords* (Ponsford 2020) and the many ways the state—and the European Union—orchestrate, for example, evictions (Paton and Cooper 2016). They also need to consider the role indebting ordinary people plays in today's capitalist system to reveal the joint strategies of the neoliberal politico-economic elites for making profits at the cost of destroying ordinary citizens' and non-citizens' life chances / chances of survival by denying them access to a vital resource.

Shifting

Shifting, the second aspect of austerity politics as a strategy of marginalizing citizens, de-democratizes political decisions by moving the sovereign power from citizens to powerful neoliberal politico-economic elites. Assaults on citizenship rights started with the rise of neoliberalism in the 1970s, with fierce attacks on welfare systems that led to a loss of social rights and the dismantling of the welfare state, marginalizing parts of the citizenry by questioning *full citizenship*.[12]

Yet, these attacks were intensified after the banking crisis, as the announcement of former president of the European Central Bank, Jean-Claude Trichet, that 'it is now time for *all* to tighten' (Trichet 2010; emphasis added) made clear. Of course, while banks and the neoliberal elites were bailed out, the *time to tighten* had come for ordinary citizens and non-citizens only, especially the most vulnerable. Further, the tightening was not restricted to welfare.

The banking crisis-as-event actually enabled neoliberal elites to envision and finally put into practice a core demand of various forms of neoliberal theory (Friedman and Friedman 1980; Hayek 2003; Buchannan 1975a; 1975b; see MacLean 2022), the *enchaining of democracy* (MacLean 2017), by means of strategies to restrict, replace, or complement democracy (Biebricher 2015). Using the crisis and referring to a *state of emergency*, the European Union shifted its politics to one of *informality* and *discretion* (White 2022), mainly characterized 'by the suspension of "normal" democratic procedures as national governments agreed to reforms imposed by international and supranational economic and governmental institutions (the Troika of IMF, ECB, European Commission, rating agencies, financial markets)' (Hayes 2017, 27–28; Berglund 2018, 905). Not only were all these institutions acting without democratic legitimacy, but at the same time national governments were shifting power from citizens to corporate interests (Hayes 2017, 28). Joseph Vogl has made this point very clear:

> A consortium of public and private actors, improvised meetings, secret arrangements, and time pressures directed at the movements of financial markets. Since at least 2008, these methods have become a new standard for

---

[12] Of course, the neoliberal attacks on the welfare state, as a first step of neoliberal elites' war against citizenship rights, came in the early 1980s, see Hasenfeld, Rafferty, and Zald 1987; King and Waldron 1988; Hall and Held 1989; Saunders 1993; Kymlicka and Norman 1994.

determining the practice of governance as well as the fate of contemporary economy and society. (Vogl 2014, 143)

How does this transfer of decision-making power in the sense of *political austerity* (Graeme Hayes) operate as a strategy of marginalization with regard to rights as a dimension of life chances / chances of survival? As a strategy of shifting rights, it triggers the mechanism of denying access by marginalizing citizens from democratic participation in at least three ways.

First is a *democracy without choices* (Bosco and Verney 2012), which results from neoliberal elites pushing their ideology by declaring the neoliberal organization of these fields a *factual constraint* or *without any alternative* (Anderson 2017). In presenting the myth of an inevitable and unchangeable working of market mechanisms, neoliberal elites succeeded in widely marginalizing citizens' decision-making in the political process, shifting the very foundation of society from democratic politics to the market. As Jean-Claude Michéa (2009, 16) has shown, in neoliberalism the law and the market replace citizens' democratic participation. Yet, this does not mean the end of politics, but rather a transfer to powerful actors who actively engage in the allegedly neutral and quasi-natural processes of markets, albeit in ways that do not have anything to do with democracy.

Second is a *democracy without citizens* (Wolin 2008, 65). The ongoing blocking of citizens from the political process and restrictions on their participation has created a system that Sheldon Wolin has characterized as *inverted totalitarianism* and a *managed democracy*. Looking at the United States, he argues:

> The fact that politically organized interest groups with vast resources operate continuously, that they are coordinated with congressional procedures and calendars, that they occupy strategic points in the political processes, is indicative of how the meaning of 'representative' government has radically changed. The citizenry is being displaced, severed from a direct connection with the legislative institutions that are supposed to 'stand in' for the people. (Wolin 2008, 59)

Such a system may be called a 'misrepresentative or clientry government' that is 'a powerful contributing factor to the depoliticization of the citizenry, as well as reason for characterizing the system as one of antidemocracy' (Wolin 2008, 59; MacLean 2022; see also Harriot 2023).

Third is a 'democracy without representation' (Hayes 2017, 27–28), which has shifted power from citizens to newly created yet democratically non-legitimized actors such as the Troika, thereby insulating critical policy fields from citizens' democratic decisions: 'Most of the government's economic, fiscal, spending, social security and social policies now elude popular choice; instead they are shaped and ultimately imposed by the external limits of markets' negative power' (D'Eramo 2013, 24). D'Eramo has further referred to 'the former governor of the German Bundesbank, Hans Tietmeyer, who in 1998 praised national governments for preferring "the permanent plebiscite of global markets" to the (implicitly less qualified) "plebiscite of the ballot box"' (D'Eramo 2013, 24–25).

All three forms of shifting power from citizens to the interests of a neoliberal elite reorganize the relations between the highly organized and powerful excluders and the weakly organized, less powerful excluded, marginalizing the citizen from democratic decision-making by curtailing his/her political right to participate. Consequently, these austerity strategies have fundamentally reorganized the social relations of exclusion in political regimes and shifted power to highly organized neoliberal elites and organizations. Denied access to their political rights of participation as they are cut off from quite a number of critical policy fields, citizens are replaced by democratically illegitimate bodies, as corporate interests influence or even make political decisions to protect private interests from citizens. This triggering of the *denial of access* mechanism has established a new and fundamentally asymmetric and unequal access to political decision-making and thus to a critical dimension of life chances / chances of survival. In these processes two developments converge. While on the one hand they show empirically the variants of what Wendy Brown (2015) has called *Undoing the Demos*, what is left for citizens on the other hand are irrelevant decisions that will not change their daily lives in a significant way (see also Brown, W. 2003). Peter Mair has characterized the fate of the citizen in the face of institutional neoliberal blockades of democratic decision-making processes as a hollowing out of Western democracy leaving nothing for citizens but a *Ruling the Void* (Mair 2013) that is celebrated as democratic participation and decision-making.

De-universalization

De-universalization, the third aspect of austerity politics as a strategy of marginalization, aims at reregulating access to critical networks or institutions from universal to conditional access. Such a strategy prevents weaker and vulnerable groups from structurally integrating into the wider society to realize their life chances / chances of survival. Strategies of de-universalization have many faces, from reducing support for the disadvantaged, homeless, and the worse off, to cutting special aid for those who have already been pushed into precarious living conditions. Further, denying access to a country or to the right to asylum, the rejection of refugees, or denying refugees a legally secured residence status and access to the labour market or their children the right to go to school are all strategies that deny access to a country's institutions. There are in fact many faces of marginalization that sideline and finally exclude social groups and individuals. I briefly explain this critical strategy with two examples from Spain again—its reorganized access to the health system and labour markets.[13]

1. Reorganized Access to the Spanish Health System

When the European Union forced Spain to adopt *strict fiscal austerity* (Karanikolos et al. 2013, 1323),[14] this strategy of de-universalization by making access to the health system conditional, triggered the mechanism *denial of access*, leaving huge parts of the citizenry in a highly problematic situation, since the health system is a critical institution to realize one's life chances / chances of survival (Papadopoulos and Roumpakis 2018; Perez and Matsaganis 2018). Cutting spending on healthcare in Spain had begun in 2009 (Ambast 2018), yet austerity measures were adopted in 2012, when

> the Spanish government in power approved Royal Decree Law 16/201 that drastically reformed the national health system the justification being that limiting universal access to services was necessary to ensure the healthcare system's sustainability during the financial crisis. Thus, it excluded publicly funded healthcare services for adult immigrants with irregular administrative status, established co-payments for medications, adversely affected the elderly and other people with the fewest resources, and imposed other administrative barriers that harmed precisely the groups most impoverished by the crisis. The supposed fiscal savings the norm was supposed to generate never emerged. (Aguilar 2018)[15]

---

[13] For an overview see OECD/European Observatory on Health Systems and Policies 2017.

[14] By forcing its member states to adapt austerity, the European Union refrained from its duty to protect its citizens' rights to health, abandoned those in need of a functioning public health system, and deliberately shifted interest from the well-being of the population to the interests of the wealthy. It is instructive and says everything about the EU's position that 'the Directorate-General for Health and Consumer Protection of the European Commission, despite its legal obligation to assess the health effects of EU politics, has not assessed the effects of the Troika's drive for austerity, and has instead limited EU commentary to advice about how health ministries can cut their budget' (Karanikolos et al. 2013, 1329).

[15] Of course, austerity measures in healthcare systems interact with the consequences of such strategies with regard to employment, food, housing, poverty, and so forth in ways that 'the most vulnerable people are those in countries facing the largest cuts to public budgets and increasing unemployment. Both job loss and fear of job loss have adverse effects on mental health, and income reduction, growing health-care costs, and cuts in services prevent patients from accessing care in time' (Karanikolos et al. 2013, 1328). Moreover, Goudriaan has shown that mass cuts and hospital privatizations have 'resulted in an upsurge in infectious diseases, including HIV, and suicides' (Goudriaan 2016). Weakened mental health, increased substance abuse, and higher suicide rates have all been linked with fiscal consolidation measures (Stuckler and Basu 2013). The European Centre for Disease Control warned that serious health hazards are emerging because of fiscal consolidation measures introduced since 2008.

Further, after the introduction of the Royal Decree implemented in September 2012, 'undocumented migrants were excluded from all but basic emergency care, prenatal care, and paediatric care' (The Lancet 2018). This strategy of de-universalizing access to services 'had a devastating effect on health and health equity' (Viens 2019, 147). As a lower quality of health-service provision generally leads to worse health outcomes (e.g., Karanikolos et al. 2013; Mladovsky et al. 2012), 'in Greece, Portugal and Spain, citizens' access to public health services has been seriously constrained to the extent that there are reported increases in mortality and morbidity' (Ortiz et al. 2015, 34).

The United Nations, while stressing the alleged successes of austerity with regard to the recovery of the Spanish economy, nevertheless took a sceptical look at the de-universalizing of access and the effects it caused in the Spanish health system for specific vulnerable social groups, unwittingly making it apparent that the Spanish government had activated strategies that marginalized both its citizens and migrants, not only in order to marginalize refugees or minorities but also to set vulnerable groups against each other:

> With reference to its previous recommendation (E/C.12/ESP/CO/5, para. 8) the Committee urges the State party to ensure that the austerity measures it adopts are temporary, necessary, proportionate and non-discriminatory, and are compatible with the core content of the rights recognized in the Covenant, with the aim of ensuring that such measures do not impinge, disproportionately, on the rights of the most disadvantaged and marginalized groups and individuals. In that regard, the Committee recommends that the State party conduct a full evaluation of the effects of such measures on the enjoyment of economic, social and cultural rights, especially by *disadvantaged and marginalized groups and individuals, including women, children, persons with disabilities, Gitanos and Roma, as well as refugees, asylum seekers and migrants*; and that, in consultation with the persons affected, it consider the possible withdrawal of those measures. (United Nations 2017; emphasis added)

Blocking access to the health system, as well as requiring co-payments for drugs, delaying necessary treatments, reducing hospital beds, and the like are all an expression of how a seemingly fiscal strategy in fact operates as a strategy to reorganize the social relations between those who can afford to pay or move to private healthcare and those who cannot. Austerity measures have also reorganized the relation of citizens versus non-citizens and affected migrants, refugees, or asylum seekers, discriminating against them, and blocking them almost completely from access. It is evident that severe cuts to healthcare provision are a far-reaching strategy of de-universalization, creating distinct and isolated *categories of individuals* within the population given differentiated access to a once universal provision of healthcare.[16]

Spanish austerity policies of de-universalizing access to the health sector have also radicalized an already existing social inequality with regard to health and life expectations, as

> around 870,000 people lost the health card that provided them with access to healthcare services. The mortality rate in the immigrant community with irregular status increased by 15 percent (Hierro 2018) over a three-year period, there was a reduction in primary care (Center for Social and Economic Rights 2018), and a greater use of emergency services, as well as multiple documented cases (REDER 2012) of illegal barriers to access to emergency services and maternal and child care. (Aguilar 2018; sources added)

The destructiveness of austerity politics in the health sector reducing personnel and services and denying access to its services could not have become more dramatically obvious than in the case of the global Covid-19 pandemic. With reduced services and personnel already exhausted, Spain's health system was strained more than it could anticipate, as is well known. In a deeply reorganized system of access to health, not only health workers were pushed beyond their limits but also the most vulnerable social groups, who, marginalized after years of strategies of de-universalization, were impacted the most with illness and death (Navarro 2020). In austerity-ridden Spain during the pandemic, the denial of access to the health system pushed human beings to the fringes and turned individuals' life chances / chances of survival into a matter of personal wealth.

2. Reorganized Access to Labour Markets

In the aftermath of the banking crisis, pressures to implement austerity politics came along with demands to fundamentally *re*-regulate (Block and Somers, 2014) the labour market, being another main institution of structural integration for both citizens and non-citizens. Demanding and enforcing measures such as labour market flexibility, revisions of the minimum wage, wage reduction, and rising numbers of atypical occupations, as well as 'decentralising collective bargaining and facilitating the ability of employers to lay off workers' (Szczepański 2013, 2), has sidelined huge numbers of citizens and non-citizens and created

---

[16] In a study that conducted qualitative interviews with healthcare professionals in Spain, the effects of reducing the breadth of services available for everyone was seen as a significant problem for public health, as 'all of the interviewees were against excluding undocumented migrants from the health care system. The reasons provided were related to a public health threat and for economic reasons, as the solutions proposed were believed to end up being more expensive if infectious diseases or other pathogens were to reach other population groups' (Heras-Mosteiro, Sanz-Barbero, and Otero-Garcia 2015, 294).

marginalizing effects especially for members of vulnerable groups. Greece has seen precarious labour market outcomes, such as in patterns of employment and unemployment, part-time employment, temporary employment, and self-employment, all of them experiencing reduced wages, creating working poverty (Kennedy 2018), and pushing individuals to the fringes of society rather than allowing them to integrate.[17] Even research at the IMF later had to acknowledge that fiscal consolidation was having adverse effects on both short- and long-term unemployment, private demand, and GDP growth, with wage earners hurt disproportionately more than profit earners and rent earners (Guajardo, Leigh and Pescatori 2011; Ball, Leigh and Loungani 2011).

Besides many other aspects of a *politics of austerity*, extensive labour market reforms were pushed through as neoliberal economists, employers, organized neoliberal elites, and politicians argued that 'increasing flexibility would encourage employers to hire more workers and boost economic growth' (Szczepański 2013, 2). Given such strategies of re-regulating labour markets, in 2017 the United Nations looked back at the effects of the *politics of austerity* and came to a clear conclusion: 'Austerity-related labour market reforms promoted by multilateral and regional financial institutions in many developed and developing countries have been shown to not help economies recover after crises, and have instead inflicted substantial harm on working people, which will be felt for many years' (Raja 2017).

Given all these disastrous effects of labour market *reforms* on citizens' and non-citizens' opportunities to integrate into a critical institution in a way that would allow them to realize their life chances / chances of survival by connecting to networks and groups in the economy, even unions, it is also obvious that austerity measures have not affected all social groups in the same way. Rather, they have fostered discrimination in labour markets, targeting social groups differently and thereby also pitting them against one another in the sense of a politics of *divide et impera* that Popitz stressed as a critical measure used by the powerful in *systems of redistribution*.

A brief look at the case of women and how they were affected by labour market reregulation after the banking crisis reveals critical effects. There can be no doubt that the EU's austerity measures are gendered (O'Dwyer 2018), affecting women in the labour market more than men, although in Portugal, Italy, Ireland, Greece, and Spain there are a lot of dynamics and differences at play with regard to the

---

[17] Summarizing the manifold reregulations and restructurations of labour markets, Alcañiz and Monteiro have concluded: 'All these jobs are characterized by de-structuring existence, and also by generalized and institutionalized insecurity that turns the mere survival into the central incentive, thereby a disciplinary tool in current society (Bourdieu 2003 [1999]; Alonso and Fernández 2013). To sum up, precariousness is characterized by three "I's": Instability, Insecurity and Insufficiency (Todaro and Yáñez 2004)' (Alcañiz and Monteiro 2016, 3–4).

gender situation (Benlloch Doménech 2017). Nevertheless, critical aspects of austerity disadvantaged women, including cuts to public spending in combination with women's double burden of being responsible for household chores and unpaid care work as well as earning money to make ends meet. Additionally, deep cuts to public sector employment, a rather feminized sector, hit women hard (Gender and Development Network 2018). Looking at reinforced labour market segregation and segmentation, austerity has created disastrous consequences that have marginalized women in the labour market, generating a degree of precariousness that is destructive for their life chances / chances of survival (Segnana and Villa, 2015; Karamessini and Rubery, 2014; European Women's Lobby 2012; Barry and Conroy 2013). Part-time work is clearly a feminized labour structure, and temporary employment creates permanent instability particularly for women; pushing them into self-employment, as the European Union does, is also a high-risk strategy. Wage differences remain while gender roles are reinforced (Lombardo 2016), increasing the precariousness of women's situation even more: 'If we add the cutbacks the States have made to their social expenditure, the situation becomes complicated for women, and in words by Rodriguez-Modroño, Addabbo and Galvez (2013), a feminine *austericide* is committed, and it especially affects women with the least resources' (Alcañiz and Monteiro 2016, 13).

This highlights the fact that analysing de-universalization as a critical dimension of austerity politics is indeed a matter of explaining variation among vulnerable social groups that are affected to different degrees and in various ways. Such is the case, for example, with less-educated women (Távora and Rodríguez-Modroño 2018) being affected to a greater degree, while Anthony Rafferty (2014) has shown for the United Kingdom that gender intersects with ethnicity, making minority women also more affected by austerity measures in the labour market.[18] These are just some examples of the different impacts on vulnerable social groups who are prevented from realizing their life chances / chances of survival through austerity measures in the labour market.

De-solidarization
Turning to de-solidarization as the fourth aspect of austerity as a strategy of marginalization, we now look at processes that activate the mechanism of *intervention into community closure*, which operates in a way that prevents the excluded from closing their own community, forming a collective identity, and creating

---

[18] Another highly vulnerable social group heavily affected in a different way by austerity measures in the labour market is the youth. It is hard to imagine the long-term consequences of neoliberal elites imposing strategies that marginalize young people from structural integration into society. See the highly interesting case studies in a supplementary issue of the *International Journal of Adolescence and Youth* in European countries, edited by Bradford and Cullen 2014.

solidarity. It is obvious that commodification/financialization, shifting, and de-universalization do not only trigger the *denial of access* mechanism in different ways with regard to various aspects of life chances / chances of survival. In addition, by marginalizing vulnerable social communities or groups, these strategies also impact their self-conception as deserving and valuable members of society. Yet pushing ahead de-solidarization and holding the excluded personally and morally responsible for their situation directly affects processes of community closure. Negative impacts on individuals' dignity and self-esteem leaves them unable to develop a sense of belonging which would allow them to close their community and act in solidarity:

> There is indeed what might be called a coherent, large-scale 'responsibilisation' process underway, led by governments and public authorities and experienced in their daily lives by citizens and employers—but also by various collective, institutional bodies (trade unions, public-sector and governmental agencies, companies, and many others. (Thompson 2007)

After the banking crisis-as-event, the strategy of responsibilization, taken from the neoliberal *anti-social textbook* of extreme individualism (see Hayek 2004 [1979]) was even more radicalized under conditions of austerity. This strategy holds the individuals and social groups that are the main targets of the *politics of austerity* responsible for their own low social status or situation. At the same time, it individualizes social risks, creating a *self-help myth* (Vallelly 2020) and radically isolating citizens via policies coming from Hayek's (2004 [1979]) rejection of any idea of the social.[19] As neoliberalism has created a *society of individuals* (Blakely 2021) and turned the individual into nothing but a market actor that has to compete and succeed, failure is conceived as a matter of individual responsibility, as in neoliberal societies all ideas of communality have been abandoned (Michéa 2009). Individuals are held responsible for the consequences of neoliberalism's destruction of societies' social fabric (Polanyi 2001 [1944]), which has a deep impact on feelings of dignity and self-esteem for members of marginalized social groups. They are confronted with the demands of responsibilization, which creates perceptions and beliefs within communities around class, gender, ethnicity, religion, and language that reduce their ability to close their communities and to generate solidarity.[20]

---

[19] Of course, Margaret Thatcher only echoed her advisor's conviction in other words when she uttered the phrase 'there is no such thing as society' (Thatcher 1987; see also Hayek 2007 [1944]).
[20] There is evidence from psychological studies that 'neoliberalism can reduce well-being by promoting a sense of social disconnection, competition, and loneliness' (Becker, Hartwich, and Haslam 2021). Such effects on the individual necessarily affect self-esteem and dignity not only for the individual but also for the social groups to which he or she belongs, and which are blamed for problems created by private actors in financial capitalism.

Neuwirth's argument is fitting here, which states that a major interest of the dominant actors is to perpetuate the powerlessness of the subordinated, intending to regulate 'those affairs and interests of the negatively privileged which, if left uncontrolled, might affect the interests and relative positions of the dominant communities within the larger society' (Neuwirth 1969, 152). Such strategies are visible with regard to many marginalized social groups that are made responsible for a social misery they have not created. The strategy targets vulnerable groups from the homeless to the jobless, from migrants to the disabled, from single parents to workers in precarious employment. However, the strategy of responsibilization in its neoliberal form was nowhere as dramatically clear as in the case of Greece and its population after the banking crisis.[21]

As the strategy of holding the Greek people responsible for the economic situation triggered the mechanism of *intervention into community closure*, it enabled the Troika to 'solve' the banking crisis to the advantage of mainly German and French banks and neoliberal elites (also within Greece) as it began to regulate the affairs of the negatively privileged—in this case the Greek nation. Declaring that Greece (and of course Italy, Spain, Portugal, and Ireland) were responsible for the mischief because their populations had lived beyond their means for a long time, the Troika took advantage of Greece's desolate situation and the obvious vulnerability of millions of citizens. As a highly organized and powerful actor, this neoliberal body even de facto suspended the countries' sovereignty, taking over the reins of government (Vogl 2015) by making decisions about how Greek society should be run according to neoliberal standards. In doing so, this actor punished and humiliated the Greeks by imposing on their society an austerity regime that caused misery for millions of citizens, marginalizing them and driving them to despair.

How could a dominant actor be any more intrusive into the ongoing social life of both a national society in general and of weak social groups in particular than by taking over the power to make sovereign decisions? Blaming the victims by declaring them responsible for the debts the neoliberal financial elite had generated allowed them to even suspend a whole nation's democratic institutions and procedures. The Troika's 'rescue plan' imposed strict austerity measures, such as

> tax increases, widespread lay-offs of public employees, and massive cuts in pensions and other social supports. Laying off so many workers and pauperizing pensioners sharply reduced demand, which triggered further

---

[21] Also, with regard to the health system, responsibilization plays a critical role insofar as 'citizens become "responsibilized" by making them see health risks and outcomes of illness or disease as their own individual responsibility, with the corollary that the policy problem of health governance is framed as one of encouraging "self-care"' (Kay and Williams, 2009, 7).

lay-offs and wage cuts in the private sector. As the depression deepened, unemployment topped 25 percent. When austerity devastated the Socialists' working-class constituency, the party was effectively destroyed. (Super 2019)[22]

Austerity measures thus necessarily contributed to the disintegration of Greek society, and by disempowering a democratically legitimate government these politics established tight economic and social controls that the Troika exacted directly on Greek citizens. Job losses, pay cuts, cuts to welfare provisions, reduction of pensions, loss of homes, and so forth—all these measures are of course a means of putting extreme pressure on individuals and communities and are therefore used to prevent community closure. Being forced to fight for everyday survival and against a catastrophic social marginalization created anxiety to lose everything, Greek citizens had to accept all conditions imposed on them and found hardly ways to fight against them. The Troika and other neoliberal agencies discriminated against the Greek citizens, setting them against 'good' EU citizens, who allegedly helped them to settle their debts. However, as these measures created mass unemployment, low-paid jobs, and poverty and reduced public services while at the same time holding Greeks responsible for the consequences of the banking crisis, this simply perpetuated their powerlessness and incapacity to organize or oppose these measures in the end. Therefore, from the perspective of closure theory, the strategy of de-solidarizing communities by separating their members and responsibilizing individuals deprives social communities of dignity and takes away their self-esteem, all of which they would need to draw boundaries, close their communities, and organize themselves.

Looking back at the cases of Spain and Greece discussed with regard to strategies of repossession and marginalization, we can see how denying access to housing, welfare institutions, and the labour market operates jointly with the exercise of control over the vulnerable social groups targeted by the excluders:

> After experiencing the austerity politics of blackmail and fear, and the dispossession of basic human rights such as the rights to housing, employment, and welfare, the—fragile—individual remains increasingly puzzled before the empire of finance, ready to obey new norms shaped by the global financial institutions. (Alexandri and Janoschka 2018, 130)

---

[22] It is obvious that the burden has been shifted to the shoulders of normal citizens. In contrast, as we know from the Panama Papers 2016, the Pandora Papers 2021, and the Crédit Suisse Leak 2022, that governments are not interested in closing loopholes or passing regulations that would force the rich class to contribute to a *common good*. Their own interests are represented as the *general interest*.

It becomes obvious how the mechanisms *denial of access* and *intervention into community closure* interact, leaving the excluded marginalized while strengthening the side of the powerful neoliberal elites.

22.1.5 Outcomes, Stabilization, and Legitimation

Looking at austerity from the perspective of social closure reveals the allegedly unavoidable economic measure to be a highly complex strategy of marginalization affecting citizens and non-citizens in any country in which neoliberal elites employ it. The critical dimensions of social relations—socio-economic, politico-legal, socio-structural, and socio-cultural—are fundamentally reorganized, thereby shifting access to resources, rights, and networks/institutions in favour of the excluders, increasing their forms of control over the excluded, affecting communities' dignity, self-respect, and self-esteem, and preventing them from organizing.

Making plausible the explanatory logic of closure analysis has shown how strategies of commodification/financialization, shifting, and de-universalization trigger the mechanism *denial of access*, blocking citizens from making use of resources, utilizing their rights, or integrating into wider society. As these derogatory measures already heavily impinge upon individuals' and social groups' dignity and self-esteem, intervening into these communities' possibilities to close their boundaries, develop a political identity, and create solidarity, the strategy of de-solidarization that triggers the mechanism *intervention into community closure* plays the crucial role here because a *politics of austerity* aims at both controlling the weaker and marginalized groups and holding their individual members responsible for their social situation.

All the strategies of marginalization discussed above in detail—transforming resources into financialized commodities; shifting democratic participation towards oligarchic rule; dismantling systems of social security, healthcare, and pensions; transforming the universal provision of welfare states to conditionality and thus restricting access to them, and the neoliberal strategy of responsibilizing the individual for social risks—have institutionalized a new social order that has pushed huge segments of the citizenry as well as non-citizens to the fringes of societies, of the European Union, but also in both the Global South, by disrupting and destroying the social fabric of these communities.

In this sense, a closure analysis of exclusionary processes enables us to explain the various dimensions of the *politics of austerity*, a programme of radical marketization that operates with a complex set of strategies allowing the wealthy and neoliberal elites to maximize their life chances / chances of survival at the expense of the excluded in daily social struggles.

While such *re*regulated social arrangements are institutionalized through legislation and administrative regulations, their legitimacy is essentially based on the reciprocal recognition and horizontal legitimacy that neoliberal elites grant one another. The political and media discourse proclaiming the inevitability of measures that are without any alternative and are in line with the logic of the markets support the interests of the excluders by creating misery and fear among the excluded to otherwise experience even worse outcomes. On this basis, critical processes of creating legitimacy in *systems of redistribution* in which a certain social order still exists, and basic securities are maintained—the *security of order*, the *value of order*, and the critical element of *investment value* (Popitz)—makes even the excluded accept and support the new order, while being positioned against one another by strategies of marginalization that push them to the edge.

22.2 Analysing and Explaining the Reorganization of Social Relations of Exploitation

In their 2017 report 'Global Estimates of Modern Slavery: Forced Labour and Forced Marriage', the International Labour Organization (ILO), Walk Free, and the International Organization for Migration (IOM) 2017, 10) showed that of 'the 24.9 million victims of forced labour, 16 million were in the private economy'. In the face of this, analysing exploitation as a second form of social closure would not make any sense without taking seriously the fact that global capital has created an accumulation regime that rests upon exploitation *and* slavery all over the globe and that has radicalized capital's emphasis on *profit over people* (Chomsky 1999; see also International Labour Organization (ILO), Walk Free, and International Organization for Migration (IOM) 2022; International Labor Organization (ILO) 2014b; LeBaron 2018).

The creation of a global market resulting from interactions and transactions among financial-economic-political elites—financial capital, nation-states, and neoliberal institutions such as the WTF, IMF, World Bank, OECD, and G7—has put powerful oligopolistic multinational companies in the driver's seat of global capitalism. Pursuing strategies of *extraction*—the basic form of exploitative strategies—these powerful actors target the global workforce in both the Global North and the Global South by reorganizing social relations between the exploiters and the exploited in *systems of profit maximization* (Popitz).

Extraction is not confined purely to strategies of capitalist economic actors. States or supranational actors, such as the European Union, play crucial roles in creating the conditions for global capital to exploit and enslave human beings wherever it sees fit. Thus, a variety of strategies lead to processes of reorganizing socio-economic relations, but also to reorganizing politico-legal, socio-structural, and socio-cultural social relations.

22.2.1 Context: The Capitalism-Slavery Nexus

Today's global capitalism cannot be understood properly by conceiving of it as simply exploiting *formally free* labour provided through a labour contract. Rather, we need to take into consideration that huge parts of the global workforce are labouring, and consequently living, in conditions representing new forms of slavery, and that global capital is making enormous profits from slave labour.

My approach to closure theory and analysis thus does not confine itself to simply looking at exploitation of formal free labour in the Global North but expands the conceptual framework and joins the debate on *the new slavery* in global capitalism (Walk Free 2023; see also Conermann and Zeuske 2020). This step immediately leads to the question of whether slave labour is compatible with the capitalist mode of production at all. Marx's own position is critical here:

> Within its process of circulation, in which industrial capital functions either as money or as commodities, the circuit of industrial capital, whether as money-capital or as commodity-capital, crosses the commodity circulation of the most diverse modes of social production, so far as they produce commodities. No matter whether commodities are the output of production based on slavery, of peasants (Chinese, Indian ryots) of communes (Dutch East Indies), of state enterprise (such as existed in former epochs of Russian history on the basis of serfdom) or of half-savage hunting tribes, etc.—as commodities and money they come face to face with the money and commodities in which the industrial capital presents itself and enter as much into its circuit as into that of the surplus-value borne in the commodity-capital, provided the surplus-value is spent as revenue; hence they enter in both branches of circulation of commodity-capital. (Marx 2010 [1885], 63)

Following this assessment leads to the rejection of two widely held convictions in Marxist thought. The first is the conceptual argument that only *formally free* labour can create value; the second is the contextual argument that slavery belongs to a premodern form of production and thus cannot be capitalist. Given that today's globalized capitalism has created working conditions for millions of people that—as in times of Manchester Capitalism—can only be described as *pure industrial slavery* (Marx), neither of the two arguments is convincing given the reality of working conditions in global production and labour processes.

Thus, taking the *capitalism-slavery nexus* seriously means that, *conceptually*, the expenditure of labour power also generates value in the form of slave labour as a matter of course. Extracting labour power from working people under capitalism does not necessarily presuppose a labour contract, the doubly free wageworker, or a wage-employment relationship at all. Considerable segments of the Marxist tradition have rejected this position on the grounds that they—in contrast to Marx—have not taken into consideration the fact that capitalism from its very beginning was a global phenomenon. In Marx' view, it depended on both colonial exploitation of raw materials, inevitable for the expansion of capitalist production, and—as a logical consequence—slave labour as a decisive moment in the global capitalist mode of production.

Therefore, disregarding the critical role of the *plantation system* and *colonial slavery*, this theoretical strand of Marxist thought conceived of capitalism as a new mode of production that emerged out of intrinsic processes, especially in England. In this view, the enclosure of farmland and its transformation into pastureland, setting free masses of peasants and transforming them into a proletariat, along with the original accumulation of capital in Europe and the liberal institutions of private property and the labour contract, all contributed to the unfolding of the capitalist mode of production due to the contradictions between the feudal systems and bourgeois revolutions.[23]

While the invention of *formally free labour* is critical for such Eurocentric interpretations of the emergence of capitalism that reject the critical role of slave labour both in the rise of and within capitalism, Christian Frings (2019) in an illuminating analysis has shown that these interpretations are misguided. He shows that Marx discusses formally free labour in a central place only to unmask economists' ideological beliefs and refutes their claims that bourgeois society had abolished exploitation by implementing an exchange of the alleged equivalents of labour and wages paid for its expenditure. Marx further explicitly characterized work in the capitalist factory *as* slavery throughout his *Critique of Political Economy* and in the *Grundrisse*, and made the link between the development of early capitalism in England and the plantation system in the colonies very clear:

---

[23] This view of the West arising out of itself of course is prominent in the entire classical sociological tradition. Nowhere does settler colonialism, the plantation system, slave trade and slavery, and the brutal exploitation of human beings in the Global South play a role (see Hall 2019 [1992]; Gilroy, 1993). For the relations of Europe and Africa in a historical perspective, see Rodney 2018 [1971], and for the ongoing colonial legacy and the concept of 'Eurafrica', see Hansen and Jonsson 2014; 2017; Berthelot 2017.

Whilst the cotton industry introduced child-slavery in England, it gave in the United States a stimulus to the transformation of the earlier, more or less patriarchal slavery, into a system of commercial exploitation. In fact, the *veiled slavery of the wage workers in Europe* needed, for its pedestal, slavery pure and simple in the new world. (Marx 2015 [1867], 538; emphasis added)

Frings, analysing Marx's writings in detail, shows that he was not only referring to the working conditions of the doubly free wage labourer *as* slavery. He also emphasizes that such slave labour naturally creates wealth, 'because for Marx there was no question that enslaved labour forces produce value and surplus value in capitalist organized production' (Frings 2019, 434, my translation; see also Barrientos, Kothari, and Phillips 2013, 1038).

Contextually, we also need to take into consideration the capitalism-slavery nexus, as according to historical transformations of capital, slavery is not simply a premodern phenomenon but occurs in various guises in different historical contexts depending on historically specific capital accumulation regimes. The global organization of the use of labour power shows an interesting pattern of strategies in the West's global outreach from its very beginnings. As Thomas A. Brady has shown for Europe's building of *Merchant Empires*, since the fifteenth century military-commercial elites 'despite a vague allegiance to "civilization" . . . respected no ecumenical ideology but the *doctrine of the market*, no common ritual but the business of exchange, and no common morality but the pursuit of profit' (Brady 1991, 159–160; emphasis added). Thus, as the historical perspective on global capitalism reveals, from its very beginnings it has been based to a considerable extent on non-free labour. The constitutive capitalism-slavery nexus starts with colonialism, as Robin Blackburn has shown:

1) The household and ancillary slavery of the early Iberian phase of colonization, 2) the colonial mercantilist plantation slavery of seventeenth-century Brazil, Barbados, Saint-Domingue and Virginia, and 3) the era of independent American slavery led by the United States and Brazil, but also involving the strange colony of Cuba—a colonial tail that often wagged the metropolitan dog. These epochs embraced three styles of slavery—the baroque linked to silver and gold (1500–1650); the mercantile linked to sugar and tobacco (1650–1800); and the industrial, linked to cotton and coffee (1800–88). (Blackburn 2013, 21)

With the creation of markets, the capitalism-slavery nexus becomes critical. As Eric Williams (2022 [1944]) has brilliantly argued in his classic study *Capitalism and Slavery*, it was slavery in the plantation system of the Caribbean islands that decisively contributed to the creation of wealth in England.[24] Williams shows that the *triangular trade* of Britain, Africa, and the Plantations—trading slaves and goods—had a major impact on *original accumulation* and the Industrial Revolution in Britain (Blackburn 2010, 517). This is not to say that slavery in the New World created capitalism, yet, as Barbara L. Solow has forcefully argued, 'Colonial slavery increased British national income and the pool of investable funds and resulted in a pattern of trade that encouraged industrialization' (Solow 1985, 99). Thus, slavery stands at the cradle of capitalism and has played an important role in the newly emerging economic system and has played a critical role in capitalism since then (Solow 1987).

The second form of the capitalism-slavery nexus refers to what Blackburn has called the *industrial nexus*. It emerges because of 'the changing character of slavery in the nineteenth century world economy', showing 'the formation and reformation of slave relations within historical processes of the capitalist world economy' (Tomich 2004 [1988], 57).[25] This new form of slavery, which Dale Tomich has called *The Second Slavery*, 'consolidated a new international division of labor and provided important industrial raw materials and foodstuffs for industrializing core powers. Far from being a moribund institution during the nineteenth century, slavery demonstrated its adaptability and vitality' (Tomich 2004 [1988], 69).

Slavery, albeit in various guises and in different economic sectors, played a central role both in the emergence of capitalism and during the reorganization of the capitalist accumulation regime and the formation of a capitalist world market. Once we see that this crystallizing of capitalism is thoroughly market dependent, the critical role of slave labour in capitalism becomes obvious: 'Insofar as it is capable of being either hired or purchased slave labor is like any other capitalist commodity' (Clegg 2015, 301). Moreover, it is, as Williams has already pointed out, the cheapest labour capitalists can buy. In view of this fundamental importance of the market for an understanding of capitalist exploitation and the capitalism-slavery nexus, John C. Clegg makes this point clear:

> Indeed, there is something pristinely capitalist about the total commodification of labor under slavery. Slaves are doubly alienated, for they lack property in both the means of production and in themselves. Nineteenth-century slave

---

[24] See for this debate, Woolfolk 1956; Temperley 1977; Meiskins Wood 2017 [1999]; Carrington 2003; Issar 2021.

[25] I cannot go into a detailed discussion of Tomich's concept, which has provoked a broad debate in history (see Tomich 2004 [1988]; Tomich 2018; Tomich and Zeuske 2008). For a debate on the situation in the Antebellum South, see Kaye 2009. Sarkar 2018; Stanziani 2018; Damir-Geilsdorf et al. 2016 discuss how slavery and indentured labour are linked; for a review of these three books, see Bosma 2018.

markets in the United States were both more unified and more competitive than markets for wage labor.... In a capitalist order of fully specified property rights, it is wage labor rather than slave labor that is the anomaly. (Clegg 2015, 302–303)

This, however, is true not only for the nineteenth century and the centuries before it, but even more so for today's global capitalism, which has resulted in 'worker exploitation that has grown to a level never before seen in our world economy, in which an estimated 40 million people are currently living as modern slaves' (Association of Ambas 2019). Although one may debate whether the term *modern slavery* is appropriate (Allain 2017 Boersma and Nolan 2022),[26] it points to the simple fact that only a naïve belief in progress with regard to the taming of capitalism or the realization of human rights or the dignity of all human beings could prevent us from soberly examining the conditions of profit maximization in the twenty-first century that quite simply show a continuity of the capitalism-slavery nexus. Although the term *modern slavery* is not yet legally defined and thus 'constitutes a broad non-legal umbrella term' (Boersma and Nolan 2022, 165), it refers to destructive working and living conditions for human beings, including the following:

> *Human trafficking.* The use of violence, threats or coercion to transport, recruit or harbour people in order to exploit them for purposes such as forced prostitution, labour, criminality, marriage or organ removal. *Forced labour.* Any work or services people are forced to do against their will under threat of punishment. *Debt bondage/bonded labour.* The world's most widespread form of slavery. People trapped in poverty borrow money and are forced to work to pay off the debt, losing control over both their employment conditions and the debt. *Descent-based slavery.* Most traditional form, where people are treated as property, and their 'slave' status was passed down the maternal line. *Slavery of children.* When a child is exploited for someone else's gain. This can include child trafficking, child soldiers, child marriage and child domestic slavery. *Forced and early marriage.* When someone is married against their will and cannot leave. Most child marriages can be considered slavery. (Anti-Slavery International 2022a)[27]

---

[26] I cannot go into detail here. Bales 2012 [1999] has made an interesting yet also problematic comparison of old and new slavery. For a discussion of problems with the use of the term *slavery* in recent debates, see Patterson 1982; Patterson and Zhuo 2018.

[27] See the report of the Special Rapporteur on the human rights of migrants; the Special Rapporteur on contemporary forms of racism, racial discrimination, xenophobia, and related intolerance; the Special Rapporteur on contemporary forms of slavery, including its causes and consequences; and the Special Rapporteur on trafficking in persons, especially women and children, 2019.

Analysing exploitation/slavery from the perspective of social closure requires taking seriously the mere fact of millions of children, women, and men working and living in conditions of modern slavery, exploited by global capital in the Global South and Global North. As added value is produced from both *formally free* and *de facto unfree* labour, and as labour is expended under extremely different working conditions, it may help to conceive of modern slavery as 'part of a continuum of exploitation', since its 'most extreme forms ... represent instances of modern slavery' (Boersma and Nolan 2022, 1, 2; see also Davies and Ollus 2019, 87). Therefore, when analysing exploitation as a form of social closure, manifestations of modern slavery or a *Third Slavery*[28] are critical with regard to processes of subjugating human beings and reorganizing the social relations between the exploiters and the exploited in the global economy. These relations not only keep alive an unholy tradition of Western civilization but certainly revive centuries-old experiences for those suffering under global capital:

> As a legally permitted labour system, traditional slavery has been abolished everywhere, but it has not been completely eradicated. It can persist as a state of mind—among victims and their descendants and among the inheritors of those who practiced it—long after it has formally ended. (OHCHR 2021; Association of Ambas 2019)

22.2.2 Event and Principal Strategy

In the chapter on exclusion, I have referred to Rodrik's distinction between the rather political dimension (exclusion) of marketization and the more economic dimension of the intertwined national economies within a global market (exploitation). As the debate on the capitalism-slavery nexus has shown, from its very beginning the creation of a capitalist global market has allowed for exploitation and slavery as ways of making use of human labour to make profits. Marketization thus also plays a critical role, when looking in detail at processes of subjugation as the basic form of exploitative strategies in at least two senses: First, as Tomich and Clegg have argued, marketization is critical because with the fundamental reorganization of capital transforming production and trade on a global scale, today we face a radicalized system of exploitation. Second, following Block's and Somers' (2014) arguments of marketization, we

---

[28] I am not aware of the term/concept *The Third Slavery* having been introduced in the academic debate. However, The Third Slavery Project at the University of Michigan at Ann Arbor makes use of it. See *Slavery and Its Aftermath* (2022). For a discussion of the *new slave narrative* from the human rights perspective, see Johnson 2013.

can understand how states and the EU have *re*regulated the frameworks and rules of capitalist production in favour of capital, creating conditions allowing for exploitation and slavery.

I identify a turning point in the creation of today's global market and the enforcing of a new global capitalist division of labour as the reorganization of the global capitalist economy following the demise of the Soviet Union, in which capital was truly allowed to go global. By including the once socialist part of the world into the capitalist market as an experiment with *shock doctrines*, the creation of the World Trade Organization in 1995 was the critical event in the sense of a *template of possibility* (Berezin) for global capital to envisage (once again) the transformation of all social relations around the globe according to market principles and thus the implementation of all social relations as self-regulating markets. A critical element of this new global capitalism with its rhetoric of the *free market* is the introduction of the *shareholder value doctrine* that Milton Friedman[29] characterized concisely and succinctly in a *New York Times* article already in 1970:

> In a free-enterprise, private-property system, a corporate executive is an employee of the owners of the business. He has direct responsibility to his employers. That responsibility is to conduct the business in accordance with their desires, which generally will be *to make as much money as possible* while conforming to the basic rules of the society, both those embodied in law and those embodied in ethical custom. (Friedman 1970; emphasis added)

Friedman forcefully argued against emerging debates around the *social responsibilities* of enterprises and organizations and declared such ideas, coming directly from socialist textbooks, posing threats to a *free society*. With the unleashing of the financial markets that US President Ronald Reagan initiated in 1982, shareholder value became the new global neoliberal doctrine of major international financial and developmental institutions. This doctrine[30] in today's global capitalism, which prioritizes the enrichment of a company's shareholders as the only measure for the company's economic success, makes comprehensible the extreme exploitation and unseen rates of slavery in the global economy today. As in centuries before, as Clegg has shown, today, to fulfil their responsibility to increase shareholder profits, for *free capitalist enterprises* in a global market slave labour is simply the cheapest labour power available and thus the means of choice in globalized production processes.

---

[29] The roots of this idea can actually be traced back to the eighteenth century.
[30] I am grateful to Martijn Boersma for having drawn my attention to the link between the doctrine of shareholder value and the rise of global value chains and its connections with the new slavery; see also Lazonick 2007; Lazonick and O'Sullivan 2010.

Advocates of a global capitalist market and the shareholder value doctrine completely disregard existing extreme power asymmetries in favour of multinational oligopolistic corporations that prefer to dictate the terms of trade down the global hierarchy to contractors, subcontractors, and—even if indirectly—to the workers in supply firms, demanding from all human beings that they make themselves employable, sell their labour power at any price, and see themselves in permanent competition with others on a global scale.

This strategy of global capital has had far-reaching consequences: In the Global South, we see a renewed colonial dependence on multinational companies of the Global North that utilize widely *un*regulated working conditions, allowing them to harness the cheapest labour available in the global labour force and expose millions to labour and living conditions of the new slavery. Yet, also in the Global North, capital makes use of *de*regulated working conditions, exposing workers in postal delivery services and firms like Amazon, Uber, and others to extreme exploitation. Taking the European Union and the United Kingdom as an example, powerful multinational firms are also given free rein to push into new forms of slavery widely disenfranchised groups such as refugees, rejected asylum seekers, seasonal workers, or labour migrants from Eastern Europe, many of them members of Sinti and Roma groups facing racial discrimination throughout the European Union in economic sectors such as the agribusiness or meat industries.

As I conceive of global capital's imposition of a new global division of labour with the liberalization of finance and trade and the critical role of the shareholder value doctrine as a critical event, I argue that the politics of *developing and implementing global chains*—differently labelled as global value chains (GVCs), global commodity chains (GCCs), global supply chains (GSCs), or global production networks (GPNs)—is the most critical and radical strategy of global capital's reorganization of social relations between the exploiters and the exploited and the strategic means to increase profits in the global capitalist market. Yet, why is this the case?

During the last decades, global chains have become dominant and critical for capitalism's accumulation regime, as 'about 70% of international trade today involves global value chains (GVCs), as services, raw materials, parts, and components cross borders—often numerous times. Once incorporated into final products they are shipped to consumers all over the world' (OECD, n.d.-b). Thus, the establishment of global chains has created what we can call

> supply chain capitalism . . . [which] refers to commodity chains based on subcontracting, outsourcing and allied arrangements in which the autonomy of component enterprises is legally established even as the enterprises are disciplined within the chain as a whole. Such supply chains link ostensibly independent entrepreneurs, making it possible for commodity processes to span

the globe. Labor, nature, and capital are mobilized in fragmented but linked economic niches. (Tsing 2009, 148–149)

Such global chains are not simply a matter of allowing multinational firms 'to optimize their production processes by locating the various stages across different sites' (OECD n.d.-a; see also OECD n.d.-c), as neoliberal organizations and authorities argue. Capital's strategy is not that innocent. Rather, these chains 'have been purposefully constructed by powerful economic and political interests to bring about a particular model of globalized production' (Phillips 2017, 434) and operate as a critical strategy of the exploiters to globally subjugate workers in a neoliberal and financialized capitalism that has radicalized the extraction of labour power and shifted exploitation towards slavery.

Therefore, from the point of view of closure theory, global chains are a strategy to fundamentally reorganize production and labour processes, establishing a new division of labour and control with lead firms (buyers) in the Global North and contractors (suppliers) and their subcontractors in the Global South, but also within the Global North,[31] thereby promoting the rise of 'the particular form of industrial organization that has come to underpin the contemporary global economy—one organized around the structures of global value chains (GVCs) and global production networks (GPNs)' (Phillips 2017, 430). Global chains are thus a means to maximize profits by making use of extreme power inequalities in the global market:

> The increasing concentration of market power is apparent in many sectors. Examples include retailing (Walmart, Amazon, Alibaba), office software and operating systems (Microsoft), smartphones (Apple and Samsung), large commercial aircraft (Boeing and Airbus), soft drinks (Coca-Cola) and credit card networks (Visa and MasterCard). A key policy support underpinning this trend is the expansion of intellectual property protections, particularly in the high-technology sector. . . . Large firms occupy oligopolistic positions—that is, positions of market dominance, and in which the lower tiers of production are characterized by densely populated and intensely competitive markets. In the context of high levels of market concentrations, asymmetry of market power is entrenched by the simple fact that suppliers face limited numbers of buyers for their goods, lending to those lead firms a form of monopsony power, while buyers often have many potential suppliers and are able to use their market power to generate intense competition between supplier firms, particularly on conditions of price and supply. (Phillips 2017, 435)

---

[31] In the debate on global chains, the focus lies on the Global North–Global South relationship. While I agree with this critical perspective on ongoing colonial dependencies, I am also interested in specific working and living conditions within the capitalist core, created by global chains. However, I will not refer to this each time the literature concentrates on the situation in the Global South.

Based on these power asymmetries in the global market, we must further consider the intimate relations in which global chains are organized with regard to extreme social inequalities, since they not only generate them but also make use of existing grave social inequalities by deciding in which country of the Global South to have their goods produced or assembled (Phillips 2017). Of course, capital logic outsources production or assembly to countries with the lowest unit labour costs, thereby generating hyper-exploitation and conditions of slavery:

> Giant oligopolistic multinationals take advantage of differential unit labour costs within an imperialist system of 'world value'; they control much of the world market through their international operations, and the fact that capital can move much more freely than labor... allows multinationals to take advantage of labor price differences on a global level, and to possess more freedom in pursuing higher profits through the substitution of higher-paid labor with low-paid labor globally. (Suwandi 2019, 20)

From the perspective of closure theory, implementing global chains is thus a strategy of exploitation that (1) is based on contracting, subcontracting, outsourcing, and offshoring, (2) guarantees lead firms' control over production processes, and (3) is an expression of extreme power differentials in the global market. Given these extreme power imbalances between buyers and suppliers, in GVCs 'cost and time pressures can generate violations of workers' rights' (Mosely 2017, 154). For the garment industry, Mark Anner has shown that increasing pressure from capital markets has exacerbated power imbalances in the last two decades, with massive consequences for workers' rights. First, the high degree of organization and the corresponding power of multinational firms have enabled them 'to reduce the real price paid for apparel by suppliers. This *price squeeze* impacts workers in the form of low wages and increased work intensity' (Anner 2020, 321). Second, due to competition for market share and the resultant fast-fashion marketing, low retail prices, and ever-changing products, the power imbalance in GVCs produces a *sourcing squeeze* that has severe impacts on workers' rights 'in the form of chronic and forced overtime, and unauthorized outsourcing to unsafe factories. Indeed, three of four worst factory disasters in the history of industrial garment production have taken place since 2012 (Nova and Wegemer 2016)' (Anner 2020, 321).[32] Given that such squeezes create specific relations of exploitation, strategies are developed out of these transactions between the exploiting and the exploited, since

---

[32] Anner 2020 develops this approach based on developments in the garment industry. Yet, although there are features specific to the garment industry, such as permanently changing products and short fashion seasons, I would argue that price squeezes and sourcing squeezes are critical for understanding why and how global marketization maximizes exploitation/slavery through the strategy of global chains; see also Anner 2011.

the sad truth for business leaders is that modern slavery is driven, in large part, by irresponsible corporate practices and unrealistic consumer demands. While criminal trafficking networks capitalise on the exploitation of the vulnerable, they are simply servicing the industries whose business models depend on cheap overseas labour and the production of consumer goods at low prices. In other words, modern slavery is deeply embedded in our global economy. (Association of Ambas 2019)

Not much has changed in global capitalism, seeing as today, just like in historically earlier times, global capital exploits formally free *and* de facto unfree labour, both of which are sources of wealth. Given the critical role of labour power in the exploitation-slavery continuum, I follow Intan Suwandi's (2019, 17) suggestion to use the term *global labour value commodity chains* or *global labour value chains* (GLVCs) to properly describe the character of global chains that are all about extracting labour power and exploiting it to maximize profits. Of course, global capital cannot and does not act alone; rather, we must take into consideration that in the global neoliberal political economy, states, supranational actors, and neoliberal agencies support capital interests and have supported and helped to create the institutional conditions in which marketization can operate.

Global marketization again dramatizes the cleavage and the us-them boundary in terms of capital situated in the Global North and the global workforce in the Global South and Global North, as powerful multinational organizations have reinforced these centuries-old power asymmetries by creating CLVCs in order to make use of both globally different labour costs and the lack of regulations regarding labour contracts, working conditions, and the safety and health of the workforce. In this sense, the new slavery fits into the picture of the historical continuity of the existing capitalism-slavery nexus and also its racialized character. It is a critical ingredient in capital's strategy of establishing GLVCs, with an exploited and enslaved working class in the Global South and Global North: 'Slavery exists in all stages of the supply chain, from the picking of raw materials such as cocoa or cotton, to the manufacturing of goods such as mobile phones or garments, and at later stages of shipping and delivery to consumers' (Anti-Slavery International 2022b).

22.2.3 Mobilizing Predominantly Economic Structural Elements of Power

Global capital's high degree of organization among oligopolistic multinationals has enabled the wealthy and super rich, bankers, hedge funds, and shareholders to increase profits and expand their life chances / chances of survival at the cost of the exploited by intensifying exploitation and slavery in the global economy.

As social relations of exploitation are based predominantly on economic power, the strategies of global capitalist elites need to draw on its structural elements to mobilize economic power and reorganize the social relations of exploitation: (1) the ownership of means of production guaranteed by the state, access to capital, and financialization; (2) human labour, natural and material features of the environment (crops, fruits, raw materials, rare earths), and instruments of production and technology; and (3) control over production and labour processes, exchange, distribution, and consumption.

Again, these abstract notions of structural elements need to be made more concrete and plausible for an analysis of the strategies of subjugation at play in GLVCs. First, we see private property as the basis of an exploitative relationship. Since from the perspective of social closure it is critical to understand how life chances / chances of survival are created and destroyed, Weber's claim is critical, namely that 'it is the most elemental economic fact that the way in which the disposition over material property is distributed among a plurality of people, meeting competitively in the market for the purpose of exchange, in itself creates specific life chances' (Weber 1978 [1922], 927). Private property in the capitalist economy, access to capital, and financialization together create economic power that allows for the exploitation of those who have nothing to sell but their labour power or accept slavery. Second, looking at production processes, such labour power is the sole indispensable resource, as it is the only one that creates value. While in the case of GLVCs capital can rely on the unproblematic supply of labour in the Global South, in the Global North it can make use of members of social groups such as asylum seekers, refugees, or harvest workers in economic sectors as different as the agribusiness or meat-packing industry. Third, control over arm's length production—the steps of production that take place across the globe and are finally assembled in one country according to labour processes—is a critical aspect of the oligopolistic character of global capitalism, allowing for extra profits from exploitation/slavery throughout the globalized production process.

To be sure, when analysing exploitation in the global economy, we are dealing predominantly with economic power and the structural elements that powerful actors need to draw upon. However, politico-legal, ideological, and military/violence structural elements are also important. Because in neoliberalism the economy and politics (national or supranational) are ever more intertwined, the politico-legal framework for establishing GLVCs (i.e., policies to promote, establish, and back them legally) is, of course, critical. Neoliberalism as an immanent ideology serves as a legitimizing resource for global marketization and a radically intensified form of exploitation/slavery to maximize profits of shareholders and slaveholders. Further, the military/violence will always be a resource with which to guarantee the global flow of goods and the undisturbed production in supply chains. As such strategies are critical not only in countries of the Global South, we also need to recognize the crucial role of states and the European Union as main actors, leaving the most vulnerable social groups like migrants, refugees, and asylum seekers unprotected from being used as modern slaves, as is the case in almost all EU countries.

22.2.4 *Global Labour Value Chains* as a Strategy of Social Closure: Processes and Mechanisms

Turning to the core of the explanation of exploitation/slavery and conceiving of GLVCs as a strategy of extraction, we now need to take a closer look at its critical dimensions by analysing how strategies of *deprivation, undermining, suppression*, and *subjugation* operate. This will require a brief outline of how these strategies trigger the mechanisms *denial of access* and *intervention into community closure*, and how they affect the different dimensions of the life chances / chances of survival of workers in GLVCs.

As a recent strategy in the ongoing reorganization of global capitalism, capital that is highly organized is mobilizing predominantly structural elements of economic power to push through strategies of extraction. Taking into consideration at the same time that global capital's strategies are backed by states, or the European Union, closure analysis reveals and explains how these strategies reorganize the social relations between the exploiters and the exploited. The implementation of GLVCs as a critical part of enforcing a new global division of labour and the creation of monopolies in neoliberal global capitalism have transformed previously established social relations of global capital (positively privileged) and global labour (negatively privileged), which is an 'intrinsically original aspect of the new order' (Popitz 2017, 134). However, this reorganization is complex and triggers effects that closure analysis has to bring to the fore, since by making profits in countries in the Global South and Global North, capital (1) refuses workers the prerequisites to enjoy vital *resources*, (2) utilizes the lack of *rights* and enforces a country's denial of citizens' or workers' rights in the production and labour process, (3) by shifting exploitation ever further on the continuum towards slavery, reinforces and stabilizes obstacles barring workers/modern slaves from *networks/institutions* that might improve their living conditions, and (4) makes use of and reinforces processes that are destructive and degrading for *communities*.

As multinational corporations are looking for low-cost countries in which to invest in production or assembly work, food picking, meat packing, and so forth, states compete in a global market offering capital the best investment options.

Thus, rather than a natural process of production, trade, exchange, or comparative cost advantages in the twenty-first century, from the perspective of closure theory, GLVCs are a purposive strategy implemented by global capital, states, the European Union, and international regulatory bodies to set the rules that make marketization and competition among states in the Global South and Global North 'key to new regimes of profitability', allowing 'capitalists to avoid high labour costs' (Tsing 2009, 149, 151), thereby maximizing exploitation, turning millions of human beings into slaves, and maintaining colonial dependencies.

To make the explanatory logic of closure analysis plausible in the case of strategies of extraction, I look at the consequences of GLVCs as a strategy of extraction in the Global South (mainly the garment industry) and the Global North (mainly European agribusiness). The garment industry is a well-known and typical example of a GLVC, with working and living conditions in the Global South that are typical of the new slavery. Oxfam's 'What She Makes' campaign that started in 2017 has revealed these conditions, stressing the gendered and racialized exploitation in this economic sector:

> Big brands are keeping the women who make our clothes living in poverty. The women who make our clothes do not make enough to live on. . . . Despite long hours away from their families, working full time plus many hours of overtime, big clothing brands do not pay garment workers enough money to cover the basics of life—food and decent shelter. (Oxfam n.d.)

As there are no official data on the distribution of value for top brands with the highest market share, Oxfam has further shown for the case of Australia that 'on average, just 4% of the price of a piece of clothing sold in Australia goes toward workers' wages in garment factories' (Oxfam n.d.), thereby revealing an extreme redistribution of produced wealth from the female workers to the brand. 'If brands absorbed the cost of paying living wages within their supply chains, it would cost them less than 1% of the price of a garment' (Oxfam n.d.).

Looking mainly at the GLVCs in the European Union agribusiness as an example of exploitation/slavery in the Global North brings us to the core of neoliberal governance. While Olivier De Schutter, United Nations special rapporteur on extreme poverty, declared that 'the situation facing migrant workers in southern Spain is a human tragedy' (de Pablo et al. 2020), the EU Commission in drafting its new common agricultural policy (CAP) for the period 2023–2027 defined ten key objectives without ever mentioning a single word about migrants' situation in EU agribusiness (European Commission n.d.). Exploitation and slavery are a matter of course for the EU, which subsidizes its agricultural sector with almost €60 billion, almost a third of the bloc's budget (Borges and Huet 2020). There is an extreme concentration in food supply chains, giving retailers an enormous market power (see figure 22.2).

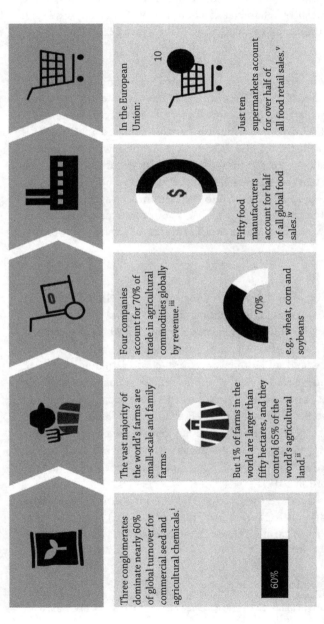

Figure 22.2 Market concentration in food supply chains

[i] Bayer-Monsanto, Dupont-Dow, and Chem-China Syngenta (Friends of the Earth Europe, Heinrich Böll Foundation & Rosa Luxemburg Foundation 2017)

[ii] Lowder, Skoet & Raney, 2016; UN Food and Agriculture Organisation 2008

[iii] Archer Daniels Midland (ADM), Bunge, Cargill and Louis Dreyfus Co. (Friends of the Earth Europe, Heinrich Böll Foundation & Rosa Luxemburg Foundation 2017)

[iv] Friends of the Earth Europe, Heinrich Böll Foundation & Rosa Luxemburg Foundation 2017

[v] Friends of the Earth Europe, Heinrich Böll Foundation & Rosa Luxemburg Foundation 2017

Source: Oxfam 2018 9

Analysing the strategies of extraction at work in both examples of GLVCs with regard to dimensions of life chances / chances of survival will also reveal the heavily gendered and racialized character of labour in GVLCs. I analyse all such strategies according to the same explanatory logic (see figure 22.3).

Deprivation

Discussing the *deprivation* of workers in the Global South and Global North of resources indispensable for realizing their life chances / chances of survival as the first dimension of GLVCs as a strategy of extraction highlights the extreme asymmetry of the distribution of value created in the global market.[33] Profits of leading firms in GLVCs are skyrocketing, while the exploitation of (mainly) female workers in the garment industry in the Global South and (mainly) migrant workers in the fields of the European agribusiness has reached unimaginable proportions. Due to the minimum wages paid by the leading companies, large sections of the global labour force have no access to vital resources and have to live under exploitative and slavery-like working and living conditions.

1. Global South

The prospects for life chances / chances of survival in the Global South are bleak for mainly female workers under labour conditions in GLVCs functioning as exploitative strategies by multinational corporations and their contractors/subcontractors, denying workers basic minimum wages and consequently access to resources that would allow them to afford 'clean drinking water and sanitation', 'decent housing', 'adequate clothing and footwear', 'education', 'a nutritious low-cost diet', 'social security schemes and basic social services', and 'savings to ensure economic resilience' (Flake, Freitag, and Gordon 2019).[34] All these vital resources are essential for human beings to realize even only basic life chances or to have any chances of survival at all, as without them it is impossible for 'a worker to afford a decent standard of living for themselves and their family' (Flake, Freitag, and Gordon 2019).

In a detailed report on wage theft in the Haitian apparel industry, where mainly US brands produce, WRC (Worker Rights Consortium) has shown 'that wage theft in Port-au-Prince garment factories robs workers of almost one third

---

[33] The extremely unequal distribution of value is apparent in all GLVCs. This is well known from the electronics sector—for example, with regard to the distribution of value for Apple's iPhone in 2010 (Clarke and Boersma 2019; Phillips 2017, 434; Kraemer, Linden and Dedrick 2011) and other devices. For a general perspective, see ILO 2014b.

[34] See LeBaron 2014 on the ethical problems of subcontracting; Barnes, Lal Das, and Pratap 2015 on the role of labour contractors with regard to the rights of workers; Ware Barrientos 2013 on the role of subcontractors in global chains.

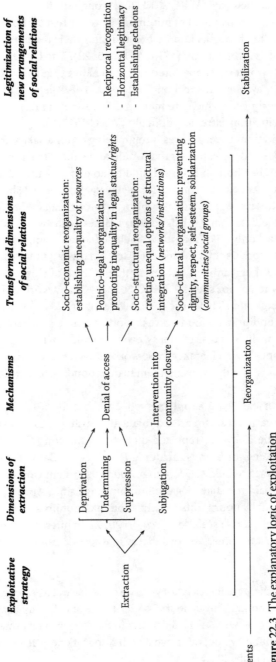

Figure 22.3 The explanatory logic of exploitation

of their legally earned pay' (WRC 2013, 20) through strategies such as minimum wage violations, non-payment of minimum wage for regular hours, work off the clock—during lunch-breaks and before and after their regular shifts—and underpayment of overtime hours (WRC 2013, 20–22). The consequences are disastrous for the workers, as one interviewed person explains: 'With this money [we can] only pay our transport and our food. This salary doesn't allow us to meet our [other] needs which are many . . . The suffering inside the factories is great and the situation extremely difficult' (WRC 2013, 8).

Such exploitation/slavery leaves human beings with a salary that pays about 19% of their basic living expenses that would allow them to simply survive—not to live decently, like human beings should be able to do—thus denying modern slaves even the most basic resources for survival, as the report shows. More than 75% of the workers 'were unable to pay for three meals a day for themselves and their immediate family'; this leaves families with 'workers' current food spending . . . [at] only 15% of a nutritionally adequate family diet. . . . Seventy-one percent of workers interviewed reported borrowing money to buy food for themselves and their families, and more than a third of workers reported borrowing money to pay for shelter' (WRC 2013, 8). Many workers have no access to clean running water. They need to buy water to drink. They bring water from wells to bathe and prepare food or wash clothes. There is hardly any electricity, and going to hospitals in case of illness, even for children, is not possible without borrowing money—which makes these workers even more vulnerable to exploitation/slavery, eventually exposing them to debt bondage as a critical form of the new slavery.

This list can easily be supplemented and extended as anywhere female workers in the garment sector are exploited and pushed into new slavery around the world. Annie Kelly has reported quite the same conditions from India in factories producing for brands including Puma, Nike, Zara, Tesco, C&A, Gap, Marks & Spencer, and H&M: 'More than 400,000 garment workers in Karnataka have not been paid the state's legal minimum wage since April 2020, according to an international labour rights organization that monitors working conditions in factories' (Kelly 2021; see also Mezzadri 2017). In interviews conducted with female workers, it becomes obvious that paid wages do not suffice to cover basic living costs:

> If we had got the wage increase last year, we could have at least eaten vegetables a few times a month. Throughout this year I have only fed my family rice and chutney sauce [she said]. . . . I tried to talk to the factory management about it, [she added], but they said, this is what we pay to work here. If you don't like it, you can leave. (Kelly, 2021)

Further, as Constance Flake, Stella Freitag and Elise Gordon state in reference to an Oxfam Australia report that

> 100 per cent of the 472 garment workers interviewed in Bangladesh, earned below the living wage. To fill this income expenditure gap 87 per cent of workers took out loans and 56 per cent made purchases on credit. In Vietnam the report found that 99 per cent of workers earned below the living wage recommended by the Asia Floor Wage and 74 per cent earned below the rate established by the Global Living Wage Coalition. (Flake, Freitag, and Gordon 2019)

Finally, a report on Ethiopia, which has only recently become a *North Star* (WRC 2018) in the global apparel sector, is an example of global capital's ruthless strategies of moving production to the places offering the cheapest labour, making use of states' rules that allow hyper-exploitation and conditions of slavery, while at the same time guaranteeing the withdrawal of profit made from the country. The minimum wages per hour and per month paid in Ethiopia to female workers reach an incredibly low point that only becomes clear in comparison to other countries where wages are also paid below minimum (see table 22.3).

Looking at the garment sector around the globe and the politics of apparel brands, there is a *race to the bottom* in terms of wages paid in order to increase profits for brands. As one worker stated, who was employed in the Port-au-Prince garment factories in Haiti mentioned above, there is no way 'to reach the

Table 22.3. Hourly and Monthly Minimum Wage for Garment Workers by Country Compared to the Lowest Garment Worker Wage in Ethiopia (USD)

Hourly Minimum Wage		Monthly Minimum Wage	
China	1,45	China	302
Honduras	1,20	Honduras	288
Cambodia	0,88	Cambodia	182
India	0,48	India	113
Pakistan	0,46	Pakistan	108
Bangladesh	0,45	Bangladesh	94
Burma	0,38	Burma	78
Ethiopia	0,12	Ethiopia	25

Source: WRC 2018

impossibly high production quota the factories require workers to meet in order to earn the minimum wage' (WRC 2013, 24).[35]

Extraction of labour power in GLVCs is also characterized by powerful brands' or retailers' ability to relocate production sites to countries that entice with lower-than-minimum wages, purposive wage theft by violating even these minimum wages, and enforced unpaid overtime. Such working and living conditions are simply *pure industrial slavery*, creating a vicious cycle because 'without a living wage, workers may be compelled to work excessive overtime hours or multiple jobs, become bonded labourers, put their children into work instead of school' (Ethical Trading Initiative n.d.; Walk Free 2019).

2. Global North

The extreme power asymmetry and resulting market power of retailers and supermarkets such as Edeka, Rewe, Aldi, Lidl, Carrefour, and Tesco in GLVCs reveal a typical structure:

> At the top, big supermarkets and other corporate food giants dominate global food markets, allowing them to squeeze value from vast supply chains that span the globe, while at the bottom the bargaining power of small-scale farmers and workers has been steadily eroded in many of the countries from which they source. The result is widespread human suffering among the women and men producing food for supermarkets around the world. (Oxfam 2018; see figure 22.4).

Under these conditions, the strategies of retailers and supermarkets are the same as those in the garment industry in the Global South, as wages in exploitation/slavery are so low that access to vital resources is denied.

In Italy, small-scale farmers and workers in vegetable and fruit chains had difficulties accessing food due to earnings that were too low: 50% severely food insecure, 36% moderately food insecure, 9% mildly food insecure, and 5% food secure, as '75% of surveyed women workers on fruit and vegetable farms said they or a family member had cut back on the number of meals in the previous month because their household could not afford sufficient food' (Oxfam 2018, 13, 14).

In Spain, in the province of Huelva, with around half a billion euros in revenue yearly, farmworkers suffer from exploitative labour conditions and are

---

[35] As we have seen in the case of exclusion, the Covid-19 pandemic clearly revealed neoliberal elites' contempt for humanity, and quite a number of investigations have shown the same for global corporations' failure to take responsibility for workers in their GLVCs during the pandemic. For reports, see Nova and Zeldenrust 2020; Kyritsis, LeBaron, and Nova 2020; WRC 2020.

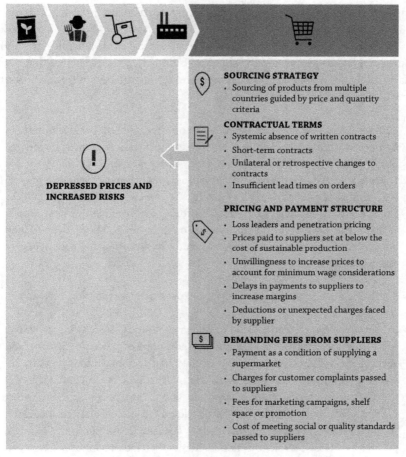

Figure 22.4 Powerful retailers depressing prices and increasing risks for supermarket suppliers

Source: Oxfam 2018 10

Figure created by Oxfam using information from Vaughan-Whitehead & Caro, 2017; Ellison 2017; European Parliament 2016. See Appendix 1 in the main report for a list of unfair trading practices and references.

treated like slaves. 'Many farmworkers in the region are undocumented migrants living in "chabolas"—shacks made up of discarded pallets, pieces of cardboard and plastic leftover from greenhouses. These have no access to electricity, sanitation or clean water' (Borges and Huet 2020). Wage withdrawal is usual for workers who fail to make the quota. 'Most of the workers we spoke to for this investigation asked not to be identified for fear of reprisal. Several had worked for Bionest—also known as Berrynest—which collected €4.4 million in CAP subsidies last year alone, according to data provided by the Spanish government' (Borges and Huet 2020).

In France, which receives €7 billion of agricultural subsidies from the European Union every year, the situation is no better. Cases such as that of the Larrère farms have been revealed, where workers are offered miserable working and living conditions:

> Up to five adults were packed together in one bedroom. Others slept in bunk beds, in violation of French laws relating to the housing of seasonal workers. No bedsheets or pillows were provided. There was no toilet paper in the restrooms. The Larrère farms are major producers of organic carrots in France, with annual sales of around €50 million. They receive more than €300,000 in European CAP subsidies each year, according to government data. We spoke to more than a dozen people who worked on these farms. They described long working days, extra hours left unpaid, and excessive housing costs. (Borges and Huet 2020)

Not only in Southern Europe are workers experiencing exploitation/slavery. Also

> in Germany, the Netherlands and Sweden agri-food restructuring processes producing a price-cost squeeze and an imbalance of power along long and verticalized supply chains are one of the main factors putting pressure on working conditions. The retail giants and international buying groups (IBGs) use their oligopolistic market power to impose prices and conditions on farmers. This leads to an unfair distribution of risks, costs and profits along supply chains. Therefore, the margin for farmers across Europe to increase prices on wholesale markets is limited. Rather than looking for other strategies that allow them to keep being competitive or to develop alternative channels or shorter supply chains, most farmers tend to depress the cost of labour by lowering pay and eroding working conditions. (Palumbo and Corrado 2020)

In Germany, as the weekly magazine *Der Spiegel* reported, migrant workers, after having arrived, found out that they had to work off the cost of the flight and the food. While they had been promised €7 per hour, they later learned that Germany's minimum wage was €9.35. Yet, one of the migrants said, '"But that was irrelevant anyway, given that the fees were calculated according to performance: 3 euros per box of strawberries." . . . "We needed at least 45 minutes for that". They often worked 10-hour days' (Klawitter, Lüdke, and Schrader 2020).

In Australia, people working in farms and factories for suppliers of Australia's biggest supermarkets and fast-food chains suffer from extreme exploitation and conditions of slavery. The *Four Corners* investigation of ABC 'revealed the food being picked, packed and processed by exploited workers is being sold to consumers nationwide. The supermarkets involved include Woolworths, Coles, Aldi, IGA and Costco' (AP Migration 2015), but also KFC and Red Rooster.

While the investigation into the Australian situation found that 'the shocking forms of exploitation are all accompanied by the gross underpayment of wages, with potentially hundreds of millions of dollars in stolen pay' (AP Migration 2015), these findings can be generalized to the situation in agribusiness GVLCs in the Global North as well. As in the Global South, exploitation/slavery with wages that do not allow workers and their families to make a decent living deny them access to vital resources such as water, food, sanitation, housing, and others. GLVCs are thus a capital-based strategy of reorganizing social relations among the exploiters and the exploited, minimizing the life chances / chances of survival of the latter at the expense of the former.

Undermining

In general, *undermining* refers to the fact that workers in GLVCs are denied the most basic human rights and protections in the production and labour process, as Genevieve LeBaron and her colleagues have shown in reference to studies pointing out some of the most 'endemic rights violations' such as 'gender-based violence (Evans 2017; Selwyn, Misiolek, and Ijarja 2020), unsafe working conditions and dangerous levels of productivity (Merk 2011; Mezzadri 2017), and infringements on freedom of association (Egels-Zandén and Merk 2014; Anner 2017)' (LeBaron et al. 2022, 9).

While 'the legal basis for international human, labour and women's rights obligations is found in the Universal Declaration of Human Rights (1948), the International Covenant on Economic Social and Cultural Rights (1966), the International Covenant on Civil and Political Rights (1966) and the UN Convention on the Elimination of All Forms of Discrimination against Women (1979)' (Oxfam 2019, 25), GLVCs operate as an exploitative and enslaving strategy of global capital to maximize profits. Yet, these practices would not be possible without states setting the rules that govern both lead firms in countries of the Global North and production and labour conditions everywhere. In this sense, processes of *re*regulation again play a critical role. While governments in countries of the Global North have done everything to pave the way for lead firms to exploit and enslave human beings in the Global South, they also turn a blind eye to the situation in their own countries that they created. Governments of states in the Global South are in a weak position with regard to both Western states' and global capital's demands to reduce minimum wages and *de*regulate working conditions. However, this does not excuse the fact that they take advantage of their powerful position vis-à-vis their own citizens, whom they expose to working conditions with hardly any labour regulations, denying them workers' rights or their citizenship rights in general, and are ready to even use violence against their citizens if necessary—at the service of global capital.

1. Global South

Rules and regulations that states in the Global South set for global capital to operate within their jurisdictions contribute to fundamentally reorganizing the social relations between global brands and ordinary workers in the garment industry. *Re*regulating conditions for global brands to produce in a country allows for multinational companies to create opportunity structures and, consequently, mobilize power that forces the exploited into *de*regulated or widely *un*regulated inhumane working and living conditions, exposing (female) workers to exploitation and conditions of slavery.

In the report on Ethiopia quoted above, the WRC (2018) points out the Ethiopian government's critical role in the hyper-exploitation/slavery, as it offers conditions for global capital characterized by 'harsh restrictions on freedom of association, speech and assembly—in particular, on the ability of non-governmental human rights organizations to function freely' (WRC 2018, 16). States offering the cheapest labour and best conditions for exploitation/slavery profit from corporate taxes—however small their share may be—by undermining the rights of their own citizens, denying them access to basic rights, and leaving them without legal protection from the exploitation and brutalized working conditions imposed at the bottom of GLVCs. Not the *formally free* labourer, but the *de facto unfree* female worker, deprived of rights, is creating global wealth without any chance of realizing her own life chances / chances of survival. Multinational brands' utilization of such conditions becomes obvious with an 'increase in the *illegal use of contract labor* in apparel factories, particularly in Asia, which has the effect of denying a large percentage of the production workers at many factories the wages, benefits, and protection from arbitrary dismissal to which they would otherwise be entitled' (Nova 2006; emphasis added).

When it comes to violently attacking, jailing, or killing workers who demand their rights, the recent situation in Myanmar (Hoskins et al. 2021)[36] is obvious, yet we have seen such assaults for a long time already in other countries, such as Cambodia, which sentenced and jailed workers (Nova and DeLaurentis 2019) following a military crackdown on strikes in 2014 (WRC 2019a). While multinational brands in GLVCs can rely on states and the military to secure their private property, they can also make use of often-unmanageable legal regulations

---

[36] While brands stopped sourcing from Myanmar after the coup in February 2021 and later resumed business, it has become obvious that workers' rights are simply a chess piece in the game of cynical Western politics that does not care about exploitation/slavery in friendly countries.

that are barely controlled and that allow them to reject responsibility for workers' wages or the working conditions of their suppliers:

> While supply chains stretch across multiple jurisdictions, they are too often effectively regulated by *none*. Meanwhile, the number of victims trapped in modern slavery . . . remains stubbornly high. Despite forced labour and slavery being a violation of customary international law, and the subject of numerous treaties, domestic regulations, and voluntary standards followed by both companies and MSIs [multi-stakeholder initiatives—J.M.], such modern slavery practices persist. (Nolan and Bott 2018, 60; emphasis added)

Both sides are critical here with regard to production in GLVCs framed by a neoliberal political economy. On the one hand, workers are denied their basic rights to unionize so that they will not demand or fight for better working conditions, running the risk of violent police or military suppression if they were to do so. On the other hand, multinational corporations' exploitative practices are backed by states that set the rules, also—in accordance with institutions such as the World Trade Organization, IMF, and World Bank, and the global financial sector—enabling GLVCs' business models of contracting[37] and subcontracting across multiple jurisdictions. From a global perspective, processes of reorganization in the course of marketization have enabled an economically induced and politico-legally enforced reorganization of inequalities that keeps workers deprived of rights while permitting organized irresponsibility and generalized impunity that protect lead firms from being held accountable.[38]

2. Global North

GLVCs operate as a strategy of global capital to systematically undermine the rights of the global workforce. In demanding not only the opening of markets in countries of the Global South, but also supporting their lead firms in *de*regulating working conditions and rejecting minimum wages, maximum daily working hours, workplace safety, and the right to unionize, governments of states of the Global North have contributed to disenfranchising workers in the Global North

---

[37] There has been an 'increase in the illegal use of contract labor in apparel factories, particularly in Asia, which has the effect of denying a large percentage of the production workers at many factories the wages, benefits, and protection from arbitrary dismissal to which they would otherwise be entitled' (Nova 2006).

[38] While this is the basic politico-legal consequence of GLVCs as a strategy of undermining rights of the global workforce, in recent years workers, their organizations, and external supporters have won quite a number of court proceedings holding multinational corporations accountable, ordering them to compensate workers for wages that had been withheld or simply stolen from them. Analysing these class struggles would be interesting cases for theorizing counterstrategies in closure struggles and explaining how exploited/enslaved workers fight back.

as much as possible, making them exploitable for lead firms and driving them into conditions of modern slavery.[39] Like in the Global South

> exploitation and systematic denial of the rights of workers—especially of migrant workers—also underpins the agri-food sector in Northern Europe. The retail giants and international buying groups (IBGs) use their oligopolistic market power to impose prices and conditions on farmers. This leads to an unfair distribution of risks, costs and profits along supply chains. Therefore, the margin for farmers across Europe to increase prices on wholesale markets is limited. (Palumbo and Corrado 2020; see also Davies 2019)

As an expression of neoliberal governance, also in countries of the Global North, states have played a crucial role in undermining the rights of workers, destroying their life chances / chances of survival in favour of maximizing profits for lead firms in GLVCs. States, as well as the European Union, have thus been supportive in undermining basic human rights, including civil, political, and social rights, such as the right to unionize, to a legally regulated working day, and others, with the end result of making migrants and seasonal workers exploitable to degrees that amount to slavery. This reserve army for global capital has been left without any protection by governments in the Global North, or the European Union as a supranational actor, which are simply fulfilling the demands of global capital and its *missionary institutions* (Stiglitz 2002) such as the WTO, IMF, and World Bank.

The situation of workers in the Irish fishing industry is so grave that, in 2019, the Special Rapporteur on the human rights of migrants; the Special Rapporteur on contemporary forms of racism, racial discrimination, xenophobia, and related intolerance; the Special Rapporteur on contemporary forms of slavery, including its causes and consequences; and the Special Rapporteur on trafficking in persons, especially women and children (2019), reported that 'they had been given evidence that laws on minimum wage, maximum hours and safety were being widely flouted, while a quarter of Asian and African migrant workers in fishing boats (Lawrence and McSweeney 2018) had experienced verbal or physical abuse, and one in five had experienced racial discrimination' (Lawrence and McSweeney 2019).

---

[39] Only after pressure from civil society after disasters such as 'the collapse of the Rana Plaza building in Dhaka, Bangladesh, which housed five garment factories [that] killed at least 1,132 people and injured more than 2,500' (ILO n.d.), there arose a debate on working conditions for female workers in the garment industry in the Global South. The governments of Western states now engage in window dressing, with an undignified spectacle of supply chain laws that are allegedly made to improve working conditions in GLVCs but are simply a staging to appease the Western public. Germany's so-called Supply Chain Act (*Lieferkettengesetz*), for example, has fulfilled all the demands of German capital and thus created a purposeless law, the consequence being that Germany now does everything to mitigate the Supply Chain Law planned by the European Union.

Even after the working and living conditions of migrant workers, undocumented migrants, rejected asylum seekers, and seasonal workers from mainly Eastern European countries became known to the population during the Covid-19 pandemic, they were not discussed as a systematically disenfranchised group of hyper-exploited human beings who had been exposed to new forms of slavery, but as isolated cases. It thus comes as little surprise that human rights, workers' rights, social rights, and legal protection for all these workers do not play any role in the most powerful instrument of the EU Commission, the CAP. As noted above, working and living conditions of migrant or seasonal workers in the EU agribusiness in the fields of Europe are not even mentioned in the CAP 2023-2027. This amounts to allowing the EU member states and lead firms of GLVCs to continue undermining the fundamental rights of the most vulnerable workers. Western states and the European Union thus contribute to, promote, and aggravate the ongoing destruction of these workers' life chances / chances of survival, creating and re-creating conditions of exploitation/slavery, as Oxfam has revealed in its 2019 report *Workers' Rights in Supermarket Supply Chains*:

> Our food supply chains are in crisis. Around the world, Oxfam has found them to be rife with violations of human, labour and women's rights. Forced labour and hidden suffering are unwanted ingredients in products ranging from tea and cocoa to fruit and vegetables, meat and seafood. In-work poverty in these supply chains is the norm, not the exception, and gender discrimination is woven into their fabric. (Oxfam 2019, 3)

The organization and strategic reorganization of life chances / chances of survival becomes clear if we look at how processes of *de-* and *re*regulation are connected to differences in how the exploiters and exploited are treated legally. While states and the EU allow the basic human, social, economic, and civil rights of the vulnerable workforce in EU agribusiness—migrants, asylum seekers, the undocumented, seasonal workers—to be undermined, lead firms are subsidized from the almost €60 billion EU budget for the agricultural sector, enabling them to make huge profits. Further, the EU operates as a tax haven, paving the way for tax avoidance instead of protecting vulnerable workers, thereby contributing to the reorganization of social relations with regard to the rights that exploiters and the exploited can legitimately claim. To name just one example

> some of Europe's biggest meat companies have avoided paying tax on more than €200 million in what experts say are 'aggressive tax avoidance' schemes. The findings involve Anglo Beef Processors (ABP), owned by Irish billionaire Larry Goodman, as well as Pilgrim's Pride and Moy Park which are both owned by Brazilian beef giant JBS, the world's largest meat company. Together the two

groups control a third of the UK's beef, and chicken production, and a quarter of its pork. They are leading suppliers to most major supermarkets, as well as fast food chains McDonalds, Nando's and KFC. ABP controls 30% of the Republic of Ireland's beef processing and up to half of the lamb processing on the island of Ireland. It operates across Europe, with plants and sales offices in Poland, France, Spain and the Netherlands. Both groups used finance companies in European tax havens to book hundreds of millions of euros in profits. But these companies employ nobody, and were taxed at less than one percent. Corporate tax rates in the UK and Ireland—where the profits would otherwise have been taxed—are 19% and 12.5% respectively. (Lighthouse Reports 2022)

At the same time

migrant workers supplying meat to supermarket shelves all over the EU face a system of exploitation and labour abuses in Spain's largest slaughterhouses. [Their rights are not secured, as they] 'can be fired any time without being compensated. . . . Many described a culture of fear and widespread racist comments in which workers were told to go back to their countries or staff refused to address them by name. 'They see us as animals,' one Senegalese worker told us. (Lighthouse Reports 2021)

Further, the Spanish meat industry makes use of contracting and subcontracting, hiring 'up to 20,000 workers . . . through "multi-service companies," under a sub-contracting model that allows employers to circumvent worker protections. Workers are made to work long hours and receive wages below the legal minimum—an entirely legal system, a legal expert told us, that allows meat companies to substantially reduce costs' (Lighthouse Reports 2021).

In a global perspective, exercising rights, if any exist, is getting more difficult for workers given the 'predominance of short-term contracts', while 'both informal work and modern slavery are growing' (Deen 2019). Further, Sharan Burrow, general secretary of the International Trade Union Confederation (ITUC), explains:

'Where wages are low and there is no decent work, where there are no unions to represent workers and defend their rights—we see the conditions which lead to modern slavery'. . . . Further, 'inequality of income and between those who can access decent work drives people to work under exploitative conditions, and the inequality of the relationship between employer and worker stops you being able to exercise your rights'. (Burrow, quoted in Deen 2019)

As the Foundation for European Progressive Studies and the think-tank TASC (FEPS & TASC, 2022) found analysing working conditions of thousands of migrants in the agricultural and care sectors in Germany, Spain, Ireland, and Greece, 'an estimated one-third of agricultural workers and just under half of all domestic workers in the EU are undeclared and therefore excluded from basic mechanisms of social protection' (Cohen, Mitchell, and Morav 2022). However, European governments and the European Union have not taken steps to protect workers from exploitation/slavery.

Suppression

Suppression, the third aspect of GLVCs as a strategy of extraction, aims at denying workers access to critical networks or institutions, such as unions or public health, both of which are codified human rights. However, from the perspective of social closure, the denial of access means that vulnerable workers are left without possibilities to either fight against being exploited and exposed to slavery or to protect themselves against health risks resulting from their working and living conditions—their lives are simply put at risk. Denying access to networks and institutions extremely diminishes the life chances / chances of survival of the exploited.

Looking at problems of unionization in the Global South from this perspective allows us to focus on the ways lead firms in GLVCs deliberately make use of social and legal conditions in the countries of their suppliers for their own benefit. These states suppress or forbid unions and struggles while arresting, imprisoning, or killing people involved in them. This perspective further reveals how lead firms have an effect on politics and legislation in these countries or demand guarantees of smooth production and labour process conditions. With regard to the situation in the Global North, I do refer to unionization, but also to the denial of access to public health systems.

1. *Global South*

The situation in Cambodia's garment sector is an example of how the joint approach of powerful actors on the side of the exploiting—a state acting on behalf of financial investors and lead firms in GLVCs—does everything to undermine the efforts of garment workers to act in solidarity, such as in January 2014, faced with their demands for a minimum wage:

> The South Korean Embassy in Phnom Penh, at the request of local Korean factory owners, actively lobbied the Cambodian military to intervene against wage protests by garment workers, and, subsequently, applauded the government's violent crackdown. Korean investors hold full or partial ownership of 84 of the 613 apparel factories that are members of the GMAC, and these plants supply many of the top brands and suppliers sourcing from Cambodia, including adidas, Gap, Kohl's, Sears, H&M, Forever 21, JCPenney, Walmart, VF, Mango, Target, Costco, Spanx, Children's Place, and Li & Fung. (WRC 2014, 25)

WRC concluded that the greatest responsibility for the brutal repression by a military combat unit lay with the Cambodian government and the country's authoritarian Prime Minister Hun Sen. Yet, WRC further made clear that 'Cambodian factory owners are also deeply implicated in this violent campaign against garment workers' call for higher wages, as are their business partners— the leading US and European apparel companies that obtain the greatest profits from these workers' labor' (WRC 2014, 4).

Since then, independent unions have been under constant political pressure, their members confronted with violence, arbitrary arrests, and remand. In contrast to compliant and short-leashed trade unions aligned with either the government or employers, independent unions and their members face severe problems with regard to their activities, as Human Rights Watch published in its report *Only 'Instant Noodle' Unions Survive* on the busting of unions in the Cambodian tourism and garment sector:

> Since 2015, the Cambodian government has adopted an array of laws that significantly restrict the rights to freedom of expression, peaceful assembly, and association. These include the Trade Union Law (TUL), which imposes restrictive and burdensome requirements around registering unions, and restrictions on independent unions on the right to strike and collectively bargain. The law makes registering unions mandatory. (HRW 2022a)

There can be no doubt that the *price squeeze* in GLVCs has created the unbearable working and living conditions of being exploited without receiving a minimum wage to make a living. It is a strategy that operates in the form of co-ordinated and common politics among states in the Global North and Global South, lead firms, investors, contractors, and subcontractors, all of whom have an interest in safeguarding exploitation/slavery in GLVCs for the sake of profits at the expense of ordinary workers, who in turn are deprived of their life chances / chances of survival by powerful and highly organized interests.

These organized policies on the part of brands in the Global North and governments in the Global South to safeguard the exploitation/enslavement of workers in the garment sector shows on the one hand that these states are ready to make use of the police and the military to violently suppress unions and unionization. In Bangladesh, workers' demand for a dollar an hour led to a mass suppression of workers through mass firings, violence, false arrests, and collective punishments through criminal charges, dismissal, and blacklisting (WRC 2019b), all measures that inevitably serve to intimidate workers so that they will not act in solidarity or organize.

On the other hand, this carte blanche for exploitation and slavery makes global brands even more inhumane in their practices and behaviour towards ordinary workers. In 2009, 'Russell Athletics, a US brand claimed in a report that unionization was unpopular in Honduras and Central America' (WRC 2009). In its reaction to this claim, WRC referred to the Central American context:

> It is profoundly cynical to claim that unionization is 'unpopular' among Central American workers without acknowledging the long and brutal history, and present reality, of anti-union repression in Honduras and throughout the region—including assassinations of trade unionists and other forms of violence. Illegal firings of union supporters, blacklisting, threats and intimidation, illegal anti-union factory closures, murders of union leaders and other tactics of repression have kept Central American factories virtually union-free for decades. In recent years, there has been another upsurge in anti-union violence, illegal firings and other forms of retaliation; yet despite this repressive environment, many workers continue to try to unionize in order to protect their rights and improve their wages and conditions of work. The stark reality... is that Central American factories remain largely without unions not because 'unionization is unpopular with workers,' but because factory operators use scorched earth tactics to terrorize workers and make unionization virtually impossible.... One cannot say that the exercise of a basic right is 'unpopular,' when every attempt at it is met with harsh repression. (WRC 2009)

2. Global North
The situation is also severe in the agricultural sector and the meat-packing industry in the Global North, where lead firms, supported by governments and the EU, deny opportunities for unionization or access to unions, thereby violating workers' rights. A Lighthouse Report revealed that, in the Spanish meat-packing industry, migrants 'face intimidation if they attempt to unionise' (Lighthouse Reports 2021). The rejection of unionization is quite strong. In an investigation of working conditions in agri-food GLVCs, Oxfam showed not only a general trend of declining union organization, but also that

> the organization of workers is particularly weak within food supply chains. In a global survey of nearly 1,500 companies in global supply chains, less than a quarter of food suppliers noted the presence of trade unions (Vaughan-Whitehead and Caro 2017). When they are present, unions are often excluded from management discussions on wages or working conditions in the workplace (Vaughan-Whitehead and Pinedo Caro 2017). (Oxfam 2018, 32)

Besides declining union power and intimidation to prevent organization in GLVCs, denying workers access to public healthcare is another critical aspect of exploitation/slavery. Apart from excessive working hours, labour in the fields has become more dangerous given high-risk environmental conditions. As Michael Sainato has reported, in the US farmworkers have to work in the heat without proper protection:

> It's really challenging to work in the heat, but the reality is we have to, we don't really have a choice, we have to keep working even when it's incredibly hot, [said Tere Cruz, a farm worker for 15 years in Immokalee, Florida.] The first thing in the morning, you don't feel it as much but then after 11am your body really starts to feel the heat. You feel like all the energy has been sucked out of you and it's really hard to keep going. (Sainato 2021)

While workers are forced to work at night to avoid the heat (Tchoubar 2021), some of them have died under these working conditions (Rubin 2021). In the face of these developments, Kristjan Bragason has made clear that

> Europe is no different. With rising temperatures, workers face a growing risk of dehydration, sunburn, —in the worst cases—death. . . . According to international and EU labour standards, employers have a clear obligation to assess all risks and to stop any operation if there is an imminent and serious danger to safety and health. (Bragason 2021)

However, having rules means nothing if there is no supervision of life-threatening working and living conditions. Bragason lists other risks:

> 'Aridification caused by climate change is also accompanied by increased ultra-violet radiations, leading to a growing incidence of non-melanoma skin cancer among outdoor workers. The prevention of skin cancer, then, requires comprehensive strategies to be defined by political institutions with the involvement of social partners' (Bragason 2021).

The already precarious situation with regard to workers' health in the agribusiness and meat-packing industries was fully revealed during the Covid-19 pandemic in the form of missing health protection for workers, exposing them to the risk of infection and death. Here

> the German meatpacking firm Tönnies came under fire when it struggled to help authorities track and trace hundreds of infected workers. Much of the company's workforce is hired in Eastern Europe, via subcontractors accused by unions of underpaying extra working hours and charging migrant workers hundreds of euros of rental fees for a bed in a shared room. (Borges and Huet 2020)

Also in the Spanish agribusiness, the situation exposed workers to life-threatening conditions, as the German magazine *Der Spiegel* reported:

> A photo taken by a worker shows harvest workers in late April under a plastic tarpaulin, shoulder to shoulder, with no masks. According to a complaint from employees to the authorities, nine large companies in the region, including Berrynest, have done nothing to protect workers. According to the letter, the workers are afraid of getting infected. Few dared to ask for more protection, it argues, because it was clear to everyone that if they did, they would be fired. 'They have stripped us of our dignity' says one Spanish worker. 'I feel like a slave'. (Klawitter, Lüdke, and Schrader 2020; see also Huet 2020)

In its investigation of working conditions and protection, former fruit pickers in Huelva (Spain) reported that 'they weren't given any masks or gloves during the COVID-19 pandemic'. As during the pandemic fewer workers were available, capital used this situation to even increase pressure on workers, who 'all complained of unpaid hours, gruelling working conditions and tremendous pressure to gather large volumes of fruit' (Borges and Huet 2020).

Strategies of actors in neoliberal governance to make use of the pandemic by reorganizing social relations of exploitation through increasing the life chances of the exploiters and minimizing the chances of survival of the exploited, intentionally exposing them to danger, become clear in the case of Germany, which changed legislation during the pandemic to deny migrant workers access to public health and the health system:

> In the second year of the pandemic, migrant workers continue to work under precarious conditions, exacerbated by the additional risks associated with Covid-19. Social security assistance in Germany, including health care provisions, requires a minimum of 70 working days before employers are required to contribute. During last year's agricultural season, the German government raised this minimum to 115 days. This made healthcare the responsibility of one's country of citizenship, not of one's employer. Infected workers could thus be sent back to their home countries for treatment and both healthcare costs and the subsequent risks of spreading infection were relegated to sending countries. This year, in April 2021, the German farming industry has successfully pressured the government to re-extend this provision to 102 days. (Bejan and Boatcă 2021)

Migrants' health and chances of survival have been compromised by joint actions between capital and the states/EU during the Covid-19 pandemic. Neoliberal governance *de*regulated—in fact removed—any kind of protection for workers and denied them access to healthcare. Integration into an essential societal institution was denied in favour of securing high profits for the EU agribusiness at the cost of the health of migrant workers, whose lives no longer count and are declared to be valueless.[40]

Subjugation

Turning to subjugation as the fourth dimension of GLVCs as a strategy of extraction, we now examine processes that activate the mechanism *intervention into community closure*, which operates in a way that prevents workers from closing their communities, impinges on processes of identity formation and the development of solidarity. Again, deprivation, undermining, and suppression as dimensions of extraction not only trigger the mechanism *denial of access* in various ways, but also activate the mechanism *intervention into community closure* as has become especially obvious in the case of denying unionization or collective action in the face of dehumanising working conditions. All these strategies have already destructive effects on both individuals and communities.

Yet, following Neuwirth's arguments, the critical aspect when it comes to triggering the mechanism *intervention into community closure* is the use of specific forms of control by the powerful to stabilize existing asymmetric social relations and keep the weaker side in its subordinate position. Looking at the working conditions of the garment industry in the Global South as well as the fields of the agribusiness in the Global North, it becomes obvious that beyond mental, psychological, and physical attacks on all workers, gender-based violence and harassment (GBVH) as well as attacks on and abuses of the female psyche and body—even murdering women—often acting together with racism, are the most pervasive forms of control that may be exerted in GLVCs, not only being unbearable for women and destroying their dignity and self-respect but also dissolving families and whole communities. Such a *culture of fear* among the most vulnerable in relations of exploitation is typical in the Global South but also well known with regard to the working conditions in the Global North, where it goes hand in hand with the strategy of *making workers invisible*.

1. Global South

To understand the impact of strategies of subjugation controlling human beings working in the garment industry, we need to look at the labour process itself. Abusing exploited/enslaved workers in GLVCs in a very general sense

---

[40] Even if there has been support, 'the measures taken by German farmers (Kinkartz 2021), such as providing lunch to workers so they do not venture out to the grocery store or paying for workers' COVID tests on a regular basis, are hardly for the sake of the workers. The tacit goal is not to protect migrants for their own sake, because workers should be cared for as workers, but to spare the farms the problem of having to deal with infected workers' (Bejan and Boatcă 2021).

has a deeply negative impact on processes of community closure. Strategies of subjugating human beings have been made public in a Human Rights Watch (HRW) report referring to rights and dignity, respect, and self-esteem—critical dimensions of life chances / chances of survival—in a discussion of human rights violations of millions of people working in GLVCs:

> Too many of these workers endure abuses such as poor working conditions, including minimum wage violations; forced overtime; child labor; sexual harassment, exposure to toxic substances and other extreme occupational hazards; and retaliation against workers who attempt to organize. (HRW 2016, 5)

Abuse, degradation, and sheer violence in the labour process are strategies of subjugation aimed at offending workers' dignity, degrading them, denying them respect, and destroying their self-esteem by refusing to recognize them as human beings: 'Workers reported that managers or supervisors addressed them with terms like "stupid" and "trash" and said they were "dumb", "deaf", and "worthless"' (WRC 2019b, 20). Again, with Neuwirth we can see that also within the production process in the economic sphere, multinational corporations, their contractors, and/or subcontractors use such practices or approve them knowingly, as they serve their critical interest in 'perpetuat[ing] the powerlessness' (Neuwirth 1969) of the subordinated to exploit their labour power.

All workers are affected by such destructive behaviour of overseers in labour processes and managers in supply firms, as the strategies aim to perpetuate an extremely asymmetric social relation of exploitation/slavery. Yet, I want to draw attention to the critical phenomenon of GBVH and thus to gender-specific violence in the form of sexual harassment in both the garment industry in the Global South and the agribusiness in the Global North, which destroys women's dignity and self-respect and poses a permanent threat to their lives.[41] As the report *Unbearable Harassment* has revealed, market pressures are creating conditions for endemic abuse while also creating a culture of impunity (Business & Human Rights Resource Center & Asia Floor Wage Alliance 2022, 9–12).

A collection of ninety testimonies from women in thirty-one factories[42] in the main centres of India's garment production—Faridabad and Kapashera,

---

[41] This problem of the abuse of women and girls in the agribusiness sector in the European Union was addressed in a study by the FEMM Committee European Parliament 2018.

[42] 'These women work at factories which supply, or have recently supplied, to at least 12 global fashion brands and retailers: American Eagle, ASDA, C&A, Carrefour, H&M, JD Sports, Kohl's, Levi Strauss & Co., Marks & Spencer, Primark, Tesco and VF Corporation (and its portfolio brands, including Vans). All 12 brands have been linked to—often multiple—allegations of GBVH in their garment supply chains prior to the release of this report' (Business & Human Rights Resource Center and Asia Floor Wage Alliance 2022, 4).

Delhi NCR; Bangalore, Karnataka; and Dindigul, Erode, and Tirupur, Tamil Nadu—has revealed the general atmosphere of fear in which female workers are working and living, and the systematic gender-based violence with which they are confronted every day. The reports of all the women reveal that global capital's strategy of GLVCs has created working conditions in which women's bodies are seen as something available to men at all hierarchical levels of the supply firms and beyond. Considering a woman to be someone else's property is a key characteristic of slavery. Understanding women's bodies as private property to be used as bargaining chips for benefits or sexually exploited to avoid arbitrary discrimination is characteristic of slavery in the labour and production processes of global capitalism, which degrades, dehumanizes, and commodifies women:

> GBVH is endemic to India's garment industry, long predating the pandemic and largely driven by brand purchasing practices. Every woman worker we spoke to reported either directly experiencing or witnessing GBVH—including workplace discipline practices and sexual violence and harassment—in their factories, perpetrated by male supervisors and managers who drive them to meet unreasonable production targets set by fashion brands. These findings demonstrate violence on the factory floor cannot be dismissed as just a factory-level problem; rather, it must be understood as an industry-wide culture of violence. Women garment workers also reported sexual harassment and violence from men in positions of authority within the factory, as well as co-workers. However, GBVH most commonly took place in the context of employment relationships, where women held subordinate roles in relation to male supervisors, line managers and mechanics tasked with fixing their machines. The most routine forms of sexual harassment disclosed included sexual jokes, catcalling, touching women on their cheeks, buttocks and breasts and sexual advances from supervisors and managers, especially among young women workers and trainees. Women also described managers offering to reduce production targets and increase pay in return for sexual favours. Other recurrent forms of abuse perpetrated by male supervisors were non-sexual physical and verbal abuse, coercion, threats of retaliation, mandatory overtime and denial of bathroom and lunch breaks. These forms of abuse constitute GBVH as the women were targeted based on their gender and this abuse disproportionately affected women. (Business & Human Rights Resource Center and Asia Floor Wage Alliance 2022, 9)

GBVH as a strategy of subjugating women and depriving them of their dignity, is a phenomenon that can be found in all GLVCs. One woman, employed at MAA Garment and Textiles, Kebire Enterprises Plc., a supplier factory in Ethiopia, reported in an interview:

I have been asked out for a date for sex by my supervisors. I know this happens to other girls too. If we say yes, they will easily cooperate with us when we are late or ask for annual leave or other things, but if not, they will use what they can in their power to make us miserable. If we ask for annual leave they will hold our refusal to their sexual advances against us saying that 'this all could be avoided'. (WCR 2018, 20)

Going back to India, Annie Kelly, reporting on Jeyasre Kathiravel, an Indian woman and garment worker who was murdered by her supervisor, has shown 'the true price of fast fashion' (Kelly 2022):

Kathiravel never escaped the factory floor. On 1 January 2021, she failed to return home from work. Despite her family's frantic attempts to find her, four days later her desolidarising body was discovered by farmers just a few miles from her village. When her supervisor, a man named by Indian media as V Thangadurai, was arrested for her murder, few of her intimate circle were surprised. Thangadurai has since been charged with her murder and is in jail awaiting trial. For months before Kathiravel's death, her family and co-workers say that Thangadurai was perpetrating a relentless campaign of sexual harassment towards her, which she felt powerless to report or stop. 'She said this man was torturing her but she didn't know what to do because she was so scared of losing her job,' says her mother, Muthuakshmi Kathiravel. (Kelly 2022)

2. Global North

In 2021, a report by the European Institute for Gender Equality (EIGE) revealed that 'the cost of gender-based violence across the EU is €366 billion a year. Violence against women makes up 79% of this cost, amounting to €289 billion' (European Institute for Gender Equality 2021). While this horrendous sum sheds light on a severe problem, the report does not mention migrant women—either in general or as specifically being exposed to harassment and gender-specific violence at their workplaces, be it the EU agribusiness or other GLVCs, such as the cleaning sector, household, or twenty-four-hour care.

Although EIGE ignores migrant women, making them invisible, the truth is that these women working in Europe's fields for the agribusiness are experiencing gender-based violence and harassment just like female workers in the Global South,[43] as Tom Strohschneider and Kathrin Gerlof have reported: 'Dozens of women harvest workers have spoken out, publicly announcing how they

---

[43] Gender-based violence is a global problem in the agribusiness sector; see the European Bank for Reconstruction and Development 2020.

were sexually harassed or raped by their supervisors. Many more speak out of their experiences of physical violence and threats' (Strohschneider and Gerlof 2019).[44]

Control exercised by governments' judiciary systems to keep the weaker side of a social relation in its rather powerless position, to destroy human beings' and social groups' dignity, self-esteem, and self-respect in Neuwirth's sense and protect the power of powerful exploiters in the GLVCs of the EU agribusiness, can be seen in the case of Moroccan women in Spain. Working in the fields, about 20,000 Moroccan women come to Spain every year to harvest strawberries for the bog supermarkets in France, the United Kingdom, and Germany.

In its report *Rape in the Fields*, *Correctiv*, a non-profit investigative newsroom in Germany, showed the unbelievable extent of raping women picking strawberries in Huelva for German supermarkets (Müller and Prandi 2018). Sexual violence and rape in the Spanish agribusiness have been well documented over the years (Alonso 2018; FEMM Committee European Parliament 2018; Yabiladi 2018; Houmann Mortensen and Prandi 2021; El Mal 2021; Ros Robollo 2021), while governments in Spain and Morocco have downplayed or even denied all allegations (Kelly 2019). As if that were not enough contempt for female workers, Annie Kelly reports that after cases of rape and sexual assault are taken to the courts

> the provincial courts in Andalucía have been obstructive, failing to launch a proper investigation, not allowing the women enough time to travel to a courtroom in Huelva to give evidence in front of a judge last June and then leaving them in legal limbo for a further eight months. The charges of rape and sexual assault have also been downgraded to sexual harassment, with the courts citing a lack of evidence. (Kelly 2019)

Since then, the lives of the women who dared to go to court have become unbearable:

> Most say they have also been divorced by their husbands and disowned by their parents in Morocco after their families learnt of the allegations of rape and sexual assault and were sent messages saying that they were working as prostitutes in Spain. Unable to return home and unwilling to leave Spain before they get their case resolved, they say clearing their name is the only way they will see their children again. 'We knew we couldn't go home because we still hadn't been paid and we had to prove that the things that we had told the police

---

[44] There is hardly any official data and only little information about gender-based violence in the EU agribusiness

were true,' said Aicha, whose baby is now nine months old. Like all the other women, she suffers from panic attacks and depression and is too scared to leave the apartment. (Kelly 2019)

It becomes obvious how, for the benefit of an important economic sector, governments and the judiciary system exercise control in Neuwirth's sense of a destructive strategy directed against the dignity of human beings and female migrant workers as a group.

Yet, this strategy becomes obvious not only with regard to the work in the fields, but also with regard to the meat industry. In December 2022, a Spanish court also rejected a case brought forward by two women and 'acquitted a manager accused of sexual advances and using the threat of dismissal to demand sex, in a blow to a landmark legal challenge that sought to cast a spotlight on sexual abuse in the country's meat processing industry' (Chávez and Kassam 2022).

Both cases are symbolic of governments' and justice systems' support of exploitative practices in the EU agribusiness and meat industries and the knowing acceptance of slavery-like conditions by national governments and the European Union. These forms of exercising control that destroy human beings' dignity and the integrity of their communities are a critical aspect of a general ongoing strategy of European states and the European Union to make exploited and enslaved migrant workers, the undocumented, asylum seekers, and seasonal workers *invisible*.

While Shana Cohen, Gerry Mitchell, and Liran Morav (2022) have shown that core economic sectors rely 'on exploited and invisible workers to fill precarious jobs', a 2022 Lighthouse Report has revealed that the idea of making exploited and enslaved human beings invisible is a larger overarching strategy in the European Union, meaning different things in different places, yet always following the same logic:

Invisibility in Brussels has meant no voice in shaping CAP (Poinssot 2020) and no seat at the table in the current round of negotiations due to conclude in 2021. In Greece, invisibility means undocumented workers who don't know who they work for or appear on company books (EfSYN 2020), where their costs are written off as fertiliser. In the Netherlands we uncover the loophole, agreed between farms and unions that enables them to evade 'equal pay for equal work' with migrant employees. In Spain we find migrants forced to work under assumed names (Borges and Huet, 2020) to earn social security credits for Spanish citizens. In all instances invisibility made it harder for migrant workers to speak out. . . . Maria, a Spanish hotel worker who tried fruit-picking in the fields of Huelva in southern Spain and was appalled at the culture of fear that she found: 'If you're at the bottom of the list and they need to fire people, it's going to be you'. (Lighthouse Reports 2020; references inserted)

Whether in the Global South or Global North, working conditions in GLVCs come along with abuse, threats, degrading practices, humiliation, sexual harassment, violence, and murder, which are all symptoms of neoliberalism and globalized capitalism and have reorganized social relations of exploitation exposing workers, especially female workers, to daily dehumanizing experiences. Necessarily, all these experiences of mistreatment by workers in GLVCs and whole communities in struggles with multinational corporations inevitably and necessarily have an effect on their self-perception, self-esteem, and sense of dignity, in turn deeply impacting their ability to close their communities and act in solidarity. Global capital's strategies of reorganizing the social relations of the exploiting and the exploited to perpetuate and aggravate already existing power asymmetries are thus critical aspects of slavery, which 'is a system of dishonouring and degrading people through the violent coercion of their labor activity in conditions that dehumanize them' (Kara 2017, 8).

22.2.5 Outcomes, Stabilization, and Legitimation

Analysing GLVCs from the perspective of social closure reveals them to be a highly complex strategy of extraction affecting the global workforce in the Global North and Global South while fundamentally reorganizing the critical dimension of social relations—socio-economic, politico-legal, socio-structural, and socio-cultural. In doing so they not only shift access to resources, rights, and networks/institutions in favour of the exploiters; they also increase their options for controlling the exploited by intervening into their communities and preventing them from organizing, thereby degrading their dignity, self-respect, and self-esteem.

Making plausible the explanatory logic of closure analysis has shown that strategies of deprivation, undermining, suppression, and subjugation trigger the critical mechanisms *denial of access* and *intervention into community closure*, fundamentally reorganizing social relations of exploitation in favour of the exploiters at the cost of the exploited, who are exposed to conditions of exploitation/slavery within a new division of labour in global capitalist production.

All strategies of extraction discussed above in detail have institutionalized a new social order that has exposed huge parts of the global workforce to new forms of slavery. These strategies include depriving workers of a minimum wage and consequently of any possibility to enjoy vital resources, as well as making use of the politico-legal framework in countries of the Global South, but also the Global North, to create conditions that deny workers basic rights and allow multinational corporations to employ a workforce that is widely disenfranchised. They also allow for waging war against unionization on the part of state and multinational corporations, the aim being to deny workers access to health protection and the public health system. They further aim at preventing workers from integrating into networks/institutions that would allow them to defend their prospects in life, also from an intergenerational perspective, and help them to escape a vicious cycle of never-ending poverty. Finally, having made GLVCs a seedbed of abuse and harassment, global capital with the support of states or the European Union targets all workers while creating extremely dangerous situations especially for women in the workplace. In this sense, a closure analysis of processes of exploitation enables us to explain the various dimensions in which GLVCs radicalize global capital's exploitation to maximize the exploiters' life chances / chances of survival at the expense of the exploited.

*Re*regulated social arrangements in a new global division of labour are stabilized by national legislation or administrative regulations that guarantee global capital maximum profits with maximum exploitation that, if necessary, may be enforced by the military or the police. The European Union, for example, stabilizes its system of agribusiness by giving retailers free rein to exploit the vulnerable and expose them to conditions of slavery, creating an unworthy game in which the responsibilities of regulation are passed back and forth between Brussels and national governments without protecting the basic human rights of the workers.

The legitimacy of such an order is again essentially based on *reciprocal recognition* and *horizontal legitimacy* that actors in neoliberal governance—states, the European Union, financial institutions, multinational corporations, and so on—grant to one another. The political and mainstream media practices of concealing and hiding working conditions, denying the existence of modern slavery while reinforcing widespread resentment and prejudices in the populace against the most vulnerable workforce of refugees, the undocumented, rejected asylum seekers, and migrant workers from Eastern Europe guarantee support for these working and living conditions in today's global capitalism. Beyond these processes, Popitz's ideas of stabilizing and legitimizing such systems of profit maximization, forming nuclei of solidarity within highly organized multinational corporations, are achieved through strategies of *helping and dividing* (Popitz) that allow headquarters to impose a distinct division of labour along GLVCs and maintain control over it. Today, the division of labour is reorganized through *coordinated activities* in GLVCs that pursue a temporal and spatial sequencing of both similar and different activities, 'to *chain* together intertwined activities' (Popitz 2017, 145; emphasis added) on a global scale. Further, through a system of outsourcing, offshoring, and (sub-)contracting, multinational corporations have created *echelons and hierarchies* that allow lead firms to reject any responsibility for the life chances / chances of survival of their workforce and enjoy the right to exploit/enslave human beings. Meanwhile, overseers, states, and the military prevent social groups from organizing on the shop floor, such as establishing unions or political representation, to combat their exploitation. In this sense, social classes, occupational groups, skilled or semi-skilled groups, women, and other various groups are kept dependent on their exploiters and reduced to nothing but exploitable labour power.

Of course, mutual recognition among the exploiters confirming that they are doing everything correctly according to the law and existing rules does not make things better. Rather, ongoing exploitation/slavery reveals that, since the fifteenth century, two critical aspects are at work in globally operating supply chain capitalism even today: 'Expansion abroad, security of property at home—reveal the two faces of Europe's empire-builders: plunderers, slavers, and extortioners abroad; prudent, law-abiding businessmen at home' (Brady 1991, 160). The fact that slavery has also returned to the capitalist core while neither politicians nor brands, retailers, or the liberal public seem interested, but all of them still praising human rights and democracy in the West, simply perpetuates the West's tradition of exploitation and slavery.

22.3 Analysing and Explaining the Reorganization of Social Relations of Elimination

Elimination as the third form of social closure addresses settler colonialism as a *distinct formation* (Veracini 2014; 2015). While the chapter on exploitation has shown that global capital has (re)colonized the Global South as a space of extreme exploitation/slavery produced by a new global accumulation regime, settler colonialism as the *worst form of colonialism* (Noam Chomsky) has no less global outreach and significance. It still creates and re-creates social relations of elimination even today, as we can see with regard to all settler-colonial societies today dominating the world as the *West*. I will show how social relations of the eliminators and those threatened with elimination work in the case of Occupied Palestine.

By pursuing strategies of *annihilation*—the basic form of strategies of elimination—highly organized settler-colonial states in alliance with western states propagate and act according to an extreme ideology backed by an organized military and, not infrequently, by militias or paramilitary groups. Settler-colonialists initiate a huge number of *events* and an almost infinite variety of strategies that threaten the colonized with being wiped out completely. These extremely asymmetric social relations between the eliminators and those threatened with being eliminated unfold within a system of *ownership and rent* in which the colonized face *sheer violence* (Popitz) from the side of the powerful. In this sense, strategies of elimination are about destroying and removing Indigenous people. Yet, why should settler-colonialism be so significant?

22.3.1 Context: Settler Colonialism

Bringing settler colonialism into sociological theory, arguing that it is one of the three major global processes and elimination one of three basic forms of closure, acknowledges that 'settler colonialism directly informs past and present processes of European colonisation, global capitalism, liberal modernity and international governance' (Morgensen 2011, 53; see also Veracini 2013; 2021; Mackert and Pappe 2024b).

While the Western narrative dates the beginning of the modern nation state back to 1648 with the Peace of Westphalia and is thus blind to any intrinsic connection between the emergence of the nation-state and colonialism, Mahmood Mamdani (2020) has rejected this idea and argued convincingly that the year 1492 is decisive here, given two critical and simultaneous developments in Spain: On the one hand, the violent internal homogenization of Christian Spain—a decisive feature of nation-building—practiced ethnic cleansing by making Muslims and Jews choose between converting (if possible), emigrating, or being eliminated by the Catholic Inquisition. On the other hand, the Spanish monarchy with support from the Catholic pope began settling in the Americas and colonizing the land by ethnically cleansing it of the Indigenous populations through genocide:

> Modern colonialism and the modern state were born together with the creation of the modern nation-state. Nationalism did not precede colonialism. Nor was colonialism the highest or the final stage in the making of a nation. The two were co-constituted. (Mamdani 2020, 1–2)

The justification and legitimation of settler colonialism are fed by two sources—the Bible from its very beginnings in the fifteenth century and later classical political liberalism from the eighteenth century on. Scholars such as Mamdani (2015), Charles W. Mills (1997), and Domenico Losurdo (2014) have shown that great liberal minds, firmly anchored in the Christian tradition, propagated all the ingredients of White racial supremacism into the world. John Stuart Mill was convinced that the '"European race" was called upon to exercise over the rest of the world' (Losurdo 2014, 225). The great liberal Aléxis de Tocqueville added in this regard:

> The European race has received from heaven, or acquired by its own efforts, such *incontestable superiority over the other races* which compose the great human family that the man placed by us, on account of his vices and ignorance, on the bottom rung of the social scale is still first among the savages. (de Tocqueville 1951, 103, 105, quoted in Losurdo 2014, 228; emphasis added)

Despotism and slavery, seeing Indigenous people as *born slaves*, distinguishing between *superior and inferior races*, and the *civilization-barbarism divide* allowed settlers to fulfil their divine mandate and civilizational task and declared Natives to be *uncivilized races* (Mill), *beasts, wild men*, or *savages* (de Tocqueville). This philosophical perception of the divine mission of Western civilization not only dehumanized the Indigenous but also served as legitimization to decimate, eliminate, and extinguish them in genocides.

John Stuart Mill argued that the *colonies of European race* were fully entitled to self-government, meaning the right of White settlers to govern themselves and create a settler democracy. Yet, the conception of *the people* as referring to White settlers only proved to be serious and catastrophic for the Indigenous. In *The Dark Side of Democracy*, Michael Mann (2005) has given a convincing explanation of why the situation in settler democracies turned out to be extremely murderous:

> In this situation two ethnic groups clashed over a monopolistic resource, land, and most settlers did not need native labor to work it. Economic power relations were uniquely the prime mover of colonial cleansings. Yet property rights also required settlers to claim exclusive legal sovereignty over the territory at present possessed by natives.... This economic-political clash was exacerbated by the military/ideological imbalance of power.... The settlers could eliminate the out-group with little military or moral risk to themselves. (Mann 2005, 109)[45]

Settler colonialism from the beginning was thus a project of White supremacism to spread Western 'civilization' across the globe at the expense of other cultures and civilizations, in which the land inhabited by the Indigenous took centre stage, as Patrick Wolfe has shown:

> *The primary object of settler colonization is the land itself* rather than the surplus value to be derived from mixing native labour with it. Though, in practice, Indigenous labour was indispensable to Europeans, settler-colonization is at base *a winner-take-all project* whose dominant feature is not exploitation but *replacement*. The logic of this project, a sustained institutional *tendency to eliminate the Indigenous population*, informs a range of historical practices that

---

[45] It is well known that most of the celebrated Founding Fathers of the United States were landowners and slaveholders and outspoken with regard to genocide if necessary. Having invaded the land, Thomas Jefferson made this explicit: 'If ever we are constrained to lift the hatchet against any tribe, we shall never lay it down till that tribe is exterminated, or driven beyond the Mississippi.... In war, they will kill some of us; we shall destroy all of them' (Thomas Jefferson, quoted in Mann 2005, 70.

might otherwise appear distinct—*invasion is a structure not an event.* (Wolfe 1999, 163; emphases added)

Taking land from Indigenous people has always come along with the creation of myths of settling in a *land without a people*, claiming to have settled in an allegedly empty land and thus propagating *pioneer lies* (Wysote and Morton 2019). Settlers' insistence on the validity of the liberal bourgeois institution of private property also in the invaded areas in other parts of the world is part of the creation of the biopolitics of settler colonialism: 'For more than five hundred years, Western law functioned as biopower in relation to ongoing practices of European settler colonialism' (Morgensen 2011, 53). Further, land grabbing imposes an us-them boundary that separates settlers and Indigenous, making the concept of the *frontier* a critical one. It has the usual physical meaning, as in the case of the United States, when settler colonialism pushed this frontier ever further from the Atlantic to the Pacific, taking all the land from the Indigenous and finally placing them in reservations. However, as Mark Rifkin has argued, the concept of the frontier is neither only a physical and spatial concept, nor a simply legal concept defining spaces, but rather one that 'translates the juridical problem of settler sovereignty into a broader, ostensibly nonjuridical, imaginary in which settler subjects can envision a kind of space beyond the political authority of the state but yet not within that of another state or polity' (Rifkin 2014, 177).

Such a space is by definition a space of lawlessness, of extreme violence, in which the logic of elimination allows for ethnic cleansing that easily turns genocidal, creating a space and *spectrum of exception* (Rifkin). Following Michel Foucault and Giorgio Agamben, settler-colonial theorizing has shown that, as settler colonialism is a highly radical racist ideological and murderous military project, the colonized are pushed into a permanent space and state of exception (Lloyd 2012; Morgensen 2011). In this spectrum of exception, settler colonialism might turn genocidal, yet, as Wolfe in his seminal article 'Settler Colonialism and the Elimination of the Native' has made clear, in all settler societies there is a 'relationship between genocide and the settler colonial tendency that I term the *logic of elimination.* I contend that, though the two have converged—which is to say, the settler colonial logic of elimination has manifested as genocidal—they should be distinguished' (Wolfe 2006, 387; emphasis added).

While it is obvious that 'in modern colonies, settler democracies in certain contexts have been truly murderous' (Mann 2005, 4),[46] we see that 'today,

---

[46] The term *settler democracies* points to the fact that democratic structures were established exclusively among the White colonizers, while the Indigenous were extinguished.

colonial cleansing continues in Palestine and in the back lands of Latin America and Asia, chasing indigenous peoples from their land' (Mann 2005, 109; see Rodinson 2014 [1973]).

Given these central features of the settler-colonial paradigm, if we consider the case of Palestine[47], we see that 'Zionist settler colonialism ... is fundamentally based on the operative logic of "eliminating the native" and failing to utterly marginalize and "minoritize" him' (Dana and Jarbawi 2017, 197). In fact, the experience with 'A Century of Settler Colonialism in Palestine' (Dana and Jarbawi 2017) and *The Hundred Years' War on Palestine* (Khalidi 2020) confirms that 'Zionism never spoke of itself unambiguously as a Jewish movement, but rather as a *Jewish movement for colonial settlement* in the Orient' (Said 1992 [1979], 69; emphasis added). Thus, settler colonialism in Palestine started in the late nineteenth century. Like with all settler-colonial regimes, taking the land from the Indigenous is at the heart of the Zionist project, which until today has turned Palestine into a completely fragmented land of unconnected separate enclaves, just like the Bantustans during South African Apartheid (OCHA 2021a; Farsakh 2005; Benvenisti 2004; Masalha 1992; see illustration 22.1).

These maps documenting the destruction of Palestine make it very clear how Zionist occupation imposed a physical frontier separating the colonizers from the colonized and how, in a historical process, the occupiers pushed this frontier further and further, usurping the homeland of the Indigenous Palestinian population. This violent occupation of Palestinian land—like in other settler-colonial contexts—was accompanied by the attempt to justify it with lies and the spreading of myths (Wysote and Morton 2019), pretending that Palestine was a land without a people for a people without a land (Pappe 2017, 11). Of course, not only the *Four Thousand Years of Palestinian History* (Masalha 2018) but also millions of Palestinian victims of the Zionist occupation in Palestine itself or in the diaspora, as well as about 15,000 Palestinians killed by Israel, including outright massacres (Middle East Eye 2021), prove these narratives wrong. Thus, by

---

[47] When writing this chapter on the settler-colonial occupation of Palestine, it was analysing the daily atrocities of the Zionist occupation as the hopefully last White European settler-colonial project in this world. I analysed how the life chances / chances of survival of the Palestinian people are systematically destroyed. In this sense I offer an empirical analysis of how to make sense of the *logic of elimination* in Palestine from the perspective of a new theory of social closure. In the meantime, history has caught up with my analysis, as the logic of elimination has become *genocidal*, which is always possible under settler-colonial circumstances as Wolfe has shown. Israel's genocidal war against the Palestinian people makes my analysis almost an historical one up to the point where the Zionist regime has turned genocidal. According to *The Lancet* (2024), one of the world's most renowned medical journals, the 'accumulative effects of Israel's war on Gaza could mean the true death toll could reach more than 186,000 people' (Al Jazeera 2024) in the beginning of July 2024. At this moment it is utterly unclear what will be after genocide. However, I hope my analysis will be of interest as a contribution to understanding what settler-colonial regimes actually do and that it helps to make sense of the many other cases in the world that may be analysed from the perspective of social closure.

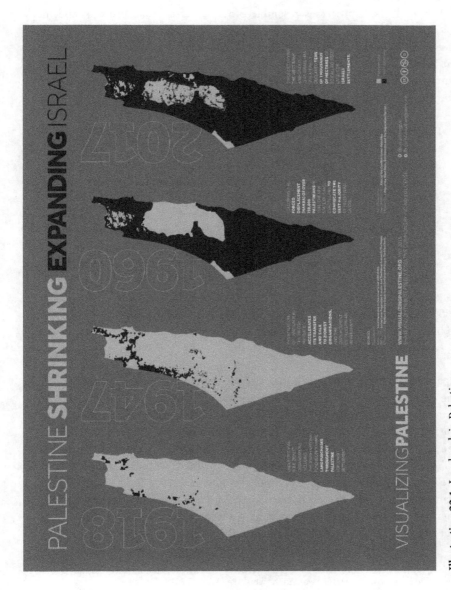

Illustration 22.1 Land grab in Palestine

Source: Visualizing Palestine 2015; see also BADIL 2021

violently grabbing Palestinian land and pushing the physical frontier forward little by little, the Zionist occupation created a space and state of exception for Palestinians.

While all these processes resemble other settler-colonial projects, specific to the Zionist one is that it exists by violating UN resolutions and international law—and is allowed to do so, not being held accountable from its supporters in *the West*.[48] Today, Israel de facto controls the West Bank, to which Zionist occupation has brought about half a million Jewish settlers now living illegally according to international law in almost 300 settlements in the West Bank:[49]

> The settlements have been condemned as illegal in many UN Security Council and other UN resolutions. As early as 1980, UN Security Council Resolution 465 called on Israel 'to dismantle the existing settlements and, in particular, to cease, on an urgent basis, the establishment, construction and planning of settlements in the Arab territories occupied since 1967, including Jerusalem. The International Committee of the Red Cross and the Conference of High Contracting Parties to the Fourth Geneva Convention have reaffirmed that settlements violate international humanitarian law. The illegality of the settlements was recently reaffirmed by UN Security Council Resolution 2334, passed in December 2016, which reiterates the Security Council's call on Israel to cease all settlement activities in the OPT [Occupied Palestinian Territories]. The serious human rights violations that stem from Israeli settlements have also been repeatedly raised and condemned by international bodies and experts. (Amnesty International 2019)

Apart from the fact that more and more new settlements are being built illegally, the ongoing process of dispossession and ethnic cleansing is further advanced by strategies of annexing Palestinian land by 'issuing military orders, declaring the area "state land", a "firing zone" or a "nature reserve"' (B'Tselem 2021b, 7; see already B'Tselem 2002). Further, the settler-colonial regime does not allow Palestinians access to their own private land. The regime uses the division of the West Bank into Areas A, B, and C created in the 1993 Oslo Accords to declare even more land as *special security areas*, barring Palestinians from reaching their land by building special roads only for settlers on which Palestinians are not allowed to set foot (see B'Tselem 2016a).[50]

---

[48] Apart from such disrespect and severe violations of international law, Israel also claims to be entitled to legislate wherever they want in the world; see MEMO 2018.

[49] The new, so-called right-wing, Israeli government, approved on 29 December 2022, has immediately announced the intention to advance illegal settlements in the West Bank and the Al-Naqab Desert (Negev Desert) and therefore push ahead with the ethnic cleansing in Palestine.

[50] Further, Palestinians are dispossessed of their land, which is taken over violently by Zionist settlers backed and supported by the Israeli Defense Forces (IDF), creating a lawless space of

On the basis of these aspects, which characterize Israel as a typical settler-colonial regime, from the perspective of closure theory we can go a step further and argue that beyond the physical *space of exception* a much broader *spectrum of exception* (Dana and Jarbawi 2023) is created through strategies of annihilation that destroy Palestinians' chances of survival by denying them access to resources, rights, and networks/institutions, and attacking their communities.[51] I will analyse some of these strategies used in the occupation's intentional creation of events that allow for ever new strategies to reinforce the logic of elimination.

22.3.2 Events and Principal Strategy

Wolfe's argument that the 'invasion of settler colonialism is not an event but a structure' (Wolfe 1999, 2; Wolfe 2006, 388) is well known and often quoted as a core assumption of the settler-colonial paradigm that points to the fact that settler colonialism is a permanent condition. As the discussion of *events* has made clear, my understanding of events as tools of methodological bracketing differs from Wolfe's understanding of the concept. In my view, a settler-colonial *invasion is an external shock* to an existing social order (see Tilly 2000, 13) and thus an *event* as it fundamentally transforms the perception of future possibilities and developments. However, this perspective does not contradict Wolfe's as in both cases, it is about the long-term and permanent establishing of a new social order by the invading settlers. While Wolfe sees this as part of the event, I discuss the long-term consequences of the invasion of settler-colonial actors as the reorganization of established social relations in struggles of elimination.

As *invasion* or *colonization* erases and fundamentally destroys established social relations among the Indigenous and allows the imposition of fundamentally new and highly asymmetrical one between *The Colonizer and the Colonized* (Memmi 1991 [1965]), this new social relation between the eliminators and those threatened with elimination—what Wolfe might call the structure—is then the characteristic social relation that imposes permanent subordination, exploitability,

---

exception for Palestinian people: 'Rather than preventing violent actions against Palestinian farmers, the military has developed a "coordination" system that treats settler violence as a given. This system ostensibly enables Palestinian farmers to access their land, but in fact denies them almost any possibility to do so by *limiting their access* to a handful of days a year. Even on these days, if settlers violently prevent farmers from cultivating their land, the military will remove the latter. Settlers, meanwhile, have unfettered access to Palestinian land all year round. Under this system, Palestinian farmers are consigned to partial cultivation of their land that keeps them from maximizing its potential, if they are able to extract anything from the land at all' (B'Tselem 2021b: 11; emphasis added).

[51] For a broad and highly informative and interesting analysis of the political economy of Palestine more than twenty-five years after the Oslo Accords, see Tartir, Dana and Seidel 2021.

and the ever-present threat of potential elimination of the Indigenous, as the colonizers envisage a future in which their phantasies of purity may be realized. For this, the regime permanently creates new events justifying and allowing it to set in motion ever new strategies designed to radicalize the social relations of elimination, making them more and more asymmetrical. Thus, I conceive of the social relations between the eliminators and those threatened with elimination as the *characteristic feature of settler colonialism and the resulting occupation*.

Given that European Jews' colonization of Palestine started in the late nineteenth century through the period of the Ottoman Empire and was, after 1918, legitimized and facilitated in the time of Great Britain's League of Nations Mandate of Palestine (1922–1948) in a colonial arrogation of power after with the Balfour Declaration (1917) the British government had already promised the Jewish settlers an own state in Palestine, first events that established the Jewish colonizers as occupiers were racist strategies like the doctrine of *Hebrew labour*, denying Palestinians access to various sectors of the labour market. However, Israel's 1948 war against the Palestinian and Arab nations needs to be seen as a critical abrupt shock to existing social arrangements in Palestine. This war brought the destruction of almost 800 Palestinian villages, a massive dispossession of Palestinians, and *The Ethnic Cleansing of Palestine* (Pappe 2006) involving huge massacres of the civil Palestinian population, about 15,000 Palestinians killed, and the expulsion of millions of them. All these crimes are preserved in the collective memory of the Palestinian people as the *Nakba* (Khoury 2020; 2022; Pappe 2020; Masalha 2008; Nabulsi 2006).

The 1967 *Naksa*,[52] another Israeli war-as-event, was officially declared to have been a war of *no choice*—another Zionist settler-colonial myth (Pappe 2017)—that allowed Israel to take 'control of Gaza and the West Bank and, since that time, the Israeli military has occupied the Palestinian lands and has enabled the establishment of illegal colonies/settlements exclusively for Israeli Jews in violation of international law' (Watts, Lee, and Aidy 2016, 8).

More lethal violence was used and more events were created to allow, enable, and justify the occupiers' enforcing ethnic cleansing and carry out even more massacres. Among them was Israel's backing of a Maronite Christian Phalange militia that, from 16 to 18 September 1982, killed between 2,000 and 3,500 Palestinian refugees and Lebanese civilians in the Lebanese refugee camps of Sabra and Shatila. Later, there were the Oslo Accords in 1993, allowing Israel to consolidate military occupation, the total siege of the Gaza Strip since 2007, imprisoning more than two million people,[53] and the Wars on Gaza in 2008/

---

[52] The *Naksa* is often referred to as Israel's Six-Day War in 1967.
[53] See Dana's 2020 analysis about Israel's experimentations with its advanced military-security technologies on Gazans during the Great March of Return in 2018/2019.

2009 (Weizman 2018), 2014 (Blumenthal 2015), 2021 (Ahmed 2022), and of course the now genocidal war that started in October 2023 (UN 2023a; OCHA 2023a; Cook 2023; UN Human Rights Council 2024). Also included was the construction of the separation wall that began in 2002, built mainly on Palestinian land and annexing it, destroying Palestinian villages and cutting off Palestinians from wells and water (see also Hass 2002). Further, among many others, there was the massacre in the Jenin refugee camp in 2002 (OCHA 2002), Ariel Sharon's intrusion into the Temple Mount and Al Aqsa Mosque with hundreds of Israeli soldiers in 2000 (Greenberg 2000; Goldenberg 2000), the proclamation of the Jewish Basic Law in 2018 (Al-Haq 2019a; Adalah 2020), and the official Annexation of the Golan Heights in 2019, when the United States officially *recognized Israel's claim on the Golan Heights* (Macaron 2019).

These events—all of them illegal according to international law and thus violating it—served as *template(s) of possibility* (Berezin) allowing the settler-colonial regime to unleash eliminatory strategies and repeatedly and permanently reorganize the social relations between the eliminators and those threatened with being eliminated. In outlining the explanatory logic of elimination as a form of social closure, I show how these events have allowed to establish a principal closure strategy that I conceive of as a *politics of erasure* (Green and Smith 2016; Gould 2023; Gregory 2005).

Under Zionist occupation, such politics have for more than seventy years imposed Israel's *sovereignty through demographic control and erasure* (Hamayel 2022),[54] trying to erase the traces of Palestinian existence in all spheres of life (Piterberg 2001).[55] Thus, while 'Zionism has relentlessly pursued a campaign to erase the Palestinian presence in Palestine' (Halper 2021),[56] as of 2022 the erasure and extermination of Palestinians can now be demanded without any intervention by the Israeli government, like in 22 April 2022, when 'hundreds of activists from the extremist movement rampaged through East Jerusalem in a march organised to "restore Jewish dignity" to the city, descending upon Damascus Gate chanting "Death to Arabs"' (Issam 2021). Amidst death threats and demands for the *deportation* of Palestinians from Israeli territory (Noy 2022), the *politics of erasure* is Israel's crucial strategy against the Indigenous that

---

[54] Since the beginning of the ethnic cleansing of Palestine, the settler regime has been obsessed with demographic questions reflecting its deeply racist character, such as when discussing the *Arab womb* (Middle East Eye 2022; Tanous 2022).

[55] I take up the term *erasure* from Piterberg's 2001 article in which he uses it to analyse the many facets of the problem of Palestinian refugees. Yet, I use it in a generalized sense, characterizing these politics with regard to all areas of Palestinian life under Zionist occupation, as the following debate will show.

[56] See the *transfer* concept in Zionism which seeks to eliminate the Palestinians through an alleged *voluntary transfer*, which in fact means using a variety of pressure methods. See Masalha 1992; Zureik 2003.

pushes for 'further eradication of their presence—a "spacio-cide"—in support of an Israeli-envisaged demographic and political vision' (Wermenbol 2020). Achille Mbembe (2016) in his *Society of Enmity* has drawn attention to some of the daily forms of politics of erasure carried out by both the IDF and Zionist settlers:

> Permanent or temporary checkpoints, cement blocks and mounds of earth serving as roadblocks, the control of aerial and marine space, of the import and export of all sorts of products, regular military incursions, home demolitions, the desecration of cemeteries, whole olive groves uprooted, infrastructure turned to rubble and obliterated, high- and medium-altitude bombardments, targeted assassinations, urban counter-insurgency techniques, the profiling of minds and bodies, constant harassment, the ever smaller subdivision of land, cellular and molecular violence, the generalization of forms adopted from the model of a camp—every feasible means is put to work in order to impose a regime of separation whose functioning paradoxically depends on an intimate proximity with those who have been separated (Parizot 2009). (Mbembe 2016, 24; see also Mbembe 2003)

As sometimes the ongoing events in the world collide with academic resonating trying to make sense of their long trajectories, in the face of Israel's genocidal war in Gaza since October 2023 after decades of settler-colonial occupation of Palestine lends the following closure analysis a sad drama and topicality. As I have already shown, events in the case of a *politics of erasure* can be manifold and—as my discussion of the concepts of events has made clear—can be created intentionally. In seventy-five years of settler-colonial occupation and seventeen years of the siege of Gaza, we have seen repeatedly how this strategy was employed by the highly organized Israeli military-ideology complex, again and again producing *events* to exert the most brutal ideological and military/violence power against Palestinian civilians. The 7 October event is no exception and fits into this pattern of decades of eliminatory occupation that in October 2023 was finally turned from strategies of elimination into a genocidal war against the civilian population in Gaza.[57]

---

[57] After seventy-five years of Zionist occupation of Palestine and after seventeen years of Israel having forced to live Palestinians in Gaza under siege, which Normal Finkelstein has described as 'the world's largest concentration camp' (quoted in Scahill 2018; see also Finkelstein 2018), Hamas's attack needs to be seen in the context of a desperate perspective that had only worsened with the new and explicitly fascist Israeli government (Hedges 2022) that had been formed after the elections of 2022. That we are dealing with Zionist fascism is obvious when taking seriously Mann's definition of 'fascism in terms of key values, actions, and power organizations of fascists. Most concisely, fascism is the pursuit of a transcendent and cleansing nation-statism through paramilitarism' (Mann 2004, 13). The five key terms following from this definition are all present in today's Israel: nationalism, statism, transcendence, cleansing, and paramilitarism. The last term refers to Israel's security

While the International Court of Justice in the case *192 – Application of the Convention on the Prevention and Punishment of the Crime of Genocide in the Gaza Strip (South Africa v. Israel)* found 'that at least some of the rights claimed by South Africa and for which it is seeking protection are plausible. This is the case with respect to the right of the Palestinians in Gaza to be protected from acts of genocide and related prohibited acts identified in Article III, and the right of South Africa to seek Israel's compliance with the latter's obligations under the Convention' (International Court of Justice 2024), the Special Rapporteur on the situation of human rights in the Palestinian territories occupied since 1967, Francesca Albanese, in the face of Israel's genocidal acts according to the constitutive elements of the Genocide Convention, concluded in her report *Anatomy of a Genocide*:

> Israel's genocide on the Palestinians in Gaza is an escalatory stage of a long-standing settler colonial process of erasure. For over seven decades this process has suffocated the Palestinian people as a group—demographically, culturally, economically and politically—, seeking to displace it and expropriate and control its land and resources. The ongoing Nakba must be stopped and remedied once and for all. This is an imperative owed to the victims of this highly preventable tragedy, and to future generations in that land. (UN Human Rights Council 2024)

Even in the face of genocide, 7 October as an *event* not only allows for different interpretations of what happened and might happen, but it also shows that there is no balance of power between the eliminators and those threatened with elimination, which means that the narrative of this event that is published, broadcasted, and repeated in public will be the eliminators' one. However, there is the fundamental difference between a common sense understanding of events as legitimate starting points to tell stories and construct simple causality and the methodological idea of events that I use in my closure analyses. To be sure, Hamas's attack on 7 October can be seen as an event at which public perception dramatically changed,[58] supported and fed by political and military propaganda and Western media that all established a dominant narrative of *security*, *terrorism*, *self-defence* and compliance with international law in defence of the

---

minister Ben-Gvir's new National Guard, which is simply his private militia that shall focus on *Arab unrest* (The Guardian 2023; Lintl 2023; Mualem 2023). Additionally, it involves his handing out of weapons to Zionist settlers, giving them free rein to kill Arabs in the West Bank, whom they dehumanize as *human animals* (Kasraoui 2023; Reuters 2023) or even *sub-human* (Middle East Eye 2023). This situation exemplifies what Mbembe (2003) described as *necropolitics*.

[58] In this sense, it is interesting to know that Israel knew about Hamas's plan but let the event happen, assuming it would be too complicated to be carried out; see Bergman and Goldman 2023.

occupying power (see Moses 2017). Yet, the analytical perspective taken here rejects this dominant discourse that uses this attack to construct it as the very starting point of a military confrontation and create a causality that does not exist. *Events* are methodological tools that allow to identify moments of a historical development, where something decisively changes. They do not allow to use what happens in these historical moments as a kind of a starting point by disregarding the historical trajectories that causally led to them. A causal argument in the case of Palestine and of the attack of 7 October needs to take seriously what I will analyse as the eliminators' seventy-five years of *strategies of annihilation* that all might trigger reactions of those threatened with elimination. From this point of view, there is no way to use the fighting back of those threatened with elimination after the experience of decades of being colonized and dehumanized as an argument that by employing the dominant and utterly ideological western discourse of *security–self-defence–terrorism* serves as justification of a genocide (UN 2023b).

Thus, in contrast to this dominant and hegemonic Western discourse dividing the world into good and evil and aiming only to justify genocide in Gaza, closure analysis concentrates on the historical processes and effects of mobilized structural elements of ideological and military/violence power to make comprehensible the processes and mechanisms of a decades-long Israeli settler-colonial *politics of erasure* against the Palestinian people, which makes 7 October only one of many events that allow for a methodological bracketing of the ongoing strategies and processes of the Israeli oppression of the Indigenous.

By looking more closely at some of these strategies, I will explain how these *politics of erasure* operate as radical strategies of annihilation that have reorganized the relations between the eliminators and those facing elimination in a created *spectrum of exception* in which Palestinian life has been turned into *bare life* (Giorgio Agamben). As Palestinians face a *colonial management of death* (Daher-Nashif 2020) and the threat of extinction (Dalley 2016) and are thus denied any *life chances* at all, I will only refer to their *chances of survival* in my analysis.

22.3.3 Mobilizing Predominantly Ideological and Military/Violence Structural Elements of Power

The Israeli state's high degree of organization has enabled it to progressively reorganize social relations of elimination by continually expanding Jewish people's *life chances* at the expense of Palestinians' *chances of survival*. All strategies of the Israeli state to this end rest mainly upon the mobilization of structural elements of both ideological and military/violence power.

Ideology

With regard to ideology, power strategies of reorganizing the social relations between the eliminators and those threatened with elimination draw on some critical structural elements: (1) transcendent visions and justifications of relations of domination creating powerful networks; (2) institutionalized ideologies, ideas, values, norms, and rituals that serve to preserve current relations of domination; and (3) immanent ideologies and justifications of relations of domination creating powerful networks. These aspects can be further examined with respect to the way the colonizers attempt to justify and legitimize the occupation of Palestine.

First, the legitimation of European Jews' settler colonialism feeds off of three transcendent visions and justifications for the relations of elimination: the Jewish religion (the Old Testament); the Western tradition of Enlightenment, humanism, and liberalism; and the impact of fascist thought. Basically, all three sources offer patterns of legitimizing White supremacism. References to the Old Testament and the alleged divine promise that the Jews would be God's chosen people, to whom this God promised a land (i.e., Palestine), establish the boundary between *the chosen ones* and the rest. Seeing themselves as part of Western European civilization allows European Jewish colonizers to take up and revitalize the tradition of Western thought that imposed the civilization-barbarism boundary as outlined above. Finally, attention must inevitably be drawn to the critical significance of Italian fascist dictator Benito Mussolini for Jewish ideologue Vladimir Jabotinsky (2011 [1923]; Jabotinsky 1940) and his creation of a Jewish youth movement in Poland that resulted in right-wing Zionism (Kupfert Heller 2017). That movement is still dominant even today in Israel's Likhud Party, but it is now being trumped by even more and outright fascist political groups.

Second, these ideologies of supremacy were institutionalized in political Zionism, a radical nationalist ideology that emerged at the end of the nineteenth century along with many other nationalist ideologies and was explained by Theodor Herzl, founding father of Zionist nationalism, as early as 1896, quite simply: 'If I wish to substitute a new building for an old one, *I must demolish before I construct*' (Herzl 1946 [1896]; emphasis added). Metaphorically, Herzl is expressing here the inevitability of a *civilized* politics of annihilation against Arab and especially Palestinian *barbarism*, drawing on the us-them boundary that classical political liberalism had propagated to justify settler-colonial projects and the ethnic cleansing of Indigenous people:

> If His Majesty the Sultan were to give us Palestine .. we should there form a portion of *a rampart of Europe against Asia, an outpost of civilization as opposed to barbarism*. We should as a neutral State remain in contact with all Europe,

which would have to guarantee our existence. The sanctuaries of Christendom would be safeguarded by assigning to them an extra-territorial status such as is well-known to the law of nations. (Herzl 1946 [1896]; emphasis added)

Moreover, though not in public, Herzl in his diaries proposed the elimination of Palestinians, as he 'dreamt of establishing a Jewish community in Palestine', writing 'that Palestinian Arabs were to be "*worked across the frontier*". Significantly, he added that this had to be done "surreptitiously"' (Veracini 2011, 2; emphasis added; Gould 2023).

Third, arguments legitimizing the occupation of Palestine are derived not only from these transcendent and institutionalized ideologies but also from politicians having at least co-coined and joined the West's ideological discourse on *security*, *self-defence*, and *terrorism*, which operate as ideological templates to justify any settler-colonial atrocity against Palestinians, while allowing politicians and the media to instrumentalize 'Palestinian resistance to de-politicize it and make it appear nothing but criminalized terror' (Halper 2021). Securitization and the T-word thus allow for any kind of legal, political, social, or cultural discrimination and degradation, as well as any kind of humiliation and dehumanization, in daily struggles against the Palestinian people. The role of politics, media, education, and the obligatory military service are of course critical here too as ideological institutions, all organized with the aim of dehumanizing Palestinians and erasing Palestinian history altogether (Masalha 2012; 2015).

Military/Violence
To understand how all these eliminatory processes are put in place, we need to turn to the critical structural elements of *military/violence power* that need to be mobilized to execute strategies of elimination: (1) means of violence systematically used in social life to defend, establish, or transform social relations among groups of people; (2) means of violence used to defend established relations of domination and social control; and (3) means of violence employed to uphold or transform social relations, mainly used against outsiders.

Since all settler-colonial societies are highly militarized and violent, all three aspects of the use of violence are critical. From the very beginning during the time of the British Mandate, Zionist military group Haganah and paramilitary group Irgun carried out terrorist attacks against the British and Palestinians, violently transforming colonial relations and, more importantly, destroying traditional Palestinian ones. As this terrorism was upheld against Palestinians and merged seamlessly into the 1948 war, terrorism basically created the state of Israel, making it a *State of Terror* (Suárez 2017; Bresheeth-Žabner 2020) that used brutal violence to replace British colonial domination over the Palestinians by establishing an eliminatory Zionist settler-colonial regime. Moreover, Palestinians' daily life today is characterized by unimaginable settler-colonial violence, exerted not only by the IDF but also by violent settlers operating as a kind of armed militia or paramilitary group operating jointly with and protected by the IDF.

The interplay of ideological and military/violence resources of power characterizes Zionism as a radical nationalist ideology of White supremacy exploiting the Jewish religion, Western philosophy, and fascist fervour that is backed and actively pushed forward by one of the most highly developed militaries on the planet, producing an obvious result: permanent violence, murderous ethnic cleansing, and brutal oppression and control of the Palestinian people. These are critical aspects of Israeli settler-colonial sovereignty, which is no longer the 'old right ... to take life or let live' but the 'opposite right ... to make live and to let die' (Foucault 2003, 239; see also Foucault 2007 [2004]) that, for Michel Foucault, signals the *birth of biopower* (Khoury 2021).

Of course, although ideology and the military/violence are the predominant structural elements of Israel as a settler-colonial society, politico-legal and economic power also play a highly important role as it orchestrates, backs, and whitewashes violence, war crimes, and crimes against humanity in Palestine. Yet, only by predominantly concentrating on the radical ideological/military character of the Zionist settler-colonial regime can we understand its strategies from the perspective of closure theory.

22.3.4 *The Politics of Erasure* as a Strategy of Social Closure: Processes and Mechanisms

Turning to the core of this explanation of elimination and conceiving of a *politics of erasure* as the critical form of a strategy of annihilation under conditions of settler colonialism, we now need to take a closer look at the most important dimensions by analysing how strategies of *letting die, disenfranchising, segregation*, and *extermination* trigger the social mechanisms *denial of access* and *intervention into community closure*.

Zionist settler-colonial strategies of elimination emerge out of strong social relations between the Israeli regime and the West—United States, Canada, Australia, United Kingdom, and the European Union and European states—sharing the fundamental ideology of the supremacy of White interests. From the very beginning at the end of the nineteenth century, the West (geo-)politically, ideologically, militarily, and financially supported the settlement movement of European Jews in Palestine, as well as Herzl's idea of European Jews building a kind of bridgehead for Europe in the Middle East to protect its interests and, of course, to protect 'Western civilization' from 'Arab barbarism'. Western powers, dominant in the United Nations, adopted in 1947 a deeply unjust partition plan in favour of the Zionist settler-colonial project. Only the support of these Western powers today enables Israel to pursue its eliminatory strategies because they back the settler-colonial regime, also guaranteeing it impunity for its predatory strategies against the Palestinian people that destroy Palestinians' survival chances with regard to resources, rights, and networks/institutions, as well as the Palestinian communities. Their explanation follows the same logic (see figure 22.5).

Letting Die

Letting die, the first dimension of a *politics of erasure* as a strategy of annihilation, denotes the settler-colonial regime's strategy of denying Palestinians access to *food* and *water*—vital *resources*—that is directly related to illegal land grab, dispossession, and ethnic cleansing, but no less recalls genocidal practices of earlier settler-colonial regimes such as Germany's genocide of the Nama and Herero in Namibia in 1904, which also involved cutting human beings off from food and water.[59] Of course, both strategies are in total contradiction of Protocol I of the Geneva Convention (1977):

> It is prohibited to attack, destroy, remove or render useless objects indispensable to the survival of a civilian population, such as foodstuffs, agricultural areas for the production of foodstuffs, crops, livestock, drinking water installations and supplies and irrigation works, for the specific purpose of denying them for their sustenance value to the civilian population or to the adverse Party, whatever the motive, whether in order to starve out civilians, to cause them to move away, or for any other motive. (Geneva Convention 1977; quoted in Dajani 2014)

Palestinian land is understood here not in the sense of Palestinians' home, history, and culture or the embeddedness of individual lives in a community, but as a vital resource that is misappropriated by Zionist occupation to prevent Palestinian communities from developing and growing by acquiring land (Segal, Tartakover, and Weizman 2003) through corresponding laws thereby depriving Palestinians of their livelihoods. Moreover, what is left is attacked, destroyed, or poisoned by either the IDF or Zionist settlers. Among such strategies are the destruction of whole farms in the West Bank (MEMO 2021), the destruction of vital harvests in the West Bank and Gaza Strip as a form of *agricultural terrorism* (Patel 2018; OCHA/WFP 2010), and the burning and uprooting of Palestinian crops and olive groves by Israeli settlers. In the West Bank (MEMO

---

[59] Of course Israel's strategy of starving almost two million people to death and letting them die of thirst in its genocidal war on Gaza is only the radicalized version of its general strategy of annihilating Palestinians that follows the logic of elimination.

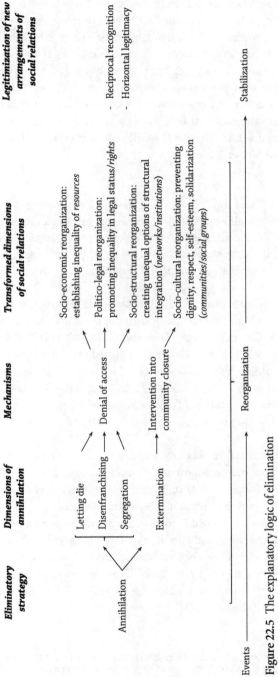

Figure 22.5 The explanatory logic of elimination

2022b; The New Arab 2021), Palestinians' animals are stolen or killed (B'Tselem 2005); Palestinian land is poisoned by Israel dumping sewage and waste on it (Ashly 2017); and the manufacturing of pesticides in illegal settlements in the Jordan Valley has serious consequences for Palestinian workers in the factories but also for all Palestinians living in the area (Watts, Lee, and Aidy 2016), which is contaminated with chemicals hazardous to health (Hass 2005). This list is by no means exhaustive, yet these examples of how Palestinian land is destroyed allows for an examination of specific consequences of this strategy of starving Palestinians to death and letting them die of thirst (Hass 2016a; 2016b; 2016c; Environmental Justice Atlas 2019).

1. Food

Depriving people of food, preventing them from growing it, and destroying what they grow are all expressions of eliminatory strategies meant to create food insecurity for the entire Palestinian population, especially children (El Bilbeisi et al. 2022), and are thus expressions of the strategy of letting the Indigenous die that triggers the mechanism *denial of access* to the vital resource.

Hunger and Malnutrition Since the *Irish Times* reported in 2002 that one in five Palestinian children were malnourished, the situation has only worsened, particularly for Gazan children (People's World 2009; NHRC 2008; Journal of Palestine Studies 2011), and has been described as a 'silent epidemic of malnutrition in Palestinian preschool children' (Tsigga and Grammatikopoulou 2012, 181; Albelbeisi et al. 2018). From a general perspective, the World Bank report *Hidden Hunger. Micronutrient Deficiencies in the West Bank and Gaza* has confirmed a catastrophic situation for the Palestinian people:

> The poor nutritional status of the Palestinian population is worrying, with a high prevalence of micronutrient deficiencies among groups for whom good nutrition is particularly important, such as children under five years old and pregnant and postnatal women. There are many reasons why: In the West Bank and Gaza, heightened food insecurity contributes to an insufficient intake of micronutrients, and poor households especially have limited access to micronutrient-rich foods, such as red meat, fresh vegetables, and milk. . . . The resulting, persistently high prevalence of micronutrient deficiency is likely to have grave consequences for human health and economic development if no action is taken. (Cieslik 2022)[60]

---

[60] In a brief paper in *The Lancet*, Horton (2022) demanded that the *WHO's erasure of Palestinians must cease*, referring to the WHO's practice of erasing Palestinians in its World Health Statistics 2022, arguing: 'Despite being a member of WHO's Eastern Mediterranean Region (EMRO), the occupied

Hidden hunger and malnutrition, caused by both invading Gaza with bulldozers protected by the military (OCHA 2020b; MEMO 2020) and spraying herbicides to poison crops and fields and soil (Gisha 2020),[61] create severe dangers such as 'the presence of parasitic, bacterial, and viral infections, and other environmental risk factors. In women and children, micronutrient deficiencies are associated with increased morbidity and mortality' (Cieslik 2022).

In Israel's bio-political war against the Palestinian people, children are prevented from growing up healthy with growth rates according to their age (Albelbeisi et al. 2018) and from developing without diseases or serious deficiencies that will affect their later health and physical, mental, and psychological capacities. The Zionist occupation permanently *exacerbates child malnutrition* (Berger 2018), leading to disastrous stunting, wasting, and underweight among children in the West Bank and Gaza Strip, as recent studies confirm (Albelbeisi et al. 2018; Watkins 2019; Hamouda and Al Hindi 2020; The Lancet 2020; Razali 2022).

Illnesses Malnutrition necessarily leads to widespread severe illnesses. Iron deficiency and anaemia appeared in the child population soon after the siege of the Gaza Strip (Sirdah, Yaghi, and Yaghi, 2013) and was confirmed again recently (Hamouda and Al Hindi 2020). Also, in other parts of Palestine, anaemia among children is at a critical level (AbuKishk et al. 2020; see also International Bank for Reconstruction and Development/World Bank 2021). In 2022, the World Bank found even more severe malnutrition, revealing not only the racist character of Israel's strategy of *letting die* but also a gender-specific dimension, making Israel's nutrition war also a war against women:

> Data from the most recent national survey conducted by the MOH in 2013—the most reliable and comprehensive source of data on micronutrient status to date—showed about 72% of children (6–59 months old) and 47% to 58% of pregnant women (depending on the trimester of pregnancy) suffered from low plasma vitamin A. About 54% to 68% of children (6–59 months old) and 99% of pregnant women (18–43 years old) in their second and third trimesters had low vitamin D. About 65% of children (6–59 months old) and 16% to 42% of pregnant women (depending on the trimester of pregnancy) had low vitamin E. (Cieslik 2022)

Palestinian territory (oPt)—3.2 million people in the West Bank and East Jerusalem and 2.2 million people in the Gaza Strip—is absent from WHO's data. There is only one mention of the oPt: in a single chart of crude death rates for COVID-19.' See also Giacaman et al. 2009.

[61] Of course, poisoning the air in Gaza with air strikes against an agrochemical warehouse is another strategy of denying access to a vital resource: *fresh air* (MacKernan and Balousha 2022).

Israel's strategy of letting Palestinians die, especially women and children, has forced the World Food Programme to launch 'a new campaign to provide nutritional support to hundreds of pregnant and nursing women in Gaza and the West Bank, aiming to combat malnutrition and high anaemia (iron deficiency) rates among them' (World Food Programme 2022). As the situation is especially grave in Gaza, another aspect plays a critical role, since for 'Gazans, living under Israeli blockade and intermittent attacks, food insecurity is further exacerbated by import restrictions and the deprivation of access to Palestinian fishing zones by Israel's coast guard' (Arab News 2022). In this vein, Jamie McGoldrick, Humanitarian Coordinator for the Occupied Palestinian Territory of the World Health Organization, argued:

> The dire humanitarian situation—particularly in the Gaza Strip and for West Bank communities in Area C, East Jerusalem and H2 area of Hebron—has profound implications for people's health. WHO's report highlights the health implications of impediments to adequate access to water and sanitation, high rates of poverty, unemployment and food insecurity and insecure housing, demolitions and displacement. (WHO 2019)

Controlling and Reducing Calories The bio-political character of Israel's *politics of erasure* and its focus on extinction become fully obvious when we look at the collective punishment of the residents of the Gaza Strip for having democratically voted for Hamas in 2006 (see Baumgarten 2006; Hroub 2006). The total blockade and siege on the Gaza Strip included a programme of *controlling and reducing calories* that could be brought into the Strip, far below the required amount (Al Jazeera 2021; Cook 2012; Reuters 2012; The New Arab 2018; The Associated Press 2012), aimed at slowly starving human beings. In June 2022, the United Nations Office for the Coordination of Humanitarian Affairs Occupied Palestinian Territory published the report *Gaza Strip. The Humanitarian Impact of 15 Years of the Blockade* (OCHA 2022a) stressing the catastrophic humanitarian impact of the siege of Gaza.

2. *Water*

Illegal land grabs and the banning of Palestinians from their land have always been connected to the control of water resources. This eliminatory strategy of denying Palestinians access to water in various ways expresses a politics of *letting Palestinians die of thirst*. Following the 1976 war-as-event when Israel

> occupied the West Bank, including East Jerusalem, and the Gaza Strip . . . the Israeli military authorities consolidated complete power over all water resources

and water-related infrastructure in the Occupied Palestinian Territories (OPT). 50 years on, Israel continues to control and restrict Palestinian access to water in the OPT to a level which neither meets their needs nor constitutes a fair distribution of shared water resources. (Amnesty International 2017; see also B'Tselem 2016a)

Israel retained all that control in the occupied territories 'under the 1995 Interim Agreement (Oslo II)' (B'Tselem 2017/21). Although the right to water is codified as a human right (United Nations Economic and Social Council 2003; Abu-Eid 2007) and occupying nations are responsible for the people in areas they have occupied, Israel is waging a water war against Palestinians (Abu-Ei 2007; Journal of Palestine Studies 2009; Amnesty International 2009a; Zeitoun 2005), employing strategies that deny access to water as a vital resource in order to uproot Palestinians. The consequences for Palestinians of both being cut off from the water supply and having to pay high prices to buy back water that has been taken illegally from their land can be compared to the conditions for Jewish settlers, who, quite often in close proximity to the Palestinians concerned, live with an abundance of water and can buy water for much lower prices, as the WHO has made clear:

> Due to access restrictions imposed by the Israeli authorities, poor infrastructure, and the risk of confiscation, the average water price ranges from two to four times the average in the West Bank generally (NIS5 or $1.50 per cubic metre), for 36 per cent of Area C communities in the Jordan Valley. For other communities (31 per cent), the access to water is even more expensive, reaching up to eight times the average price. Water consumption for these communities drops to less than 50 litres/capita/day (l/c/d), compared with the WHO recommendation of 100 l/c/d. In comparison, all households in nearby Israeli settlements are connected to piped water services. These households have access to permanent and unlimited water supply at affordable prices (NIS9 or $2.8 per cubic metre for drinking use, and NIS2.8 or $0.9 per cubic metre for agricultural use). Such unlimited access to water results in water consumption rates of 300-440 l/c/d, particularly in Israeli settlements focusing on agriculture. (OCHA 2021b; see also ECHO 2004)

Three graphs from the United Nations Office for the Coordination of Humanitarian Affairs show the effects of denying Palestinians access to water in the West Bank (OCHA 2021) and the high costs they must pay to get back the stolen water (OCHA 2021, Najib 2021) (see illustrations 22.2 and 22.3).

Strategies that promote the mechanism of denying access to water in general (Dajani 2014), and to the *scarce, polluted, and mostly unfit* (OCHA 2020a) water

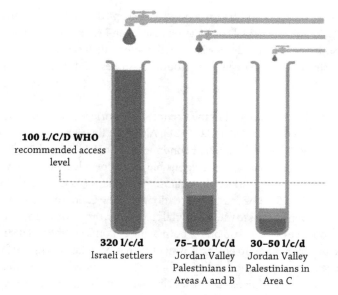

Illustration 22.2. Different amounts of water per person and day in the Jordan Valley (Palestinians/Settlers)
Source: OCHA 2021

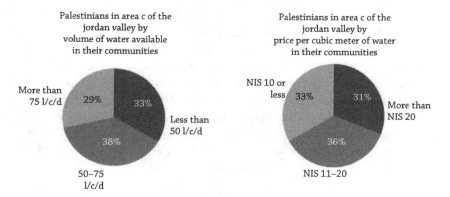

Illustration 22.3 Volume of water and prices to pay
Source: OCHA 2021; see Najib 2021

for use in Gaza in particular, cause severe illnesses, as described in a statement from the EU Commission reporting a

> wide range of diseases such as parathyroid fever, hepatitis and poliomyelitis, and in particular to the prevalence of intestinal parasites such as amoeba,

giardia, and roundworm. Surveys indicate a marked increase in the prevalence of diarrhea from 2002 to 2003, with two-week diarrhea prevalence rising from 12% to 17%. (ECHO 2004; see also EWASH 2012)

Such problems arising from Israel's strategies of annihilation have only grown in recent decades, as has been shown more recently (see Abu Shawish and Weibel 2017; Baroud 2022). The consequences of letting Palestinians die of thirst and, of course, letting their harvests dry up were revealed by the United Nations already in 2012 (OCHA 2012; see also Assadi 2008), showing a number of different actions taken by both the state and settlers to uproot Palestinians following strategies immediately triggering the mechanism of denying access to water. I refer briefly to only three of them: prohibition, annexation, and destruction.

Prohibition on Water Use Israel's *water war* against Palestinians (Gumas 2021) has many facets, grounded in the Israeli Military Order 158 from 1976 that is still valid today and was another *event* that served as a template for possibilities to dramatically worsen the situation of the Indigenous Palestinians. According to this military order, Palestinians hardly ever receive a permit to construct water installations. Moreover

> they are unable to drill new water wells, install pumps or deepen existing wells, in addition to being denied access to the Jordan River and fresh water springs. Israel even controls the collection of rain water throughout most of the West Bank, and rain water harvesting cisterns owned by Palestinian communities are often destroyed by the Israeli army. As a result, some 180 Palestinian communities in rural areas in the occupied West Bank have no access to running water, according to OCHA. (Amnesty International 2017)

Prohibiting Palestinians from accessing water has a huge number of consequences directly aimed at threatening their chances of survival. It is a basic strategy there to dry out Palestine—for the Palestinians, not for the settlers (Dajani 2014)—and to allow access to this vital resource to one people only (Al-Haq 2013), with serious consequences also for public health in the Occupied Territories (Gumas 2021; WHO 2019).

Annexing Palestinian Water The United Nations (OCHA 2012) has outlined the humanitarian impact of the takeover of Palestinian water springs by Israeli settlers in detail. Palestinians are driven from their land and thus from water by the growing illegal Jewish settlements and the transformation of wells into tourist attractions accessible to Jews and tourists only. In contrast, the legitimate owners of the land are confronted with a variety of practices such as 'trespass, intimidation, theft, and building without permit—[that] are illegal under both international and Israeli military legislation' (OCHA 2012).

In June 2020, the Stop the Wall Campaign made explicit the eliminatory character of Israel's politics, arguing that the water crisis is a consequence of Israel's 'weaponizing water for annexation', and that cutting Palestinians off from water is a means to '*coerce Palestinians into leaving the land*', and that legalizing water confiscation is one critical aspect of 'the continuous deprivation of Palestinians of their natural resources' (Stop the Wall Campaign 2020; emphasis added).[62]

From the perspective of closure analysis, also building the separation wall that Israel started in 2002 was and still is a strategy to trigger the mechanism of denying access to resources by annexing land and barring Palestinians from water, thereby exposing them to the threat of being eliminated:

> A 700-kilometer fence/wall that has been under construction by Israel since 2002 has further *reduced Palestinian access to water* in the West Bank.... The route of the fence/wall has been planned in such a way that it *prevents access by Palestinians* to areas of the West Bank that include some of the best access to water, notably the Western Aquifer. (Amnesty International 2009b)[63]

As the separation wall cuts through Palestinian land, the consequences of this strategy of annihilation designed to uproot human beings is obvious: 'We are here and our water is there. Many farmers don't have permits to go to cultivate their land where the water is, and on this side of the wall we suffer from lack of water (Abdellatif Khaled, a hydrologist from Jayyus, describing the impact of the fence/wall to Amnesty International)' (Amnesty International 2009b). Also, Human Rights Watch in its report *A Threshold Crossed. Israeli Authorities and the Crime of Apartheid and Persecution* pointed out Israel's real reason for building the separation wall, namely to initiate processes of social closure:

> The separation barrier, for example, separates Palestinians from more than 20 wells in the 'seam zone', between the barrier and the Green Line, limiting their ability to use these water sources, as well as cutting them off from about 70 percent of the Western Aquifer Basin (United Nations 2021).

Destruction of Water Resources and Water Infrastructure Destroying water resources and water infrastructure has consistently been a strategy of both the

---

[62] Of course, a specific means of using water to harass Palestinian Muslims is when Israel's national water company cuts off water supply to the West Bank during a Muslim holiday; see Yeung 2016.
[63] For an excellent study of the impact of the Israeli separation wall on Palestinian water rights and agriculture from the perspective of International Law, see Malone 2004.

IDF and settlers to cut Palestinians off from water, like the destruction of a Palestinian water well in the West Bank village of Ras Atiyeh that served 400 farmers in the area (MEMO 2022a), or the destruction of an agricultural pool by bulldozers. One of the most critical cases in 2022 was certainly that of Masafer Yatta, an area in which Bedouin communities have been threatened for years, their 'water pipelines cut by Israeli occupation forces' (Environmental Justice Atlas 2019). This 'cutting the lifeline' (Stop the Wall Campaign 2020) through the destruction of both natural resources and infrastructure comes along with restrictions on building new infrastructure to access water, since 'in the years 2010–2016 Palestinians received approval for two new water wells, one in Hizme and the second in Janzoor. During this time period the CA [Civil Administration] carried out enforcement measurements against 28 Palestinian wells, 11 of which were demolished' (ACRI 2018). Further

> authorities have also denied permits for Palestinians to build water pipelines and demolished water infrastructure built without permits. Between 2009 and July 2019, Israeli authorities demolished or seized 547 structures providing water and related sanitation services, including cisterns, water pipes, and mobile latrines, according to OCHA. (HRW 2021)

Of course, both state means are designed to deny Palestinians access to water and make up a critical aspect of strategies of elimination and ethnic cleansing:

> Water is life. Without water we cannot live; not us, not the animals, or the plants. Before we had some water, but after the army destroyed everything we have to bring water from far away; it's very difficult and expensive. They make our life very difficult, *to make us leave* (Fatima al-Nawajah, a resident of Susya, speaking to Amnesty International). (Amnesty International 2009b; emphasis added)

Disenfranchising

Disenfranchising, the second dimension of a *politics of erasure* as a strategy of annihilation, encompasses a wide range of strategies with which the Israeli settler-colonial regime denies the colonized *access to rights*. The eliminatory character of this strategy is so extreme that Israel was declared an apartheid state by three main human rights organizations and the United Nations, after the Russell Tribunal on Palestine had done so ten years before in 2011 (Russell Tribunal on Palestine 2013). In 2021, the human rights organizations B'Tselem (The Israeli Information Center for Human Rights in the Occupied Territories) (2021a), Human Rights Watch (2021), and Amnesty International (2022a) did so in their reports as well, and in May 2022 even the United Nations Human

Rights Office of the High Commissioner (OHCHR 2022a) joined them. Human Rights Watch characterized the apartheid situation on the ground in Palestine in these words:

> Laws, policies, and statements by leading Israeli officials make plain that the objective of maintaining Jewish Israeli control over demographics, political power, and land has long guided government policy. In pursuit of this goal, authorities have dispossessed, confined, forcibly separated, and subjugated Palestinians by virtue of their identity to varying degrees of intensity. In certain areas, as described in this report, these deprivations are so severe that they amount to the crimes against humanity of apartheid and persecution. (HRW 2021)

As Susan Power has shown in her analysis *The Legal Character of Apartheid*, the Israeli state's legal architecture has always had the intention of establishing a system of domination of Jews over Palestinians:

> Israel maintains its apartheid regime through a complex framework of laws that enable demographic engineering, widespread land appropriation and the fragmentation of the Palestinian people and territory. These laws also introduce illegally transferred Jewish settlers to colonize both sides of the Green Line. Finally, racially discriminatory laws seek to subordinate the Palestinian population as a whole through denying their collective rights of return, self-determination and permanent sovereignty (over lands on both sides of the Green Line). (Power 2021)

From the perspective of closure theory, progressively and comprehensively disenfranchising Palestinians through laws providing for Jewish supremacy and domination, in addition to the citizenship and nationality laws, the law providing for land appropriation, the physical fragmentation of Palestine, and laws to prevent Palestinian resistance (see Power 2021), lie at the heart of the Zionist settler-colonial project and reorganize the social relations of elimination dramatically. To make plausible the logic of disenfranchising, I will highlight three examples of ways Israel maintains Jewish superiority over Palestinians, thereby eliminating the latter as legal subjects: the definition of citizens, the dividing of the Palestinian people by attributing to them different legal statuses, and the Israeli judiciary system's strategy of *whitewashing*.

1. *Defining Citizens*

On 29 July 2018, the Israeli parliament passed 'The Basic Law: Israel—The Nation-State of the Jewish People', a critical event that finally allowed for the

Table 22.4 Articles 1–7 of the Jewish Nation State Basic Law

Article 1 states that the Land of Israel ("Eretz Israel") is the historic national home of the Jewish people, in which the State of Israel was established, and in which the Jewish people exercises its natural, cultural, and historic right to self-determination. It adds that the right to exercise national self-determination in the State of Israel is solely for the Jewish people

Article 2 sets forth the symbols of the state, all specifically Jewish in character

Article 3 defines the capital of Israel as Jerusalem, which includes occupied East Jerusalem

Article 4 states that the official language of the state is Hebrew, demoting Arabic, which was previously a second official language, to a language with an undefined "special status"

Article 5 establishes that immigration leading to automatic citizenship is exclusive to Jews

Article 6 provides that the state will strengthen ties between the state and Jewish people around the world, and preserve the cultural, historic, and religious heritage of the Jewish people in the Diaspora

Article 7 provides that the state views development of Jewish settlement as a national value, and will act to encourage, promote and consolidate its establishment, thereby instituting segregation as a new legal norm, and allowing for the annexation of the West Bank

Source: Adalah 2018

codification of the long-practiced discrimination against non-Jews. The establishment of a regime of religious and ethnic purity by enshrining Jewish supremacy permanently in the law assigned Palestinians a legally subordinate status in the territory of the state of Israel, but no less in the Occupied Palestinian Territories. Articles 1–7 of the Jewish Nation State Basic Law expose its racist character grounded in White Jewish supremacy (see table 22.4).

As a critical event, the passing of the Basic Law has created a legal reality for Palestinians in which their basic rights are denied, and their chances of survival compromised. They are confronted with an ever-growing legal vacuum, a lawless space. For example

> Article 7 of the Nation State Law establishes that the State considers the development of Jewish settlements to be a national priority. In November 2020, Israel's Krayot Magistrate's Court cited this Article when upholding a municipal policy that denied Palestinian children access to schools in the Israeli city of Karmiel. In justification, it observed: 'Karmiel is a Jewish city intended to solidify Jewish settlement in the Galilee. The establishment of an Arabic-language school or

even the funding of school transportation for Arab students is liable to alter the demographic balance and damage the city's character'. (Al-Haq 2021)

Obviously, the passing of the Nation State Law has anchored norms to which courts now refer to deny Palestinians basic rights such as the right to education. This eliminatory strategy denies Palestinian children not only their fundamental right to education but also compromises their chances of survival.

As the Basic Law mainly just codified a racist legal validation of practices that had already been carried out for a long time, reports have already criticized the 'unconstitutionality of the 2008 amendment to Israel's Citizenship Law that authorizes the court to approve requests from the interior minister to revoke the citizenship of Israeli citizens for "breach of loyalty"' (Adalah 2017b). This instrument is used as a legal weapon only against Palestinians, threatening to revoke their citizenship and, eventually, make them stateless. This happened for the first time on Sunday, 6 August 2017, when 'the Haifa District Court ruled ... to revoke the citizenship of Alaa Zayoud, a Palestinian citizen of Israel serving time in prison on attempted murder conviction' (Adalah 2017b). On 1 December 2022, the strategic argument of a *breach of loyalty* was also used in the 'Israeli decision to deport Palestinian French human rights defender and resident of occupied East Jerusalem, Salah Hamouri, 37, after revoking his Jerusalem residency rights' (WAFA 2022). Hamouri, whom the Israeli state accused of supporting terrorism was deported in the morning of 18 December (The Guardian 2022), which shows that Israeli law is used strategically to silence any criticism by threatening Palestinians with stripping them of their basic human rights.

2. Different Legal Statuses and Different Rights for Palestinians

The Basic Law codifies a decades-old settler-colonial practise of bestowing all citizenship rights upon Jewish people living in Israel as well as in the illegally Occupied Palestinian Territories, while disenfranchising the Palestinian people. Analysing the legal discrimination against Palestinians, Adalah's *Discriminatory Laws Database* presents a list that encompasses almost seventy laws that

> discriminate directly or indirectly against Palestinian citizens in Israel and/or Palestinian residents of the Occupied Palestinian Territory (OPT) on the basis of their national belonging. The discrimination in these laws is either explicit— 'discrimination on its face'—or, more often, the laws are worded in a seemingly neutral manner, but have or will likely have a disparate impact on Palestinians in their implementation. These laws limit the rights of Palestinians in all areas of life, from citizenship rights to the right to political participation, land and housing rights, education rights, cultural and language rights, religious rights, and due process rights during detention. Some of the laws also discriminate

against other groups such as gays, non-religious Jews, and Palestinian refugees. (Adalah 2017a)

Of course, any one of these discriminatory laws would be a case worthy of a closure analysis to understand in detail the ways and degree to which these strategies disenfranchise Palestinians, who are not all granted the same rights but are rather confronted with the strategy of *divide and conquer*. This strategy divides Palestinians into distinct groups, conceding them different legal statuses on the basis of which they are granted different rights—or no rights at all. There are four such groups under occupation that are denied access to rights in different ways.

Israeli Territory (within the Green Line): Palestinians as Second-Class Citizens In the 1948 war against the Palestinians, the Zionists did not succeed in completely ethnically cleanse the territory that in 1949 became the state of Israel. Some Palestinians survived the war and the massacres and managed to stay, driven out of their destroyed villages and finding a place in other villages or cities, while others who had fled to Jordan or Lebanon somehow managed to return after the Nakba. Today, 20% of Israel's citizens are Palestinian—called *48-Palestinians*. Around 1.5 million people, they are—as the discussion of the effects of the Basic Law has shown—discriminated against in many ways and denied rights that are exclusive to Jews, which bestows upon them the status of second-class citizens.

East Jerusalem: Palestinians as Residents East Jerusalem was annexed by Israel in the *Naksa*, its 1967 war against the Palestinians, Jordan, and Egypt. This step, illegal according to international law, has turned its approximately 350,000 Palestinian inhabitants into

> permanent residents of Israel a status that allows them to live and work in Israel without needing special permits, to receive social benefits and health insurance, and to vote in municipal elections. Yet permanent residency, unlike citizenship, may be revoked at any time, at the complete discretion of the Minister of the Interior. In certain circumstances, it can also expire. (B'Tselem 2021a)

West Bank: Palestinians as Subjected More than 2.6 million Palestinians are living in the West Bank in a permanent state and space of exception, as Israel has imposed its military rule since 1967. Here, as the above maps of Israel's illegal land grab show, Palestinians live in disconnected islands, fragmented into areas A, B, and C, each having its own legal treatment, deprived of all political and civil rights. Although the Palestinian Authority (PA) officially exercises civilian power in the West Bank, having established a kind of deeply corrupt police state that aids and abets the settler-colonial regime, Palestinians remain *born without civil rights* (HRW 2019a) under the repressive Israeli regime which exercises power by means of *draconian military orders* (HRW 2019a; ACRI 2014; ACRI 2022).

Gaza Strip: Palestinians as Outlawed Until October 2023, the Gaza Strip was inhabited by approximately 2.2 million Palestinians. In 2005, Israel dismantled Jewish settlements in the Strip and, after Hamas won the democratic elections and took power in 2006, imposed a total blockade of the Gaza Strip over land, air, and water, withholding all human rights from the inhabitants. At the same time, Israel 'abdicated any responsibility for the fate of the Palestinian population' (B'Tselem 2021a). The control is absolute and

> continues to have a devastating effect as people's movement to and from the Gaza Strip, as well as access to markets, remains severely restricted. The UN Secretary-General has found that the blockade and related restrictions contravene international humanitarian law as they target and impose hardship on the civilian population, effectively penalizing them for acts they have not committed. (UNRWA n.d.)

This state of being divided into groups with different legal statuses is further exacerbated, as

> Israel accords Palestinians a different package of rights in every one of these units—all of which are inferior compared to the rights afforded to Jewish citizens. The goal of Jewish supremacy is advanced differently in every unit, and the resulting forms of injustice differ: the lived experience of Palestinians in blockaded Gaza is unlike that of Palestinian subjects in the West Bank, permanent residents in East Jerusalem or Palestinian citizens within sovereign Israeli territory. Yet these are variations on the fact that all Palestinians living under Israeli rule are treated as inferior in rights and status to Jews who live in the very same area. (B'Tselem 2021a)

In the face of these and, of course, many more strategies completely disenfranchising Palestinians, Agnès Callamard, Amnesty International's Secretary General, concluded in the organization's report *Israel's Apartheid against Palestinians: Cruel system of domination and crime against humanity*:

> Our report reveals the true extent of Israel's apartheid regime. Whether they live in Gaza, East Jerusalem and the rest of the West Bank, or Israel itself, *Palestinians are treated as an inferior racial group and systematically deprived of their rights*. We found that Israel's cruel policies of segregation, dispossession

and exclusion across all territories under its control clearly amount to apartheid. The international community has an obligation to act. (Amnesty International 2022a; emphasis added)

3. A Legal System of Whitewashing Elimination
While one essential core aspect of a democratic society is an impartial legal system, a third critical institutionalized legal strategy of the Israeli settler-colonial regime operating as a means to disenfranchise Palestinians is the partisan nature of the regime's judiciary system. In this system, the Israeli Supreme Court plays a critical role in defending, safeguarding, and legitimizing Israeli politics that breach international law and compromise Palestinians' chances of survival.[64]

The court upholds and legitimizes racist political decisions, such as the already mentioned strategy of revoking citizenship from 48-Palestinians for an alleged *breach of loyalty*, even if this means rendering them stateless (Adalah 2022). It also gives the authorization for torture and mistreatment (Ben-Natan 2019) and justifies targeted killings (Eichensehr 2007). Further, it upholds Israel's policy of withholding the bodies of Palestinians killed by the IDF (Al-Haq 2019b), not to mention the 'Supreme Court's decision to demolish Khan Al-Ahmar Bedouin Community, east of occupied Jerusalem' (Palestinian Center for Human Rights, 2018), which amounts to legalizing a case of ethnic cleansing. Moreover, there is Israel's '[utilizing] the Israeli Supreme Court's security-based reasoning, ... [to justify] punitive house demolitions in reference to the Defence Emergency Regulations of 1945' (Al-Haq 2011). The Israeli Supreme Court has also ruled that

> Israel can expel some 1,000 Palestinians who live in an area declared a firing zone in the South Hebron Hills. In a judgment filled with lies and errors, the court ignored Israel's longstanding aim to bring the area under Jewish control, dismissed international law as irrelevant, and ruled the residents had 'invaded' the area to 'establish facts on the ground' as it is not their real home. In doing so, the justices permitted the state to commit a war crime for which they, too, will bear liability if it is committed. (B'Tselem 2022a)

Thus, the Israeli justice system is a system of juridically *whitewashing* any of the regime's eliminatory strategies against Palestinians (B'Tselem 2020b; 2020c).[65] It confers legitimacy to the regime's extrajudicial killings and the practice of

---

[64] For a detailed analysis of the Israeli legal system, see the impressive study *The Occupation of Justice. The Supreme Court of Israel and the Occupied Territories* by Kretzmer and Ronen 2021.
[65] 'The duties of the occupying power are spelled out primarily in the 1907 Hague Regulations (arts 42-56) and the Fourth Geneva Convention (GC IV, art. 27–34 and 47–78), as well as in certain provisions of Additional Protocol I and customary international humanitarian law' (International Committee of the Red Cross 2004).

administrative detention, in which individuals are detained for an initial period of six months without being given any reason, a period of time that can be arbitrarily extended indefinitely, also without giving reasons, and can include torture of prisoners (OMCT 2019; Addameer 2017). Consequently, we observe 'the perversion of the justice system and rule of law ... [that is] nothing more than a weapon to legitimize even the most destructive state actions, while punishing those who oppose them'. The primary function of such a kind of justice system is to simply 'shield government actors from accountability' (Greenwald 2012). This is also true with regard to all the atrocities committed by the Israeli military during the Great March of Return in 2018. In a joint report by the Palestinian Centre for Human Rights (P.C.H.R.) and B'Tselem (2021), it was revealed that the Israeli justice system is *unable and unwilling* to hold anyone in the Israeli military or politics accountable for the targeted killings (see also Amnesty International 2001) and war crimes committed (see also Dana 2020).

One of the most critical aspects of this whole legal system is the role of the military justice system that was implemented after Israel's 1967 war and that enables the occupation regime to pursue any kind of eliminatory strategy against Palestinians, thus reducing their chances of survival to a minimum (see El-AD 2016). In her analysis of Israel's military justice system and its relation to international law, Valentina Azarova reveals the pathological nature of this system:

> States that obey international law transform it into domestic law and internalise the imperative of compliance with international law. But the inverse is also true. The Israeli military justice system is based ... on rule and practice that mandate Israeli entities to reject the status of Palestinians as a protected population and the status of the territory as 'occupied' (as in the case of international law). This pathology of this legal system entails a certain posture and attitude towards Israel's legal obligations under international law that predetermines the ability of its authorities to will action in compliance with international law. (Azarova 2017, 13–14)

Moreover, Luigi Daniele in his discussion of the military justice system in the West Bank concludes that the military courts simply serve as 'courts of exception for endless occupation' (Daniele 2017, 37). In accordance with this, a detailed report on the practices of the military law enforcement system in the West Bank concludes that this system simply serves to whitewash Israeli soldiers' abuses of Palestinians (B'Tselem 2016b; Baker 2016). As a whole, the Israeli judicial system does not fulfil the requirements of a democratic society, which must guarantee the same rights to all human beings under its rule. Rather it is clear that the Israeli judicial system is nothing more than a tool for inflicting more suffering on the Palestinians in collusion with the military and other occupation institutions. In an official response to the Israeli Supreme Court regarding aggressive acts against Palestinian property, the Israeli government claimed boldly that it 'is allowed to ignore the directives of international law in any field it desires' (MEMO 2018). This provides the green light for the judicial system in Israel to whitewash the crimes of its soldiers. The people of Palestine can expect no justice from the self-proclaimed occupation state. (Dalloul 2018; reference inserted)

While Israel, as Tony Judt argued back in 2003, as a system striving for religious or ethnic purity is *an anachronism* of the nineteenth century (Judt 2003), like any other settler-colonial regime it has created a White supremacist 'democracy' that disenfranchises the Indigenous, exposing them to a *politics of erasure*. As Israel rejects international law as a guiding principle stipulating how modern pluralistic democracies work and which duties must be fulfilled, the regime resembles much more anti-democratic systems of the first half of the twentieth century. Like them, Israel has

> developed two distinct pillars of its jurisdiction—one for Jews only and the other for Palestinians and other non-Jewish groups. While Jews have full citizenship subject to the laws of a 'Legal State', Palestinians are subject to the laws of a 'Prerogative State' that arbitrarily refers to Israeli military law, Ottoman law, British colonial law, Jordanian law, the laws from Oslo I and II, and so forth to punish Palestinians. (Mackert 2022, 10)

Israel has thus established a regime that Ernst Fraenkel (2017 [1941]) has called a *dual state* and declared to be a dictatorship. We may thus call the Israeli regime a *settler-colonial dual state* (Mackert 2022, 10; see also Daniele 2017) that allows any kind of eliminatory and genocidal strategies against the Palestinian people in an environment of impunity guaranteed by its western allies.

Segregation
Segregation, as the third dimension of a *politics of erasure* as a strategy of annihilation, describes colonizers' strategy of denying the colonized access to critical *institutions* or *networks* to avoid the Indigenous peoples' integration into the occupiers' societal infrastructure. Looking at the system of public health, Médecins Sans Frontières (2021) has reported several critical issues in structures operating in a way that keeps Palestinians at a distance from the public health system. There are infrastructural problems in the health system itself, including

poorly maintained roads and streets blocked or destroyed by the IDF preventing access to hospitals and ambulances. There is also a lack of public transport as well as financial resources enabling people to reach the nearest hospital. Yet, lowering Palestinians' survival chances through strategies of segregation finds immediate expression in the many ways Israel purposively fails to meet its obligations as an occupation power. In its 2019 report *Right to Health in the Occupied Palestinian Territory, 2018*, Gerald Rockenschaub, Head of the WHO office in the occupied Palestinian territory, addressed this problem among many others:

> Palestinians in the West Bank and Gaza Strip continue to face major barriers to the realization of the right to health. Sustainability of quality healthcare services is challenged by chronic occupation and fragmentation; restrictions on movement have a profound impact on access to healthcare, including for some of the most vulnerable Palestinian patients. A study completed by WHO this year demonstrates that cancer patients initially denied or delayed permits to access chemotherapy and/or radiotherapy outside Gaza from 2015 to 2017 were 1.5 times less likely to survive in the following six months or more, compared to those initially approved permits. The findings highlight the urgent need for reform to remove access barriers to protect patients from harm. (WHO 2019)

Following this report, B'Tselem made explicit the consequences of such measures for severely ill people:

> In comparison, from March 2019 to February 2020 (just before the pandemic), according to World Health Organization figures, almost 24,000 Gazans applied for permits to enter Israel for vital medical treatment. Some 65% of the requests related to treatment at hospitals in East Jerusalem, about 22% to hospitals in the rest of the West Bank, and some 13% to hospitals in Israel. Of all these applications, more than a third (about 8,500) were rejected or not answered before the scheduled appointment, including at least 2,274 minors and about 996 persons over 60. Among the persons who were rejected or went unanswered, at least 1,996 had cancer, 597 had a heart condition, and 210 required neurosurgical treatment. (B'Tselem 2021d)

Denying cancer patients necessary medical treatment by making them miss their appointments, which must be arranged in a complicated process and according to a time-consuming schedule, is a cruel measure exposing human beings to death that shows the fundamentally racist character of the Israeli settler-colonial regime. It becomes especially obvious that these strategies mainly intersect with gender, because 'women living in the area, in particular, face challenges accessing healthcare.... Women usually work around the clock on farms and, as they have no replacement, many tend to neglect their health and wait until their condition becomes serious before seeking medical attention' (Médecins Sans Frontières 2021). Moreover, with regard to both preventive medical check-ups and treatment, we see the mobilized us-them boundary working also between Palestinian and Israeli women in the system the occupation set up, intentionally reducing Palestinian women's chances of survival:

> Early diagnosis is one of the most important factors for breast cancer recovery. In Gaza, screening is very limited and the MoH [Ministry of Health] has only one mammography machine dedicated for screening, which is currently broken. In Israel, however, 84% of women aged 50 to 69 receive mammogram screening. (Medical Aid for Palestinians 2021)

Refusing ill women access to the Israeli health system is thus nothing but a death sentence. Israel's annihilation strategy of radical segregation with regard to accessing the health system and the consequences it has especially for Palestinian women is obvious. Yet, it has become even more obvious in the face of the Covid-19 pandemic, which Israel has used even to intensify its *politics of erasure*. Against the background of these politics, international legal scholar Marco Longobardo (2020) has referred to Article 56 of the 1949 Fourth Geneva Convention (GCIV) that holds Israel, as an occupying power, responsible for the health of Palestinians in the occupied territories in general, and under conditions of pandemics in particular. Article 56(1) reads:

> To the fullest extent of the means available to it, the occupying power has the duty of ensuring and maintaining, with the cooperation of national and local authorities, the medical and hospital establishments and services, public health and hygiene in the occupied territory, with particular reference to the adoption and application of the prophylactic and preventive measures necessary to combat the spread of contagious diseases and epidemics. (GCIV Article 56(1))

From this, Longobardo concludes:

> The object of the duty is insurance and maintenance of the healthcare system in the occupied territory, with particular attention in relation to 'prophylactic and preventive measures necessary to combat the spread of contagious diseases and epidemics'. This is a particularly topical provision in relation to Covid-19. (Longobardo 2020)

However, Israel has in no way fulfilled its obligations to the people it has occupied. Rather, in 2021 B'Tselem stated that 'the Israeli Ministry of Health has not yet publicly formulated an allocation policy that includes reserving specific amounts for Palestinians in the OPT, nor has it established a timeline for the transfer of these vaccines'. In the face of the pandemic, it thus willingly failed to provide 'support for the purchase and distribution of vaccines to the Palestinian population under its control' (B'Tselem 2021c). One year later, in 2022, Human Rights Watch made public that

> the Israeli government had vaccinated more than two-thirds of its citizens and residents and begun offering third booster shots, as of October. Israeli authorities provided vaccines to Palestinian citizens of Israel and residents of occupied East Jerusalem, as well as Israeli settlers in the West Bank, but not to most of the more than 4.7 million Palestinians living under Israeli control in the occupied West Bank and Gaza. Israeli authorities claim this responsibility falls on the PA, but the Fourth Geneva Convention obliges occupying powers to ensure medical supplies, including to combat the spread of pandemics, to the occupied population. More than 1 million Palestinians in the West Bank, excluding Jerusalem residents, and 466,000 Palestinians in Gaza, were vaccinated as of October 21, according to the WHO, largely through vaccines obtained from external sources and administered by Palestinian authorities. (HRW 2022b)[66]

Besides withholding vaccinations, Israel also prohibits the development of Palestinian healthcare infrastructure, for example by confiscating tents meant to serve as a clinic in the Northern West Bank. Such measures reveal not only Israel's attack on Palestinians' health and their right to healthcare, but also the goal beyond, which is the ethnic cleansing of the area:

> As the whole world battles an unprecedented and paralyzing healthcare crisis, Israel's military is devoting time and resources to harassing the most vulnerable Palestinian communities in the West Bank that Israel has attempted *to drive out of the area for decades*. Shutting down a first-aid community initiative during a health crisis is an especially cruel example of the regular abuse inflicted on

---

[66] See also B'Tselem 2021c for the joint statement '15 Israeli, Palestinian and international health and human rights organizations: Israel must provide necessary vaccines to Palestinian health care systems' signed by Adalah, the Legal Center for Arab Minority Rights in Israel; Al Mezan Center for Human Rights; Amnesty International Israel; B'Tselem, the Israeli Information Center for Human Rights in the Occupied Territories; Gisha, Legal Center for Freedom of Movement; Lawyers for Palestinian Human Rights; Medical Human Rights Network IFHHRO; MEDACT; Physicians for Human Rights Israel; The Palestinian Center for Human Rights; Hamoked: Center for the Defence of the Individual; Rabbis for Human Rights; Medecins du Monde France; Medici per i Diritti Umani, MEDU (Physicians for Human Rights Italy); Combatants for Peace.

these communities, and it goes against basic human and humanitarian principles during an emergency. (B'Tselem 2020a; emphasis added)

As one last aspect of such inhumane strategies, Middle East Eye reported on 'Israel's attempt to swap soon-to-expire Covid-19 vaccines with a future shipment of Pfizer doses earmarked for Palestinians in the occupied West Bank' (Uddin 2021), showing the cynical character of the Occupation's *politics of erasure* designed to eliminate Palestinian lives.

Extermination

Turning to extermination, the fourth dimension of a *politics of erasure* as a strategy of annihilation, we now look at the eliminators' strategies that activate the mechanism *intervention into community closure*. While strategies of letting die, disenfranchising, and segregation inevitably have a deep impact on Palestinian communities and civil society, strategies of extermination impinge directly on individuals and communities to prevent them from organizing or to discredit and destroy organizations that have been able to do so and are politically active. As Israel dehumanizes Palestinians, denying them human rights and a life in dignity, strategies of extermination aim to destroy the colonized mentally, physically, and psychologically to annihilate individuals and eradicate the Palestinian people.

Neuwirth's argument that state agencies prevent the closing of a subordinate community by exerting control over it to regulate its internal affairs and its members' everyday lives is nowhere as fitting as with regard to the eliminators' excessive strategies of individual, communal, economic, social, political, and cultural control of Palestinian lives. The regime's control in fact ranges from suppression of individual lives to surveillance of the whole Palestinian population (Sa'di 2014; see also Halper 2009). To make plausible the explanatory logic of the reorganization of socio-cultural relations to deny those threatened with elimination a life of dignity, respect, self-esteem, and possibilities for solidarization, I again describe only three strategies in more detail: the exertion of sheer violence, the destruction of human rights organizations, and the wiping out of Palestinian collective memory, culture and history, all of which trigger the mechanism *intervention into community closure*.

1. Sheer Violence: Killings, Targeted Killings, Imprisonment, and Torture

The destructiveness of *sheer violence* (Popitz) is the daily experience of the Palestinian people living under military rule. They are exposed to permanent harassment—even children are the targets of IDF soldiers and Zionist settlers—which can lead to imprisonment and eventually torture (see B'Tselem 2022b).[67]

---

[67] Israel's notorious torture regime has finally been exposed by whistleblowers from Sde Teiman torture camp and B'Tselem's (2024) report *Welcome to Hell*.

Given the IDF's readiness to immediately kill Palestinians, military raids of Palestinian refugee camps in the OPT and of Palestinians' private homes pose a permanent threat to life. Shooting at peaceful demonstrators and arbitrarily executing human beings at checkpoints or any other place of daily life clearly exposes the regime's eliminatory character.

Further, targeted killings of prominent personalities of Palestinian civil society are intended to show Palestinians who controls their lives and who has the power to prevent them from building communities. Among many other cases, Israeli snipers assassinated the prominent Palestinian journalist Shireen Abu Akleh in June 2022 (Abdulrahim et al. 2022; Hammad 2022; Al-Haq and Forensic Architecture 2022), who had played an important role in reporting during the Second Intifada, with no consequences for the assassinators in the IDF and without further investigation of the extrajudicial execution:

> The law of occupation grants occupiers wide authority to restrict rights, but also imposes key limitations, including the requirement to facilitate public life for the occupied population. The Israeli army has for over 50 years used broadly worded military orders to arrest Palestinian journalists, activists and others for their speech and activities—much of it non-violent—protesting, criticizing or opposing Israeli policies. (HRW 2019a; see also Amnesty International 2022b)

Moreover, the settler-colonial regime's policies of arbitrary imprisonment and administrative detention as well as torturing prisoners are an instrument for exercising control aimed at destroying Palestinian organizations. According to Addameer, the total number of political prisoners in 2022 amounted to 4,700 Palestinians, including 30 Palestinian women imprisoned, 190 children,[68] and 800 human beings held in administrative detention, which means that the imprisoned do not learn why they have been arrested because the occupiers refer only to so-called *secret evidence*. These prisoners have no legal aid, and while administrative detention theoretically lasts six months, it can be renewed indefinitely without giving any reasons. This lawless system creates a *spectrum of exception*, since the detainees have no way of knowing what charges are being brought against them, nor do they have the right to legal assistance.

For decades, torture has been a widespread practice in Israeli prisons (Ballas 2020; HRW 1994), yet in 2019 '"Israel's Supreme Court . . . clarified, this time explicitly, that interrogational torture is lawful in certain circumstances in

---

[68] Following Viterbo's 2021 analysis, Aburabia has made clear that 'Israel forced upon Palestinian children a certain legal model of childhood that is detrimental to them, using the law, the judiciary, and the rhetoric of human rights to operate its violence while politically exploiting international human rights law and the principle of the child's best interest to enable the regime of control and occupation' (Aburabia 2022).

Israel's legal system" referring to practices such as "sleep deprivation, beating and slapping, holding in the painful 'banana' and 'frog' positions, threats, curses, humiliations and much more"' (OMCT 2019; B'Tselem 2022b; HRW 2021; Amnesty International 2022b; Ben-Natan 2019).

Sheer violence, also a permanent threat and means of control, aims at preventing any closure of Palestinian communities or civil society groups that would allow them to act. Spreading fear and terror are strategies of annihilation destroying survival chances, attacking political identities, and degrading Palestinians. All this amounts to what the UN's Office of the High Commissioner of Human Rights has described as a

> *denial of the right to life and liberty*: Israel's rule is requiring increasingly more violence and confinement to be maintained: between January 2008 and February 2022, 5,988 Palestinians have been killed in the context of the occupation and conflict. (262 Israelis have died during the same time period).... State-sanctioned extra-judicial killings by Israel continues to be part of its toolbox, including the killings of civilians posing no immediate threat to Israeli troops, and with little or no internal accountability (Al-Haq 2022c). In addition, Israel's military courts incarcerates thousands of Palestinians on security charges through a judicial system that offers few of the international protections regarding due process, and the prevention of arbitrary arrest and detention (Daniele, 2017). Additionally, hundreds of Palestinians languish in administrative detention under open-ended confinement (Addameer 2017). Collective punishment is frequently employed, whether it is the blockade of Gaza, the demolition of family homes of terror suspects or the withholding of bodies (OHCHR 2020). (OHCHR 2022b; references inserted, emphasis added)[69]

There is growing lethal violence against Palestinians coming from both the Israeli state and radical Zionist settlers (OHCHR 2022c), who go unpunished for killing Palestinians. While in 2022 the United Nations Office for the Coordination of Humanitarian Affairs reported that 2021 had been the deadliest year for Palestinians since 2014 (OCHA 2022b), 2022 was even worse, with more than 150 Palestinians killed, making it the deadliest year for them since 2005 according to the United Nations—especially with regard to children killed (MEMO 2022c; OCHA 2022c; 2022d; Fayyad 2022; Berger 2022). However, in 2023 the numbers continued to rise. While in the first quarter of 2023 already 95 Palestinians had been killed by the IDF in the West Bank (Muaddi 2023), in the beginning of June the number had risen to 112 (WAFA 2023). Yet, already

---

[69] For a general analysis of collective punishment in the occupied territories, see OHCHR 2020.

in April 2023 the Knesset had approved Israel's security minister Ben-Gvir's demands for a new National Guard that should focus on *Arab unrest* (The Guardian 2023), and while Israel unleashed its genocidal war against the civilian population in Gaza in October 2023, the same minister ordered to hand out assault rifles to Zionist settlers (DAWN 2023; The New Arab 2023), who do not have to fear persecution when killing Arabs. Consequently

> Between 7 October and 23 November in the West Bank, including East Jerusalem, Israeli forces killed 211 Palestinians (including 54 children),[70] while Israeli settlers killed an additional eight Palestinians (including one child).... The number of Palestinians killed in the West Bank since 7 October accounts for 48% of the total Palestinian deaths (452) reported in the West Bank for 2023. (OCHA 2023b; see also HRW 2023)

2. Human Rights as Terrorism

Controlling the Palestinian people and preventing them from forming civil society organizations has long been a strategy of the Zionist settler-colonial regime (Dana 2015). Here, too, the strategies are almost innumerable. Not only has the space for civil society in Palestine been constantly shrinking during the last decades (Burkert 2022a; 2022b), but the organizations of Palestinian civil society have been persecuted (Muhareb et al. 2022; Baumgarten 2022; Bollens 2022; see Dana 2015). In 2022, such strategies of extermination were escalated by Israel declaring internationally respected Palestinian human rights organizations as *terrorist groups* and *unlawful organizations*, a move that 'effectively outlaws the most prominent organisations in the Palestinian human rights community' (Cook 2021), crushing them with the T-word (Buttu 2022). This move threatens with criminalization any kind of civil society organization that defends the rights of Palestinian people and threatens the organizations' staff and members with years in prison. As Al-Haq, one of the targeted groups, made public:

> On 18 August 2022, at approximately 3:00 am, Israeli Occupying Forces (IOF) entered Ramallah, forcibly entering, raiding the offices and confiscating property from the six designated Palestinian civil society organisations, Al-Haq, Addameer, the Bisan Center for Research and Development, Defence for Children International-Palestine, Union of Agricultural Workers Committees (UAWC), and the Union of Palestinian Women's Committees (UPWC). The IOF also raided the offices of the Health Workers Committees. The organisations are designated by Israel under its Counter Terrorism Law of

---

[70] This number has risen to sixty on November 27 according to DCIP (Defense for Children International-Palestine) 2023.

2016, and under military order issued on 3 November 2021, as 'terrorist' and 'unlawful associations'. (Al-Haq 2022a)

It is obvious that all groups declared to be terrorist organizations have been making an impact on the situation of the Palestinian people by revealing information about the settler-colonial regime's crimes against humanity that Israel wants to conceal. First, Al-Haq, which since 1979 has worked as a human rights organization specialized in international law and international human rights law, has documented and reported the eliminators' crimes against human rights in the OPT. Second is Addameer, Prisoner Support and Human Rights Organization, which concentrates on the rights of Palestinian prisoners in Israel and Palestine (Addameer n.d.). According to the organization, in August 2022 there were a total of 4,450 political prisoners, including 27 female prisoners, 175 child prisoners, and 670 administrative detainees (Addameer n.d.). Third is the Bisan Center for Research and Development, which according to its self-description 'aligns itself with the poor and marginalized in the Palestinian society, by working to support their struggle in advancing their socio- economic rights in the context of national liberation, through the production and application of critical development knowledge and the building of partnerships with progressive bodies and entities' (Bisan Center for Research and Development, n.d.). Fourth is the Defence for Children International-Palestine (DCIP), which defends the rights of Palestinian children. By offering legal support and aid, it also documents cases of violations against children's rights, such as keeping them in solitary confinement and treating them as *security detainees*, documenting what it means to grow up under Israeli occupation and reporting and documenting child fatalities (DCIP n.d.). Fifth, the Union of Agricultural Workers Committees (UAWC)

> is an independent agricultural developmental organization, politically neutral as per its by-laws, policies, vision, mission and practices. UAWC abides, and is guided by the national sectorial strategies and policies as well as the international laws and standards set by the UN's Security Council and General Assembly resolutions that focus on Palestinian rights of freedom, development, and decent life on their land that is recognized as 'Occupied Territories'. (UAWC n.d.)

Sixth is the Union of Palestinian Women's Committees (UPWC), which since 1980 has fought for a democratic Palestinian civil society, equality for men and women, and social justice. UPWC sees itself as

> an integral part of the Palestinian national movement, which is struggling to get rid of the Israeli occupation. Together with all Arab and global progressive

movements, it fights against the aggressiveness of globalization and against all forms of discrimination and injustice to which any social group in the world, specifically women, is exposed. (UPWC n.d.)

All these groups are defending Palestinian human rights, giving legal support to political prisoners and dedicating themselves to building a community for those suffering most from occupation in economic and social respects. These groups defend the rights and lives of Palestinian children, look for new ways of achieving food security for Palestinians given the consequences of the illegitimate Israeli land grab discussed above, and strengthen the rights of Palestinian women and thus of Palestinian civil society in general. All these groups have succeeded in lengthy struggles to close their communities and develop a political identity, enabling them to act in solidarity. Thus, they face fierce and violent strategies of extermination trying to silence and erase them. While smear campaigns have long been part of the settler-colonial regime's strategies against civil society organizations, discrediting and defaming them as 'terrorist' groups is of course also aimed at putting pressure on international donors to give up funding them (Cook 2021).

Moreover, Israel also directly targets international civil society groups for supporting Palestinians in their fight for human rights and their struggle for chances of survival, thus preventing important coalitions and processes of organizing. Two cases are instructive regarding this strategy. First, in 2016, Mohammad el Halabi, 'the former head of the US-based charity World Vision's Gaza office, was arrested . . . after being accused by Israel's Shin Bet security service of transferring tens of millions of dollars to Hamas.' However, 'his employer, independent auditors and the Australian government, a major World Vision donor, found no evidence of wrongdoing or diversion of funds' (MacKernan 2022). After six years of being imprisoned and a lengthy trial during this period that was widely held in secrecy, on 30 August 2022, 'disregarding UN concerns over a lack of evidence . . . the district court in the southern city of Beersheba said Mohammad el Halabi . . . would have to serve six years in prison taking into account the deduction of the amount he was held during the trial' (Lynfield 2022). Second, in an assault on human rights and an attempt to silence one of the most important and internationally respected human rights organizations, on 29 November 2019 Israel expelled Human Rights Watch's Israel and Palestine director Omar Shakir from the country (HRW 2019b; OHCHR 2019; Holmes 2019; see also Kershner 2019).

3. *Erasing Palestinian Culture, Memory, and History*
A third critical strategy of extermination aims at erasing the memory of Indigenous Palestinian history and culture, since Zionist settlers—just like any

other settler-colonialists—desperately want to be seen and recognized not as a settler-colonial regime but as the *real* Indigenous (Veracini 2011, 3). However, referring to the most recent archaeological evidence, Nur Masalha (2018) has presented scientific proof that Palestinian life and culture historically preceded the stories in the Old Testament that Zionism relies on to make claims to the land. Thus, the Zionist claim requires that not only the Palestinian people have to be extinguished, but so must the history, culture, and (collective) memory of the real Indigenous people at any cost:

> The founding myths of Israel have dictated the conceptual removal of Palestinians before, during and after their physical removal in 1948.... The de-Arabisation of Palestine, the erasure of Palestinian history and the elimination of the Palestinians' collective memory by the Israeli state are no less violent than the ethnic cleansing of the Palestinians in 1948 and the destruction of historic Palestine: this elimination is central to the construction of a hegemonic collective Israeli-Zionist-Jewish identity in the State of Israel. (Masalha 2012, 89)

Starting with Israel's 1948 war and the Nakba, rewriting history has been a common strategy just like in other settler-colonial regimes, suppressing the Indigenous peoples' history and concealing the eliminators' strategies of elimination, genocidal atrocities, and ethnic cleansing. This is well known for all settler societies, and just as much with regard to the Israeli regime. A

> 2019 investigation by the Israeli NGO Akevot and Haaretz newspaper has uncovered official suppression of crucial documents about the Nakba in Israeli archives. The *Journal of Palestine Studies* is publishing print excerpts and a full online version of the buried 'migration report', which details Israel's depopulation of Palestinian villages in the first six months of the 1948 war, a document that clearly undermines official Israeli state narratives about the course of events. (Anziska 2019)[71]

Rewriting history by concealing the historical truth about Israel's settler-colonial regime, the ethnic cleansing of Palestine, the killings and massacres, and the making of millions of Palestinian refugees also lies at the heart of the settler-colonial regime's strategies of erasing the truth about the Jewish occupation of Palestine.

---

[71] Of course, as has been shown by testimonies in Lyons's 2021 *Dateline Jerusalem: Journalism's Toughest Assignment*, all these politics of erasure could not be concealed without the effective lobbying of 'pro-Israel lobby groups in the media's coverage of Israel and Palestine' (Abdel Fattah 2021).

In 2022, Israeli authorities 'rescinded the permanent licenses previously granted to six Palestinian schools in occupied east Jerusalem, claiming that their textbooks "incite against the State of Israel and the Israeli army"' (Jundi 2022). In an interview, the director of the Jerusalem affairs unit at the Palestinian Ministry of Education, Dima al-Samman, explained that 'the danger of the Israeli or "distorted Palestinian" curriculum lies in its falsification of history... It attempts to eliminate the national awareness of the children of Jerusalem and create a sense of inferiority within them' (Jundi 2022).

A closer look at censored content in the curriculum reveals the attack on historical truth and efforts to erase memories of sheer violence, ethnic cleansing, genocide, and even national symbols from Palestinian collective memory:

> The censored content... includes the logo of the Palestinian Authority, the Palestinian flag, lessons that discuss the Palestinian struggle against occupation, adherence to the land, the right of return and prisoners, settlements, the immigration of settlers to Palestine, military checkpoints, the intifada, displaced villages, and considering Zionism a racist political movement. (Jundi 2022)

The Israeli *politics of erasure* is also directed against Palestinian symbols, as Farrah Najjar (2022) has shown in her report on Israeli soldiers trying to violently tear down Palestinian flags and remove one from Palestinian-American journalist Shireen Abu Akleh's coffin (Abdellatif 2022; Vohra 2022; Al Jazeera 2022). Al-Haq and Forensic Architecture (2022) proved that Abu Akleh had been assassinated by an Israeli sniper while reporting on an IDF raid of the Palestinian refugee camp in Jenin. For the occupation regime, 'even a flag is seen as a threat' (Najjar 2022), as it is the symbol of Palestinian life in Jerusalem that should be erased: 'The very existence of the Palestinian flag threatens Israeli identity', said Marwa Fatafta, a policy member of the think-tank Al Shabaka. 'When a regime is hell bent on your erasure, even a flag is seen as a threat,' Fatafta told *Al Jazeera*. The Israeli occupation is 'adamant in its mission to ethnically erase Palestinians from Jerusalem'. 'They steal and demolish homes, they attack worshippers, they crack down on public spaces, they exile Jerusalemites from their city', she said. 'For Palestinians to raise a flag in Jerusalem, despite this brutal violence, is to remind them of what they dread the most: We are still here', she said (Najjar 2022).[72]

What's more, not only is the Palestinian flag banned as a cultural symbol, but the politics of erasure extends to all cultural testimonies of the 4,000 years of Palestinian history:

---

[72] The Israeli regime is also planning to ban the Palestinian flag from Palestinian university campuses, declaring it the flag of an enemy and threatening students with six-month suspensions should they exhibit the flag; see Middle East Eye 2022.

Israeli authorities carried out excavations in the historic Al-Bahr Mosque in the city of Tiberias, on the western shores of the Sea of Galilee. In its place, Israel aims to establish a museum, a practice it has used many times in the past in order to erase historic symbols of Palestinian existence. Israel's disregard for the historical rights of Palestinians is deeply rooted in Zionist ideology. Indeed, from the very start, Zionist ideologues promoted the idea that Palestine was a place bereft of culture or heritage—an arid desert, waiting for Zionist pioneers to make it 'bloom'. (Baroud 2019)[73]

While erasing Palestinian lives, history, culture, and memory lies at the heart of Israeli eliminatory strategies against Palestinians, the settler-colonial regime's politics of cultural erasure in all of Palestine completely contradicts

> the framework of the Hague Regulations (1907), the Fourth Geneva Convention (1949), international human rights law, customary international law and relevant treaties to which it is bound. However, during this time [since 1967], Israel has conducted a series of unlawful acts that run counter to internationally recognized human rights and humanitarian norms in order to entrench its colonial domination, employing a policy of cultural erasure (Tamimi 2019), the military targeting of cultural property (WAFA 2021), and the appropriation of cultural heritage (Al-Haq 2021). Such actions have included removing artefacts of scientific, historical and archaeological interest (Shaveh and Din 2017), carrying out illegal archaeological excavations whose outcomes directly serve Israel's colonial narrative, and strategically targeting and destroying any cultural sites that are not directly exploitable to confirm this narrative. (Al-Haq 2022b; references inserted)

Masalha (2015) has further analysed the renaming of Palestinian places and villages with Israeli towns built on their ruins giving them Hebrew names. On signs announcing the names of towns and regions, we sometimes find the Arabic translation of the Hebrew names, but not the original Arabic names. The politics of erasure in the field of art and culture start with the destruction and burning of books during the Nakba, and in '1982, during its occupation of Lebanon, Israeli invasion troops would storm the homes, offices, and libraries of Palestinians and walk away with thousands of books, films, and other records documenting Palestinian history' (Sheety 2015). The cultural

---

[73] See also Al-Haq's 2022 highly interesting report on Israel's systematic destruction of Gaza's cultural heritage: *Cultural Apartheid Israel's Erasure of Palestinian Heritage in Gaza* (Al-Haq 2022b). Further, see UNESCO's Executive Board position paper on Israel's erasure of Palestinian cultural heritage; UNESCO 2016.

erasure further includes the sealing of huge numbers of Palestinian books in official archives, the erasure of Palestine from official maps, the appropriation and redefinition of classical Palestinian embroidery designs and clothing as traditions from the 'Holy Land', and renaming the classical Palestinian cuisine as *Mediterranean*.[74] All these practices are part of the politics of cultural eradication that follow the logics of elimination of the Zionist settler-colonial regime:

> Stealing and appropriating the culture and history of indigenous peoples is a typical characteristic of all modern colonial-settler states, but usually accomplished once the indigenous people in question has been eliminated, dispossessed, or otherwise seemingly defeated therefore making it safe to do so. The colonial-settler state of 'Israel', established on the ruins of Palestine and through the expulsion of the majority of its indigenous population in 1948 and after, is no different. The Israeli theft of all things Palestinian, however, ... is rather a conscious political policy of the state that seeks to erase Palestine from historical memory, particularly within Western discourse. Indeed, the continuing ethnic cleansing of Palestinians from their historic homeland goes hand in hand with the theft of Palestinian land, homes, history, and culture. It is an essential part of the larger, long-term Zionist project of eradicating the Palestinian nation altogether, literally writing it out of history while simultaneously assuming its place. (Sheety 2015)[75]

Following Neuwirth's analysis (Neuwirth 1969, 155–157), the perspective of closure theory contributes to understanding the highly problematic situation faced by the Palestinian community in terms of violent and highly destructive interventions from the eliminating settler-colonial regime. Administrative procedures, targeted killings, imprisonment of leaders of civil society organizations and intellectuals, defamation of human rights organizations as terrorist groups, and the destruction of Palestinian cultural heritage—all these strategies are elements of an encompassing system of control that the settler-colonial regime imposes directly on Palestinian people to prevent processes of organizing and thus Palestinians' ability to *act in solidarity*.

---

[74] It suffices to refer to the huge success of Ottolenghi's cookbooks that proceed in precisely this way by redefining cuisine from Palestinian to Mediterranean, which makes them part of a cultural strategy of expropriation of Palestinian tradition.

[75] This is, of course, also becoming apparent in the settler-colonial regime's demolishing of Palestinian buildings, houses, and homes, destroying spaces and places, realizing an *architecture of erasure*; see Makdisi 2010; Segal, Tartakover, and Weizman 2003; Weizman 2007; see also Barclay 2020.

22.3.5 Outcomes, Stabilization, and Legitimation

Looking at Israel's strategies of annihilation from the perspective of closure theory exposes them as inconceivably violent and variable strategies against the Palestinian people. It reveals the fundamental transformation of social relations of elimination in socio-economic, politico-legal, socio-structural, and socio-cultural terms. With regard to the dimensions of life chances / chances of survival, access to resources, rights, and networks/institutions is minimized to a degree that has reduced Palestinians' life chances to mere chances of survival. While access to resources, rights, and networks/institutions is fundamentally shifted in favour of the eliminators, their increasing options for control over those they threaten with elimination degrade the latter's dignity, respect, and self-esteem. These forms of control prevent Palestinian communities from organizing and destroy their existing organizations, showing clearly that the dehumanization of the Indigenous is a core aspect of the settler-colonial regime's *politics of erasure*.

Making plausible the explanatory logic of closure analysis has shown how strategies of letting die, disenfranchising, and segregation trigger the mechanism *denial of access*, which operates in various ways to block the Indigenous from making use of vital resources, rights, and integrating into settler society. As these dehumanizing measures already heavily impinge upon Palestinians' dignity and self-esteem, controlling them because of trying to realize eliminatory phantasies of religious purity is critical for the settler-colonial regime in its pursuit of strategies to exterminate Palestinians as a people.[76]

All strategies of annihilation discussed above in detail—denying access to land, food, and water; dividing the Palestinian population, creating different legal statuses that accord different, if any, rights, while all of them are subordinate to Jewish citizens; denying access to social institutions, exposing Palestinians knowingly to illnesses, reducing their life-expectancy, poisoning them, or cynically refusing them assistance even during the Covid-19 pandemic; and finally politicide, memoricide, spaciocide, and the destruction of cultural heritage—are permanently creating new and racially radicalized social orders

---

[76] Such effects have been famously described by Memmi: 'The most serious blow suffered by the colonized is being removed from history and from the community. Colonization usurps any free role in either war or peace, every decision contributing to his destiny and that of the world, and all cultural and social responsibility.... The colonized ... feels neither responsible nor guilty nor skeptical, for he is out of the game. He is in no way a subject of history any more. Of course, he carries its burden, often more cruelly than others, but always as an object. He has forgotten how to participate actively in history and no longer even asks to do so. No matter how briefly colonization may have lasted, all memory of freedom seems distant; he forgets what it costs or else he no longer dares to pay the price for it' (Memmi 1991 [1965], 91, 92).

that are institutionalized, only to be reorganized, reinforced, and exacerbated for Palestinians in short periods of time.

While the institutionalization and thus stabilization of these conditions takes place through the establishment of a 'Dual State' and a judicial system that positively sanctions all strategies of annihilation by whitewashing them, granting impunity to perpetrators, and legitimizing the *state and space of exception* into which Palestinians are forced, their legitimation in the settler-colonial regime rests upon reciprocal recognition and horizontal legitimacy. This does not include the consent of Palestinians, which makes Israeli domination illegitimate per se, but rather actors and settlers in the Zionist regime, which all offer each other immediate advantages of annihilating the Palestinian people, taking their space, their land, and replacing them with White Jewish settlers. Of course, the full support from Western states—United States, Canada, Australia, United Kingdom, and the European Union and European states—for all that and even for Israel's genocide against the Palestinians plays a critical role in legitimizing the settler-colonial regime's eliminatory strategies.

These processes of conferring legitimacy bring us back to a critical ideological source of the Zionist settler-colonial project. As we have seen, claiming the right to a 'promised land' as Herzl did by referring to the Old Testament to justify the occupation of Palestine, plays a critical role. The narrative goes against all historical evidence of Palestine having always been a multicultural land, not a land for Jewish dreams of religious purity. Yet the Old Testament also provides a justification for Israel's genocidal strategies against the Palestinians:

> Avenge the children of Israel of the Medianites: afterward shalt thou be gathered unto thy people. And Moses spoke unto the people saying, Arm ye men from among you for the war, that they may go against Median, to execute the LORD's vengeance on Median.... And they warred against Median, as the LORD commanded Moses, and they slew every male.... And the children of Israel took captive the women of Median and their little ones; and all their cattle, and all their flocks, and all their goods, they took for a prey. And all their cities in the places wherein they dwelt, and all their encampments, they burnt with fire. And they took the spoil, and all the prey, both of man and beast.... And Moses said unto them, Have you saved all the women alive? Behold, these caused the children of Israel, through the counsel of Balaam, to commit trespass against the LORD in the matters of Peor, and so the plague was among the congregation of the Lord. Now therefore, kill every male among the little ones, and kill every woman that hath known man by lying with him. But all the women children that have not known man by lying with him, keep alive for ourselves. (Numbers 31: 9–10; quoted in Mamdani 2001, 9)

The Old Testament offers nothing less than a script for the genocidal realization of the eliminatory logic of settler colonialism. Of course, 'Israeli authorities are deliberately concealing historical documents to undermine evidence of the state's dark and violent origins' (Iraqi 2019) and the beginnings of the ongoing ethnic cleansing and genocidal strategies, thereby perpetuating the atrocities of occupation (IMEMC 2019). Yet, there is, as the world has seen every day since October 7, really no way to conceal the Zionist regime's genocidal character, since 'racist tendencies latent in Israeli society and its institutions are erupting, with bloody consequences. Looking at the ground, it is hard to imagine a future other than further dispossession, settlements, and violent repression' (Weizman 2018, 134).

A a second aspect of horizontal legitimacy becomes clear and gains importance, as Israel, whatever eliminatory or genocidal strategies it deploys against Palestinians, as a state is supported and legitimized by most states of the West that defend the White settler-colonial project Herzl promised them. Guaranteed impunity, along with rejecting as anti-Semitic human rights reports declaring Israel to be an apartheid system, denouncing official investigations of Israel's war crimes as illegitimate and unjustified, and many more strategies that could be added, make it obvious that Europe and the United States support the illegitimate settler-colonial Dual State that perpetuates their own histories and legacies as settler-colonial states.

23
The Explanatory Logic of Social Closure

Based on a new conceptualization of social closure and a typology that cross-tabulates forms of closure and the associated forms of strategies with dimensions of life chances / chances of survival, I identified twelve distinct strategies of closure. Analysing how these strategies of the powerful function in social relations of exclusion, exploitation, and elimination in ongoing closure struggles, and what consequences they have for the less powerful, laid the groundwork to suggest the explanatory logic of social closure.

Emirbayer's observation that social life is to be understood from a relational perspective as dynamic, continuous, and processual has informed my understanding of social life as struggle in general, as ongoing closure struggles in particular. From this perspective, the unfolding of the explanatory logic of such struggles expresses the primacy of *contextuality* and *processes* of a relational approach (Emirbayer 1997, 290). Against the backdrop of specific contexts—neoliberal austerity policies, capitalist exploitation/slavery in GLVCs, and Israeli settler-colonial politics of erasure—the processuality of a relational explanation becomes clear through the identification of two critical relational social mechanisms.

Explaining closure, as I have suggested, is thus based on the operation of the mechanisms *denial of access* and *intervention into community closure*. They are relational in the sense that they are neither based on the logic of a system nor on 'changes in individual or collective perceptions' (Tilly 2003b, 20) that lead to closure, but denote processes that result from communications, interactions, or transactions among social actors that then deploy strategies to exacerbate or radicalize social relations of exclusion, exploitation, or elimination.

In summarizing the logic of explanation, two aspects should be highlighted. First we need to consider the organization of collective actors on the side of the excluders, exploiters, and the eliminators. This step precedes what we actually have to explain, but it is critical because without considering their organization we cannot explain why the less powerful sides in the social relations of closure eventually might not be able to organize. The second step involves explanations of strategies of social closure proper—the ways the mechanisms *denial of access* and *intervention into community closure* actually work.

First, as in a relational perspective, closure strategies result from communications, interactions, and transactions of collective actors. I have referred to the plurality of these actors in the empirical analyses. *Neoliberal strategies of exclusion* result from the way neoliberal elites of the financial system, central banks, IMF, World Bank, hedge funds, rating agencies, and states interact. The way the elements of the Troika—European Central Bank, European Commission, and IMF—interacted after the financial collapse of 2008/2009, developing strategies of austerity to save the international financial system while exerting maximum pressure on ordinary people, is only one recent interesting example of how communication, interactions, and transactions result in specific strategies.

The situation is similar with global *capitalist strategies of exploitation/ slavery*. Since multinational corporations need capital, we find similar actors from the world of finance and politics, but above all powerful actors from all sectors where, for example, GLVCs produce through the exploitation of *valueless* life in the interest of huge profits. The way they interact creates ever-new strategies to reorganize the capitalist global division of labour, to increase the *price-cost squeeze*, and to exploit the almost infinite reservoir of labour power in a globalized capitalist world economy.

As far as the *eliminatory strategies of settler colonialism* are concerned, the main actors are states, the military, and organized paramilitary groups of settlers. These groups interact with other or former settler-colonial states, and their eliminatory strategies can be adopted or imitated. Unsurprisingly, the Zionist settler-colonial regime is supported by the United States, the United Kingdom, Canada, and Australia (as the classic *liberal* settler-colonial societies), but no less by the European Union and, as one of its member states, Germany, with its own history of brutal settler-colonial regimes, among others in today's Namibia but also during the Nazi regime with the settlement of the Ostland (Zimmerer 2004) and the killing of up to 27 million human beings in a settler-colonial war (Mackert and Pappe 2024a). These same ideas and ideologies, and further the same geopolitical interests and deep-rooted prejudices against non-White people, especially a pronounced anti-Arabism against people from the Middle East, led to a White settler-colonial outpost in the Middle East at the end of the nineteenth century led by European Jews against Arab *barbarism*, as Herzl (1946 [1896]) put it.

The organization of an interest, as practised by all these collective actors, gives them a decisive advantage when it comes to closure struggles, because they act in them from a position of strength, which is based on asymmetrical power relationships that are constitutive of closure relations and form the basis for the powerful to deploy strategies of closure.

Second, to explain how these strategies work, I have analysed how the mechanisms *denial of access* and *intervention into community closure* operate. Because these social mechanisms have identical effects—denial of access to resources, for example, happens in relations of exclusion, exploitation, and elimination alike—they show variability, which is a crucial aspect of their functioning. This variability becomes apparent in different social relations, but also with regard to the different dimensions of life chances / chances of survival. Explaining social closure is not about uniformity as in Weber or the theory of social closure, which both reduced all processes of closure to exclusion and monopolization in an economic perspective; instead, it is about variability. As with resources, this is the case with the denial of access to rights and to networks/institutions. This explanatory logic of the operation of the denial-of-access mechanism and the variability of effects it generates was made plausible empirically in the analysis.

Having argued earlier that it is only by considering processes of closing the boundaries of a community, developing a shared political identity, and organizing an interest as the requisite conditions for being able to act as a collective actor, the second mechanism could be introduced, which I call *intervention into community closure* (a concept that owes much to a critical idea from Neuwirth's seminal but unfortunately neglected early contribution to closure theory). It is crucial not only to consider how groups or classes are denied access to resources, rights, and networks/institutions but also to explain why certain groups, classes, or others are unable to close their communities and develop a political identity that enables them to act in solidarity and resist being excluded, exploited/enslaved, or eliminated. The strategies of powerful collective actors to prevent the less-powerful sides from organizing—to even destroy their being organized or their eventually existing formal organizations—is a central aspect of what happens in social closure struggles and must be part of an explanation of how social relations of the excluders and the excluded, the exploiters and the exploited, and the eliminators and those who are threatened with elimination are organized and reorganized in social closure struggles. Only by including these processes in an explanation of processes of closure does such an analysis become a comprehensive one.

All the closure strategies I have systematized and discussed in detail work independently of each other and thus trigger specific closure effects. However, these strategies can interact and even reinforce each other in social reality. While this is obvious within one form of closure, it is also possible between the three forms, as transitions can be, and often are, fluid. As I showed, the exclusionary strategies of the European Union against migrants often turn into eliminatory ones. The same is true for hyper-exploitation. But the reverse is also true: elimination in settler-colonial societies can and does involve hyper-exploitation and severe exclusionary processes against the Indigenous. In this respect, analyses of complex social problems should start from the form of closure that is dominant in such a context, as it is based on the dominant form of power in the social relation in question. However, which forms of closure strategies are dominant in a particular temporal/spatial context is then the subject of empirical analysis. In all these cases, the two social mechanisms interact and produce to the reorganization of established social relations at a given point in time.

What about the excluded, the exploited, and those threatened with elimination? While Weber argued that groups facing social closure in certain circumstances might respond to their exclusion, for Parkin the response seemed a necessity and solidarity among the excluded simply inevitable. Finally, Murphy differentiated the strategies of the excluded as either inclusionary or revolutionary.

All this is neither convincing nor sufficient. Unsurprisingly, however, we see here the consequences of the fact that they all lack a concept of collective action and *how acting in solidarity* is possible. With introducing the second mechanism, I have provided the point of reference, since before we can analyse possible strategies of those who face strategies of marginalization, extraction, and annihilation, we need to know to what extent the control of powerful groups over them prevents them from closing their communities and from developing a common political idea, thus leaving them in a *subordinate position* (Neuwirth 1969).

In some of the empirical fields in which I have made the explanatory logic of the approach presented plausible, I have referred to actors or strategies of the less powerful in everyday closure struggles, who might to certain degrees be able to react. The fact that I have not done so systematically does not mean that the options and possibilities for action of the weaker sides are not of interest. On the contrary, it is of utmost interest to learn more about what enables the less powerful to fight back and what prevents them from doing so and how they can develop their own strategies to defend their life chances / chances of survival—or not. However, to develop an approach to what might be called *theorizing counterstrategies* (Hartmann 2011) goes beyond the aim of this book, which has set itself the task of developing a new approach to social closure, to re-conceptualize it in order to systematize the closure strategies of the powerful in closure relations and unfold the explanatory logic of social closure, thereby hopefully contributing to revitalizing sociological thinking on social closure.

Conclusion

Social Closure and the Global Struggle for Life Chances / Chances of Survival

In the twenty-first century, the global dynamics of neoliberalism, capitalism, and settler colonialism have finally created a world of radically intensified struggles for life chances / chances of survival that cannot be brought to a halt. I have presented a new approach to closure theory with the intention of developing a sociological tool that enables us to analyse and explain ongoing struggles for life chances / chances of survival not only within one society, as closure theory has been doing for a long time, but also to do so in a global perspective and to prepare sociological reasoning and analysis for already emerging new and radical closure struggles in the world. I have pointed to several specific problems, and some of these will become general and universal, such as struggles for access to basic resources like water and land, which have long since become tradable commodities to speculate with on financial markets and are therefore already being withdrawn and denied to millions of people; access to rights such as citizenship, which are increasingly withdrawn from citizens and blocked for migrants; and human rights, which have long since been selectively applied and are pawns of ideological, economic, political, and geopolitical power relations. Access to institutions or networks that enable integration into societies is increasingly limited for those who seem to have no economic value. Finally, among other strategies, the West's destructive discourses on *security*, *self-defence*, and *terrorism* increasingly serve to defame any group or organization that resists the destruction of their life chances / chances of survival in a *Society of Enmity* (Mbembe 2016), while giving a free hand to the powerful for a supposedly legitimate destruction of such groups and organizations.

Sociological theories, analyses, diagnoses of the time, and analytical tools are still too focused on the West, so-called Western modernity, *advanced* societies, modern and allegedly *pluralist* societies, and so forth. Sociology is still fraught with the conviction of a *peculiarity of the Occident*, as Max Weber put it, which simply conceals and hides the fact that the Occident is nothing without the Orient and cannot even define itself without it. However, as Edward Said (1978) has taught us, this powerful discourse of *Orientalism* that is difficult to attack and to challenge has allowed the West to develop fantasies about its own alleged grandeur and superiority over the East. Looking at historical dynamics from a Eurocentric or Westernized standpoint will get us nowhere. I agree with Go's (2016) argument that only a sociology that takes a relational approach will enable it to abandon its narrow adherence to reproducing ideologies and fantasies about the West and its noble norms and values. Only when sociology abandons its dearly held fascination with the Western world and systematically begins to look at the relations between the West and the Rest and takes into account that the Global North is what it is today only because of its centuries-long exclusionary, exploitative, and eliminatory relations with the Global South, will it be relevant as a critical science in the future.

This book has proposed a fundamentally new approach to an underappreciated and misconceived basic notion and sociological concept that was forgotten in the late 1980s. This decline resulted in part through the concept's own limitations, in part because it could not envisage the dynamics and the global reach of neoliberalism and capitalism, and in part because it was in no way aware of the significance of the settler-colonial roots of the world. At that time, it was therefore not possible for closure theorists to understand and consider the dynamics that these three major global processes created. Presenting a new approach to social closure and reframing the idea of closure from the ground up and transforming it into a sociological tool that can be used to analyse today's global struggles for life chances / chances of survival was one of the main goals of newly theorizing social closure. If the assessment is correct that the struggle for life chances / chances of survival has not only become a global struggle today but also that we are confronted with the old problem of the West subjugating the Rest—where powerful actors in the Global North exclude people throughout the Global South, exploit and enslave them, and often threaten Indigenous people with elimination—we need more sociological tools that take into account the power asymmetries underlying these social relations. This is also true because the most brutal forms of exclusion, exploitation, and threats to eliminate human beings that were tried in the Global South are returning to the core of capitalism—the advanced West or the Global North. As has been shown, extremely radical forms of exclusion and exploitation have been re-imported into the core countries of neoliberal capitalism, always on the verge of sliding into the elimination of *valueless* life.

Social closure, as I have argued, is one of the most fundamental processes of social life, if not the most fundamental. If this is the case, it needs to be conceptualized and theorized in a way that makes it applicable beyond the boundaries of societies and thus allows us to analyse how the strategies of marginalization, extraction, and annihilation developed by powerful collective Western actors minimize or destroy the life chances / chances of survival of billions of people. These life chances / chances of survival and their modifications, limitations, or destructions, which I have analysed from their objective side by identifying processes, dynamics, and mechanisms, also have their subjective counterpart, namely the experience of those who suffer from being excluded, exploited, or threatened with elimination.

Housing evictions, as I have shown, are a brutal strategy to keep the financial system alive and to drive the transformation of housing into an object of speculation—at the expense of millions of victims all over the world. Their fate reveals not only the personal consequences of the shifting relations between rich and poor but, more importantly, the brutal experience of being marginalized and having their life chances destroyed. This was made explicit by a Spanish victim, Carmen Arnedo, who stated that

> people, who don't know what an eviction is, can't put themselves in our shoes. Thinking that the police are going to come. You feel really frightened. Frightened and afraid. The banks are on the side of the rich. Nobody knows what we're going through, the people whose houses are taken. (Carmen Arnedo in Redfish, 2021)

Millions of women, children, and men are exploited and subjected to conditions akin to a *new slavery* at the end of global value chains created, organized, and controlled by Western multinational corporations, backed by their states or the European Union. What is happening here is a systematic destruction of life chances within the global capitalist division of labour. But even if we turn to the Global North and look at the working conditions in a global value chain of the European Union agricultural industry, we find highly exploitative working conditions with unimaginable suffering of Eastern European workers, seasonal workers, refugees, or rejected asylum seekers, such as a man from Zambia, who had lived a long time in Germany, spoke German, but was rejected there and ended up in Calabria, Italy. He said:

> It's brutal. Bad. Work is hard and you are not paid normally.... Everybody lives just like that, like animals. Europeans see all that, but nobody is doing anything.... There is no future in Italy. Nobody is going to school. You see that. Nobody is making a formation. Nobody is getting good work.... That really makes me desperate. Every human being is a human being, regardless of the colour of your skin. This is what I learned from my parents. (Bayerischer Rundfunk, Fernsehen 2019; my own translation)[1]

---

[1] Interestingly, the video was removed from YouTube. It could for a while be viewed on ARD Mediathek 2019 under a different title, but without the interview with the man from Zambia at the very end of the film whom I quoted. Now, in a minor quality it has been uploaded again with the interview.

Finally, to this day, neither for the descendants of the Indigenous peoples of the Americas, Australia, New Zealand, Algeria, Namibia, and many other countries, nor for the Palestinians—the Indigenous people of Palestine who have suffered from eliminatory politics for more than a hundred years—continue to endure the consequences of eliminatory settler-colonial politics. The theft of their land by White settlers from Europe, having been completed, remains an ongoing issue. The settler-colonial logic of elimination—expressed in ethnic cleansing, massacres, daily atrocities, and a genocidal war that Israel has unleashed against the Palestinian civil population—is present in the daily lives and memories of Indigenous people and is a source of permanent traumatization and re-traumatization, often going back centuries. In Palestine, in the aftermath of the 1948 Nakba (the destruction of hundreds of villages and the ethnic cleansing of Palestine by White European Zionists), thousands of Indigenous Palestinians were killed in atrocities, massacres, or targeted killings, and millions were expelled from their homeland. Survivors were left with memories of their land, history, homes, and lives, while their life chances were destroyed, and their chances of survival reduced to a minimum (Karmi 2015). Nazerah Issa, a survivor of the Nakba and the ethnic cleansing, who was expelled with her family from her native village Bir'im, close to the Lebanese border, addressed this explicitly:

> When I was a little girl during the occupation, I remember someone from the army came. 15 days later they told us we were too close to the border and had to leave the village.... When I think back it hurts.... You think I'm not sad about not being in my village? Everything would be different if we were still there. I live like a refugee here. There are too many dead for us to visit them all. They [the IDF] told us to go anywhere we want, it's just for fifteen days, then we could come back. But then they said: 'We'll take you back tomorrow, the day after, etc.' That's how 52 years went by [in 2002].... The planes were bombing us, the village. So, we'd have no hope of returning.... They took the bricks of the village and built their kibbutz. They built Moshav Dorev on the land of Bir'im ... on *our* land. (Nazerah Issa in *Ashes*, 2002)

References

Aalbers, Manuel B. 2008. 'The Financialization of Home and the Mortgage Market Crisis'. *Competition & Change* 12 (2): 148–166.
Aalbers, Manuel B. 2017. 'The Variegated Financialization of Housing'. *International Journal of Urban and Regional Research* 41 (4): 542–554.
Abbott, Andrew. 1995. 'Things of Boundaries'. *Social Research* 62 (4): 857–882.
Abbott, Andrew. 2016. *Processual Sociology*. Chicago: The University of Chicago Press.
Abbott, Andrew. 2020. *Zeit zählt. Grundzüge einer prozessualen Soziologie*. Hamburg: Hamburger Edition.
Abdel Fattah, Randa. 2021. 'Lobbied: The Palestinian Erasure'. *MEANJIN Quarterly*. https://meanjin.com.au/blog/lobbied-the-palestinian-erasure/.
Abdellatif, Latifeh. 2022. 'Shireen Abu Akleh: "Pallbearers Nearly Drop Coffin as Israeli Police Hit Mourners"'. *Middle East Eye*. May 13. https://www.middleeasteye.net/news/shireen-abu-akleh-pallbearers-nearly-drop-coffin-israeli-police-hit-mourners.
Abdulrahim, Raja, Patrick Kingsley, Christiaan Triebert, and Hiba Yazbek. 2022. 'The Killing of Shireen Abu Akleh: Tracing a Bullet to an Israeli Convoy'. *The New York Times*. June 20 (Update June 28). https://www.nytimes.com/2022/06/20/world/middleeast/palestian-journalist-killing-shireen.html.
Abellan Matamoros, Christina. 2019. 'Forced Labour Most Prevalent Form of Modern Slavery in Europe, Says Report'. https://www.euronews.com/2019/07/17/forced-labour-most-prevalent-form-of-modern-slavery-in-europe-says-report.
Abu-Eid, Abdulla. 2007. 'Water as a Human Right: The Palestinian Occupied Territories as an Example'. *International Journal of Water Resources Development* 23 (2): 285–301.
AbuKishk, Nada, Yassir Turki, Suha Saleh, Shatha Albaik, Majed Hababeh, Soheir el-Khatib, Nimer Kassim, Hasan Arab, Khawalah Abu-Diab, Wafaa Zeidan, and Akihiro Seita. 2020. 'Anaemia Prevalence in Children Newly Registered at UNRWA Schools: A Cross-Sectional Study'. *BMJ Open*. https://bmjopen.bmj.com/content/10/9/e034705.
Aburabia, Rawia. 2022. 'Settler-colonial Childhood: Viterbo's Problematizing Law, Rights and Childhood in Israel/Palestine'. *Critical Legal Thinking*. April 12. https://criticallegalthinking.com/2022/04/12/settler-colonial-childhood-viterbos-problematizing-law-rights-and-childhood-in-israel-palestine%EF%BF%BC/.
Abu Shawish, Abeer, and Catherine Weibel. 2017. 'Gaza Children Face Acute Water and Pollution Crisis. Water and Power Shortages Put Children's Health at Risk'. UNICEF. September 1. https://www.unicef.org/stories/gaza-children-face-acute-water-sanitation-crisis.
ACRI (Association for Civil Rights in Israel). 2014. 'One Rule, Two Legal Systems. Israel's Regime of Laws in the West Bank'. October. https://222e6473-52e0-40bd-a823-198568ef361d.usrfiles.com/ugd/222e64_c33776e6a5844002b84de13853a463af.pdf.
ACRI (Association for Civil Rights in Israel). 2018. 'Water Provision and Drilling in the West Bank 2010-2016'. June 5. https://law.acri.org.il/en/2018/06/05/water-provision-and-drillings-in-the-west-bank-2010-2016/.
ACRI (Association for Civil Rights in Israel). 2022. 'One Rule, Two Legal Systems. Israel's Regime of Laws in the West Bank'. June 16. https://www.english.acri.org.il/post/__401.
Adalah (The Legal Center for Arab Minority Rights in Israel). 2017a. 'Discriminatory Laws in Israel'. https://www.adalah.org/en/law/index?page=4.
Adalah (The Legal Center for Arab Minority Rights in Israel). 2017b. 'First Time Ever: Israeli Court Rules to Strip Citizenship from Palestinian Citizen of Israel'. August 6. https://www.adalah.org/en/content/view/9182.

Adalah (The Legal Center for Arab Minority Rights in Israel). 2018. 'The Basic Law: Israel—The Nation-state of the Jewish People'. November 27. https://www.adalah.org/uploads/uploads/Final_2_pager_on_the_JNSL_27.11.2018%20.pdf.

Adalah (The Legal Center for Arab Minority Rights in Israel). 2020. 'Israel's Jewish Nation-State Law'. December 20. https://www.adalah.org/en/content/view/9569.

Adalah (The Legal Center for Arab Minority Rights in Israel). 2022. 'Israeli Supreme Court Allows Government to Strip Citizenship for "Breach of Loyalty"'. September 14. https://www.adalah.org/en/content/view/10693.

Addameer (Prisoner Support and Human Rights Organisation). 2017. 'On Administrative Detention'. July 20. https://www.addameer.org/israeli_military_judicial_system/administrative_detention#:~:text=Administrative%20detention%20is%20a%20procedure,allowing%20them%20to%20stand%20trial.

Addameer (Prisoner Support and Human Rights Organisation). (n.d.). 'Our Work'. https://www.addameer.org/.

Agamben, Giorgio. 1998 [1995]. *Homo Sacer. Sovereign Power and Bare Life.* Stanford, CA: Stanford University Press.

Aguilar, Gaby Oré. 2018. 'Overturning Austerity: Spain Reestablishes Universal Access to Healthcare'. *Centre for Economic and Social Rights.* June 21. https://www.cesr.org/overturning-austerity-spain-reestablishes-universal-access-healthcare/.

Agyemang, Emma. 2019. 'HMRC Quadruples Spending on Private Debt Collectors'. *Financial Times.* April 29. https://www.ft.com/content/56e1e4f6-6825-11e9-9adc-98bf1d35a056.

Ahmed, Kaamil. 2020. 'EU Accused of Abandoning Migrants to the Sea with Shift to Drone Surveillance'. *The Guardian.* October 28. https://www.theguardian.com/global-development/2020/oct/28/eu-accused-of-abandoning-migrants-to-the-sea-with-shift-to-drone-surveillance.

Ahmed, Nasim. 2022. 'Remembering Israel's 2021 Onslaught on Gaza'. *Middle East Monitor.* May 6. https://www.middleeastmonitor.com/20220506-remembering-israels-2021-onslaught-on-gaza/.

Albelbeisi, Ali, Shariff Mohd, Chan Zalilah, Mun Yoke, Hejar Abdul-Rahman, and Yehia Abed. 2018. 'Growth Patterns of Palestinian Children from Birth to 24 Months'. *World Health Organization Eastern Mediterranean Health Journal* 24 (3). http://www.emro.who.int/emhj-volume-24-2018/volume-24-issue-3/growth-patterns-of-palestinian-children-from-birth-to-24-months.html.

Albiston, Catherine, and Tristin K. Green. 2018. 'Social Closure Discrimination'. *Berkeley Journal of Employment and Law* 39 (1): 1–35.

Alcañiz, Mercedes, and Rosa Monteiro. 2016. 'She-Austerity. Women's Precariousness and Labor Inequality in Southern Europe'. *Convergencia. Revista de Ciencias Sociales* 23 (72): 39–68.

Alexander, Jeffrey C., and Philipp Smith. 1993. 'The Discourse of American Civil Society. A New Proposal for Cultural Studies'. *Theory and Society* 22 (2): 151–207.

Alexandri, Georgia, and Michael Janoschka. 2018. 'Who Loses and Who Wins in a Housing Crisis? Lessons from Spain and Greece for a Nuanced Understanding of Dispossession'. *Housing Policy Debate* 28 (1): 117–134.

Al-Haq. 2011. 'Israel's Punitive House Demolition Policy: Collective Punishment in Violation of International Law'. July 19. https://www.alhaq.org/publications/8101.html.

Al-Haq. 2013. 'Water for One People Only: Discriminatory Access and "Water-Apartheid" in the OPT'. April 8. https://www.alhaq.org/publications/8073.html.

Al-Haq. 2019a. 'Factsheet: Israel's "Jewish Nation-State Law" and the Occupied Palestinian Territory'. January 23. https://www.alhaq.org/advocacy/6115.html.

Al-Haq. 2019b. 'Israeli High Court of Justice Upholds Israel's Policy of Withholding the Bodies of Palestinians Killed'. September 16. https://www.alhaq.org/advocacy/15175.html

Al-Haq. 2021. 'Special Focus on Sebastia for World Tourism Day: Palestinian Tourism Remains a Major Target of Israel's Colonial Strategy'. September 27. https://www.alhaq.org/cached_uploads/download/2021/09/27/world-tourism-day-casestudy-ag-1632765728.pdf.

Al-Haq. 2022a. 'Alert: Israeli Occupying Forces Raid, Damage and Close Offices of Al-Haq and Other Designated Organisations. International Community Must Intervene'. August 18. https://www.alhaq.org/advocacy/20442.html.

Al-Haq. 2022b. 'Cultural Apartheid, Israel's Erasure of Palestinian Heritage in Gaza'. February 22. https://www.alhaq.org/publications/19542.html.

Al-Haq. 2022c. 'Al-Haq Sends Urgent Appeal to UN Special Procedures on Israel's Extrajudicial Killing of Three Palestinian Men in Nablus'. March 13. https://www.alhaq.org/advocacy/19710.html.

Al-Haq, and Forensic Architecture. 2022. 'Shireen Abu Akleh: The Extrajudicial Killing of a Journalist'. https://forensic-architecture.org/investigation/shireen-abu-akleh-the-targeted-killing-of-a-journalist.

Al Jazeera. 2021. 'Israel Set Calorie Limit during Gaza Blockade'. October 18. https://www.aljazeera.com/news/2012/10/18/israel-set-calorie-limit-during-gaza-blockade.

Al Jazeera. 2022. 'No Israeli Police to be Punished for Attacking Abu Akleh Funeral'. June 16. https://www.aljazeera.com/news/2022/6/16/israeli-probe-into-abu-aklehs-funeral-finds-police-misconduct.

Al Jazeera. 2024. 'Gaza Toll could exceed 186,000, Lancet Study says'. July 8. https://www.aljazeera.com/news/2024/7/8/gaza-toll-could-exceed-186000-lancet-study-says.

Allain, Jean. 2017. 'Contemporary Slavery and its Definition in Law'. In *Contemporary Slavery: The Rhetoric of Global Human Rights Campaigns*, edited by Annie Bunting and Joel Quirk, pp. 37–66. Ithaca, NY, and London: Cornell University Press.

Alonso, Judit. 2018. 'Harassment and Rape: Migrant Women Abused in European Fields'. *Info Migrants*. August 9. https://www.infomigrants.net/fr/post/11169/harassment-and-rape-migrant-women-abused-in-european-fields.

Alonso, Luis Enrique, and Carlos J. Fernández. 2013. *Los Discursos del Presente. Un Análisis de los Imaginarios Sociales Contemporáneos*. Madrid: Siglo XXI.

Ambast, Sanhita. 2018. 'Paying a High Cost: EU's Role in Spain's Painful Health Cuts'. *EU Observer*. April 30. https://euobserver.com/opinion/141711.

Amnesty International. 2001. 'Israel and the Occupied Territories: State Assassination and Other Unlawful Killings'. https://www.amnesty.org/en/documents/mde15/005/2001/en/.

Amnesty International. 2009a. 'Israel/Occupied Palestinian Territories: Thirsting for Justice: Palestinian Access to Water Restricted. (Demand Dignity Campaign Digest)'. October 29. https://www.amnesty.org/en/documents/mde15/028/2009/en/.

Amnesty International. 2009b. 'Israel/Occupied Palestinian Territories: Demand Dignity: Troubled Waters—Palestinians Denied Fair Access to Water'. October 27. https://www.amnesty.org/en/documents/MDE15/027/2009/en/.

Amnesty International. 2017. 'The Occupation of Water'. November 29. https://www.amnesty.org/en/latest/campaigns/2017/11/the-occupation-of-water/.

Amnesty International. 2019. 'Chapter 3: Israeli Settlements and International Law'. https://www.amnesty.org/en/latest/campaigns/2019/01/chapter-3-israeli-settlements-and-international-law/.

Amnesty International. 2022a. 'Israel's Apartheid against Palestinians: Cruel System of Domination and Crime against Humanity'. February 1. https://www.amnesty.org/en/documents/mde15/5141/2022/en/.

Amnesty International. 2022b. 'Israel/OPT: Increase in Unlawful Killings and Other Crimes Highlights Urgent Need to End Israel's Apartheid against Palestinians'. May 11. https://www.amnesty.org/en/latest/news/2022/05/israel-opt-increase-in-unlawful-killings-and-other-crimes-highlights-urgent-need-to-end-israels-apartheid-against-palestinians/.

Anderson, Perry. 2017. 'Why the System Will Still Win'. *Le Monde diplomatique*, March. https://mondediplo.com/2017/03/02brexit.

Anner, Mark. 2011. 'The Impact of International Outsourcing on Unionization and Wages: Evidence from the Apparel Sector in Central America'. *Industrial and Labor Relations Review* 64 (2): 305–322.

Anner, Mark. 2017. 'Monitoring Workers' Rights: The Limits of Voluntary Social Compliance Initiatives in Labor Repressive Regimes'. *Global Policy* 8 (3): 56–65.

Anner, Mark. 2020. 'Squeezing Workers' Rights in Global Supply Chains: Purchasing Practices in the Bangladesh Garment Export Sector in Comparative Perspective'. *Review of International Political Economy* 27 (2): 320–347.

Anti-Slavery International. 2022a. 'What Is Modern Slavery?'. https://www.antislavery.org/slavery-today/modern-slavery/.

Anti-Slavery International. 2022b. 'Slavery in Supply Chains'. https://www.antislavery.org/slavery-today/slavery-in-global-supply-chains/.

Anziska, Seth. 2019. 'The Erasure of the Nakba in Israel's Archive'. *Journal of Palestine Studies* 49 (1): 64–76.

AP Migration. 2015. 'Labour Exploitation, Slave-Like Conditions Found on Farms Supplying Biggest Supermarkets'. May 4. https://apmigration.ilo.org/news/labour-exploitation-slave-like-conditions-found-on-farms-supplying-biggest-supermarkets.

Arab News. 2022. 'World Food Programme Launches Nutrition Campaign in Palestine'. February 4. https://www.arabnews.com/node/2018266/middle-east.

ARD Mediathek. 2019. 'BR *Fernsehen: Europas dreckige Ernte: Das Leid hinter dem Geschäft mit dem Obst und Gemüse*'. https://www.ardmediathek.de/video/dokthema/europas-dreckige-ernte-das-leid-hinter-dem-geschaeft-mit-dem-obst-und-gemuese/br-fernsehen/Y3JpZDovL2JyLmRlL3ZpZGVvL2E5OWRiM2JlLTZhNTUtNGUxOC05YWFkLTBiMjE2MTY2MTUzMQ.

Arendt, Hannah. 2017 [1951]. *The Origins of Totalitarianism*. London: Penguin.

Aron, Raymond. 1964. '*Max Weber und die Machtpolitik*'. *Zeitschrift für Politik*. Neue Folge 11 (2): 100–113.

Ashes. 2002. Documentary film by Rima Issa. *The Sam Spiegel Film & Television School*. Jerusalem.

Ashly, Jaclynn. 2017. 'Drowning in The Waste of Israeli Settlers'. *Al Jazeera*. September 18. https://www.aljazeera.com/features/2017/9/18/drowning-in-the-waste-of-israeli-settlers.

Assadi, Mohammed. 2008. 'Water Shortage Cripples Palestinian Farming'. *Reuters*. September 18. https://www.reuters.com/article/us-palestinians-water-idUSLA43722220080918.

Association of Ambas. 2019. 'Addressing the Root Causes of Modern Slavery'. February 5. https://www.associationofmbas.com/addressing-the-root-causes-of-modern-slavery/.

Azarova, Valentina. 2017. 'The Pathology of a Legal System: Israel's Military Justice System and International Law. (Special issue: The Israeli Military Justice System and International Law). *Questions of International Law*. Zoom-in 44: 5–20.

BADIL (Resource Center for Palestinian Residency and Refugee Rights). 2021. *The Ongoing Nakba Since 1917 (End of 2021): Israeli Colonial-Apartheid Regime*. https://www.badil.org/news-media-coverage/486.html.

Baker, Luke. 2016. 'Israeli Rights Group Accuses Military of Whitewashing Soldiers' Abuses'. *Reuters*. May 25. https://www.reuters.com/article/cnews-us-israel-palestinians-ngo-idCAKCN0YG1W3.

Bales, Kevin 2012 [1999]. *Disposable People. New Slavery in the Global Economy*. Berkeley, Los Angeles, and London: University of California Press.

Ball, Laurence, Daniel Leigh, and Prakash Loungani, 2011. 'Painful Medicine'. *International Monetary Fund*. https://www.imf.org/external/pubs/ft/fandd/2011/09/pdf/ball.pdf.

Ballas, Irit. 2020. 'Fracturing the "Exception": The Legal Sanctioning of Violent Interrogation Methods in Israel since 1987'. *Law & Social Inquiry* 45 (3): 818–838.

Balog, Andreas, and Eva Cyba. 1990. *Geschlecht als Ursache von Ungleichheiten. Frauendiskriminierung und soziale Schließung*. Wien: IHS.

Barbalet, Jack M. 1982. 'Social Closure in Class Analysis: A Critique of Parkin', *Sociology* 16 (4): 484–497.

Barclay, Ahmad. 2020. 'Mapping Palestine: Erasure and Unerasure. In *Sharpening the Haze*, edited by Giulia Carabelli, Miloš Jovanović, Annika Kirkbis, and Jeremy F. Walton, pp. 177–189. London: Ubiquity Press.

Barnes, Tom, Krishna Shekhar Lal Das, and Surendra Pratap. 2015. 'Labour Contractors and Global Production Networks: The Case of India's Auto Supply Chain'. *Journal of Development Studies* 51 (4): 355–369.

Baroud, Ramzy. 2019. 'Remapping of Palestine: Why Israel's Erasure of Palestinian Culture Will Not Succeed'. *MEMO.* March 1. https://www.middleeastmonitor.com/20190301-remapping-of-palestine-why-israels-erasure-of-palestinian-culture-will-not-succeed/.

Baroud, Ramzy. 2022. 'Gaza's Next Crisis Might be Worse Than Anything We Have Ever Seen'. *MEMO.* March 29. https://www.middleeastmonitor.com/20220329-gazas-next-crisis-might-be-worse-than-anything-we-have-ever-seen/.

Barrell, Ray, and E. Philip Davis. 2008. 'The Evolution of the Financial Crisis of 2007–8'. *National Institute Economic Review* 206 (1): 5–14.

Barrientos, Stephanie, Uma Kothari, and Nicola Phillips. 2013. 'Dynamics of Unfree Labour in the Contemporary Global Economy'. *The Journal of Development Studies* 49 (8): 1037–1041.

Barry, Ursula, and Pauline Conroy. 2013. 'Ireland in Crisis 2008-2012. Women, Austerity and Inequality'. *Research Repository UCD.* https://researchrepository.ucd.ie/handle/10197/4820.

Barth, Frederik. 1969. 'Introduction'. In *Ethnic Groups and Boundaries: The Social Organization of Cultural Differences*, edited by Frederik Barth, pp. 9–38. Boston: Little, Brown.

Baumgarten, Helga. 2006. *Hamas. Der politische Islam in Palästina.* Kreuzlingen/München: Heinrich Hugendubel Verlag.

Baumgarten, Helga. 2022. 'The Struggle for Democratic Space under Violent Settler Colonialism and Authoritarian Rule'. In *The Condition of Democracy. Vol. 3. Postcolonial and Settler Colonial Contexts*, edited by Jürgen Mackert, Hannah Wolf, and Bryan S. Turner, pp. 90–109. London: Routledge.

Becker, Julia C., Lea Hartwich, and S. Alexander Haslam. 2021. 'Neoliberalism Can Reduce Well-Being by Promoting a Sense of Social Disconnection, Competition, and Loneliness'. *British Journal of Social Psychology* 60 (3): 947–965.

Bejan, Raluca, and Manuela Boatcă. 2021. 'Migrant Workers' Safety Concerns Should be a Pandemic Priority'. *Verfassungsblog.* April 28. https://verfassungsblog.de/migrant-workers-safety-concerns-should-be-a-pandemic-priority/.

Bendix, Reinhard. 1960. *Max Weber. An Intellectual Portrait.* Berkeley, Los Angeles, and London: University of California Press.

Benlloch Doménech, Cristina. 2017. 'The Effects of Austerity Policies on Gender Inequality in the PIIGS'. *Studia Diplomatica* LVIII (4): 21–36.

Ben-Natan, Smadar. 2019. 'Revise Your Syllabi: Israeli Supreme Court Upholds Authorization for Torture and Ill-Treatment'. *Journal of International Humanitarian Legal Studies* 10 (1): 41–57.

Benvenisti, Meron. 2004. 'Bantustan Plan for an Apartheid Israel'. *The Guardian.* April 26. https://www.theguardian.com/world/2004/apr/26/comment.

Berezin, Mabel. 2012. 'Events as Templates of Possibility. An Analytic Typology of Political Facts'. In *The Oxford Handbook of Cultural Sociology*, edited by Jeffrey C. Alexander, Ronald N. Jacobs, and Philip Smith, pp. 613–635. Oxford/New York: Oxford University Press.

Berger, Miriam. 2018. 'In Besieged Gaza, Poverty Exacerbates Child Malnutrition'. *The National.* November 17. https://www.thenationalnews.com/world/mena/in-besieged-gaza-poverty-exacerbates-child-malnutrition-1.792942.

Berger, Miriam. 2022. '2022 was Deadliest Year for West Bank in Nearly Two Decades'. December 29. https://www.washingtonpost.com/world/2022/12/29/palestinians-killed-west-bank-israel/.

Berglund, Oscar. 2018. 'Contesting Actually Existing Austerity'. *New Political Economy* 23 (6): 804–818.

Bergman, Ronen, and Adam Goldman. 2023. 'Israel Knew Hamas's Attack Plan More Than a Year Ago'. *The New York Times.* November 30. https://www.nytimes.com/2023/11/30/world/middleeast/israel-hamas-attack-intelligence.html.

Berthelot, Jacques. 2017. 'Why Free Trade Will Be a Disaster for Africa'. Le Monde Diplomatique. https://mondediplo.com/2017/11/10Africa-freetrade.

Beswick, Joe, Georgia Alexandri, Michael Byrne, Sònia Vives-Miró, Desire Fields, Stuart Hodkinson, and Michael Janoschka. 2016. 'Speculating on London's Housing Future. The Rise of Global Corporate Landlords in "Post-Crisis" Urban Landscapes'. *City. Analysis of Urban Change, Theory, Action* 20 (2): 321–341.

Biebricher, Thomas. 2015. 'Neoliberalism and Democracy'. *Constellations* 22 (2): 255–266.

Bisan Center for Research and Development. (n.d.). http://www.bisan.org/.

Blackburn, Robin. 2010. *The Making of New World Slavery. From the Baroque to the Modern, 1492-1800*. London: Verso.

Blackburn, Robin. 2013. *The American Crucible. Slavery, Emancipation and Human Rights*. London: Verso.

Blakely, Grace. 2021. 'How Neoliberalism Created a Society of Individuals'. *The Tribune*. January 22. https://tribunemag.co.uk/2021/01/how-neoliberalism-created-a-society-of-individuals.

Blau, Peter M. 1990. 'Structural Constraints and Opportunities: Merton's Contribution to General Theory'. In *Robert K. Merton. Consensus and Controversy*, edited by John Clark, Celia Modgil, and Sohan Modgil, pp. 141–155. London: The Falmer Press.

Block, Fred. 1994. 'The Roles of the State in the Economy'. In *The Handbook of Economic Sociology*, edited by Neil J. Smelser and Richard Swedberg, pp. 691–710. Princeton and Oxford: Princeton University Press.

Block, Fred. 2011. 'Innovation and the Invisible Hand of Government'. In *State of Innovation: The U.S. Government's Role in Technology and Development*, edited by Fred Block and Matthew R. Keller, pp. 1–30. Boulder: Paradigm Publishers.

Block, Fred. 2015. 'A Neo-Polanyian Theory of Economic Crises'. *The American Journal of Economics and Sociology* 74 (2): 362–378.

Block, Fred, and Margaret R. Somers. 2014. *The Power of Market Fundamentalism. Karl Polanyi's Critique*. Cambridge and London: Harvard University Press.

Block, Fred, and Matthew R. Keller, eds. 2011. *State of Innovation: The U.S. Government's Role in Technology and Development*. Boulder, CO: Paradigm Publishers.

Blumenthal, Max. 2015. *Ruin and Resistance in Gaza. The 51 Day War*. London: Verso.

Blyth, Mark. 2013a. *Austerity. History of a Dangerous Idea*. Oxford and New York: Oxford University Press.

Blyth, Mark. 2013b. 'The Austerity Delusion. Why a Bad Idea Won Over the West'. *Foreign Affairs* 92 (3): 41–56.

Blyth, Mark. 2014. 'The Sovereign Debt Crisis That Isn't: Or, How to Turn a Lending Crisis into a Spending Crisis and Pocket the Spread'. *American Consortium on European Union Studies (ACES)*. http://aei.pitt.edu/59147/1/ACES_Case_Blythe_2014.pdf.

Boersma, Martijn, and Justine Nolan. 2022. 'Modern Slavery and the Employment Relationship: Exploring the Continuum of Exploitation'. *Journal of Industrial Relation* 64 (2): 165–176.

Bollens, Scott. 2022. 'Political Resistance and Contested Citizenship'. In *The Condition of Democracy. Vol. 3. Postcolonial and Settler Colonial Contexts*, edited by Jürgen Mackert, Hannah Wolf and Bryan S. Turner, pp. 128–145. London: Routledge.

Borges, Anelise, and Natalie Huet. 2020. 'Invisible Workers: Underpaid, Exploited and Put at Risk on Europe's Farms'. *Lighthouse Reports* in collaboration with *Euronews*. July 20. https://www.euronews.com/my-europe/2020/07/17/invisible-workers-underpaid-exploited-and-put-at-risk-on-europe-s-farms.

Bosco, Anna, and Susannah Verney. 2012. 'Electoral Epidemic: The Political Cost of Economic Crisis in Southern Europe, 2010–11'. *South European Society and Politics* 17 (2): 129–154.

Bosma, Ulbe. 2018. 'Slavery and Labour Contracts: Rethinking Their Nexus'. *International Review of Social History* 63 (3): 503–520.

Boudon, Raymond. 1996a. 'The "Rational Choice" Model: A Particular Case of the "Cogntive Model"'. *Rationality and Society*, 8 (2): 123–150.

Boudon, Raymond. 1996b. 'Social Mechanisms without Black Boxes. In *Social Mechanisms: An Analytical Approach to Social Theory*, edited by Peter Hedström and Richard Swedberg, pp. 173–203. Cambridge: Cambridge University Press.

Bourdieu, Pierre. 1984 [1979]. *Distinction. A Social Critique of the Judgement of Taste.* Cambridge, MA: Harvard University Press.

Bourdieu, Pierre. 1986. 'The Forms of Capital'. In *Handbook of Theory and Research for the Sociology of Education*, edited by John G. Richardson, pp. 241–258. Westport, CT: Greenwood.

Bourdieu, Pierre. 2003 [1999]. *Contrafuegos. (Firing back: Against the Tyranny of the Market).* London: Verso.

Bourdieu, Pierre, and Jean-Claude Passeron. 1977. *Reproduction in Education, Society and Culture.* Beverly Hills, CA: Sage.

Bradford, Simon, and Fi Cullen, eds. 2014. 'Youth Policy in Austerity Europe'. *International Journal of Adolescence and Youth*, 19 (Suppl. 1). https://www.tandfonline.com/doi/pdf/10.1080/02673843.2013.874104?needAccess=true, 1–4.

Brady, Thomas A. Jr. 1991. 'The Rise of Merchant Empires, 1400–1700. A European Counterpoint'. In *The Political Economy of Merchant Empires. State Power and World Trade 1350–1750*, edited by James D. Tracy, pp. 117–160. Cambridge: Cambridge University Press.

Bragason, Kristjan. 2021. 'Agricultural Workers are Left Out of Europe's Green Deal'. *IPS Journal.* September 7. https://www.ips-journal.eu/topics/economy-and-ecology/agricultural-workers-are-left-out-of-europes-green-deal-5407/.

Brenner, Neil, and Nik Theodore. 2002. 'Cities and the Geographies of "Actually Existing Neoliberalism"'. *Antipode* 34 (3): 356–386.

Bresheeth-Žabner, Haim. 2020. *An Army Like No Other. How the Israel Defence Forces Made a Nation.* London: Verso.

Brey, Marlene. 2023. 'Migrationskrise. Die EU will einen Zaun um Europas Grenzen bauen'. *Der Freitag.* July. https://www.freitag.de/autoren/marlene-brey/migrationskrise-die-eu-will-keine-mauer-aber-doch-einen-zaun-um-europa-bauen.

BR Fernsehen. 2019. 'Europas dreckige Ernte. Ausbeutung mit EU Geldern'. *Bayerischer Rundfunk Fernsehen.* https://www.youtube.com/watch?v=cZXGHspYW9E.

Brown, Phillip. 2000. 'The Globalisation of Positional Competition?'. *Sociology* 34 (4): 633–653.

Brown, Wendy. 2003. 'Neoliberalism and the End of Liberal Democracy'. *Theory & Event* 7 (1). https://muse.jhu.edu/article/48659.

Brown, Wendy. 2015. *Undoing the Demos. Neoliberalism's Stealth Revolution.* New York: Zone Books.

Brown, Wendy. 2016. 'Sacrificial Citizenship: Neoliberalism, Human Capital, and Austerity Politics'. *Constellations. An International Journal of Critical and Democratic Theory.* https://doi.org/10.1111/1467-8675.12166.

Brubaker, Rogers. 1992. *Citizenship and Nationhood in France and Germany.* Cambridge, MA: Harvard University Press.

Brubaker, Rogers. 2006. *Ethnicity Without Groups.* Cambridge, MA: Harvard University Press.

B'Tselem (The Israeli Information Center for Human Rights in the Occupied Territories). 2002. 'Land Grab: Israel's Settlement Policy in the West Bank'. https://www.btselem.org/download/200205_land_grab_eng.pdf.

B'Tselem (The Israeli Information Center for Human Rights in the Occupied Territories). 2005. 'Settlers Scattered Poison in Pasture Fields, Killing Sheep and Deer, Khirbet a-Tawaneh, the Southern Hebron Hills, March 2005'. https://www.btselem.org/testimonies/20050324_poisoning_of_flock_by_settlers.

B'Tselem (The Israeli Information Center for Human Rights in the Occupied Territories). 2016a. 'Expel and Exploit. The Israeli Practice of Taking Over Rural Palestinian Land'. https://www.btselem.org/publications/summaries/201612_expel_and_exploit.

B'Tselem (The Israeli Information Center for Human Rights in the Occupied Territories). 2016b. 'The Occupation's Fig Leaf: Israel's Military Law Enforcement System as a Whitewash Mechanism'. May 16. https://www.btselem.org/sites/default/files/publications/201605_occupations_fig_leaf_eng.pdf.

B'Tselem (The Israeli Information Center for Human Rights in the Occupied Territories). 2020a. 'During the Coronavirus Crisis, Israel Confiscates Tents Designated for Clinic in the Northern West Bank'. March 26. https://www.btselem.org/press_release/20200326_israel_confiscates_clinic_tents_during_coronavirus_crisis.

B'Tselem (The Israeli Information Center for Human Rights in the Occupied Territories). 2020b. 'The Supreme Court of the Occupation'. February 25. https://www.btselem.org/supreme_court_of_occupation.

B'Tselem (The Israeli Information Center for Human Rights in the Occupied Territories). 2020c. 'The Israeli Attorney General's Memorandum: Everything the ICC Is Not Meant to Be'. https://www.btselem.org/publications/summaries/202003_position_paper_on_israel_ag_icc_memorandum.

B'Tselem (The Israeli Information Center for Human Rights in the Occupied Territories). 2017/21. 'Water Crisis'. November 11. https://www.btselem.org/water.

B'Tselem (The Israeli Information Center for Human Rights in the Occupied Territories). 2021a. 'A Regime of Jewish Supremacy from the Jordan River to the Mediterranean Sea: This is Apartheid'. January 12. https://www.btselem.org/publications/fulltext/202101_this_is_apartheid.

B'Tselem (The Israeli Information Center for Human Rights in the Occupied Territories). 2021b. 'State Business. Israel's Misappropriation of Land in the West Bank through Settler Violence'. https://www.btselem.org/publications/202111_state_business.

B'Tselem (The Israeli Information Center for Human Rights in the Occupied Territories). 2021c. 'Israel Must Provide Necessary Vaccines to Palestinian Health Care Systems'. January 5. https://www.btselem.org/press_releases/20210105_joint_statement_israel_must_provide_vaccines_to_palestinians.

B'Tselem (The Israeli Information Center for Human Rights in the Occupied Territories). 2021d. 'Since Pandemic, has Israel Allowed Almost no Palestinians out of Gaza for Medical Treatment'. May 3. https://www.btselem.org/gaza_strip/20210503_gaza_patients_denied_treatment_since_covid_19_outbreak.

B'Tselem (The Israeli Information Center for Human Rights in the Occupied Territories). 2022a. 'Supreme Court Rules: Israel Above the Law'. May 29. https://www.btselem.org/ota/164/all.

B'Tselem (The Israeli Information Center for Human Rights in the Occupied Territories). 2022b. 'Routine Torture: Painful Binding, Isolation from the Outside World and Deprivation of Food, Drink, and Toilet Access: This Is What the ISA's "Interrogation System" Looks Like'. May 23. https://www.btselem.org/torture/20230523_painful_binding_isolation_and_deprivation_of_food_drink_and_toilet_access_in_isa_interrogation_system.

B'Tselem (The Israeli Information Center for Human Rights in the Occupied Territories). 2024. 'Welcome to Hell. The Israeli Prison System as a Network of Torture Camps'. https://www.btselem.org/publications/202408_welcome_to_hell.

Buchannan, James M. 1975a. *The Limits of Liberty. Between Anarchy and Leviathan*. Chicago: The Chicago University Press.

Buchannan, James M. 1975b. 'The Samaritan's Dilemma'. In *Altruism, Morality and Economic Theory*, edited by Edmund S. Phelps, pp. 71–85. New York: Russell Sage.

Bunge, Mario. 1996. *Finding Philosophy in the Social Sciences*. New Haven, CT and London: Yale University Press,

Bunge, Mario. 1997. 'Mechanism and Explanation'. *Philosophy of the Social Sciences* 27 (4): 410–465.

Burkert, Rebecca. 2022a. *Struggle for Existence. Acts of Subjecthood as Contentious Claim-making in the West Bank*. PhD thesis at the University of Potsdam, Germany. https://doi.org/10.25932/publishup-54293.

Burkert, Rebecca. 2022b. 'Moving Mountains? Palestinian Claim Making from Oslo Onwards. In *The Condition of Democracy. Vol. 3. Postcolonial and Settler Colonial Contexts*, edited by Jürgen Mackert, Hannah Wolf, and Bryan S. Turner. pp. 110–127. London: Routledge.

Business and Human Rights Resource Center, and Asia Floor Wage Alliance. 2022. 'Unbearable Harassment. The Fashion Industry and Widespread Abuse of Female Garment Workers in Indian Factories'. https://media.business-humanrights.org/media/documents/2022_GBVH_Briefing_latvnJb.pdf.

Buttu, Diana. 2022. 'How to Crush Palestinian NGOs: Just Use the "T" Word'. *Journal of Palestine Studies* 51 (2): 57–61.

Cable, Vincent. 1995. 'The Diminished Nation-State: A Study in the Loss of Economic Power'. *Daedalus* 124 (2): 23–53.

Caliskan, Koray, and Michel Callon. 2009. 'Economization, Part 1: Shifting Attention from the Economy Towards Processes of Economization'. *Economy and Society* 38 (3): 369–398.

Callinicos, Alex. 2012. 'Commentary: Contradictions of Austerity'. *Cambridge Journal of Economics* 36 (1): 65–77.

Cano Fuentes, Gala, Aitziber Etxezarreta Etxarri, Kes Dol, and Joris Hoekstra. 2013. 'From Housing Bubble to Repossessions: Spain Compared to Other West European Countries'. *Housing Studies* 28 (8): 1197–1217.

Carrington, Selwyn H. H. 2003. 'Capitalism & Slavery and Caribbean Historiography: An Evaluation'. *The Journal of African American History* 88 (3): 304–312.

Centeno, Miguel A., and Joseph N. Cohen. 2012. 'The Arch of Neo-Liberalism'. *Annual Review of Sociology* 38: 317–340.

Center for Social and Economic Rights. 2012. 'Fiscal Fallacies: 8 Myths About the "Age of Austerity" and Human Rights Responses'. Rights in Crisis Series Briefing Paper. New York.

Center for Social and Economic Rights. 2018. '*España*. Ficha Informative No. 17'. https://www.cesr.org/sites/default/files/FACTSHEET-Espa%C3%B1a%28SP%29-Print-Final_0.pdf.

Challand, Benoit 2023. *Violence and Representation in the Arab Uprisings*. New York: Columbia University Press.

Chávez, Brenda, and Ashifa Kassam. 2022. 'Women Lose Landmark Challenge to Sexual Abuse in Spanish Meat Industry'. The Guardian. December 22. https://www.theguardian.com/environment/2022/dec/22/spain-women-lose-landmark-challenge-sexual-abuse-meat-industry.

Chomsky, Noam. 1999. *Profit over People. Neoliberalism and Global Order*. New York: Seven Stories Press.

Chomsky, Noam. 2014 [1983]. *The Fateful Triangle. The United States, Israel, and the Palestinians*. Updated edition. Chicago: Haymarket Books.

Christophers, Brett. 2010. 'On Voodoo Economics: Theorising Relations of Property, Value and Contemporary Capitalism'. *Transactions of the Institute of British Geographers* 35 (1): 94–108.

Cieslik, Natalia. 2022. 'Hidden Hunger. Micronutrient Deficiencies in the West Bank and Gaza'. *World Bank*. Feature Story. June 20. https://www.worldbank.org/en/news/feature/2022/06/20/hidden-hunger-micronutrient-deficiencies-in-the-west-bank-and-gaza.

Clark, John, and Janet Newman. 2012. 'The Alchemy of Austerity'. *Critical Social Policy* 32 (3): 299–319.

Clarke, Thomas, and Martijn Boersma. 2019. 'Global Corporations and Global Value Chains. The Disaggregation of Corporations?'. In *The Oxford Handbook of the Corporation*, edited by Thomas Clarke, Justin O'Brien, and Charles R. T. Kelley, pp. 319–365. Oxford et al.: Oxford University Press.

Clegg, John C. 2015. 'Capitalism and Slavery'. *Critical Historical Studies* 2 (2): 281–304.

Coffee John C. Jr. 2009. 'What Went Wrong? An Initial Inquiry into the Causes of the 2008 Financial Crisis'. *Journal of Corporate Law Studies* 9 (1): 1–22.

Cohen, Shana, Gerry Mitchell, and Liran Morav. 2022. 'Europe's Agriculture and Care—Mistreated Migrants'. *Social Europe*. March 9. https://www.socialeurope.eu/europes-agriculture-and-care-mistreated-migrants.

Collins, Randall. 1971. 'Functional and Conflict Theories of Educational Stratification'. *American Sociological Review* 36 (6): 1002–1018.

Collins, Randall. 1975. *Conflict Sociology: Toward an Explanatory Science*. New York: Academic Press.
Collins, Randall. 1979. *The Credential Society. An Historical Sociology of Education and Stratification*. New York: Academic Press.
Conermann, Stephan, and Michael Zeuske eds. 2020. 'The Slavery/Capitalism Debate Global. From "Capitalism and Slavery" to Slavery as Capitalism'. *Comparativ. Zeitschrift für Globalgeschichte und vergleichende Gesellschaftsforschung* (5/6).
Cook, Jonathan 2012. 'Israel's Formula for a Starvation Diet'. October 24. https://www.jonathan-cook.net/2012-10-24/israels-formula-for-a-starvation-diet/.
Cook, Jonathan. 2021. 'Israel Calls the Palestinian Fight for Rights "Terror" —And So Turns Reality on Its Head'. *Middle East Eye*. October 25. https://www.middleeasteye.net/opinion/israel-palestine-rights-fight-terror-reality-on-head.
Cook, Jonathan. 2023. 'Israel-Palestine War: How Israel Uses AI Genocide Programme to Obliterate Gaza'. *Middle East Eye*. December 5. https://www.middleeasteye.net/opinion/israel-palestine-war-genocide-programme-ai-obliterate-gaza.
Cooper, Vickie, and Kirsteen Paton. 2018. 'Everyday Evictions in the 21st Century'. In *Rent and Its Discontents: A Century of Housing Struggle*, edited by Neil Gray, pp. 71–84. Lanham, MD: Rowman and Littlefield.
Cooper, Vickie, and Kirsteen Paton. 2021. 'Accumulation by Repossession: The Political Economy of Evictions Under Austerity'. *Urban Geography* 42 (5): 583–602.
Cox, Robert W. 1986. 'Social Forces, States and World Orders: Beyond International Relations Theory'. In *Neorealism and Its Critics*, edited by Robert O. Keohane, pp. 204–254. New York: Columbia University Press.
Crisis. 2022. 'No Fault Evictions Rise by 52% In Just Three Months—Crisis Responds'. August 11. https://www.crisis.org.uk/about-us/media-centre/no-fault-evictions-rise-by-52-in-just-three-months-crisis-responds/.
Crotty, James. 2009. 'Structural Causes of the Global Financial Crisis: A Critical Assessment of the "New Financial Architecture"'. *Cambridge Journal of Economics* 33 (4): 563–580.
Crouch, Colin. 2001. 'Citizenship and Markets in Recent British Education Policy'. In *Citizenship, Markets, and the State*, edited by Colin Crouch, Klaus Eder, and Damian Tambini, pp. 111–133. Oxford: Oxford University Press.
Crouch, Colin. 2011. *The Strange Non-death of Neo-Liberalism*. Cambridge: Polity Press.
Cuerpo, Carlos, Sona Kalantaryan, and Peter Pontuch. 2014. 'Rental Market Regulation in the European Union'. Economic Papers 515. *European Commission*. https://ec.europa.eu/economy_finance/publications/economic_paper/2014/pdf/ecp515_en.pdf.
Cuneo, Carl J. 1989. 'Review Essay: Social Closure: The Theory of Monopolization and Exclusion'. *Contemporary Sociology*, 18 (2): 304–305.
Cyba, Eva. 1985. '*Schließungsstrategien und Arbeitsteilungsmythen: Die Praxis betrieblicher Diskriminierung von Frauen*'. *Österreichische Zeitschrift für Soziologie* 10 (1): 49–61.
Cyba, Eva and Andreas Balog. 1989. 'Frauendiskriminierung und Klassenanalyse'. *Österreichische Zeitschrift für Soziologie* 4 (1): 4–18.
Daher-Nashif, Suhad. 2020. 'Colonial Management of Death: To Be or Not to Be Dead in Palestine'. *Current Sociology* 69 (7): 945–962.
Dahrendorf, Ralf. 1979. *Life Chances. Approaches to Social and Political Theory*. Chicago: The University of Chicago Press.
Dajani, Muna. 2014. 'Drying Palestine. Israel's Systemic Water War'. *Al Shabaka. The Palestinian Policy Network*. https://al-shabaka.org/wp-content/uploads/2015/01/Dajani_PolicyBrief_En_Sep_2014.pdf.
Dalley, Hamish. 2016. 'The Deaths of Settler Colonialism: Extinction as a Metaphor of Decolonization in Contemporary Settler Literature'. *Settler Colonial Studies* 9 (1): 30–46.
Dalloul, Motasem A. 2018. 'Israel's Judicial System Whitewashes the Crimes of Its Soldiers'. *MEMO*. September 25. https://www.middleeastmonitor.com/20180925-israels-judicial-system-whitewashes-the-crimes-of-its-soldiers/.

Damir-Geilsdorf, Sabine, Ulrike Lindner, Gesine Müller, Oliver Tappe, and Michael Zeuske eds. 2016. *Bonded Labor. Global and Comparative Perspectives (18th–21st Century)*. Bielefeld, Germany: transcript.

Dana, Tariq. 2015. 'The Structural Transformation of Palestinian Civil Society: Key Paradigm Shifts'. *Middle East Critique* 24 (2): 191–210.

Dana, Tariq. 2020. 'A Cruel Innovation: Israeli Experiments on Gaza's Great March of Return'. *Sociology of Islam* 8 (2): 175–198.

Dana, Tariq, and Jarbawi, Ali. 2017. 'A Century of Settler Colonialism in Palestine: Zionism's Entangled Project'. *Brown Journal of World Affairs* 24 (1): 197–219.

Dana, Tariq, and Jarbawi, Ali. 2023. 'Whose Autonomy? Conceptualising "Colonial Extraterritorial Autonomy" in the Occupied Palestinian Territories'. *Politics* 34 (1): 106–121.

Daniele, Luigi. 2017. 'Enforcing Illegality: Israel's Military Justice in the West Bank'. (Special issue: The Israeli Military Justice System and International Law). *Questions of International Law. Zoom-in* 44: 21–44.

Davies, Jon. 2019. 'Corporate Harm and Embedded Labour Exploitation in Agri-Food Supply Networks'. *European Journal of Criminology* 17 (1): 70–85.

Davies, Jon, and Natalia Ollus. 2019. 'Labour Exploitation as Corporate Crime and Harm: Outsourcing Responsibility in Food Production and Cleaning Services Supply Chains'. *Crime, Law and Social Change* 72 (1): 87–106.

DAWN (Democracy for The Arab World Now). 2023. 'Ben-Gvir is Arming Thousands of Israelis—And Playing with Fire'. November 3. https://dawnmena.org/ben-gvir-is-arming-thousands-of-israelis-and-playing-with-fire/.

DCIP (Defense for Children International-Palestine) 2023. 'Grave Violations against Palestinian Children. UN's Children and Armed Conflict Agenda'. November 27. https://www.dci-palestine.org/grave_violations_against_palestinian_children_in_gaza_november_27.

DCIP (Defence for Children International-Palestine). (n.d.). https://www.dci-palestine.org/.

Debt and Development Coalition Ireland. 2017. 'From Puerto Rico to the Dublin Docklands. Vulture Funds and Debt in Ireland and the Global South'. March 27. https://www.cadtm.org/From-Puerto-Rico-to-the-Dublin.

Deen, Thalif. 2019. 'Modern Day Slavery Rated World's Largest Single Crime Industry'. *OCHA*. Februar 25. https://reliefweb.int/report/world/modern-day-slavery-rated-world-s-largest-single-crime-industry.

Del Rosso Jr., Stephen J. 1995. 'The Insecure State: Reflections on the "State" and "Security" in a Changing World'. *Daedalus* 124 (2): 175–207.

de Pablo, Ofelia, Javier Zurita, Annie Kelly, and Clare Carlile. 2020. '"We Pick Your Food": Migrant Workers Speak Out from Spain's "Plastic Sea". Human Rights in Focus'. *The Guardian*. September 20. https://www.theguardian.com/global-development/2020/sep/20/we-pick-your-food-migrant-workers-speak-out-from-spains-plastic-sea.

D'Eramo, Marco. 2013. 'Populism and the New Oligarchy'. *New Left Review* 82 (July/August): 5–28.

Desmond, Matthew. 2012. 'Eviction and the Reproduction of Urban Poverty'. *American Journal of Sociology* 118 (1): 88–133.

Desmond, Matthew. 2016. *Evicted: Poverty and Profit in the American City*. New York: Crown.

De Tocqueville, Aléxis. 1994 [1835-1840]. *Democracy in America*. Vol. 1. London: Everyman's Library.

De Tocqueville, Aléxis. 1984 [1846]. 'Unpublished Letters', in André Jardin, *Aléxis de Tocqueville*. Paris: Hachette.

De Tocqueville, Aléxis. 1951. *OEuvres Complètes*. Paris: Gallimard.

Deudney, Daniel. 1995. 'Nuclear Weapons and the Waning of the Real-State'. *Daedalus* 124 (2): 209–231.

Di Feliciantonio, Cesare, and Manuel B. Aalbers. 2018. 'The Prehistories of Neoliberal Housing Policies in Italy and Spain and Their Reification in Times of Crisis'. *Housing Policy Debate* 28 (1): 135–151.

Djelic, Marie-Laure. 2006. 'Marketization: From Intellectual Agenda to Global Policy-making'. In *Transnational Governance. Institutional Dynamics of Regulation*, edited by Marie-Laure Djelic and Kerstin Sahlin-Andersson, pp. 53–73. Cambridge: Cambridge University Press.

Durkheim, Émile. 1992 [1950]. *Professional Ethics and Civic Morals*. Edited and with a new Preface by Bryan S. Turner. London and New York: Routledge.

ECHO (European Commission Humanitarian Aid Offices). 2004. 'Humanitarian Aid for the Victims of the Ongoing Crisis in the Palestinian Territories, Palestinian Populations in Lebanon, and Refugees from Iraq'. https://ec.europa.eu/echo/files/funding/decisions/2004/dec_me_01000_en.pdf.

Edmunds, June, and Bryan S. Turner. 2004. 'Generationen und soziale Schließung. Die britische Nachkriegsgeneration'. In *Die Theorie sozialer Schließung. Tradition, Analysen, Perspektiven*, edited by Jürgen Mackert, pp. 177–192. Wiesbaden: VS.

EfSYN. 2020. 'Οι «αόρατοι» σκλάβοι της Ελλάδας και της Ευρώπης'. July 18. https://www.efsyn.gr/themata/thema-tis-efsyn/252555_oi-aoratoi-sklaboi-tis-elladas-kai-tis-eyropis.

Egels-Zandén, Niklas, and Jeroen Merk. 2014. 'Private Regulation and Trade Union Rights: Why Codes of Conduct Have Limited Impact on Trade Union Rights'. *Journal of Business Ethics* 123: 461–473.

Eichensehr, Kristen E. 2007. 'On Target? The Israeli Supreme Court and the Expansion of Targeted Killings'. *The Yale Law Journal* 116 (8): 1873–1881.

El-Ad, Hagai. 2016. 'How the Israeli Military's "Justice" System Shields an Illegal Occupation'. *Open Society Foundations*. June 29. https://www.opensocietyfoundations.org/voices/how-israeli-military-s-justice-system-shields-illegal-occupation.

El Bilbeisi, Abdel, Ayoub Al-Jawaldeh, Ali Albelbeisi, Samer Abuzerr, Ibrahim Elmadfa, and Lara Nasreddine. 2022. 'Households' Food Insecurity and Their Association with Dietary Intakes, Nutrition-Related Knowledge, Attitudes and Practices among Under-Five Children in Gaza Strip, Palestine'. *Frontiers in Public Health*. February 25. https://pubmed.ncbi.nlm.nih.gov/35284364/.

Elias, Norbert, and John L. Scotson. 1994. *The Established and the Outsiders. A Sociological Inquiry into Community Problems*. London: Sage.

El Mal, Jessica. 2021. 'Locked Down, Locked In and Locked Out: The Forbidden Fruits of Female Labour'. *Ethical Consumer*. https://research.ethicalconsumer.org/research-hub/ethical-consumption-review/forbidden-fruits-female-labour.

Ellison, Gavin. 2017. 'Grocery Code Adjudicator: Annual Survey Results'. London: YouGov. https://www.gov.uk/government/uploads/system/uploads/attachment_data/file/623564/GCA_Annual_Sector_Survey_Results.pdf.

Elster, Jon. 1996. 'A Plea for Mechanisms'. In *Social Mechanisms: An Analytical Approach to Social Theory*, edited by Peter Hedström and Richard Swedberg, pp. 55–73. Cambridge: Cambridge University Press.

Emirbayer, Mustafa. 1997. 'Manifesto for a Relational Sociology'. *American Journal of Sociology* 103 (2): 281–317.

Environmental Justice Atlas. 2019. 'Masafir Yatta's Water Pipelines Cut by Israeli Forces, Palestine'. https://ejatlas.org/conflict/mafasir-yattas-water-pipelines-cut-by-israeli-occupation-forces-palestine/?translate=tr.

Ethical Trading Initiative. (n.d.). 'A Living Wage for Workers'. https://www.ethicaltrade.org/issues/living-wage-workers.

European Action Coalition for the Right to Housing and to the City. 2016. 'Resisting Evictions Across Europe'. https://housingnotprofit.org/wp-content/uploads/2019/08/Resisting-Evictions-Across-Europe.pdf.

European Bank for Reconstruction and Development. 2020. 'Addressing Gender-Based Violence and Harassment (GVBH) in the Agribusiness Sector'. https://www.ifc.org/content/dam/ifc/doc/mgrt/sectorbrief-addressinggbvh-agribusiness.pdf.

European Commission. (n.d.). *Key Policy Objectives of the new CAP*. https://agriculture.ec.europa.eu/common-agricultural-policy/cap-overview/new-cap-2023-27/key-policy-objectives-new-cap_en.

European Institute for Gender Equality (EIGE). 2021. 'Gender-Based Violence Costs the EU €366 Billion a Year'. July 7. https://eige.europa.eu/news/gender-based-violence-costs-eu-eu366-billion-year.
European Mortgage Federation. 2022. 'EMF Hypostat 2022: An In-Depth Look at European Housing & Mortgage Markets in 2021'. September 7. https://hypo.org/emf/press-release/emf-hypostat-2022-an-in-depth-look-at-european-housing-mortgage-markets-in-2021/.
European Parliament. 2016. 'Report on Unfair Trading Practices in the Food Supply Chain'. Committee on Internal Market and Consumer Protection. Brussels: European Parliament. http://www.europarl.europa.eu/sides/getDoc.do?pubRef=-//EP//TEXT+REPORT+A8-2016-0173+0+DOC+XML+V0//EN.
European Women's Lobby/Lobby Européen des femmes. 2012. 'The Price of Austerity: The Impact on Women's Rights and Gender Equality in Europe'. https://www.womenlobby.org/IMG/pdf/the_price_of_austerity_-_web_edition.pdf.
Evans, Alice. 2017. 'Patriarchal Unions = Weaker Unions? Industrial Relations in the Asian Garment Industry'. *Third World Quarterly* 38 (7): 1619–1638.
Evans, Peter, and William H. Sewell Jr. 2013. 'Neo-Liberalism. Policy Regimes, International Regimes, and Social Effects'. In *Social Resilience in the Neo-Liberal Era*, edited by Peter A. Hall and Michèle Lamont, pp. 35–68. Cambridge: Cambridge University Press.
Eviction Lab. 2022. 'In a Typical Year, Landlords file 3.6 million Eviction Cases'. https://evictionlab.org/.
EWASH (Emergency Water Sanitation and Hygiene Group in the Occupied Territories). 2012. '"Down the Drain". Israeli Restrictions on the WASH Sector in the Occupied Palestinian Territory and Their Impact on Vulnerable Communities'. March. https://bit.ly/2z9zYpD.
Fanon, Frantz. 2004 [1961]. *The Wretched of The Earth*. With commentary by Jean-Paul Sartre and Homi K. Bhabha. New York: Grove Press.
Farha, Leilani, and Bruce Porter. 2017. 'Commodification Over Community: Financialization of the Housing Sector and Its Threat to SDG 11 and the Right to Housing'. *Spotlight in Sustainable Development*. https://www.2030spotlight.org/en/book/1165/chapter/11-commodification-over-community-financialization-housing-sector-and-its-threat.
Farnsworth, Kevin, and Zoë Irving. 2018. 'Austerity: Neoliberal Dreams Come True?' *Critical Social Policy* 38 (3): 461–481.
Farsakh, Leila. 2005. Independence, Cantons, or Bantustans: Wither a Palestinian State? *The Middle East Journal*, 59 (2): 230–245.
Fasang, Anette Eva, William Mangino, and Hannah Brückner. 2014. 'Social Closure and Educational Attainment. *Sociological Forum* 29 (1): 137–164.
Fayyad, Huthifa. 2022. 'The Deadliest Year for West Bank Palestinians since the Second Intifada in Numbers'. *Middle East Eye*. December 31. https://www.middleeasteye.net/news/palestine-west-bank-deadliest-year-second-intifada.
FEANTSA & Abbé Pierre Foundation. 2017. 'Second Overview of Housing Exclusion in Europe'. https://ec.europa.eu/futurium/sites/futurium/files/overview_housing_exclusion_2017_en_2.pdf.
FEANTSA & Abbé Pierre Foundation. 2018. 'Third Overview of Housing Exclusion in Europe'. https://www.feantsa.org/download/full-report-en1029873431323901915.pdf.
FEANTSA & Abbé Pierre Foundation. 2021. 'Sixth Overview of Housing Exclusion in Europe'. https://www.feantsa.org/public/user/Resources/reports/2021/6th_Overview_of_Housing_Exclusion_in_Europe_2021_EN.pdf.
FEMM Committee European Parliament. 2018. 'The Vulnerability to Exploitation of Women Migrant Workers in Agriculture in the EU: The Need for a Human Rights and Gender Based Approach'. *Policy Department for Citizens' Rights and Constitutional Affairs*. https://www.europarl.europa.eu/RegData/etudes/STUD/2018/604966/IPOL_STU(2018)604966_EN.pdf.
FEPS, and TASC (Foundation for European Progressive Studies & Think Tank for Action on Social Change). 2022. *Migrant Key Workers and Social Cohesion in Europe. A Comparative Field Study*. https://www.tasc.ie/assets/files/pdf/feps_tasc__policy_study_migrant_key_workers_11_jan_2022.pdf.

Fields, Desiree, and Sabina Uffer. 2016. 'The Financialization of Rental Housing: A Comparative Analysis of New York City and Berlin'. *Urban Studies* 53 (7): 1486–1502.
Finkelstein, Norman G. 2018. *Gaza: An Inquest into Its Martyrdom*. Oakland: University of California Press.
Flake, Constance, Stella Freitag, and Elise Gordon. 2019. 'A Living Wage: A Crucial Tool in the Fight Against Modern Slavery'. *Walk Free*. March 7. https://www.walkfree.org/news/2019/a-living-wage-a-crucial-tool-in-the-fight-against-modern-slavery/.
Florida, Richard. 2017. *The New Urban Crisis: How Our Cities Are Increasing Inequality, Deepening Segregation, and Failing the Middle Class—And What We Can Do About It*. New York: Basic Books.
Foucault, Michel. 2003. *Society Must Be Defended: Lectures at the Collège de France 1975–76*. Edited by Mauro Bertani and Alessandro Fontana. New York: Picador.
Foucault, Michel. 2007 [2004]. *Security, Territory, Population: Lectures at the College de France, 1977-78*. Houndmills, Basingstoke, and New York: Palgrave Macmillan.
Fraenkel, Ernst. 2017 [1941]. *The Dual State. A Contribution to the Theory of Dictatorship*. Oxford: Oxford University Press.
Friedman, Milton. 1970. 'A Friedman Doctrine—The Social Responsibility of Business is to Increase its Profits'. *The New York Times*. September 13. https://www.nytimes.com/1970/09/13/archives/a-friedman-doctrine-the-social-responsibility-of-business-is-to.html.
Friedman, Milton, and Rose Friedman. 1980. *Tyranny of the Status Quo*. New York and London: Harcourt Brace Jovanovich.
Friends of the Earth Europe, Heinrich Böll Foundation, and Rosa Luxemburg Foundation. 2017. 'Agrifood Atlas: Facts and Figures About the Corporations That Control What we Eat'. https://www.boell.de/sites/default/files/agrifoodatlas2017_facts-and-figures-about-the-corporations-that-control-what-we-eat.pdf.
Frings, Christian. 2019. 'Sklaverei und Lohnarbeit bei Marx. Zur Diskussion um Gewalt und „unfreie Arbeit" im Kapitalismus'. *PROKLA* 49 (196): 427–448.
Ganti, Tejaswini. 2014. 'Neoliberalism'. *Annual Review of Anthropology* 43: 89–104.
Garnham, Juan Pablo, Carl Gershenson, and Matthew Desmond. 2022. 'New Data Release Shows that 3.6 million Eviction Cases Were Filed in the United States in 2018'. *The Eviction Lab*. July 11. https://evictionlab.org/new-eviction-data-2022/.
Gender and Development Network. 2018. 'Submission to the Independent Expert in Foreign Debt and Human Rights on the Links and the Impacts of Economic Reforms and Austerity Measures on Women's Human Rights'. https://gadnetwork.org/gadn-resources/2018/4/4/the-impact-of-economic-reforms-and-austerity-measures-on-womens-human-rights-gadn-submission.
Geneva Convention. 1977. 'Protocol I'. June 8. https://treaties.un.org/doc/Publication/UNTS/Volume%201125/volume-1125-I-17512-English.pdf.
Giacaman, Rita, Rana Khatib, Luay Shabaneh, Asad Ramlawi, Belgacem Sabri, Guido Sabatinelli, Marwan Khawaja, and Tony Laurance. 2009. 'Health Status and Health Services in the Occupied Palestinian Territory'. *The Lancet* 373. March 7. https://www.thelancet.com/journals/lancet/article/PIIS0140-6736(09)60107-0/fulltext.
Giddens, Anthony. 1973. *The Class Structure of the Advanced Societies*. London: Hutchinson.
Giddens, Anthony. 1976a. 'Functionalism: *Après la Lutte*'. *Social Research* 43 (2): 325–366.
Giddens, Anthony. 1976b. *New Rules of Sociological Method. A Positive Critique of Interpretive Sociologies*. New York: Basic Books.
Giddens, Anthony. 1979. *Central Problems in Social Theory. Action, Structure and Contradiction in Social Analysis*. Berkeley and Los Angeles: University of California Press.
Giddens, Anthony. 1980. 'Classes, Capitalism, and the State: A Discussion of Frank Parkin, Marxism and Class Theory: A Bourgeois Critique'. *Theory and Society* 9 (6): 877–890.
Giddens, Anthony. 1981. *A Contemporary Critique of Historical Materialism*. Houndmills, Basingstoke, and London: Macmillan.

Giddens, Anthony. 1982. 'Power, the Dialectic of Control and Class Structuration'. In *Social Class and the Division of Labour. Essays in Honour of Ilya Neustadt*, edited by Anthony Giddens and Gavin MacKenzie, pp. 29–45. Cambridge: Polity Press.

Giddens, Anthony. 1984. *The Constitution of Society. Outline of the Theory of Structuration*. Cambridge: Polity Press.

Giddens, Anthony. 1985. *The Nation-State and Violence. Volume 2 of A Contemporary Critique of Historical Materialism*. Cambridge: Polity Press.

Giddens, Anthony. 1990. *The Consequences of Modernity*. Stanford, CA: Sanford University Press.

Giesecke, Johannes, and Roland Verwiebe. 2009. 'The Changing Wage Distribution in Germany Between 1985 and 2006'. *Journal of Applied Social Science Studies* 129 (2): 191–202.

Gilroy, Paul. 1993. *The Black Atlantic. Modernity and Double Consciousness*. Cambridge, MA: Harvard University Press.

Gisha—Legal Center for Freedom of Movement. 2020. 'Hundreds of Dunams of Crops in Gaza Destroyed by Aerial Herbicide Spraying Conducted by Israel'. May 7. https://gisha.org/en/hundreds-of-dunams-of-crops-in-gaza-destroyed-by-aerial-herbicide-spraying-conducted-by-israel/.

Go, Julian. 2013. 'A Global-Historical Sociology of Power: On Mann's Concluding Volumes to *The Sources of Social Power*'. *International Affairs* 89 (6): 1469–1477.

Go, Julian. 2016. *Postcolonial Thought and Social Theory*. Oxford: Oxford University Press.

Göttlich, Andreas, and Jochen Dreher. 2017. 'Editors' Introduction'. In *Heinrich Popitz. Phenomena of Power. Authority, Domination, and Violence*, edited by Andreas Göttlich and Jochen Dreher, pp. ix–xxvi. Translated by Gianfranco Poggi. New York: Columbia University Press.

Goldenberg, Suzanne. 2000. 'Rioting as Sharon visits Islam Holy Site'. *The Guardian*. September 29. https://www.theguardian.com/world/2000/sep/29/israel.

Gotev, Georgi. 2019. 'Eurozone Delays Greece Debt ReliefOver Household Insolvency Law'. *Euractiv*. March 12. https://www.euractiv.com/section/economy-jobs/news/eurozone-delays-greece-debt-relief-over-household-insolvency-law/.

Goudriaan, Jan-Willem. 2016. 'The Rising Wave of Privatization Damages Health Care in Europe'. *Euractiv*. April 7. https://www.euractiv.com/section/health-consumers/opinion/the-rising-wave-of-privatisation-damages-healthcare-in-europe/.

Gould, Rebecca. 2023. *The Erasure of Palestine*. London: Penguin.

Green, Penny, and Amelia Smith. 2016. 'Evicting Palestine'. *State Crime Journal* 5 (1): 81–108.

Greenberg, Joel. 2000. 'Sharon Touches a Nerve, and Jerusalem Explodes'. *New York Times*. September 29. https://www.nytimes.com/2000/09/29/world/sharon-touches-a-nerve-and-jerusalem-explodes.html.

Greenwald, Glen. 2012. 'How the US and Israeli Justice Systems Whitewash State Crimes'. *The Guardian*. August 28. https://www.theguardian.com/commentisfree/2012/aug/28/us-israel-justice-whitewash-state-crimes.

Gregory, Derek. 2005. 'Splintering Palestine'. In *B/ordering Space*, edited by Henk van Houtum, Olivier Kramsch, and Wolfgang Zierhofer, pp. 123–137. Aldershot, UK: Ashgate.

Gromis, Ashley, Ian Fellows, James R. Hendrickson, Lavar Edmonds, Lillian Leung, Adam Porton, and Matthew Desmond. 2022. 'Estimating Eviction Prevalence across the United States'. *Proceedings of the National Academy of Sciences of the United States of America* 119 (21). https://www.pnas.org/doi/full/10.1073/pnas.2116169119.

Groß, Martin. 2009. 'Markt oder Schließung? Zu den Ursachen der Steigerung der Einkommensungleichheit'. *Berliner Journal für Soziologie* 19 (4): 499–530.

Guajardo, Jaime, Daniel Leigh, and Andrea Pescatori. 2011. 'Expansionary Austerity: New International Evidence'. *IMF Working paper 11/158*. https://www.imf.org/external/pubs/ft/wp/2011/wp11158.pdf.

Gualerzi, Davide. 2017. 'Crisis in the Eurozone: Austerity and Economic Transformation'. *Review of Radical Economics* 49 (3): 394–403.

Gumas, Evan D. 2021. 'The Use of Water as a Weapon Against Public Health in Palestine and Kashmir'. *Fordham University. Fordham Research Commons.* https://research.library.fordham.edu/cgi/viewcontent.cgi?article=1051&context=international_senior.

Haines, Valerie, H. 1984. 'A Critical Note on Langton's "The Behavioural Theory of Evolution and the Weber thesis"'. *Sociology* 18 (3): 411–412.

Hall, Stuart. 2019 [1992]. 'The West and the Rest: Discourse and Power'. In *Stuart Hall. Essential Essays Vol.2. Identity and Diaspora*, edited by David Morley, pp. 141–184. Durham, NC and London: Duke University Press.

Hall, Stuart, and Held David. 1989. 'Citizenship and Inequality. Historical and Global Perspectives'. *Social Problems* 47 (1): 1–20.

Halper, Jeff. 2009. 'Dismantling the Matrix of Control'. *MERIP (Middle East Research and Information Project.* November 9. https://merip.org/2009/09/dismantling-the-matrix-of-control/.

Halper, Jeff. 2021. 'The Palestinian Struggle with Erasure and Instrumentality'. *ICAHD (The Israeli Committee Against House Demolitions).* May 27. https://icahd.org/2021/05/27/the-palestinian-struggle-with-erasure-and-instrumentality/.

Hamayel, Mohammad. 2022. '55 Years On: Sovereignty Through Demographic Control and Erasure'. *Jerusalem 24.* June 21. https://jerusalem.24fm.ps/14704.html.

Hammad, Shatha. 2022. 'West Bank: Israeli Troops Kill Palestinian Al Jazeera Journalist During Jenin Raid'. *Middle East Eye.* May 11. https://www.middleeasteye.net/news/israel-palestine-al-jazeera-journalist-shireen-abu-akleh-shot-dead-jenin.

Hamouda, May, and Adnan Ibrahim al Hindi. 2020. 'Prevalence of Anaemia and Malnutrition Among Hospitalized Patients Attending Al-Nasser Paediatric Hospital, Gaza, Palestine'. *British Journal of Medical and Health Journal* 7 (6): 127–137.

Hansen, Peo, and Stefan Jonsson. 2014. *Eurafrica: The Untold History of European Integration and Colonialism.* London: Bloomsbury.

Hansen, Peo, and Stefan Jonsson. 2017. 'Eurafrica Incognita: The Colonial Origins of the European Union'. *History of the Present: A Journal of Critical History* 7 (1): 1–32.

Harrington, Austin. 2018. 'Review of Heinrich Popitz: Phenomena of Power. Authority, Domination, and Violence'. *Theory, Culture, & Society.* January 16. https://www.theoryculturesociety.org/review-heinrich-popitz-phenomena-power-authority-domination-violence/.

Harriot, Michael. 2023. 'Removing Black Lawmakers is Voter Suppression—and the US has Done it for Centuries'. *The Guardian.* April 12. https://www.theguardian.com/us-news/2023/apr/12/tennessee-three-justin-pearson-justin-jones.

Hartman, Chester, and David Robinson. 2003. 'Evictions: The Hidden Housing Problem'. *Housing Policy Debate* 14 (4): 461–501.

Hartmann, Eddie. 2011. *Strategien des Gegenhandelns. Zur Soziodynamik symbolischer Kämpfe um Zugehörigkeit.* Konstanz, Germany: UVK.

Harvey, David. 2003. *The New Imperialism.* New York: Oxford University Press.

Harvey, David. 2005. *A Brief History of Neoliberalism.* Oxford and New York: Oxford University Press.

Hasenfeld, Yeheskel, Jane A. Rafferty, and Mayer N. Zald. 1987. The Welfare State, Citizenship and Bureaucratic Encounters. *Annual Review of Sociology*, 13, 387–415.

Hass, Amira. 2002. 'Israel's Closure Policy: An Ineffective Strategy of Containment and Repression'. *Journal of Palestinian Studies* 31 (3): 5–20.

Hass, Amira. 2005. 'OPT: The Settlers are Gone, the Polluted Water Remains'. *OCHA.* August 25. https://reliefweb.int/report/occupied-palestinian-territory/opt-settlers-are-gone-polluted-water-remains.

Hass, Amira. 2016a. 'Think of the Gaza Strip the Next Time You Drink Tap Water'. *Haaretz,* March 22. https://www.haaretz.com/opinion/2016-03-22/ty-article/.premium/think-of-gaza-the-next-time-you-drink-tap-water/0000017f-e1bb-d7b2-a77f-e3bf7dfc0000.

Hass, Amira. 2016b. 'Israel Plans to Destroy Only Water Source of Shepherds in West Bank Village'. *Haaretz.* June 18. https://www.haaretz.com/israel-news/2016-06-18/ty-article/

israel-plans-to-destroy-only-water-source-of-shepherds-in-west-bank-village/0000017f-da72-dc0c-afff-db7bc4a70000.

Hass, Amira. 2016c. 'Israel Admits Cutting West Bank Water Supply, but Blames Palestinian Authority'. *Haaretz*. June 21. https://www.haaretz.com/israel-news/2016-06-21/ty-article/palestinians-hit-by-local-drought-after-water-cuts/0000017f-e01b-d75c-a7ff-fc9f308b0000.

Hayek v., Friedrich A. 2003. *Law, Legislation and Liberty. A New Statement of the Liberal Principles of Justice and Political Economy*. Vol. 3. London and New York: Routledge.

Hayek v., Friedrich A. 2004 [1979]. 'Wissenschaft und Sozialismus', in Friedrich A. v. Hayek, *Gesammelte Schriften in deutscher Sprache, Bd. 7*, pp. 52–62. Tübingen, Germany: Mohr Siebeck.

Hayek v., Friedrich A. 2007 [1944]. *The Road to Serfdom*. Chicago: The University of Chicago Press.

Hayes, Graeme. 2017. 'Regimes of Austerity'. *Social Movement Studies* 16 (1): 21–35.

Heaney, Steven. 2022. 'Temporary Eviction Ban Signed into Law'. *Irish Examiner*. October 29. https://www.irishexaminer.com/news/arid-40994915.html.

Hedges, Chris. 2022. 'Israel and the Rise of Jewish Fascism'. *The Chris Hedges Report*. December 12. https://chrishedges.substack.com/p/israel-and-the-rise-of-jewish-fascism?publication_id=778851&isFreemail=true.

Helleiner, Eric. 1994. 'Freeing Money: Why Have States Been More Willing to Liberalize Capital Controls Than Trade Barriers?' *Policy Science* 27 (4): 299–318.

Hennis, Wilhelm. 1987. *Max Webers Fragestellung*. Tübingen, Germany: Mohr Siebeck.

Heras-Mosteiro, Julio, Belén Sanz-Barbero, and Laura Otero-Garcia. 2015. 'Health Care Austerity Measures in Times of Crisis: The Perspectives of Primary Health Care Physicians in Madrid, Spain'. *International Journal of Health Services* 46 (2): 283–299.

Herzl, Theodor. 1946 [1896]. *The Jewish State*. https://www.jewishvirtuallibrary.org/quot-the-jewish-state-quot-theodor-herzl.

Hierro, Lola. 2018. '*La Mortalidad Entre Sin Papeles sube un 15% desde la Reforma Sanitaria*'. *El País*. April 14. https://elpais.com/elpais/2018/04/13/migrados/1523601349_887544.html.

Hills, John, Julian Le Grand and David Piachaud, eds. 2002. *Understanding Social Exclusion*. Oxford: Oxford University Press.

Holmes, Oliver. 2019. '"Israel Is Joining an Ugly Club", Says Rights Group as Director Expelled'. *The Guardian*. 25 November. https://www.theguardian.com/world/2019/nov/25/israel-expels-director-of-human-rights-watch-for-supporting-boycott.

Horton, Richard. 2022. 'Offline: WHO's Erasure of Palestinians Must Cease'. *The Lancet* 399 (10341). June 4. https://www.thelancet.com/journals/lancet/article/PIIS0140-6736(22)01010-8/fulltext.

Hoskins, Tansy, Dil Afrose Jahan, Nidia Bautista, and Juan Mayorga. 2021. 'Report says Soldiers Shot Three Dead at Myanmar Factory making US Cowboy Boots'. *openDemocracy*. June 17. https://www.opendemocracy.net/en/oureconomy/report-says-soldiers-shot-three-dead-myanmar-factory-making-us-cowboy-boots/.

Houmann Mortensen, Nikolaj, and Stefania Prandi. 2021. 'In Spain's Strawberry Fields, Migrant Women Face Sexual Abuse'. *Al Jazeera*. July 10. https://www.aljazeera.com/news/2021/7/10/in-spains-strawberry-fields-migrant-women-face-sexual-abuse.

House Rights Watch. 2019. 'A Brief Assessment of the Portuguese Framework Law for Housing'. December 3. https://www.housingrightswatch.org/content/brief-assessment-portuguese-framework-law-housing.

Hroub, Khaled. 2006. *Hamas. A Beginner's Guide*. London: Pluto Press.

HRW (Human Rights Watch) (1994). 'Torture and Ill-Treatment: Israel's Interrogation of Palestinians from the Occupied Territories'. https://www.hrw.org/reports/pdfs/i/israel/israel946.pdf.

HRW (Human Rights Watch). 2014. 'Shattered Dreams. Impact of Spain's Housing Crisis on Vulnerable Groups'. 27 May. https://www.hrw.org/report/2014/05/27/shattered-dreams/impact-spains-housing-crisis-vulnerable-groups.

HRW (Human Rights Watch). 2016. 'Human Rights in Supply Chains. A Call for a Binding Global Standard on Due Diligence'. https://www.hrw.org/sites/default/files/report_pdf/human_rights_in_supply_chains_brochure_lowres_final.pdf.

HRW (Human Rights Watch). 2019a. 'Born without Civil Rights. Israel's Use of Draconian Military Orders to Repress Palestinians in the West Bank'. December 17. https://www.hrw.org/report/2019/12/17/born-without-civil-rights/israels-use-of-draconian-military-orders-repress.

HRW (Human Rights Watch). 2019b. 'Israel Expels Human Rights Watch Director Today'. 25 November. https://www.hrw.org/news/2019/11/25/israel-expels-human-rights-watch-director-today.

HRW (Human Rights Watch). 2021. 'A Threshold Crossed. Israeli Authorities and the Crime of Apartheid and Persecution'. April 27. https://www.hrw.org/report/2021/04/27/threshold-crossed/israeli-authorities-and-crimes-apartheid-and-persecution.

HRW (Human Rights Watch). 2022a. 'Only "Instant Noodle" Unions Survive. Union Busting in Cambodia's Garment and Tourism Sectors'. November 21. https://www.hrw.org/report/2022/11/21/only-instant-noodle-unions-survive/union-busting-cambodias-garment-and-tourism.

HRW (Human Rights Watch). 2022b. 'Israel and Palestine. Events of 2021'. https://www.hrw.org/world-report/2022/country-chapters/israel-and-palestine.

HRW (Human Rights Watch). 2023. 'West Bank: Spike in Israeli Killings of Palestinian Children. End Systematic Impunity for Unlawful Lethal Force'. August 28. https://www.hrw.org/news/2023/08/28/west-bank-spike-israeli-killings-palestinian-children.

Huet, Natalie. 2020. 'COVID-19 Outbreaks in German Slaughterhouses Expose Grim Working Conditions in Meat Industry'. *Euronews*. May 13. https://www.euronews.com/2020/05/12/covid-19-outbreaks-in-german-slaughterhouses-expose-grim-working-conditions-in-meat-indust.

Hutchinson, John. 2008. 'Anatomizing Michael Mann. Review Article'. *Journal of Power* 1 (1): 87–93.

ILO (The International Labour Office). 2012. 'World of Work Report 2012: Better Jobs for a Better Economy'. https://www.ilo.org/wcmsp5/groups/public/---dgreports/---dcomm/---publ/documents/publication/wcms_179453.pdf.

ILO (The International Labour Office). 2014a. 'World Social Protection Report'. https://www.ilo.org/wcmsp5/groups/public/---dgreports/---dcomm/documents/publication/wcms_245201.pdf.

ILO (International Labor Organization). 2014b. 'Profits and Poverty: The Economics of Forced Labor'. https://www.ilo.org/global/topics/forced-labour/publications/WCMS_243391/lang--en/index.htm.

ILO (International Labour Organization), Walk Free, and International Organization for Migration (IOM). 2017. 'Global Estimates of Modern Slavery'. https://www.ilo.org/wcmsp5/groups/public/@dgreports/@dcomm/documents/publication/wcms_575479.pdf.

ILO (International Labour Organization), Walk Free, and International Organization for Migration (IOM) (2022). 'Global Estimates of Modern Slavery. Forced Labour and Forced Marriage'. https://cdn.walkfree.org/content/uploads/2022/09/12142341/GEMS-2022_Report_EN_V8.pdf.

ILO (International Labour Organization. (n.d.). 'The Rana Plaza Accident and Its Aftermath'. https://www.ilo.org/global/topics/geip/WCMS_614394/lang--en/index.htm.

IMEMC (International Middle East Media Center) News. 2019. 'How Israel's Erasure of Palestinian History Perpetuates Occupation'. August 16. https://imemc.org/article/how-israels-erasure-of-palestinian-history-perpetuates-occupation/.

International Bank for Reconstruction and Development/World Bank. 2021. 'Micronutrient Deficiencies in Palestinian Territories: Identifying the Bottlenecks of Anemia Prevention and Control and Assessing the Feasibility of an Oil Fortification Program'. https://documents1.worldbank.org/curated/en/099520002012243108/pdf/P172739016041009409f2806df69b10a8d3.pdf.

International Committee of the Red Cross (ICRC). 2004. 'Occupation and International Humanitarian Law: Questions and Answers'. August 4. https://www.icrc.org/en/doc/resources/documents/misc/634kfc.htm.

International Court of Justice 2024. 'Application of the Convention on the Prevention and Punishment of the Crime of Genocide in the Gaza Strip (South Africa v. Israel). Request for the Indication of Provisional Measures'. 26 January. https://www.icj-cij.org/sites/default/files/case-related/192/192-20240126-sum-01-00-en.pdf.

Iraqi, Amjad. 2019. 'Don't Wait for Israeli Archives to Prove What Palestinians Already Know'. *+972 Magazine*. July 7. https://www.972mag.com/dont-wait-israeli-archives-prove-palestinians-already-know/.

Issam, Farah. 2021. 'Fighting Israel's Erasure of Palestinian Identity in Jerusalem'. *The New Arab*. May 6. https://english.alaraby.co.uk/analysis/fighting-israels-erasure-palestinian-identity-jerusalem.

Issar, Siddhant. 2021. 'Theorising "Racial/Colonial Primitive Accumulation": Settler Colonialism, Slavery and Racial Capitalism'. *Race & Class* 63 (1): 23–50.

Jabotinsky, Vladimir. 2011 [1923]. 'On The Iron Wall'. In *The Origins of Israel: A Documentary History*, edited by Eran Kaplan and Derek Penslar, pp. 257–263. Madison: University of Wisconsin Press.

Jabotinsky, Vladimir. 1940. *The Jewish War Front*. London: George, Allen & Unwin.

Johnson, Kelly L. 2013. 'The New Slave Narrative: Advocacy and Human Rights in Stories of Contemporary Slavery'. *Journal of Human Rights* 12 (2): 242–258.

Joppke, Christian. 1999. *Immigration and the Nation-State: The United States, Germany and Great Britain*. Oxford and New York: Oxford University Press.

Jordan, Bill. 1996. *A Theory of Poverty & Social Exclusion*. Cambridge: Polity Press.

Journal of Palestine Studies (2009). 'A4. Amnesty International, "Troubled Waters—Palestinians Denied Fair Access to Water" (Excerpts)': 197–200. London, October 27. https://online.ucpress.edu/jps/article-abstract/39/2/197/54237/A4-Amnesty-International-Troubled-Waters?redirectedFrom=fulltext.

Journal of Palestine Studies. 2011. 'A1. United Nations Office for the Coordination of Humanitarian Affairs (OCHA), and World Food Program (WFP), Report on the Humanitarian Impact of Israeli-Imposed Restrictions on Access to Land and Sea in the Gaza Strip. Executive Summary, Jerusalem and Gaza', pp. 170–171. August. https://www.tandfonline.com/doi/abs/10.1525/jps.2011.XL.2.170.

Judt, Tony. 2003. 'Israel: The Alternative'. *The New York Review of Books*. October 23. https://www.nybooks.com/articles/2003/10/23/israel-the-alternative/.

Jundi, Aseel. 2022. 'Israel Revokes Permanent Licences at Six Palestinian Schools in Jerusalem'. *Middle East Eye*. July 29. https://www.middleeasteye.net/news/israel-withdraws-permanent-licences-palestinian-schools-jerusalem.

Kalberg, Steven. 1980. 'Max Weber's Types of Rationality: Cornerstones for the Analysis of Rationalization Processes in History'. *American Journal of Sociology* 85 (5): 1145–1179.

Kara, Siddharth. 2017. *Modern Slavery. A Global Perspective*. New York: Columbia University Press.

Karamessini, Maria, and Jill Rubery. 2014. 'The Challenge of Austerity for Equality. A Consideration of Eight European Countries in the Crisis'. *Revue de l'OFCE* 2 (133): 15–39.

Karanikolos, Marina, Philipa Mladovsky, Jonathan Cylus, Sarah Thomson, Sanjay Basu, David Stuckler, Johan P. Mackenbach, and Martin McKee. 2013. 'Financial Crisis, Austerity, and Health in Europe. *The Lancet* 381: 1323–1331. March 27. https://www.thelancet.com/journals/lancet/article/PIIS0140-6736(13)60102-6/fulltext?origen=app.

Karmi, Ghada. 2015. *Return. A Palestinian Memoir*. London: Verso.

Kasraoui, Safaa. 2023. 'Israel Defense Minister calls Palestinians "Human Animals" amid Israeli Aggression'. *Morocco World News*. October 9. https://www.moroccoworldnews.com/2023/10/358170/israel-defense-minister-calls-palestinians-human-animals-amid-israeli-aggression.

Kay, Adrian, and Owain Williams. 2009. 'Introduction: The International Political Economy of Global Health Governance'. In *Global Health Governance: Crisis, Institutions, and Political Economy*, edited by Geoff Kennedy and Owain Williams, pp. 1–23. London: Palgrave MacMillan.

Kaye, Anthony E. 2009. 'The Second Slavery: Modernity in the Nineteenth-Century South and the Atlantic World'. *The Journal of Southern History* 75 (3): 627–650.

Kelly, Annie. 2019. 'Rape and Abuse: The Price of a Job in Spain's Strawberry Industry?' *The Guardian*. April 14. https://www.theguardian.com/global-development/2019/apr/14/rape-abuse-claims-spains-strawberry-industry.

Kelly, Annie. 2021. '"Worst Fashion Wage Theft": Workers Go Hungry as Indian Suppliers to Top UK Brands Refuse to Pay Minimum Wage'. *The Guardian*. December 16. https://www.theguardian.com/global-development/2021/dec/16/worst-fashion-wage-theft-workers-go-hungry-as-indian-suppliers-to-top-uk-brands-refuse-to-pay-minimum-wage.

Kelly, Annie. 2022. 'Murder, Rape and Abuse in Asia's Factories: The True Price of Fast Fashion'. *The Guardian*. May 22. https://www.theguardian.com/global-development/2022/may/22/murder-rape-and-abuse-in-asia-factories-the-true-price-of-uk-fast-fashion-jeyasre-kathiravel.

Kennedy, Geoff. 2018. 'Austerity, Labour Market Reform and the Growth of Precarious Employment in Greece during the Eurozone Crisis'. *Global Labour Journal* 9 (3): 281–302.

Kershner, Isabel. 2019. 'Israel to Expel Human Rights Worker, Citing Anti-Boycott Law'. *The New York Times*. 5 November. https://www.nytimes.com/2019/11/05/world/middleeast/israel-human-rights-watch-bds.html.

Khalidi, Rashid. 2020. *The Hundred Years' War in Palestine*. New York: Henry Holt and Company.

Khoury, Nadim. 2020. 'Postnational Memory: Narrating the Holocaust and the Nakba'. *Philosophy & Social Criticism* 46 (1): 91–110.

Khoury, Nadim. 2021. 'Israel and Palestinian Peoplehood: The Power to Eliminate and the Power to Constitute'. *Confluences Méditerrannée* 2 (117): 61–71.

Khoury, Nadim. 2022. Memory and Forgetting at the Negotiating Table: The Case of the Israeli-Palestinian Peace Process (1993-2001)'. *FAIR Case Brief*, 7. Oslo: PRIO. https://www.prio.org/publications/13155.

King, Desmond, and Jeremy Waldron. 1988. 'Citizenship, Social Citizenship and the Defence of Welfare Provision'. *British Journal of Political Science* 18 (4): 415–443.

Kinkartz, Sabine. 2021. 'Harvest Time and COVID Restrictions'. *Deutsche Welle*. March 18. https://www.dw.com/en/seasonal-workers-flock-to-germany-for-asparagus-harvest-under-covid-restrictions/a-56919559.

Kiser, Edgar. 2006. 'Mann's Microfoundations: Addressing Neo-Weberian Dilemmas'. In *An Anatomy of Power. The Social Theory of Michael Mann*, edited by John A. Hall and Ralph Schroeder, pp. 56–70. Cambridge: Cambridge University Press.

Kitchin, Rob, Cian O'Callaghan, Mark Boyle, Justin Gleeson, and Karen Keaveney. 2012. 'Placing Neoliberalism: The Rise and Fall of Ireland's Celtic Tiger'. *Environment & Planning A. Economy and Space* 44 (6): 1302–1326.

Klawitter, Nils, Steffen Lüdke, and Hannes Schrader. 2020. 'The Systematic Exploitation of Harvest Workers in Europe'. *Der Spiegel*. July 22. https://www.spiegel.de/international/germany/cheap-and-expendible-the-systematic-exploitation-of-harvest-workers-in-europe-a-b9237b95-f212-493d-b96f-e207b9ca82d9.

Kraemer, Kenneth L., Greg Linden, and Jason Dedrick. 2011. 'Capturing Value in Global Networks: Apple's iPad and iPhone'. *PCIC Working paper*. https://docplayer.net/13426565-Capturing-value-in-global-networks-apple-s-ipad-and-iphone.html.

Kreckel, Reinhard. 1992. *Politische Soziologie der sozialen Ungleichheit*. Frankfurt a.M. and New York: Campus.

Kretzmer, David, and Yaël Ronen. 2021. *The Occupation of Justice. The Supreme Court of Israel and the Occupied Territories*. Second edition. Oxford: Oxford University Press.

Krugman, Paul. 2010. 'Myths of Austerity'. *The New York Times.* July 2. https://www.nytimes.com/2010/07/02/opinion/02krugman.html.
Krugman, Paul. 2012. *End This Depression Now!* New York: W.W. Norton.
Kupfert Heller, David. 2017. *Jabotinsky's Children. Polish Jews and the Rise of Right-wing Zionism.* Princeton, NJ: Princeton University Press.
Kymlicka, Will, and Wayne Norman. 1994. 'Return of the Citizen: A Survey of Recent Work on Citizenship'. *Ethics* 104 (2): 352–381.
Kyritsis, Penelope, Genevieve LeBaron, and Scott Nova. 2020. 'Hunger in the Apparel Supply Chain. Survey Findings on Workers' Access to Nutrition during Covid-19'. *Worker Rights Consortium.* November. https://www.workersrights.org/wp-content/uploads/2020/11/Hunger-in-the-Apparel-Supply-Chain.pdf.
Lamont, Michèle, and Virág Molnár. 2002. 'The Study of Boundaries in the Social Sciences'. *Annual Review of Sociology* 28: 167–195.
Langton, John. 1982. 'The Behavioural Theory of Evolution and the Weber Thesis'. *Sociology* 16 (3): 341–358.
Langton, John. 1984. 'Weber, Darwinism, and Sociocultural Evolution. A Reply to Haines'. *Sociology* 18 (3): 413–416.
Lawrence, Felicity, and Ella McSweeney. 2018. '"We Thought Slavery Had Gone Away": African Men Exploited on Irish Boats'. *The Guardian.* May 18. https://www.theguardian.com/world/2018/may/18/we-thought-slavery-had-gone-away-african-men-exploited-on-irish-boats.
Lawrence, Felicity, and Ella McSweeney. 2019. 'UN Experts Condemn Ireland's Migrant Fishing Workers Scheme'. *The Guardian.* February 19. https://www.theguardian.com/world/2019/feb/19/un-experts-condemn-irelands-migrant-fishing-workers-scheme.
Lawson, George. 2006. 'The Social Sources of Life, the Universe and Everything: A Conversation with Michael Mann'. *Millennium: Journal of International Studies* 34 (2): 487–508.
Lazonick, William. 2007. 'The New Normal Is "Maximizing Shareholder Value": Predatory Value Extraction, Slowing Productivity, and the Vanishing American Middle Class'. *International Journal of Political Economy* 46 (4): 217–226.
Lazonick, William, and Mary O'Sullivan. 2010. 'Maximizing Shareholder Value: A New Ideology for Corporate Governance'. *Economy & Society* 29 (1): 13–35.
LeBaron, Genevieve. 2014. 'Subcontracting Is Not Illegal. But Is It Unethical? Business Ethics, Forced Labor, and Economic Success'. *The Brown Journal of World Affairs* 20 (2): 237–249.
LeBaron, Genevieve. 2018. 'Report of Findings. The Global Business of Forced Labour'. *The University of Sheffield.* https://respect.international/wp-content/uploads/2018/06/The-Global-Business-of-Forced-Labour-Report-of-Findings-University-of-Sheffield-2018.pdf.
LeBaron, Genevieve, Remi Edwards, Tom Hunt, and Charline Sempéré. 2022. 'The Ineffectiveness of CSR: Understanding Garment Company Commitments to Living Wages in Global Supply Chains'. *New Political Economy* 27 (1): 99–115.
Lepsius. Rainer M. 1990. *Ideen, Interessen und Institutionen.* Opladen, Germany: Westdeutscher Verlag.
Liberti, Stefano. 2013. *Land Grabbing. Journeys in The New Colonialism.* London: Verso.
Lighthouse Reports. 2020. 'Invisible Workers. Modern Slavery Conditions for Migrant Workers on EU's Farms at Height of Pandemic'. https://www.lighthousereports.com/investigation/invisible-workers/.
Lighthouse Reports. 2021. 'Dark Side of Spain Slaughterhouses. Fear, Racism, and Exploitation in Publicly Subsidised Pork Companies'. October 13. https://www.lighthousereports.com/investigation/fear-and-loathing-in-spains-slaughterhouses/.
Lighthouse Reports. 2022. 'Big Meat. How Europe's Biggest Meat Companies Avoid Tax While Raking in Subsidies'. September 26. https://www.lighthousereports.nl/investigation/big-meat-fat-subsidies-thin-taxes/.
Lima, Valesca. 2020. 'The Financialization of Rental Housing: Evictions and Rent Regulation'. *Cities* 105. https://doi.org/10.1016/j.cities.2020.102787.

Lintl, Peter. 2023. 'A Private Militia for an Arsonist'. *IPS-Journal*. April 3. https://www.ips-journal.eu/topics/democracy-and-society/a-private-militia-for-an-arsonist-6620/.
Lloyd, David. 2012. 'Settler Colonialism and The State of Exception: The Example of Palestine/Israel'. *Settler Colonial Studies* 2 (1): 59–80.
Lombardo, Emanuela. 2016. 'The Spanish Gender Regime in the EU Context: Changes and Struggles in Times of Austerity'. *Gender, Work and Organization* 24 (1): 20–33.
Longobardo, Marco. 2020. 'The Duties of Occupying Powers in Relation to the Fight against Covid-19'. *EJIL: Talk!* (Blog of the European Journal of International Law). April 8. https://www.ejiltalk.org/the-duties-of-occupying-powers-in-relation-to-the-fight-against-covid-19/.
Losurdo, Domenico. 2014. *Liberalism. A Counter-History*. London: Verso.
Lowder, Sarah K., Jakob Skoet, and Terri Raney. 2016. 'The Number, Size and Distribution of Farms, Smallholder Farms and Family Farms Worldwide'. *World Development* 87: 16–29.
Lukes, Steven. 1974. *Power. A Radical View*. London and New York: Macmillan.
Lynfield, Ben. 2022. 'Israeli Court Sentences Director of Gaza Charity to 12 Years in Prison'. *The Guardian*. 30. August. https://www.theguardian.com/world/2022/aug/30/israeli-court-sentences-mohammad-el-halabi-director-of-gaza-charity-to-12-years-in-prison.
Macaron, Joe. 2019. 'Why Trump Recognised Israel's Claim on the Golan Heights'. *Al Jazeera*. March 26. https://www.aljazeera.com/opinions/2019/3/26/why-trump-recognised-israels-claim-on-the-golan-heights.
MacDonald, Keith M. 1985. 'Social Closure and Occupational Registration'. *Sociology* 19 (4): 541–556.
Mackenzie, Gavin. 1980. 'Book Review: Marxism and Class Theory: A Contemporary Critique'. *The British Journal of Sociology* 31 (4): 582–584.
MacKernan, Bethan. 2022. 'Israeli Court Finds Gaza Aid Worker Guilty of Financing Terrorism'. June 15. https://www.theguardian.com/world/2022/jun/15/israeli-court-finds-gaza-aid-worker-guilty-of-financing-terrorism.
MacKernan, Bethan, and Hazam Balousha. 2022. 'Impact of Israeli Strike in Gaza Akin to Chemical Weapons, NGO Report Finds'. *The Guardian*, May 30. https://www.theguardian.com/world/2022/may/30/impact-of-israeli-strike-in-gaza-akin-to-chemical-weapons-ngo-report-finds.
Mackert, Jürgen. 1999. *Kampf um Zugehörigkeit. Nationale Staatsbürgerschaft als Modus sozialer Schließung*. Opladen, Germany: Westdeutscher Verlag.
Mackert, Jürgen. 2004a. 'Die Theorie sozialer Schließung. Das analytische Potenzial einer Theorie mittlerer Reichweite'. In *Die Theorie sozialer Schließung. Tradition, Analysen, Perspektiven*, edited by Jürgen Mackert, pp. 9–24. Wiesbaden, Germany: Verlag für Sozialwissenschaften.
Mackert, Jürgen. 2004b. 'Reorganization and Stabilization. Social Mechanisms in Emile Durkheim's "Professional Ethics and Civic Morals". A Contribution to the Explanation of Social Processes'. *Classical Sociology* 4 (3): 311–336.
Mackert, Jürgen. 2006. *Staatsbürgerschaft. Eine Einführung*. Wiesbaden, Germany: Verlag für Sozialwissenschaften.
Mackert, Jürgen. 2010. 'Opportunitätsstrukturen und Lebenschancen'. *Berliner Journal für Soziologie* 20 (4): 401–420.
Mackert, Jürgen. 2012. 'Social Closure'. In *Oxford Bibliographies Online*, edited by Jeff Manza. https://www.oxfordbibliographies.com/display/document/obo-9780199756384/obo-9780199756384-0084.xml.
Mackert, Jürgen. 2014. 'Explaining Terrorist Behavior. Secrecy, Social Relations, and the Dynamics of Terrorism'. *Revue de Synthèse* 135 (4): 331–359.
Mackert, Jürgen. 2015. 'The Secret Society of Torturers. Explaining the Social Generation of Extremely Violent Behaviour'. *International Journal of Conflict and Violence* 9 (1): 106–120.
Mackert, Jürgen. 2017. 'Why We Need a New Political Economy of Citizenship'. In *The Transformation of Citizenship. Vol. 1. Political Economy*, edited by Jürgen Mackert and Bryan S. Turner, pp. 99–117. London and New York: Routledge.

Mackert, Jürgen. 2021. 'Social Life as Collective Struggle. Closure Theory and the Problem of Solidarity'. *Sozialpolitik.CH*. https://www.sozialpolitik.ch/article/view/3742.

Mackert, Jürgen. 2022. 'Introduction. A "Master-Race Democracy". Myths and Lies of Western Liberal Civilization'. In *The Condition of Democracy. Vol. 3. Postcolonial and Settler Colonial Contexts*, edited by Jürgen Mackert, Hannah Wolf, and Bryan S. Turner, pp. 1–13. London and New York: Routledge.

Mackert, Jürgen, and Bryan S. Turner. 2017a. 'Introduction: A Political Economy of Citizenship'. In *The Transformation of Citizenship. Vol. 1. Political Economy*, edited by Jürgen Mackert and Bryan S. Turner, pp. 1–12. London and New York: Routledge.

Mackert, Jürgen, and Bryan S. Turner. 2017b. 'Introduction: Citizenship and Its Boundaries. In *The Transformation of Citizenship. Vol. 2. Boundaries of Inclusion and Exclusion*, edited by Jürgen Mackert and Bryan S. Turner, pp. 1–14. London and New York: Routledge.

Mackert, Jürgen, and Ilan Pappe. 2024a. 'Das Paradigma des Siedlerkolonialismus. Eine Leerstelle in der deutschen Soziologie und Geschichtswissenschaft'. In *Siedlerkolonialismus. Grundlagentexte des Paradigmas und aktuelle Analysen*, edited by Jürgen Mackert and Ilan Pappe, pp. 11–54. Baden-Baden: Nomos.

Mackert, Jürgen, and Ilan Pappe eds. 2024b. *Siedlerkolonialismus. Grundlagentexte des Paradigmas und aktuelle Analysen*. Baden-Baden: Nomos.

MacLean, Nancy. 2017. *Democracy in Chains. The Deep History of the Radical Right's Stealth Plan for America*. Melbourne and London: Scribe.

MacLean, Nancy. 2022. 'Enchaining Democracy: The Now-Transnational Project of the US Corporate Libertarian Right'. In *The Condition of Democracy. Vol. 1. Neoliberal Politics and Sociological Perspectives* edited by Jürgen Mackert, Hannah Wolf and Bryan S. Turner, pp. 19–36. London: Routledge.

Macpherson, C. B. 2012 [1977]. *The Life and Times of Liberal Democracy*. Oxford: Oxford University Press.

Madrid No Frills. 2021. 'Understanding Evictions in Spain'. June 14. https://madridnofrills.com/understanding-evictions/.

Mair, Peter. 2013. *Ruling the Void. The Hollowing of Western Democracy*. London: Verso.

Makdisi, Saree. 2010. 'The Architecture of Erasure'. *Critical Inquiry* 36 (3): 519–559.

Malone, Andrew R. 2004. 'Water Now: The Impact of Israel's Security Fence on Palestinian Water Rights and Agriculture in the West Bank'. *Case Western Reserve Journal of International Law* 36 (2): 639–671.

Mamdani, Mahmood. 2001. *When Victims Become Killers. Colonialism, Nativism, and the Genocide in Rwanda*. Princeton: Princeton University Press.

Mamdani, Mahmood. 2015. 'Settler Colonialism: Then and Now'. *Critical Inquiry* 41 (3): 596–614.

Mamdani, Mahmood. 2020. *Neither Settler nor Native. The Making and Unmaking of Permanent Minorities*. Cambridge and London: The Belknap Press of Harvard University Press.

Mann, Michael. 1986. *The Sources of Social Power. Vol. 1: A History of Power from the Beginning to AD 1760*. Cambridge: Cambridge University Press.

Mann, Michael. 2004. *Fascists*. Cambridge: Cambridge University Press.

Mann, Michael. 2005. *The Dark Side of Democracy. Explaining Ethnic Cleansing*. Cambridge: Cambridge University Press.

Mann, Michael. 2006. 'The Sources of Social Power Revisited: A Response to Criticism'. In *An Anatomy of Power. The Social Theory of Michael Mann*, edited by John A. Hall and Ralph Schroeder, pp. 343–396. Cambridge: Cambridge University Press.

Mann, Michael. 2013. *The Sources of Social Power. Vol. 4: Globalizations, 1945-2011*. Cambridge: Cambridge University Press.

Manza, Jeff. 1992. 'Classes, Status Groups, and Social Closure. A Critique of Neo-Weberian Social Theory'. *Current Perspectives in Social Theory* 12: 275–302.

Marshall, Thomas H. 1950. 'Citizenship and Social Class'. In T. H. Marshall, *Citizenship and Social Class and Other Essays*, pp. 1–85. Cambridge: Cambridge University Press.

Marx, Karl. 2015 [1867]. *Capital. A Critique of Political Economy*. Vol. I. https://www.marxists.org/archive/marx/works/download/pdf/Capital-Volume-I.pdf.

Marx, Karl. 2010 [1885]. *Capital. A Critique of Political Economy*. Vol. II. https://www.marxists.org/archive/marx/works/1885-c2/index.htm.

Marx, Karl. 1977 [1939-1941]. *Grundrisse. Foundations of the Critique of Political Economy*. Penguin Books in association with New Left Review. https://www.marxists.org/archive/marx/works/download/pdf/grundrisse.pdf.

Masalha, Nur. 1992. *The Expulsion of the Palestinians. The Concept of 'Transfer' in Zionist Political Thought, 1882-1948*. Beirut, Ramallah, and Washington: Institute for Palestine Studies.

Masalha, Nur. 2008. 'Remembering the Palestinian Nakba. Commemoration, Oral History, and Narratives of Memory'. *Holy Land Studies* 7 (2): 123–156.

Masalha, Nur. 2012. *The Palestine Nakba: Decolonising History, Narrating the Subaltern, Reclaiming Memory*. London: ZED Books.

Masalha, Nur. 2015. 'Settler-Colonialism, Memoricide and Indigenous Toponymic Memory: The Appropriation of Palestinian Place Names'. *The Journal of Holy Land and Palestine Studies* 14 (1): 3–57.

Masalha, Nur. 2018. *Palestine. A Four Thousand Year History*. London: ZED Books.

Mavelli, Luca. 2022. *Neoliberal Citizenship. Sacred Markets, Sacrificial Lives*. Oxford: Oxford University Press.

Mbembe, Achille. 2003. 'Necropolitics'. *Public Culture* 15 (1): 11–40.

Mbembe, Achille. 2016. 'Society of Enmity'. *Radical Philosophy* 200 (November/December). https://www.radicalphilosophyarchive.com/issue-files/rp200_article_mbembe_society_of_enmity.pdf.

Médecins Sans Frontières. 2021. '"For One Year No One Came Here" to Provide Medical Care in the West Bank'. January 5. https://www.msf.org/west-bank-palestine-communities-face-healthcare-access-challenges.

Medical Aid for Palestinians. 2021. 'How Restrictions on Gaza Are a Matter of Life and Death for Breast Cancer Patients'. October 20. https://www.map.org.uk/news/archive/post/1302-how-restrictions-on-gaza-are-a-matter-of-life-and-death-for-breast-cancer-patients.

Meiskins Wood, Ellen. 2017 [1999]. *The Origin of Capitalism. A Longer View*. London: Verso.

Memmi, Albert. 1991 [1965]. *The Colonizer and the Colonized*. Boston: Beacon Press.

MEMO (Middle East Monitor). 2018. 'Israel Declares It Is Above the Law'. September 21. https://www.middleeastmonitor.com/20180921-israel-declares-it-is-above-the-law/.

MEMO (Middle East Monitor). 2020. 'Gaza Farmers: "Israel Destroyed All of Our Crops"'. January 16. https://www.middleeastmonitor.com/20200116-gaza-farmers-israel-destroyed-all-of-our-crops/.

MEMO (Middle East Monitor). 2021. 'Israel "Defence" Forces to Destroy Palestinian Farms in Occupied West Bank'. September 6. https://www.middleeastmonitor.com/20210906-israel-defence-forces-to-destroy-palestinian-farms-in-occupied-west-bank/.

MEMO (Middle East Monitor). 2022a. 'Israel Soldiers Demolish Water Well in West Bank'. May 31. https://www.middleeastmonitor.com/20220531-israel-soldiers-demolish-water-well-in-west-bank/.

MEMO (Middle East Monitor). 2022b. 'Israel Settlers Uproot Hundreds of Olive Trees in West Bank'. January 22. https://www.middleeastmonitor.com/20220122-israel-settlers-uproot-hundreds-of-olive-trees-in-west-bank/.

MEMO (Middle East Monitor). 2022c. 'UN Condemns Israel for Making 2022 the Deadliest Year for Palestinians'. December 16. https://www.middleeastmonitor.com/20221216-un-condemns-israel-for-making-2022-the-deadliest-year-for-palestinians/.

Merk, Jeroen. 2011. 'Production Beyond the Horizon of Consumption: Spatial Fixes and Anti-Sweatshop Struggles in the Global Athletic Footwear Industry'. *Global Society* 25 (1): 73–95.

Merton, Robert K. 1968 [1957]. 'On Sociological Theories of the Middle Range'. In Robert K. Merton, *Social Theory and Social Structure*, pp. 39–72. 1968 enlarged edition. New York and London: The Free Press.

Merton, Robert K. 1995. 'Opportunity Structure: The Emergence, Diffusion, and Differentiation of a Sociological Concept'. In *The Legacy of Anomie Theory. Advances in Criminological Theory. Vol. 6*, edited by Freda Adler and William S. Laufer, pp. 3–78. New Brunswick: Transaction Publishers.

Metz, Caroline. 2016. 'Turning Debts into a Market: The Wonderful Promises of Securitization'. *The Broker*. August 15. https://www.thebrokeronline.eu/turning-debts-into-a-market-the-wonderful-promises-of-securitization/.

Metz, Caroline. 2020. 'The Financialisation of Distressed Debts in Europe'. *Finance Watch*. June 19. https://www.finance-watch.org/the-financialisation-of-distressed-debts-in-europe/.

Mezzadri, Alessandra. 2017. *The Sweatshop Regime: Labouring Bodies, Exploitation and Garments Made in India*. Cambridge: Cambridge University Press.

Middle East Eye. 2021. 'Israel: Documents Detail 1948 Nakba Massacres of Palestinians. *Middle East Eye*. December 10. https://www.middleeasteye.net/news/israel-palestine-documents-detail-massacres-nakba.

Middle East Eye. 2022. 'Israel: Top Doctor Says "Arab Womb" Is Overwhelming Country with High Birthrate'. October 24. https://www.middleeasteye.net/news/israel-doctor-arab-womb-overwhelming-country-high-birthrate.

Middle East Eye. 2023. 'Israeli Official Calls for Burying Alive "Subhuman" Palestinian Civilians'. December 8. https://www.middleeasteye.net/live-blog/live-blog-update/israeli-municipality-official-calls-burying-alive-subhuman-palestinian.

Michéa, Jean-Claude. 2009. *The Realm of Lesser Evil*. Cambridge and Malden, MA: Polity.

Mill, John Stuart. 2001 [1859]. *On Liberty*. Kitchener: Ontario: Batoche Books Limited.

Mills, Charles W. 1997. *The Racial Contract*. Ithaca, NY: Cornell University Press.

Mirowski, Philip. 2013. *Never Let a Serious Crisis Go to Waste: How Neo-Liberalism Survived the Financial Meltdown*. New York: Verso/New Left Books.

Mladovsky, Philipa, Divya Srivastava, Jonathan Cylus, Marina Karanikolos, Tamás Evetovits, Sarah Thomson, and Martin McKee. 2012. 'Health Policy Responses to the Financial Crisis in Europe'. *Eurohealth* 18 (1): 3–6.

Montgomery, Johanna, and Daniela Tepe-Belfrage. 2016. 'Caring for Debts: How the Household Economy Exposes the Limits of Financialisation. *Critical Sociology* 43 (4-5): 653–668.

Morgensen, Scott Lauria. 2011. 'The Biopolitics of Settler Colonialism: Right Here, Right Now'. *Settler Colonial Studies* 1 (1): 52–76.

Morrow, Raymond A. 1990. 'Review Essay/Note de Lecture: Social Closure: The Theory of Monopolization and Exclusion. By Raymond Murphy'. *The Canadian Journal of Sociology/Cahiers canadiens der sociologie* 15 (4): 477–482.

Moses, A. Dirk 2017. 'Empire, Resistance, and Security: International Law and the Transformative Occupation of Palestine'. *Humanity: An International Journal of Human Rights, Humanitarianism, and Development* 8 (2): 379–409.

Mosley, Layna. 2017. 'Workers' Rights in Global Value Chains: Possibilities for Protection and for Peril'. *New Political Economy* 22 (2): 153–158.

Muaddi, Quassam. 2023. '95 Palestinians Killed in Occupied West Bank by Israel Since Beginning of 2023: Health Ministry'. *The New Arab*. April 4. https://www.newarab.com/news/95-palestinians-killed-israel-first-quarter-2023.

Mualem, Mazal. 2023. 'Israel's Ben-Gvir's Push for a National Guard Could Give Him Own Militia'. *El-Monitor*. April 12. https://www.al-monitor.com/originals/2023/04/israels-ben-gvirs-push-national-guard-could-give-him-own-militia#ixzz7ztJQl9nT.

Müller, Hans-Peter. 2007. *Max Weber. Eine Einführung in sein Werk*. Köln, Weimar, und Wien: Böhlau Verlag UTB.

Müller, Hans-Peter. 2014. 'Rationalität, Rationalisierung, Rationalismus'. In *Max Weber Handbuch. Leben-Werk-Wirkung*, edited by Hans-Peter Müller and Steffen Sigmund, pp. 108–113. Stuttgart und Weimar, Germany: Verlag J.B. Metzler.

Müller, Pascale, and Stefania Prandi. 2018. 'Rape in the Fields'. *Correctiv*. April 30. https://correctiv.org/en/top-stories/2018/04/30/rape-in-the-fields/.

Muhareb, Rania, Elizabeth Rghebi, Susan Power, and Pearce Clancy. 2022. 'Persecution of Palestinian Civil Society: Epistemic Violence, Silencing, and the Apartheid Framework'. *Current Issues in Depth*. No. 9. Washington DC: Institute for Palestine Studies.

Murphy, Raymond. 1984. 'The Structure of Closure: A Critique and Development of the Theories of Weber, Collins and Parkin'. *British Journal of Sociology* 35 (4): 547–567.

Murhpy, Raymond. 1985. 'Exploitation or Exclusion?' *Sociology* 19 (2): 225–243.

Murphy, Raymond. 1986. 'Weberian Closure Theory: A Contribution to the Ongoing Assessment'. *British Journal of Sociology* 37 (1): 21–41.

Murphy, Raymond. 1988. *Social Closure. The Theory of Monopolization and Exclusion*. Oxford: Clarendon Press.

Murphy, Richard. 2019. 'The European Tax Gap'. *Socialists and Democrats*. https://www.socialistsanddemocrats.eu/publications/european-tax-gap.

Nabulsi, Karma. 2006. 'From Generation to Generation'. *The Electronic Intifada*. May 15. https://electronicintifada.net/content/generation-generation/5966.

Najib, Mohammed. 2021. 'Palestine Runs Dry: "Our Water They Steal and Sell to Us"'. *Al Jazeera*. July 15. https://www.aljazeera.com/news/2021/7/15/water-war-palestinians-demand-more-water-access-from-israel.

Najjar, Farah. 2022. 'The Palestinian Flag: A Target for "Erasure" by Israeli Forces'. *Al Jazeera*. May 13. https://www.aljazeera.com/news/2022/5/13/why-is-israel-afraid-of-the-palestinian-flag.

National Low Income Housing Commission. 2022. 'New Research Finds 2.7 Million Households Receive Eviction Filings Annually'. May 23. https://nlihc.org/resource/new-research-finds-27-million-households-receive-eviction-filings-annually.

Navarro, Vicente. 2020. 'The Consequences of Neoliberalism in the Current Pandemic'. *International Journal of Health Services* 50 (3): 271–275.

Neckel, Sighard. 1995. Politische Ethnizität. Das Beispiel der Vereinigten Staaten. In *Politische Institutionen im Wandel. Special Issue of the Kölner Zeitschrift für Soziologie und Sozialpsychologie*, edited by Birgitta Nedelmann, pp. 217–236. Opladen, Germany: Westdeutscher Verlag.

Neuwirth, Gertrude. 1969. 'A Weberian Outline of a Theory of Community: Its Application to the "Dark Ghetto"'. *British Journal of Sociology* 20 (1): 148–163.

NHRC (National Human Rights Committee). 2008. 'UN Officials Warn of Malnutrition Threat as Closure of Gaza Border Continues'. January 30. https://www.un.org/unispal/document/auto-insert-208155/.

Nolan, Justine, and Gregory Bott. 2018. 'Global Supply Chains and Human Rights: Spotlight on Forced Labour and Modern Slasvery Practices'. *Australian Journal of Human Rights* 24 (1): 44–69.

Norris, Michelle, and Tony Fahey. 2011. 'From Asset Based Welfare to Welfare Housing? The Changing Function of Social Housing in Ireland'. *Housing Studies* 26 (3): 459–469.

Nova, Scott. 2006. 'WRC Factory Assessment Update'. *Worker Rights Consortium*. December 19. https://www.workersrights.org/communications-to-affiliates/wrc-factory-assessment-update/.

Nova, Scott, and Chris Wegemer (2016). 'Outsourcing Horror: Why Apparel Workers Are Still Dying, One Hundred Years after Triangle Shirtwaist'. In *Achieving Workers' Rights in the Global Economy*, edited by Richard P. Appelbaum and Nelson Lichtenstein, pp. 17–31. Ithaca, New York: Cornell University Press.

Nova, Scott and, Vincent DeLaurentis. 2019. 'Illegitimate Criminal Conviction of Union Leaders in Cambodia'. *Worker Rights Consortium*. March 7. https://www.workersrights.org/communications-to-affiliates/illegitimate-criminal-conviction-of-union-leaders-in-cambodia/.

Nova, Scott, and Ineke Zeldenrust. 2020. 'Who Will Bail Out the Workers That Make Our Clothes?' White Paper. *Worker Rights Consortium*. https://www.workersrights.org/wp-content/uploads/2020/03/Who-Will-Bail-Out-the-Workers-March-2020.pdf.

Noy, Orly. 2022. 'Israel: Ben-Gvir's Threats to Deport Palestinians Are No Joke'. *Middle East Eye*. August 18. https://www.middleeasteye.net/opinion/israel-ben-gvir-threats-deport-palestinians-no-joke.

Observatory of Economic, Social and Cultural Rights and Platform of Mortgage Victims. 2013. 'Housing Emergency in Spain: The Crisis of Foreclosures and Evictions from a Human Rights Perspective'. December 2013. http://observatoridesc.org/sites/default/files/2013-housing-emergency-spain-observatory-desc.pdf.

OCHA (United Nations Office for the Coordination of Humanitarian Affairs). 2002. 'Israeli Forces Commit Massacre in Jenin Refugee Camp'. *Reliefweb*. April 8. https://reliefweb.int/report/israel/israeli-forces-commit-massacre-jenin-refugee-camp.

OCHA (United Nations Office for the Coordination of Humanitarian Affairs). 2012. 'The Humanitarian Impact of the Takeover of Palestinian Water Springs by Israeli Settlers'. March. https://www.ochaopt.org/sites/default/files/ocha_opt_springs_factSheet_march_2012_english.pdf.

OCHA (United Nations Office for the Coordination of Humanitarian Affairs). 2020a. 'Water in Gaza: Scarce, Polluted and Mostly Unfit for Use'. *Reliefweb*. August 21. https://reliefweb.int/report/occupied-palestinian-territory/water-gaza-scarce-polluted-and-mostly-unfit-use.

OCHA (United Nations Office for the Coordination of Humanitarian Affairs). 2020b. 'Incursion of Israeli Bulldozers into the Strip Destroys Crop'. *Reliefweb*. October 18. https://reliefweb.int/report/occupied-palestinian-territory/incursion-israeli-bulldozers-strip-destroys-crops.

OCHA (United Nations Office for the Coordination of Humanitarian Affairs). 2021a. 'The Gaza Bantustan—Israeli Apartheid in the Gaza Strip'. *Reliefweb*. November 29. https://reliefweb.int/report/occupied-palestinian-territory/gaza-bantustan-israeli-aparth eid-gaza-strip.

OCHA (United Nations Office for the Coordination of Humanitarian Affairs). 2021b. 'Palestinians Strive to Access Water in the Jordan Valley'. June 22. https://www.ochaopt.org/content/palestinians-strive-access-water-jordan-valley.

OCHA (United Nations Office for the Coordination of Humanitarian Affairs). 2022a. 'Gaza Strip. The Humanitarian Impact of 15 Years of the Blockade'. June. https://reliefweb.int/report/occupied-palestinian-territory/gaza-strip-humanitarian-impact-15-years-blockade-june-2022-enarhe.

OCHA (United Nations Office for the Coordination of Humanitarian Affairs). 2022b. 'Data on Casualties'. https://www.ochaopt.org/data/casualties.

OCHA (United Nations Office for the Coordination of Humanitarian Affairs). 2022c. '2022 Becomes the Deadliest Year for Palestinian Children in the West Bank in over 15 Years'. November 23. https://reliefweb.int/report/occupied-palestinian-territory/2022-becomes-deadliest-year-palestinian-children-west-bank-over-15-years.

OCHA (United Nations Office for the Coordination of Humanitarian Affairs). 2022d. 'Protection of Civilians Report. 6-19 December 2022'. December 22. https://www.ochaopt.org/poc/6-19-december-2022.

OCHA (United Nations Office for the Coordination of Humanitarian Affairs). 2023a. 'Euro-Med Monitor to UN: Recognise Israel's Actions in Gaza as Genocide'. *Reliefweb*. November 22. https://reliefweb.int/report/occupied-palestinian-territory/euro-med-monitor-un-recogn ise-israels-actions-gaza-genocide.

OCHA (United Nations Office for the Coordination of Humanitarian Affairs). 2023b. Hostilities in the Gaza Strip and Israel. Flash Update #48 [EN/AR/HE]. November 24. https://reliefweb.int/report/occupied-palestinian-territory/hostilities-gaza-strip-and-isr ael-flash-update-48-enarhe.

OCHA/WFP (United Nations Office for the Coordination of Humanitarian Affairs/World Food Programme). 2010. 'Between the Fence and a Hard Place. The Humanitarian Impact of Israeli-Imposed Restriction on Access to Land and Sea in the Gaza Strip'. August. https://www.un.org/unispal/document/auto-insert-196584/.

O'Dwyer, Muireann. 2018. 'Making Sense of Austerity: The Gendered Ideas of European Economic Policy'. *Comparative European Politics* 16 (5): 745–761.

OECD (Organization for Economic Co-operation and Development) (n.d.-a). 'Global Value Chains (GVCs)'. https://www.oecd.org/sti/ind/global-value-chains.htm.

OECD (Organization for Economic Co-operation and Development). n.d.-b). 'Global Value Chains and Trade'. https://www.oecd.org/trade/topics/global-value-chains-and-trade/.

OECD (Organization for Economic Co-operation and Development). (n.d.-c). 'Global Value Chains and Agriculture'. https://www.oecd.org/agriculture/topics/global-value-chains-and-agriculture/.

OECD/European Observatory on Health Systems and Policies. 2017. 'State of Health in the EU. Spain Country Health Profile 2017'. https://doi.org/10.1787/9789264283565-en.

Offe, Claus. 1972. 'Political Authority and Class Structure—An Analysis of Late Capitalist Societies'. *International Journal of Sociology* 2 (1): 73–108.

OHCHR (Office of the High Commissioner for Human Rights). 2013. 'Report on Austerity Measures and Social and Economic Rights'. https://www.ohchr.org/sites/default/files/E-2013-82_en.pdf.

OHCHR (Office of the High Commissioner for Human Rights). 2019. 'Portugal: UN Expert Welcomes New Law Protecting the Right to Housing'. October 1. https://www.ohchr.org/en/press-releases/2019/09/portugal-un-expert-welcomes-new-law-protecting-right-housing.

OHCHR (Office of the High Commissioner for Human Rights). 2020. 'A/HRC/44/60: Report on the Situation of Human Rights in the Occupied Palestinian Territory, including East Jerusalem, with a Focus on Collective Punishment'. December 22. https://www.ohchr.org/en/documents/country-reports/ahrc4460-report-situation-human-rights-occupied-palestinian-territory.

OHCHR (Office of the High Commissioner for Human Rights). 2021. 'Report of the Special Rapporteur on Contemporary Forms of Slavery, Including its Causes and Consequences. Report on the Nexus between Displacement and Contemporary Forms of Slavery'. https://www.ohchr.org/en/documents/thematic-reports/ahrc4852-report-nexus-between-displacement-and-contemporary-forms.

OHCHR (Office of the High Commissioner for Human Rights). 2022a. 'Report of the Special Rapporteur on the Situation of Human Rights in the Occupied Palestinian Territories: Israel Has Imposed Upon Palestine an Apartheid Reality in a Post-Apartheid World'. March 25. https://www.ohchr.org/en/press-releases/2022/03/special-rapporteur-situation-human-rights-occupied-palestinian-territories.

OHCHR (Office of the High Commissioner for Human Rights). 2022b. 'Report of the Special Rapporteur on the Situation of Human Rights in the Palestinian Territories Occupied since 1967'. March 25. https://www.ohchr.org/en/special-procedures/sr-palestine.

OHCHR (Office of the High Commissioner for Human Rights). 2022c. 'Israel: UN Experts Condemn Record Year of Israeli Violence in the Occupied West Bank'. December 15. https://www.ohchr.org/en/press-releases/2022/12/israel-un-experts-condemn-record-year-israeli-violence-occupied-west-bank#:~:text=At%20least%20two%20Palestinians%20were,occupied%20West%20Bank%20in%202022.

OHCHR (Office of the High Commissioner for Human Rights). 2023, 'UN Experts Condemn Israeli Decision to Expel Omar Shakir of Human Rights Watch'. November 8. https://www.ohchr.org/en/press-releases/2019/11/un-experts-condemn-israeli-decision-expel-omar-shakir-human-rights-watch.

Olson, Mancur. 1965. *The Logic of Collective Action. Public Goods and the Theory of Groups.* Cambridge: Harvard University Press.

OMCT (World Organisation Against Torture). 2019. 'It's Now (Even More) Official: Torture is Legal in Israel'. March 21. https://www.omct.org/en/resources/blog/its-now-even-more-official-torture-is-legal-in-israel.

Ortiz, Isabel, Matthew Cummins, Jeronim Capaldo, and Kalaivani Karunaneth. 2015. 'The Decade of Adjustment: A Review of Austerity Trends 2010-2020 in 187 Countries'. *Initiative* for Policy Dialogue, the South Centre and International Labour Organization. Working Paper. https://www.ilo.org/wcmsp5/groups/public/---ed_protect/---soc_sec/documents/publication/wcms_431730.pdf.

Oxfam. 2013. 'The True Cost of Austerity and Inequality. Spain Case Study'. https://oxfamilibrary.openrepository.com/bitstream/handle/10546/301384/cs-true-cost-austerity-inequality-spain-120913-en.pdf;jsessionid=0A9527FC8179FA4A554CEF318AF5106E?sequence=111.

Oxfam. 2018. 'Ripe for Change: Ending Human Suffering in Supermarket Supply Chains'. June. https://oi-files-d8-prod.s3.eu-west-2.amazonaws.com/s3fs-public/file_attachments/cr-ripe-for-change-supermarket-supply-chains-210618-en.pdf.

Oxfam. 2019. 'Human-Rights Abuses Commonplace in Farms Linked to Major European Supermarkets, Oxfam Finds'. October 19. https://www.oxfam.org/en/press-releases/human-rights-abuses-commonplace-farms-linked-major-european-supermarkets-oxfam-finds.

Oxfam. (n.d.). '"What She Makes" About the Campaign'. https://www.oxfam.org.au/what-she-makes/about-the-campaign/.

Palestinian Center for Human Rights (P.C.H.R.). 2018. 'Israeli Supreme Court Issues Decision to Demolish Khan Al-Ahmar Bedouin Community, East of Jerusalem'. June 5. https://pchrgaza.org/en/israeli-supreme-court-issues-decision-to-demolish-khan-al-ahmar-bedouin-community-east-of-jerusalem/.

Palestinian Center for Human Rights (P.C.H.R.) and B'Tselem. 2021. 'Unable and Unwilling. Israel's Whitewashed Investigations of the Great March of Return Protests'. https://pchrgaza.org/en/wp-content/uploads/2021/12/202112_unwilling_and_unable_eng.pdf.

Palumbo, Letizia, and Alexandra Corrado. 2020. 'Are Agri-Food Workers Only Exploited in Southern Europe?' European University Institute. MPC Blog. November 4. https://blogs.eui.eu/migrationpolicycentre/are-agri-food-workers-only-exploited-in-southern-europe/.

Papadopoulos, Theodoros, and Antonios Roumpakis. 2018. 'Rattling Europe's Ordoliberal "Iron Cage": The Contestation of Austerity in Southern Europe'. *Critical Social Policy* 38 (3): 505–526.

Pappe, Ilan. 2006. *The Ethnic Cleansing of Palestine*. Oxford: Oneworld Publications.

Pappe, Ilan. 2017. *Ten Myths About Israel*. London: Verso.

Pappe, Ilan. 2020. 'An Indicative Archive: Salvaging Nakba Documents'. *Journal of Palestine Studies* 49 (3): 22–40.

Parizot, Cédric. 2009. 'Après le Mur: Les Représentations Israéliennes de la Séparation avec les Palestiniens'. *Cultures & Conflits* 73 (1): 53–72.

Parker, Brad. 2023. 'Israel's Slaughter of Palestinian Children Must End'. *Al Jazeera*. November 19. https://www.aljazeera.com/opinions/2023/11/19/israels-slaughter-of-palestinian-children-must-end.

Parkin, Frank. 1974. 'Strategies of Social Closure in Class Formation'. In *The Social Analysis of Class Structure*, edited by Frank Parkin, pp. 1–18. London: Tavistock.

Parkin, Frank. 1979. *Marxism and Class Theory. A Bourgeois Critique*. New York: Columbia University Press.

Parkin, Frank. 1980. 'Reply to Giddens'. *Theory and Society* 9 (6): 891–894.

Patel, Yumna. 2018. '"Agricultural Terrorism": Palestinian Crops Face Destruction by Israeli Settlers'. *Middle East Eye*. June 3. https://www.middleeasteye.net/news/agricultural-terrorism-palestinian-crops-face-destruction-israeli-settlers.

Paton, Kirsteen, and Vickie Cooper. 2016. 'It's the State, Stupid: 21st Gentrification and State-Led Evictions'. *Sociological Research Online* 21 (3). https://doi.org/10.5153/sro.4064.

Patterson, Orlando. 1982. *Slavery and Social Death. A Comparative Study*. Cambridge and London: Harvard University Press.

Patterson, Orlando. 2007. 'Review of William H. Sewell, Jr., Logics of History'. *American Journal of Sociology* 112 (4): 1287–1290.

Patterson, Orlando, and Xiaolin Zhuo. 2018. 'Modern Trafficking, Slavery, and Other Forms of Servitude'. *Annual Review of Sociology* 44: 407–439.

Peck, Jamie. 2012. 'Austerity Urbanism. American Cities Under Extreme Economy'. *City* 16 (6): 626–655.

People's World. 2009. 'Signs of Worsening Malnutrition among Gazan Children'. April 22. https://peoplesworld.org/article/signs-of-worsening-malnutrition-among-gazan-children/.

Perez, Sofia A., and Manos Matsaganis. 2018. 'The Political Economy of Austerity in Southern Europe'. *New Political Economy* 32 (2): 192–207.

Phelan, Ciara. 2022. 'Cabinet Approves One-Off Eviction Ban from November to March'. *Irish Examiner*. October 18. https://www.irishexaminer.com/news/politics/arid-40986191.html.

Phillips, Nicola. 2017. 'Power and Inequality in the Global Political Economy'. *International Affairs* 93 (2): 429–444.

Piterberg, Gabriel. 2001. 'Erasures'. *New Left Review* 10 (July-August): 31–46.

Plaut, Martin. 2017. 'Europe's Crackdown on African Immigration Is Hitting Vulnerable Refugees'. *The Guardian*. January 26. https://www.theguardian.com/commentisfree/2017/jan/26/europe-crackdown-africa-immigration-vulnerable-refugees-sudan-eritrea.

Poinssot, Amélie. 2020. '*Exploitation de la main-d'œuvre immigrée: un système cautionné par la PAC*'. *Mediapart*. July 17. https://www.mediapart.fr/journal/international/170720/exploitation-de-la-main-d-oeuvre-immigree-un-systeme-cautionne-par-la-pac.

Polanyi, Karl. 2001 [1944]. *The Great Transformation. The Political and Economic Origins of Our Time*. Boston: Beacon.

Ponsford, Matthew. 2020. 'The Hypocrisy of Europe's Big Corporate Landlords'. City Monitor. August 28. https://citymonitor.ai/environment/hypocrisy-europes-big-corporate-landlords-5239.

Popitz, Heinrich. 1968. *Prozesse der Machtbildung*. Tübingen, Germany: J.C.B. Mohr (Paul Siebeck).

Popitz, Heinrich. 1986. *Phänomene der Macht*. Tübingen, Germany: J.C.B. Mohr (Paul Siebeck).

Popitz, Heinrich. 2017. *Phenomena of Power. Authority, Domination, and Violence*. Translated by Gianfranco Poggi. New York: Columbia University Press.

Power, Susan. 2021. 'The Legal Architecture of Apartheid'. *Al-Haq*. April 2. https://aardi.org/2021/04/02/the-legal-architecture-of-apartheid-by-dr-susan-powers-al-haq/.

Preston, John. 2019. *Grenfell Tower. Preparedness, Race and Disaster Capitalism*. Cham: Palgrave Macmillan.

Rafferty, Anthony. 2014. 'Gender Equality and the Impact of Recession and Austerity in the UK'. *Revue de l'OFCE* 2 (133): 335–361.

Raja, Kanaga. 2017. 'United Nations: Austerity-Related Labour Reforms Harmful to Working People'. *Social Watch*. https://www.socialwatch.org/node/17571.

Razali, Nurul Ain. 2022. 'Undernutrition, Stunting Rife: Dire State of Diets among Palestinian Kids Underlined by New Study'. *FoodNavigator-Asia*. May 30. https://www.foodnavigator-asia.com/Article/2022/05/31/acute-undernutrition-stunting-rife-among-kids-under-five-in-gaza-strip-palestine-study.

REDER (Red De Denuncia y Resistencia). 2012. '*La Sociedad Civil frente la Exclusión Sanitaria. Defender nuestra Sanidad*'. https://www.reder162012.org/images/InformeOct2017/REDERsep17ESP.pdf.

Redfish. 2021. 'Spain's Housing Crisis: Banks, Scams and Evictions'. July 2. https://redfish.media/spains-housing-crisis-banks-scams-and-evictions/.

Reemtsma, Jan Philipp. 2012 [2009]. *Trust and Violence. An Essay on a Modern Relationship*. Princeton and Oxford: Princeton University Press.

Reuters. 2012. 'Israel Gaza Blockade Study Calculated Palestinians' Calories'. October 17. https://www.reuters.com/article/us-palestinians-israel-gaza-idUSBRE89G0NM20121017.

Reuters. 2023. 'UN Committee Voices Concern about Rising Israeli Hate Speech against Palestinians'. October 27. https://www.reuters.com/world/un-committee-voices-concern-about-rising-israeli-hate-speech-against-2023-10-27/.

Rex, John. 1979. 'Towards an Understanding of Society. *New Society* 50: 200–202.

Rifkin, Mark. 2014. 'The Frontier as (Movable) Space of Exception'. *Settler Colonial Studies* 4 (2): 176–180.
Right to the City Alliance. 2014. 'Renting from Wall Street: Blackstone's Invitation Homes in Los Angeles and Riverside'. https://www.saje.net/wp-content/uploads/2021/04/SAJE_RentingfromWallstreet_2014.pdf.
Rodinson, Maxime. 2014 [1973]. *Israel. A Colonial-Settler State?* New York et. al: Pathfinder.
Rodney, Walter. 2018 [1971]. *How Europe Underdeveloped Africa.* London: Verso.
Rodriguez-Modroño, Paula, Tindara Addabbo, and Lina Galvez. 2013. 'The Impact of European Austerity Policy of Women's Work in Southern Europe'. Modena: *DEMB* Working papers. Series 18. https://www.researchgate.net/publication/277770949_The_impact_of_European_Union_austerity_policy_on_women%27s_work_in_Southern_Europe.
Rodrik, Dani. 1996. *Has Globalization Gone Too Far?* New York: Columbia University Press.
Rolnik, Raquel. 2013. 'Late Neoliberalism: The Financialization of Homeownership and Housing Rights'. *International Journal of Urban and Regional Research* 37 (3): 1058–1066.
Roscigno, Vincent J., Sherry Mong, Reginald Byron, and Griff Tester. 2007. 'Age Discrimination, Social Closure and Employment'. *Social Forces* 86 (1): 313–343.
Roscigno, Vincent J, Lisette M. Garcia, and Donna Bobbitt-Zeher. 2018. 'Social Closure and Processes of Race/Sex Employment Discrimination'. *The Annals of the American Academy of Political and Social Science* 609 (1): 16–48.
Ros Robollo, Rocio. 2021. '"If You Report Abuse, You Lose Your Job": Spain's Labourers Fight Back'. *Open Democracy.* July 6. https://www.opendemocracy.net/en/5050/if-you-report-abuse-you-lose-your-job-spains-labourers-fight-back/.
Roth, Guenther. 1980. 'Book Review: Marxism and Class Theory: A Bourgeois Critique'. *Contemporary Sociology* 9 (2): 307.
Rubin, April. 2021. '"We Don't Want More Death; We Don't Want More Sadness": Man Who Yearned to Become Parent Died of Heat Working to Provide Oregonians with Food, Shade'. *The Oregonian/Oregon live.* July 3. https://www.oregonlive.com/business/2021/07/we-dont-want-more-death-we-dont-want-more-sadness-man-who-yearned-to-become-parent-died-of-heat-working-to-provide-oregonians-with-food-shade.html.
Ruggie, J. G. 1982. 'International Regime, Transactions, and Change: Embedded Liberalism in the Postwar Economic Order'. *International Organization* 36 (2): 379–415.
Runciman, W. G. 2001. 'Was Max Weber a Selectionist in Spite of Himself?' *Journal for Classical Sociology* 1 (1): 13–32.
Russell Tribunal on Palestine. 2013. 'Findings of the Final Session of the Russell Tribunal on Palestine'. Brussels. 16–17 March. http://www.russelltribunalonpalestine.com/en/full-findings-of-the-final-session-en.html.
Sa'di, Ahmad H. 2014. *Thorough Surveillance: The Genesis of Israeli Policies of Population Management, Surveillance and Political Control towards the Palestinian Minority.* Manchester, UK: Manchester University Press.
Said, Edward W. 1978. *Orientalism.* New York: Pantheon Books.
Said, Edward W. 1992 [1979]. *The Question of Palestine.* New York: Vintage Books.
Sainato, Michael. 2021. '"We're Not Animals, We're Human Beings": US Farm Workers Labor in Deadly Heat with few Protections'. *The Guardian.* July 16. https://www.theguardian.com/environment/2021/jul/16/farmworkers-labor-deadly-heat-few-protections.
Salmon, Keith. 2017. 'A Decade of Lost Growth: Economic Policy in Spain through the Great Recession'. *South European Society and Politics* 22 (2): 239–260.
Sarkar, Mahua ed. 2018. *Work Out of Place.* Berlin: De Gruyter.
Sassen, Saskia. 2014a. *Expulsions: Brutality and Complexity in the Global Economy.* Cambridge and London: Harvard University Press.
Sassen, Saskia. 2014b. 'Finance as Capability: Good, Bad, Dangerous'. http://arcade.stanford.edu/occasion/finance-capability-good-bad-dangerous.
Saunders, Peter. 1993. 'Citizenship in a Liberal Society'. In *Citizenship and Social Theory,* edited by Bryan S. Turner, pp. 57–90. London, Newbury Park, and New Delhi: Sage.

Savills World Research Forum. 2016. 'What Price the World?'. www.savills.co.uk/research_articles/188297/198669-0.
Scahill, Jeremy.2018. 'Blacklisted Academic Norman Finkelstein on Gaza, "the World's Largest Concentration Camp"'. *The Intercept.* May 20. https://theintercept.com/2018/05/20/norman-finkelstein-gaza-iran-israel-jerusalem-embassy/.
Schluchter, Wolfgang. 2005. *Handlung, Ordnung und Kultur.* Tübingen, Germany: Mohr Siebeck.
Schluchter, Wolfgang. 2008. 'Ideen, Interessen, Institutionen. Schlüsselbegriffe einer an Max Weber orientierten Soziologie'. In *Soziale Konstellation und historische Perspektive. Festschrift für Rainer M. Lepsius,* edited by Steffen Sigmund, pp. 57–80. Wiesbaden, Germany: Verlag für Sozialwissenschaften.
Schmid, Michael. 1998. 'Individuelles Handeln und strukturelle Selektion: Eine Rekonstruktion des Erklärungsprogramms von Robert K. Merton'. In Michael Schmid, *Soziales Handeln und strukturelle Selektion. Beiträge zur Theorie sozialer Systeme,* pp. 71–89. Opladen, Germany: Westdeutscher Verlag.
Schmidt, Max Oliver 2021. *Seenotrettung und Kirchenasyl. Organisationale Schließungskämpfe im Feld der europäischen Asylverwaltung.* Wiesbaden, Germany: Verlag für Sozialwissenschaften.
Schmidt, Vivien A. 1995. 'The New World Order, Incorporated: The Rise of Business and the Decline of the Nation-State'. *Daedalus* 124 (2): 75–106.
Schmidt-Wellenburg, Christian. 2020. 'Kampf/Konflikt'. In *Max Weber Handbuch. Leben-Werk-Wirkung,* edited by Hans-Peter Müller and Steffen Sigmund, pp. 97–98. Stuttgart: J.B. Metzler.
Schmidtke, Oliver. 2008. 'National Closure and Beyond'. In *Of States, Rights, and Social Closure. Governing Migration and Citizenship,* edited by Oliver Schmidtke and Saime Ozcurumez, pp. 91–110, New York: Palgrave Macmillan.
Schmidtke, Oliver, and Saime Ozcurumez, eds. 2008. *Of States, Rights, and Social Closure. Governing Migration and Citizenship.* New York: Palgrave Macmillan.
Schönig, Barbara, and Sebastian Schipper, eds. 2016. *Urban Austerity. Impact of the Global Financial Crisis on Cities in Europe.* Edition Gegenstand und Raum. Berlin: Theater der Zeit.
Schroeder, Ralph. 2006. 'Introduction: The IEMP Model and its Critics. In *An Anatomy of Power. The Social Theory of Michael Mann,* edited by John A. Hall and Ralph Schroeder, pp. 1–16. Cambridge: Cambridge University Press.
Schwartz, Herman M., and Leonard Seabrooke. 2009. 'Varieties of Residential Capitalism in the International Political Economy: Old Welfare States and the New Politics of Housing'. In *The Politics of Housing Booms and Busts,* edited by Herman M. Schwartz and Leonard Seabrooke, pp. 1–27. International Political Economy Series. London: Palgrave Macmillan UK.
Segal, Rafi, David Tartakover, and Eyal Weizman, eds. 2003. *A Civilian Occupation. The Politics of Israeli Architecture.* London: Babel and Verso.
Segnana, Maria Luigia, and Paola Villa. 2015. 'Women and Austerity in Italy'. *ex æquo* 32: 15–32.
Selwyn, Benjamin, Bettina Misiolek, and Artemisa Ijarja. 2020. 'Making a Global Poverty Chain: Export Footwear Production and Gendered Labour Exploitation in Eastern and Central Europe'. *Review of International Political Economy* 27 (2): 377–403.
Sewell, William H. Jr. 1996. 'Historical Events as Transformations of Structures'. *Theory and Society* 25 (6): 841–881.
Sewell, William H. Jr. 2005. *Logics of History. Social Theory and Social Transformation.* Chicago: Chicago University Press.
Seymour, Richard. 2014. *Against Austerity: How We Can Fix the Crisis They Made.* London: Pluto Press.
Shaveh, Emek, and Yesh Din. 2017. 'Appropriating the Past: Israel's Archaeological Practices in the West Bank'. December 26. https://emekshaveh.org/en/appropriating-the-past-israels-archaeological-practices-in-the-west-bank/.

Sheety, Roger. 2015. 'Stealing Palestine: A Study of Historical and Cultural Theft'. *Middle East Eye*. July 14. https://www.middleeasteye.net/big-story/stealing-palestine-study-historical-and-cultural-theft.

Shelter. 2022. 'Bailiff Evictions Rise by 39% in just Three Months as Private Renters Run Out of Options'. *Shelter* August 11. https://england.shelter.org.uk/media/press_release/bailiff_evictions_rise_by_39_per_cent_in_just_three_months_as_private_renters_run_out_of_options.

Siedentop, Larry. 2015. *Inventing the Individual. The Origins of Western Liberalism*. London: Penguin.

Sigmund, Steffen. 2014. 'Ideen und Interessen'. In *Max Weber Handbuch. Leben-Werk-Wirkung*, edited by Hans-Peter Müller and Steffen Sigmund pp. 66–69. Stuttgart und Weimar, Germany: Verlag J.B. Metzler.

Silver, Hilary. 1994. 'Social Exclusion and Social Solidarity'. Three Paradigms'. *International Labour Review* 5-6 (133): 531–578.

Silver, Hilary. 2007a. 'Social Exclusion'. In *The Blackwell Encyclopedia of Sociology*. Vol. IX, edited by George Ritzer. pp. 4411–4413. Malden, Oxford, and Victoria: Blackwell Publishing.

Silver, Hilary. 2007b. 'The Process of Social Exclusion: The Dynamics of an Evolving Concept'. *CPRC Working Paper 95*. Chronic Poverty Research Centre. Brown University. https://papers.ssrn.com/sol3/papers.cfm?abstract_id=1629282.

Silver, Hilary. 2019. 'Social Exclusion'. In *The Wiley Blackwell Encyclopedia of Urban and Regional Studies*, edited by Anthony Orum. Hoboken: Wiley. DOI: 10.1002/9781118568446.eurs0486.

Silver, Hilary, and S. M. Miller. 2003. 'Social Exclusion. The European Approach to Social Disadvantage'. *Indicators* 2 (2): 5–21.

Sirdah, Mahmoud Mohammed, Ayed Yaghi, and Abdallah R. Yaghi. 2013. 'Iron Deficiency Anemia among Kindergarten Children Living in the Marginalized Areas of Gaza Strip, Palestine'. *Brazilian Journal of Hematology and Hemotherapy* 36 (2): 132–138. https://www.ncbi.nlm.nih.gov/pmc/articles/PMC4005512/.

Slavery and its Aftermath. 2022. 'The Third Slavery Project'. https://lsa.umich.edu/social-solutions/history-and-slavery/third-slavery.html.

Smith, Michael D. 2017. 'Counting the Dead: Estimating the Loss of Life in the Indigenous Holocaust, 1492–Present'. *Proceedings of the Twelfth Native American Symposium, 2017*. Southeastern Oklahoma State University. https://www.se.edu/native-american/wp-content/uploads/sites/49/2019/09/A-NAS-2017-Proceedings-Smith.pdf.

Smith, Michael D. 2023. *Endless Holocausts. Mass Death in the History of the United States Empire*. New York: Monthly Review Press.

Soederberg, Susanne. 2018. 'Evictions. A Global Capitalist Phenomenon'. *Development and Change* 49 (2): 286–301.

Sørensen, Aage B. 1996. 'The Structural Basis of Social Inequality'. *American Journal of Sociology* 101 (5): 1333–1365.

Solow, Barbara L. 1985. 'Caribbean Slavery and British Growth: The Eric Williams Hypothesis'. *Journal of Development Economics* 17 (1-2): 99–115.

Solow, Barbara L. 1987. 'Capitalism and Slavery in the Exceedingly Long Run'. *Journal of Interdisciplinary History* 17 (4): 711–737.

Somers, Margaret R. 2008. *Genealogies of Citizenship. Markets, Statelessness and the Right to Have Rights*. Cambridge: Cambridge University Press.

Special Rapporteur on the Human Rights of Migrants, the Special Rapporteur on Contemporary Forms of Racism, Racial Discrimination, Xenophobia and Related Intolerance, the Special Rapporteur on Contemporary Forms of Slavery, Including Its Causes and Consequences, and the Special Rapporteur on Trafficking in Persons, Especially Women and Children. 2019. https://spcommreports.ohchr.org/TMResultsBase/DownLoadPublicCommunicationFile?gId=24331.

Spivak, Gayatri Chakravorty. 2010 [1985]. *Can the Subaltern Speak? Reflections on the History of an Idea*, edited by Rosalind Morris. New York: Columbia University Press.

Stannard, David E. 1992. *American Holocaust: The Conquest of the New World*. New York: Oxford University Press.
Stanziani, Alessandro. 2018. *Labor on the Fringes of Empire. Voice, Exit and the Law*. New York: Springer.
Stein, Ben. 2006. 'In Class Warfare, Guess Which Class Is Winning'. *New York Times*. November 26. https://www.nytimes.com/2006/11/26/business/yourmoney/26every.html.
Steinert, Heinz. 2003. '*Die kurze Geschichte und offene Zukunft eines Begriffs: Soziale Ausschließung*'. *Berliner Journal für Soziologie* 13 (2): 275–285.
Steinert, Heinz. 2004. '*Schließung und Ausschließung. Eine Typologie der Schließungen und ihrer Folgen*'. In *Die Theorie sozialer Schließung. Tradition, Analysen, Perspektiven*, edited by Jürgen Mackert, pp. 193–212. Wiesbaden, Germany: Verlag für Sozialwissenschaften.
Steinmetz, George. 2008a. *The Devil's Handwriting: Precoloniality and the German Colonial State in Qingdao, Samoa, and Southwest Africa*. Chicago: The University of Chicago Press.
Steinmetz, George. 2008b. 'Sewell's Logics of History as a Framework for an Integrated Social Science'. *Social Science History* 32 (4): 535–553.
Steinmetz, George. 2023. *The Colonial Origins of Modern Social Thought*. Princeton: Princeton University Press.
Stiglitz, Joseph E. 2002. *Globalization and Its Discontents*. New York: W. W. Norton.
Stiglitz, Joseph E. 2014. 'Europe's Austerity Zombies'. *Project Syndicate*. September 26. https://www.project-syndicate.org/commentary/joseph-e--stiglitz-wonders-why-eu-leaders-are-nursing-a-dead-theory.
Stinchcombe, Arthur L. 1975. 'Merton's Theory of Social Structure'. In *The Idea of Social Structure. Papers in Honor of Robert K. Merton*, edited by Lewis A. Coser, pp. 11–33. New York: Harcourt Brace Jovanovich.
Stinchcombe, Arthur L. 1990. 'Social Structure in the Work of Robert Merton'. In *Robert K. Merton. Consensus and Controversy*, edited by John Clark, Celia Modgil, and Sohan Modgil, pp. 81–93. London: The Falmer Press.
Stopford, John, and Susan Strange. 1991. *Rival States, Rival Firms: Competition for World Market Shares*. Cambridge: Cambridge University Press.
Stop the Wall Campaign. 2020. 'Factsheet: Cutting the Lifeline—Stop the Annexation of Palestinian Water'. June 26. https://stopthewall.org/wp-content/uploads/2020/11/water-factsheet-final.pdf.
Strange, Susan. 1995. 'The Defective State'. *Daedalus* 124 (2): 55–74.
Strange, Susan. 1996. *The Retreat of the State: The Diffusion of Power in the World Economy*. Cambridge: Cambridge University Press.
Streeck, Wolfgang. 2014. *Buying Time: The Delayed Crisis of Democratic Capitalism*. London: Verso.
Strohschneider, Tom, and Kathrin Gerlof. 2019. 'Slaves in Europe's Fields. On the Exploitation of Migrants during the Harvest and Grassroots Union Resistance in Italy, Austria, and Spain'. *Rosa-Luxemburg-Foundation*. https://www.rosalux.de/en/publication/id/41102/slaves-in-europes-fields.
Stuckler, David, and Sanjay Basu. 2013. *The Body Economic. Why Austerity Kills*. New York: Basic Books.
Suárez, Thomas. 2017. *State of Terror. How Terrorism Created Modern Israel*. Northampton: Olive Branch Press.
Super, David A. 2019. 'Will We Learn from the Greece Austerity Debacle?' *The Hill*. July 14. https://thehill.com/opinion/finance/452939-will-we-learn-from-the-greece-austerity-debacle.
Suwandi, Intan. 2019. *Value Chains. The New Economic Imperialism*. New York: Monthly Review Press.
Swartz, David. 1990. 'Review Essay: Social Closure: The Theory of Monopolization and Exclusion. By Raymond Murphy'. *American Journal of Sociology* 96 (2): 480–482.

Swedberg, Richard. 2014. *The Art of Social Theory*. Princeton. Princeton University Press.
Szczepański, Marcin. 2013. 'Austerity, Labour Market and International Treaties'. *Briefing. European Parliamentary Research Service*. https://www.europarl.europa.eu/meetdocs/2009_2014/documents/empl/dv/austerity_labour_market_int_treaties_/austerity_labour_market_int_treaties_en.pdf.
Tamimi, Tamara. 2019. 'Israeli Appropriation of Palestinian Cultural Heritage in Jerusalem'. MIFTAH (The Palestinian Initiative for the Promotion of Global Dialogue and Democracy). July 1. https://www.un.org/unispal/wp-content/uploads/2019/06/MIFTAH_Submission_1July2019.pdf.
Tanous, Osama. 2022. 'Israel and the Palestinian "Womb": Racism by Numbers Rears Its Ugly Head'. *Middle East Eye*. October 25. https://www.middleeasteye.net/opinion/israel-palestinian-birthrate-racism-numbers.
Tartir, Alaa, Tariq Dana, and Timothy Seidel, eds. 2021. *Political Economy of Palestine. Critical, Interdisciplinary, and Decolonial Perspectives*. London: Palgrave Macmillan.
Távora, Isabel, and Paula Rodríguez-Modroño. 2018. 'The Impact of the Crisis and Asterity on Low Educated Women: The Cases of Spain and Portugal'. *Gender, Work & Orgnization* 25 (6): 621–636.
Tchoubar, Poline. 2021. 'US Heatwave Pushes Agricultural Workers to Work at Night: "Even So, It's Horrible"'. *France 24*. July 5. https://observers.france24.com/en/americas/20210706-heatwave-united-states-washington-agricultural-workers.
Temperley, Howard. 1977. 'Capitalism, Slavery and Ideology'. *Past & Present* 75 (1): 94–118.
Tenbruck, Friedrich. 1975. 'Das Werk Max Webers'. *Kölner Zeitschrift für Soziologie und Sozialpsychologie* 27 (4): 663–702.
Thatcher, Margaret. 1987. 'Epitaph for the Eighties? "There Is No Such Thing as Society"'. *The Sunday Times*. October 31. https://briandeer.com/social/thatcher-society.htm.
The Associated Press. 2012. 'Documents on Calorie Figures in Gaza Blockade Stirs Dispute'. *The New York Times*. October 17. https://www.nytimes.com/2012/10/18/world/middleast/israel-counted-calories-needed-for-gazans-in-blockade.html.
The Guardian. 2021. 'Third Night of Protests in Poland after Abortion Ban Takes Effect'. January 29. https://www.theguardian.com/world/2021/jan/29/third-night-of-protests-in-poland-after-abortion-ban-takes-effect.
The Guardian. 2022. 'Israel Deports Palestinian-French Human Rights Lawyer Salah Hamouri'. December 18. https://www.theguardian.com/world/2022/dec/18/israel-deports-palestinian-french-human-rights-lawyer-salah-hamouri.
The Guardian 2023. 'Israeli Government Approves Far-Right Minister's Proposal of National Guard'. April 2. https://www.theguardian.com/world/2023/apr/02/israel-government-approves-national-guard-itamar-ben-gvir.
The Irish Times. 2002. '1 in 5 Palestinian Children Malnourished—Study'. August 6. https://www.irishtimes.com/news/1-in-5-palestinian-children-malnourished-study-1.1090975.
The Lancet. 2018. 'Austerity in Spain: Time to Loosen the Grip'. Vol. 391. https://www.thelancet.com/journals/lancet/article/PIIS0140-6736(18)30983-8/fulltext.
The Lancet. 2020. 'Research in the Occupied Palestinian Territory'. Vol. 399, Supplement 1: pp. S1–S44. https://www.sciencedirect.com/journal/the-lancet/vol/399/suppl/S1.
The Lancet. 2024. 'Counting the Dead in Gaza: Difficult but Essential'. July 5. Vol. 404, Issue 10449: pp. 237–238. https://www.thelancet.com/journals/lancet/article/PIIS0140-6736(24)01169-3/fulltext.
The New Arab. 2018. 'The Gaza Diet: How Israel's Calorie Control Left Palestinians Food-Insecure'. September 10. https://english.alaraby.co.uk/opinion/gaza-diet-how-israels-calorie-control-left-palestinians-hungry.
The New Arab. 2021. 'Israeli Settlers Destroy Olive Trees in Palestinian Community'. December 9. https://english.alaraby.co.uk/news/israeli-settlers-destroy-palestinian-olive-trees-hebron.

The New Arab. 2023. 'Israeli Extreme-Right Minister Ben Gvir to Arm Civilians with Assault Rifles'. October 12. https://www.newarab.com/news/israels-ben-gvir-arm-civilians-assault-rifles.

Theodore, Nik, Jamie Peck, and Neil Brenner. 2011. 'Neoliberal Urbanism: Cities and the Rule of Markets'. In *The New Blackwell Companion to the City*, edited by Gary Bridge and Sophie Watson, pp. 15–25. Oxford: Wiley.

Thiemann, Matthias. 2016. 'Capital Markets Union and the Mirage of Resilience'. *The Broker*. June 2. https://www.thebrokeronline.eu/capital-markets-union-and-the-mirage-of-resilience-d54/.

Thompson, Graeme. 2007. 'Responsibility and Neo-Liberalism'. *Open Democracy*. July 31. https://www.opendemocracy.net/en/responsibility_and_neo_liberalism/.

Thornton, Russell. 1987. *American Indian Holocaust and Survival: A Population History Since 1492*. Norman: University of Oklahoma Press.

Tilly, Charles. 1998. *Durable Inequality*. Berkeley, Los Angeles, and London: University of California Press.

Tilly, Charles. 1999. 'The Trouble with Stories'. In *The Social Worlds of Higher Education. Handbook for Teaching in a New Century*, edited by Bernice A. Pescosolido and Ronald Aminzade, pp. 256–270. Thousand Oaks, London, and New Delhi: Pine Forge Press.

Tilly, Charles. 2000. 'Processes and Mechanisms of Democratization'. *Sociological Theory* 8 (1): 1–16.

Tilly, Charles. 2003a. 'Political Identities in Changing Polities'. *Social Research* 70 (2): 605–620.

Tilly, Charles. 2003b. *The Politics of Collective Violence*. Cambridge: Cambridge University Press.

Tilly, Charles. 2005a. 'Terror as Strategy and Relational Process'. *International Journal of Comparative Sociology* 46 (1-2): 11–32.

Tilly, Charles. 2005b. *Identities, Boundaries and Social Ties*. Boulder: Paradigm Publishers.

Tilly, Charles. 2008. 'Method and Explanation'. In Charles Tilly, *Explaining Social Processes*, pp. 2–23. Boulder: Paradigm Publishers.

Tilly Charles, and Robert E. Goodin. 2006. 'It Depends'. In *The Oxford Handbook of Contextual Political Analysis*, edited by Robert E. Goodin and Charles Tilly, pp. 7–32. Oxford and New York: Oxford University Press.

Todaro, Rosalba, and Sonia Yáñez eds. 2004. *El tabajo se transforma. Relaciones de propducción y relaciones de género*. Santiago de Chile: Cetro de Estudios de la Mujer.

Tomich, Dale. 2004 [1988]. 'The "Second Slavery": Bonded Labor and the Transformations of the Nineteenth-Century World Economy'. In Dale Tomich, *Through the Prism of Slavery: Labour, Capital, and World Economy*, pp. 56–71. Lanham: Rowman & Littlefield.

Tomich, Dale. 2018. 'The Second Slavery and World Capitalism: A Perspective for Historical Inquiry'. *International Review of Social History* 63 (3): 477–501.

Tomich, Dale, and Michael Zeuske. 2008. 'Introduction. The Second Slavery. Mass Slavery, World-Economy, and Comparative Microhistories'. *Review* 31 (2): 91–100.

Toussaint, Eric, and Eva Betavatzi. 2021. 'How Private and Public Debt Crisis Exacerbate Housing Problems in the EU'. *CADTM* (Committee for the Abolition of Illegitimate Debt). June 9. https://www.cadtm.org/spip.php?page=imprimer&id_article=19934.

Trichet, Jean-Claude. 2010. 'Stimulate No More—It Is Now Time for All to Tighten'. *Financial Times*. July 22. https://www.ft.com/content/1b3ae97e-95c6-11df-b5ad-00144feab49a.

Tsigga, Maria, and Maria G. Grammatikopoulou. 2012. 'Assessing the Silent Epidemic of Malnutrition in Palestinian Preschool Children'. *Journal of Epidemiology and Global Health*, 2 (4): 181–191.

Tsing, Anna. 2009. 'Supply Chains and the Human Condition'. *Rethinking Marxism* 21 (2): 148–176.

UAWC (Union of Agricultural Workers Committees). (n.d.). 'About Us'. https://www.uawc-pal.org/UAWCAbout.php.

Uddin, Rayhan. 2021. '"Dumping Ground": Israel Blasted for Bid to Swap Expiring Vaccines with PA'. *Middle East Eye*. June 19. https://www.middleeasteye.net/news/israel-palestine-covid-vaccine-swap-expired-cynical-dumping-ground.

UNCTAD (United Nations Conference on Trade and Development). 2011. 'On the Brink: Fiscal Austerity Threatens a Global Recession'. *Policy Brief No. 24*. December. https://unctad.org/system/files/official-document/presspb2011d12_en.pdf.

UNESCO (United Nations Educational, Scientific and Cultural Organization). 2016. 'Occupied Palestine'. Executive Board. Two Hundredth Session. Programme and External Relations Commission (PX). October 12. https://unesdoc.unesco.org/ark:/48223/pf0000246215.

UN HABITAT and OHCHR. 2014. 'Forced Evictions'. *Fact Sheet No. 25/Rev.1*. https://www.ohchr.org/sites/default/files/Documents/Publications/FS25.Rev.1.pdf.

United Nations. 2013. 'Austerity Measures in Greece undermining Human Rights'. May 1. https://news.un.org/en/story/2013/05/438592-austerity-measures-greece-undermining-human-rights-says-un-independent-expert.

United Nations. 2017. 'Report of The Special Rapporteur on Adequate Housing as a Component of the Right to an Adequate Standard of Living, and on the Right to Non-Discrimination in this Context'. *General Assembly. Human Rights Council*. January 18. https://digitallibrary.un.org/record/861179?ln=en.

United Nations. 2021. 'Allocation of Water Resources in the Occupied Palestinian Territory, Including East Jerusalem'. *Report of the United Nations High Commissioner for Human Rights and Reports of the Office of the High Commissioner and the Secretary-General*. https://www.un.org/unispal/document/the-allocation-of-water-resources-in-the-opt-including-east-jerusalem-report-of-the-united-nations-high-commissioner-for-human-rights-advance-unedited-version-a-hrc-48-43/.

United Nations. 2023a. 'Palestine: Preventing a Genocide in Gaza and a New "Nakba"'. November 21. https://unric.org/en/palestine-preventing-a-genocide-in-gaza-and-a-new-nakba/.

United Nations. 2023b. 'Gaza: UN Experts Call on International Community to Prevent Genocide against the Palestinian People'. November 16. https://www.ohchr.org/en/press-releases/2023/11/gaza-un-experts-call-international-community-prevent-genocide-against.

United Nations Economic and Social Council. 2003. 'General Comment No. 15 (2002). The Right to Water'. (Arts. 11 and 12 of the International Covenant on Economic, Social and Cultural Rights). E/C.12/2002/11. https://digitallibrary.un.org/record/486454?ln=en.

UN Food and Agriculture Organisation. 2008. 'The State of Food and Agriculture'. Rome: *FAO*. https://www.fao.org/3/i0100e/i0100e.pdf.

UN Human Rights Council 2024. 'Anatomy of a Genocide - Report of the Special Rapporteur on the Situation of Human Rights in the Palestinian Territories Occupied Since 1967, Francesca Albanese (A/HRC/55/73) (Advance unedited version)'. March 25. https://reliefweb.int/report/occupied-palestinian-territory/anatomy-genocide-report-special-rapporteur-situation-human-rights-palestinian-territories-occupied-1967-francesca-albanese-ahrc5573-advance-unedited-version.

UNRWA (United Nations Relief and Works Agency for Palestine Refugees in the Near East). (n.d.). 'Where We Work'. https://www.unrwa.org/where-we-work/gaza-strip.

UPWC (Union of Palestinian Women's Committees). (n.d.). 'About Us'. https://upwc.org.ps/.

Urbina, Ian. 2021. 'The Secret Prisons that keep Migrants out of Europe'. *The New Yorker*. November 28. https://www.newyorker.com/magazine/2021/12/06/the-secretive-libyan-prisons-that-keep-migrants-out-of-europe.

Vallelly, Neil. 2020. 'The Self-Help Myth'. *New Internationalist*. June 2. https://newint.org/features/2020/04/07/feature.

Van de Werfhorst, Herman G. 2011. 'Skills, Positional Good or Social Closure? The Role of Education across Structural-Institutional Labour Market Settings'. *Journal of Education and Work* 24 (5): 521–548.

Vaughan-Whitehead, Daniel, and Luis Pinedo Caro. 2017. 'Purchasing Practices and Working Conditions in Global Supply Chains: Global Survey Results'. Geneva: *ILO*. https://www.ilo.org/wcmsp5/groups/public/---ed_protect/---protrav/---travail/documents/publication/wcms_556336.pdf.

Veracini, Lorenzo. 2011. 'Introducing *Settler Colonial Studies*'. *Settler Colonial Studies* 1 (1): 1–12.

Veracini, Lorenzo. 2013. 'The other Shift: Settler Colonialism, Israel, and the Occupation'. *Journal of Palestine Studies* XLII (2): 26–42.

Veracini, Lorenzo. 2014. 'Understanding Colonialism and Settler Colonialism as Distinct Formations'. *Interventions* 16 (5): 615–633.

Veracini, Lorenzo. 2015. *The Settler Colonial Project*. New York: Springer.

Veracini, Lorenzo. 2021. *The World Turned Inside Out. Settler Colonialism as a Political Idea*. London: Verso.

Viens, A. M. 2019. 'Neo-Liberalism, Austerity and the Political Determinants of Health'. *Health Care Analysis* 27 (3): 147–152.

Visualizing Palestine 2015. 'Shrinking Palestine Expanding Israel https://s3.amazonaws.com/VP2/visuals/en/high_resolution/708289912c4716e6a976a640559265be.pdf?1634248159.

Viterbo, Hedi. 2021. *Problematizing Law, Rights, and Childhood in Israel/Palestine*. Cambridge: Cambridge University Press.

Voce, Antonio, Leyland Cecco, and Chris Michael. 2021. '"Cultural Genocide". The Shameful History of Canada's Residential Schools—Mapped'. *The Guardian*. September 6. https://www.theguardian.com/world/ng-interactive/2021/sep/06/canada-residential-schools-indigenous-children-cultural-genocide-map.

Vogl, Joseph. 2014. 'The Sovereignty Effect: Market and Power in the Economic Regime'. *Qui parle: Critical Humanities and Social Sciences* 23 (1): 125–155.

Vogl, Joseph. 2015. *The Ascendancy of Finance*. Cambridge and Malden, MA: Polity Press.

Vohra, Anchal. 2022. 'Why Israel is afraid of Palestinian Funerals'. *Foreign Policy*. May 25. https://foreignpolicy.com/2022/05/25/shireen-abu-akleh-funeral-israeli-palestinian-conflict-journalist-killing/.

Wacquant, Loïc J.D. 1996. 'The Rise of Advanced Marginality. Notes on Its Nature and Implications'. *Acta Sociologica* 39 (2): 121–140.

WAFA (Palestine News & Info Agency). 2021. 'Ministry of Culture Details Israel's Attack on Gaza's Cultural Institutions'. May 19. https://english.wafa.ps/Pages/Details/124612.

WAFA (Palestinian News & Info Agency). 2022. 'Palestinians Condemn Israeli Decision to Deport Palestinian French Human Rights Defender Hammouri'. December 1. https://english.wafa.ps/Pages/Details/132154.

WAFA (Palestinian News & Info Agency). 2023. '112 Palestinians Killed by Israel in the West Bank in 2023: UN'. June 4. https://english.wafa.ps/Pages/Details/136145.

Walk Free. 2019. 'A Living Wage: A Crucial Tool in the Fight against Modern Slavery'. *Opinion*. March 9. https://www.walkfree.org/news/2019/a-living-wage-a-crucial-tool-in-the-fight-against-modern-slavery/.

Walk Free. 2023. 'Global Slavery Index'. *Walk Free*. https://www.walkfree.org/global-slavery-index/.

Walks, Alan, and Susanne Soederberg. 2021. 'The New Urban Displacements? Finance-Led Capitalism, Austerity, and Rental Housing Dynamics'. *Urban Geography* 42 (5): 571–582.

Ware Barrientos, Stephanie. 2013. '"Labour Chains": Analysing the Role of Labour Contractors in Global Production Networks'. *The Journal of Developmental Studies* 49 (8): 1058–1071.

Watkins, Kevin. 2019. 'The Tragedy of Gaza's Children'. *Project Syndicate*. August 8. https://www.project-syndicate.org/commentary/gaza-children-humanitarian-emergency-by-kevin-watkins-2019-08?barrier=accesspaylog.

Watts, Meriel, Tanya Lee, and Heather Aidy. 2016. 'Pesticides and Agroecology in the Occupied West Bank'. APN-PANAP Mission. https://www.apnature.org/sites/default/files/2019-12/pestiagroeco-palest-web.pdf.

Weber, Max. 1946. 'The Social Psychology of World Religions'. In *From Max Weber*, edited by H. H. Gerth and C. W. Mills, pp. 267–301. New York: Oxford University Press.

Weber, Max. 1949. 'Objectivity in Social Science and Social Policy'. In *The Methodology of the Social Sciences*. Translated and edited by Edward A. Shils and Henry A. Finch, pp. 50–112. Glencoe, UK: The Free Press.

Weber, Max (1978) [1922]. *Economy and Society. An Outline of Interpretive Sociology*. Edited by Guenther Roth and Claus Wittich. Berkeley, Los Angeles, and London: University of California Press.

Weber, Max (1985) [1922] *Wirtschaft und Gesellschaft. Grundriss der verstehenden Soziologie*. Tübingen, Germany: Mohr Siebeck.

Weber, Max. 1992 [1930]. *The Protestant Ethic and the Spirit of Capitalism*. London and New York: Routledge.

Weber, Max. 2010 [1895]. 'The Nation State and Economic Policy'. In *Weber. Political Writings*, edited by Peter Lassman and Ronald Speirs, pp. 1–28. Cambridge: Cambridge University Press.

Weber, Max. 2012 [1922]. 'The Meaning of "Value Freedom" in the Sociological and Economic Sciences'. In *Max Weber. Collected Methodological Writings*, edited by Henrik H. Bruun and Sam Whimster, pp. 304–334. London and New York: Routledge.

Weisbrot, Mark, and Helene Jorgensen. 2013. 'Macroeconomic Policy Advice and the Article IV Consultations: A European Union Case Study'. *International Labour Organisation*. Research Paper No. 7. https://www.ilo.org/wcmsp5/groups/public/---dgreports/---inst/documents/publication/wcms_218547.pdf.

Weizman, Eyal. 2007. *Hollow Land. Israel's Architecture of Occupation*. London: Verso.

Weizman, Eyal. 2018. *Forensic Architecture. Violence at the Threshold of Detectability*. London: Zone Books.

Wermenbol, Grace. 2020. 'For Palestinians, Annexation Spells Further Erasure of Their History'. *Middle East Institute*. July 8. https://www.mei.edu/publications/palestinians-annexation-spells-further-erasure-their-history.

White, Jonathan. 2022. 'The De-Institutionalisation of Power beyond the State'. *European Journal of International Relations* 28 (1): 187–208.

WHO (World Health Organization). 2019. 'Right to Health in the Occupied Palestinian Territory 2018'. Cairo: *WHO Regional Office for the Eastern Mediterranean*. http://www.emro.who.int/opt/news/who-launches-report-on-the-right-to-health-2018-october-2019.html.

Williams, Eric. 2022 [1944]. *Capitalism and Slavery*. London: Penguin Classics.

Williamson, John. 1999. 'What Should the World Bank Think About the Washington Consensus?' *Peterson Institute for International Economics*. July 1. https://www.piie.com/commentary/speeches-papers/what-should-world-bank-think-about-washington-consensus.

Wilson, Jade. 2022. 'Termination Notices by Landlords Rise by 58% in Six Months'. *The Irish Times*. August 8. https://www.irishtimes.com/ireland/housing-planning/2022/08/08/termination-notices-rise-58-at-residential-tenancies-board/.

Wilterdink, Nico 2018. 'Driving in a Dead-end Street: Critical Remarks on Andrew Abbott's Processual Sociology'. *Theory and Society* 47 (4): 539–557.

Wilz, Sylvia M. 2004. 'Für und wider einen weiten Begriff von Schließung. Überlegungen zur Theorie sozialer Schießung am Beispiel von Geschlechterungleichheiten'. In *Die Theorie sozialer Schließung. Tradition, Analysen, Perspektiven*, edited by Jürgen Mackert, pp. 213–231. Wiesbaden, Germany: VS.

Wimmer, Andreas. 2008. 'The Making and Unmaking of Ethnic Boundaries: A Multilevel Process Theory. *American Journal of Sociology* 113 (4): 970–1022.

Witz, Anne. 1988. 'Review Essay. Social Closure: The Theory of Monopolization and Exclusion. By Raymond Murphy'. *Sociology* 22 (4): 660–661.

Wolf, Hannah, and Jürgen Mackert. 2020. 'Introduction. Urban Warfare. Neo-Liberalism's Assault on Democratic Life in the City. In *Urban Change and Citizenship in Times of Crisis*.

Vol. 2. Urban Neo-liberalisation, edited by Bryan S. Turner, Hannah Wolf, Gregor Fitzi, and Jürgen Mackert, pp. 1–14. London and New York: Routledge.

Wolfe, Patrick. 1999. *Settler Colonialism and the Transformation of Anthropology. The Politics and Poetics of an Ethnographic Event*. London and New York: Cassell.

Wolfe, Patrick. 2006. 'Settler Colonialism and the Elimination of the Native'. *Journal of Genocide Research* 8 (4): 387–409.

Wolin, Sheldon S. 2008. *Democracy Incorporated. Managed Democracy and the Spectre of Inverted Totalitarianism*. Princeton, NJ: Princeton University Press.

Woolfolk, George R. 1956. 'Planter Capitalism and Slavery: The Labor Thesis'. *The Journal of Negro History* 41 (2): 103–116.

WRC (Worker Rights Consortium). 2009. 'Russell Says Workers in Honduras Don't Want to Exercise Their Associational Rights'. March 17. https://www.workersrights.org/communications-to-affiliates/russell-says-workers-in-honduras-dont-want-to-exercise-their-associational-rights/.

WRC (Worker Rights Consortium). 2013. 'Stealing from the Poor: Wage Theft in the Haitian Apparel Industry'. October 15. https://www.workersrights.org/wp-content/uploads/2016/02/WRC-Haiti-Minimum-Wage-Report-10-15-13-5.pdf.

WRC (Worker Rights Consortium). 2014. 'Report: Crackdown in Cambodia. Workers Seeking Higher Wages Meet Violent Repression'. March 24. https://www.workersrights.org/wp-content/uploads/2016/06/WRC-Report-Crackdown-in-Cambodia-3.24.14.pdf.

WRC (Worker Rights Consortium). 2018. '"Ethiopia Is a North Star". Grim Conditions and Miserable Wages Guide Apparel Brands in their Race to the Bottom'. December 31. https://www.workersrights.org/wp-content/uploads/2019/03/Ethiopia_isa_North_Star_FINAL.pdf.

WRC (Worker Rights Consortium). 2019a. 'Brands Should Consult Unions Before Resuming Sourcing in Myanmar'. June 1. https://www.workersrights.org/commentary/brands-should-consult-unions-before-resuming-sourcing-in-myanmar/.

WRC (Worker Rights Consortium). 2019b. 'Banning Hope. Bangladesh Garment Workers Seeking a Dollar an Hour Face Mass Firings, Violence and False Arrests'. April. https://www.workersrights.org/wp-content/uploads/2019/04/Crackdown-on-Bangladesh.pdf.

WRC (Worker Rights Consortium). 2020. '"My Children Don't Have Food. I Can Withstand This Hunger, but They can't." What the Crisis Means for People Who Make Collegiate Apparel'. June. https://www.workersrights.org/wp-content/uploads/2020/06/My-children-dont-have-food_June-2020.pdf.

World Food Programme. 2022. 'WFP Launches a Campaign to Improve the Nutrition of Vulnerable Women and Children in Palestine'. February 4. https://www.wfp.org/news/wfp-launches-campaign-improve-nutrition-vulnerable-women-and-children-palestine.

Wright, Erik Olin. 1985. *Classes*. London and New York: Verso.

Wrong, Denis. 1981. 'Survey Essay Marxism: The Disunity of Theory and Practice'. *Contemporary Sociology* 10 (1): 36.

Wysote, Travis, and Erin Morton. 2019. '"The Depth of the Plough": White Settler Tautologies and Pioneer Lies'. *Settler Colonial Studies* 9 (4): 479–504.

Yabiladi. 2018. 'Moroccan Women in Huelva: Nine Farm Workers File Complaints against Their Managers'. April 6. https://en.yabiladi.com/articles/details/65636/moroccan-women-huelva-nine-farm.html.

Yeung, Peter. 2016. 'Israel's National Water Company Cuts Off Water Supply to West Bank During Muslim Holiday'. *Business & Human Rights Resource Center*. June 14. https://www.business-humanrights.org/en/latest-news/israels-national-water-company-cuts-off-water-supply-to-west-bank-during-muslim-holy-month/.

Young, Robert. 2001. *Postcolonialism. An Historical Introduction*. Malden: Blackwell Publishing.

Zeitoun, Mark. 2005. 'Conflict and Water in Palestine. The Consequences of Armed Conflict on Drinking-Water Systems in Jenin, West Bank'. In *Water Values and Rights,* edited by Imad Khatib, Karen Assaf, Dominique Claeys and Ayman Al Haj Daoud. Palestine: Palestine Academy Press. http://citeseerx.ist.psu.edu/viewdoc/download?doi=10.1.1.514.5191&rep=rep1&type=pdf.

Zimmerer, Jürgen. 2004. '*Die Eroberung des "Ostlandes" aus dem Geiste des Kolonialismus. Die nationalsozialistische Eroberungs- und Beherrschungspolitik aus (post-)kolonialer Perspektive*'. *Sozial.Geschichte* 19 (1), 10–43.

Zonszein, Mairav. 2014. 'Jaffa "Ethnic Cleansing"'. *Al Jazeera*. April 16. https://www.aljazeera.com/news/2014/4/16/israels-ethnic-cleansing-of-jaffa-city.

Zureik, Elia. 2003. 'Demography and Transfer. Israel's Road to Nowhere'. *Third World Quarterly* 24 (4): 619–630.

All websites accessed last time 2 December 2023.

Index

For the benefit of digital users, indexed terms that span two pages (e.g., 52–53) may, on occasion, appear on only one of those pages.

accumulation by dispossession, 197–98, 202
Adalah (The Legal Center for Arab Minority Rights in Israel), 285t, 286–87, 289, 296
Addameer (Prisoner Support and Human Rights Organisation), 289–90, 296, 297, 298–99
austerity, 188–89, 188n.3
   commodification/fiancialization, 192, 195
   effects on communities, 212, 213–14, 215
   evictions, 200, 201
   health system, Spain, 207, 207n.15, 208, 209
   labour markets, Spain, 209–11
   political, 205–6
   politics of, 14, 186–89, 191, 192
   welfare reforms, 197

Berezin, M., 176, 177
   events as template of possibility, 186, 194, 223, 267, 281
boundaries, us-them, 149, 227, 271
Bourdieu P., 21–22, 36
Brady, T.A. Jr., 219, 258
Bunge, M., 84–85, 86

CAP (common agricultural policy), 230, 243, 255
capitalism, 7, 143–44
   financial, 34, 188, 225
   global, 8–9, 143–44, 150–51, 219, 221, 227, 229
   major global dynamic, 6, 8
   powerful actors, 204, 216, 241, 242, 309
   shareholder, 150–51, 223, 224, 227–28
   strategies of extraction, 14, 143–44, 146, 147t, 165, 216, 229, 232
capitalism-slavery nexus, 218, 219–21, 222–23, 227
   exploitation/slavery in Global North, 236, 239, 241–42, 243, 247–48, 253, 254
   exploitation/slavery in Global South, 232, 236, 240, 241, 245, 246, 250–52
Chomsky, N., 216, 258

collective memory, Palestinian, 266, 295, 300–1, 302, 303, 304

Dahrendorf, R., 129–30, 131–32, 131n.3, 156
Dana, T., 262, 265, 266n.53, 289–90, 298
De Tocqueville, A., 259, 260

elimination in closure theory, 115, 124, 144, 146, 147t, 165, 166
   dimensions of life chances/chances of survival, 169, 171–72
   explanation, 165–66
   form of social closure, 143, 165
   processes of, 148, 178
   relational, 133
   in settler colonialism, 258, 261 (*see also* settler colonialism)
   social relations of, 6–7, 15, 107, 133, 149
   strategies of, 178–79
   struggles of, 128
Emirbayer, M., 137–38, 139, 166, 308
erasure, politics of, 267–68, 268–69n.57, 291
   colonial process of, 269
   disenfranchising, 283–84
   extermination, 295
   letting die, 274, 278
   Palestinian history and collective memory, 301, 302, 303–4
   segregation, 291–92
ethnic cleansing, 9–11, 116n.5
   Palestine, 264, 265n.51, 266–67, 267n.56, 271, 273
   settler colonialism, 259, 261
   strategy of annihilation, 301, 302, 304, 307
   strategy of disenfranchising, 283, 289
   strategy of letting die, 274, 283
   strategy of segregation, 294
Europe/EU (European Union), 7–8
   actor in closure struggles, 197–98
   austerity, 189, 191, 194, 207n.15
   excluding migrants, 181
   housing/evictions, 195–96, 197, 199

European Action Coalition for the Right to Housing and to the City, 199–201
European Central Bank, 187–88, 204, 308–9
events in closure analysis, 178, 178f
  in elimination, 258, 260–61, 263f, 265–66, 269–70
  in exclusion, 186, 189, 190, 193f, 204, 212
  in exploitation, 223, 224, 225, 233f
exclusion in closure theory, 115, 124, 143, 146, 147t, 165, 166
  dimensions of life chances/chances of survival, 169, 171–72
  explanation, 165–66
  form of social closure, 143, 165, 180
  in neoliberalism, 7–8 (*see also* neoliberalism)
  processes of, 148, 178
  relational, 133
  social relations of, 6–7, 15, 107, 133, 149, 185–86, 190
  strategies of, 178–79
  strategies of marginalization, 180–81, 193f, 201
  struggles of, 128
exploitation in closure theory, 115, 124, 143–44, 146, 147t, 165, 166
  in capitalism/slavery, 221, 222, 227 (*see also* capitalism)
  dimensions of life chances/chances of survival, 169, 171–72
  explanation, 165–66
  form of social closure, 143, 165
  processes of, 148, 178, 182
  radical exploitation and slavery, 222–23, 225, 226
  relational, 133
  social relations of, 107, 133, 149, 185–86, 190, 226, 228
  strategies of, 178–79
  structural elements of economic power, 228–29
  struggles of, 128, 191

Fourth Geneva Convention (GCIV), 264, 274, 293, 294, 297n.69, 303

GBVH (gender-based violence and harassment), 250–56, 251n.42
genocide, 10, 259
  Gaza, 264n.49, 269–70
  Namibia, 274
  settler colonialism and, 260, 261, 261n.46, 302

Giddens, A., 108
  agency, 108
  capability, 108–9, 110, 112
  critique of Weber, 94
  dialectic of control, 112, 113
  duality of structure, 113–14
  institutions, 114, 115
  power, 114
  structures as resources, 110–11
Gilroy, P., 218n.23
GLVC (global labour value chain), 180, 227, 229, 245, 250, 256
  human rights, 239–40
GVC (global value chain), 8–9, 224, 225
  price squeezes and sourcing squeezes, 226, 238, 246, 309

Hall, S., 132, 218n.23
Harvey, D., 181, 185–86, 196–98, 202
Herzl, T., 271–72, 273–74, 306, 307, 309
HRW (Human Rights Watch), 246, 250–51, 283, 300
  apartheid in Israel, 284, 287–88
  killings of Palestinians, 298
  law of occupation, 296
  torture as lawful in Israel, 296–97
  vaccination of Palestinians, 294

IDF (Israeli Defence Forces), 267–68, 272–73, 274–76, 282–83, 291–92, 296, 297–98, 302
IMF (International Monetary Fund), 180, 184, 194, 216, 241, 242, 308–9
Israel, 1–2, 10–11, 291, 295–97, 306, 307

Mamdani, M., 259, 306
Mann, M., 93–94, 116, 117–18
  economic power, 120
  ethnic cleansing in settler colonialism, 260, 261–62
  ideological power, 118–19
  military power, 120, 121
  political power, 122
Manza, J., 22, 22n.1, 29–30, 51, 65, 130
Marx, K., 137, 217–18, 219
Masalha, N., 262–64, 266, 272, 300–1, 303–4
Mbembe, A., 10–11, 16, 267–68, 312
mechanism of social closure/denial of access, 139, 158, 161f, 165–66, 175, 179, 192–94
  democracy, 205, 206
  disenfranchising Palestinians, 283–84, 285t, 286–87, 288–89
  health system Germany, 248, 249–50

health system Palestine, 291–92, 293, 294–95
health system Spain, 207
housing Spain, 197, 199
labour market Spain, 209–11
malnutrition in Palestine, 276, 277, 278
minimum wages in GLVCs, 232–34, 236
rights in CLVCs, 239, 240
unionization in GLVCs, 245, 246, 247
vital resources in GLVCs, 236–38, 239
vital resources in Palestine, 276, 282
water in Palestine, 278, 279–80, 281–83
mechanism of social closure/intervention into community closure, 139, 159, 161f, 165–66, 175, 179
   degradation/violence, 251
   gender-based violence and harassment (GBVH), 251–52, 253–55
   human rights as terrorism, 298, 299, 300
   invisibility, 255
   Palestinian collective memory, 301, 303–4
   Palestinian culture, 300–1, 302
   responsibilization in neoliberalism, 211–12, 213
   sheer violence against Palestinians, 264n.49, 295, 296, 297
   unionization in GLVCs, 250
mechanisms (social), 17–18, 100, 138, 158, 166
memoricide, 171–72, 305–6
Merton, R.K., 129–32, 131n.3, 156

neoliberalism, 143, 181, 183, 185, 191–92, 195, 204, 212
   as ideology, 149, 190, 191, 228–29
   major global dynamic, 6, 7
   marketization, 9–10, 181, 182, 184–85, 186, 189, 212
Neuwirth, G., 82, 129, 162, 250
   community closure and control, 159–60
   new approach to social closure, 162–63, 213, 251, 254, 295, 304

Occupied Palestinian Territories (OPT), 264, 278–79, 284–85, 286
OMCT, 289–90, 296–97

Pappe, I., 121, 262–64, 266
plantation system, 218, 218n.23, 219–20
   and slavery, 218
Polanyi, K., 181–82, 183–84, 184n.1, 212
Popitz, H., 93–94, 95
   anthropological dimension of power, 95, 96
   conceptualization of power, 95, 96–97, 98, 99t

contexts of power, 100
emerging power relations, 98–99
organizing power, 94, 95, 101–2, 105, 106, 146–47
processes of power formation, 101–2, 103–4, 105–6
relational character of power, 99, 150
systematics of power, 96

Rodinson, M., 261–62
Rodney, W., 218n.23

Said, E.W., 9–10, 262, 312–13
settler colonialism, 10–11, 14, 261, 265, 144
   distinct formation, 258
   legitimation of settler colonialism, 259
   logic of elimination, 9–10, 261
   major global dynamic, 6, 7, 9–10, 14
   racism, 261
   relationship Global North and Global South, 15
   social struggles, 12, 72
   strategies of annihilation, 144, 146, 147t, 165, 258, 265 (*see also* erasure)
Silver, H., 4, 127
slavery, 219–20
   and exploitation, 14, 16, 183, 222, 230, 232
   in Marx, 217–18, 219
   second slavery, 220
   in sociological tradition, 218n.23
   third slavery, 222, 222n.28
slavery new/modern, 8–9, 14, 216, 217, 224, 230, 234, 314
   definition/term, 221
   historical continuity, 227
   social closure and, 222, 227–28, 229
   See also GLVC
social closure
   acting in solidarity, 17–18, 75–76, 91, 133–34, 138, 159, 311
   explanatory logic of elimination, 263f, 267, 295, 305
   explanatory logic of exclusion, 193f, 215
   explanatory logic of exploitation, 230, 233f, 256
   explanatory logics of, 178, 308, 309–10, 311
   group action, 17–18, 89, 91, 101–2, 138, 160
   life chances/chances of survival, 126, 127, 139, 154–55, 156
   life chances/chances of survival, definition/typology, 157
   power, 145, 146, 147t

social closure (*cont.*)
    power, social relations of, 6–7, 91, 145, 164, 175, 178, 308
    power, structural elements, 148, 149, 150–53
social exclusion, 2–4, 5
social relations of actors in closure struggles, 100–1, 133–34, 143, 147*t*, 162–63, 166, 178
    reorganization in global capitalism, 224, 229, 239, 243
    reorganization in neoliberalism, 187–88, 189, 191–94, 203–4
    reorganization in settler colonialism, 258, 267, 270, 271, 295
Steinert, H., 3–4, 55–56, 89, 91–92, 133–34
Suwandi, I., 226, 227

theory of social closure, 21, 22
    closure and exploitation, 29, 30, 31–32
    deep structure of domination, 41, 43, 57–58
    dual closure, 40
    framework for the theory of social closure, 43–44, 45, 46–47
    group action missing, 55, 133–34
    reciprocal strategies of action, 30, 56
    social closure equation, 26–27, 52, 59–60
    social closure as strategies of social action, 25–27, 28
    social closure as usurpation, 37–38, 39
Tilly, C., 90, 91, 133, 158, 159, 308
    methodological relationalism, 90, 138, 156
    social relations, 137–38, 175
Tomich, D., 220, 220n.25, 222–23

Troika, 187–88, 309
    austerity, 199–200, 207n.14, 214
    rescue programmes, 189n.4, 213

Veracini, L., 121, 258, 259, 272, 300–1

Weber, M., 69
    associative and communal relationships, 73
    closure, 69, 74–75
    distribution of power within the community, 78–80
    economic relationships of communities, 77, 78
    individualism, 129, 133, 134, 137
    life chances, 74, 127, 128–30
    open and closed relationships, 74
    relations between ethnic groups, 81, 82
    selection, 71, 128
    struggle, 69–70, 74
Weizman, E., 266–67, 274–76, 307
WHO, 278, 279, 281, 292
Williams, E., 219–20
Wolfe, P., 1–2, 9–10, 121, 260–61, 265
Wolin, S., 205
Worker Rights Consortium (WRC), 234, 235*t*, 240–41, 246, 251
    cases, 232–34, 235–36, 240, 246–47
World Organisation Against Torture. *See* OMCT
World Trade Organization, 223, 241, 242

Zionism, 262, 267–68, 267n.56, 271, 273, 302